D0082309

Conflict Resolution for the Helping Professions

SECOND EDITION

Allan Edward Barsky
Florida Atlantic University
at Fort Lauderdale

BROOKS/COLE
CENGAGE Learning·

Australia · Brazil · Japan · Korea · Mexico · Singapore · Spain · United Kingdom · United States

BROOKS/COLE
CENGAGE Learning™

Conflict Resolution for the Helping Professions, Second Edition
Allan Edward Barsky

Social Work Editor:
Dan Alpert

Assistant Editor:
Alma Dea Michelena

Editorial Assistant:
Ann Lee Richards

Marketing Manager:
Meghan McCullough

Marketing Communications
Manager: Tami Strang

Project Manager, Editorial
Production: Trudy Brown

Creative Director: Rob Hugel

Art Director: Vernon Boes

Print Buyer: Karen Hunt

Permissions Editor:
Roberta Broyer

Production Service:
Interactive Composition
Corporation

Copy Editor: Laura Larson

Cover Designer:
Cheryl Carrington

Cover Image:
Doris Cyrette, "Harmony"

Compositor: Interactive
Composition Corporation

© 2007, 2000 Brooks/Cole, Cengage Learning

ALL RIGHTS RESERVED. No part of this work covered by the copyright herein may be reproduced, transmitted, stored, or used in any form or by any means graphic, electronic, or mechanical, including but not limited to photocopying, recording, scanning, digitizing, taping, Web distribution, information networks, or information storage and retrieval systems, except as permitted under Section 107 or 108 of the 1976 United States Copyright Act, without the prior written permission of the publisher.

For product information and technology assistance, contact us at **Cengage Learning Customer & Sales Support, 1-800-354-9706.**

For permission to use material from this text or product, submit all requests online at **www.cengage.com/permissions**. Further permissions questions can be emailed to **permissionrequest@cengage.com**.

Library of Congress Control Number: 2006927248

ISBN-13: 978-0-495-09225-4
ISBN-10: 0-495-09225-8

Brooks/Cole
20 Davis Drive
Belmont, CA 94002-3098
USA

Cengage Learning is a leading provider of customized learning solutions with office locations around the globe, including Singapore, the United Kingdom, Australia, Mexico, Brazil, and Japan. Locate your local office at: **www.cengage.com/global**.

Cengage Learning products are represented in Canada by Nelson Education, Ltd.

To learn more about Brooks/Cole, visit **www.cengage.com/brookscole**.

Purchase any of our products at your local college store or at our preferred online store **www.cengagebrain.com**.

Printed in the United States of America
5 6 7 8 9 10 13 12 11

*To the memory of Coretta Scott King
whose life embodied the spirit of nonviolence,
peace, and justice even when challenged by the
faces of bloodshed, acrimony, and bigotry*

Contents

CHAPTER 1

CHAPTER 2

The Reflective CR Practitioner   37

CHAPTER 7

CHAPTER 8

Preface

Helping professionals deal with conflict in virtually all aspects of their work—with supervisors, coworkers, clients, families, social systems, and other community members. In order to deal effectively with conflict, helping professionals need to understand the nature of conflict and the range of approaches for dealing with it. This text and its companion *Instructor's Manual* provide educational materials designed to help adult learners integrate the theories, values, skills, and practice of conflict resolution through the development of knowledge, critical thinking skills, moral imagination and self-awareness.

Whereas conflict resolution *training courses* typically teach students how to follow one particular model of practice, this text offers a broad educational experience. In terms of knowledge base, this text compares and contrasts four approaches to conflict resolution: power based, rights based, interest based, and transformative. In addition, the discussion questions and exercises encourage students to explore a range of theories and models that inform conflict resolution, including loss theory, systems theory, restorative justice, forgiveness, and narrative conflict resolution. By understanding a wide spectrum of theories, models, and skills, helping professionals can assess each conflict situation and make informed, deliberate choices about how to intervene.

Each helping profession has its own body of knowledge, skills, and approaches to practice. This text encourages helping professionals to integrate their existing knowledge, skills, and approaches, with the conflict resolution knowledge, skills, and approaches presented in this text: What do I know from my professional education and experience? How does this compare and contrast with what I am learning about conflict resolution? What types of conflict resolution roles can or should I assume in my practice? What types of conflict resolution roles are inconsistent with my ordinary practice?

Given the value-driven nature of conflict resolution, discussion questions and exercises in this text provide opportunities for students to explore and clarify their personal and professional values. In particular, students need to examine their values, attitudes, and beliefs toward anger, power, autonomy, privacy, paternalism, and social justice. Although most helping professionals would say they value collaboration and peaceful means of dealing with conflict, these values are often challenged in practice—particularly when concerns such as power, emotions, miscommunication, greed, and limited resources come into play.

To help learners translate conflict resolution theories into practice, this text provides detailed case examples to demonstrate the use of common conflict resolution strategies and processes. Skills inventories provide learners with checklists of behaviors and activities that can be used to help them plan and evaluate their conflict interventions. Learners can experiment and practice skills through the use of role-plays. Learners can also reflect on their experience of dealing with conflict with family, friends, and clients. How have they dealt with conflict in the past, and how has the material in this text affected how they might respond differently in the future? Most learners find that conflict resolution education has very practical and immediate applications, in both their personal and professional lives.

Chapter 1 provides an overview of conflict resolution terminology, roles, and theories. Chapter 2 builds on this introduction by examining the roles of helping professionals as reflective practitioners who use knowledge, values, skills, and self-awareness to guide their practice, including the use of conflict resolution. Although this text takes a broad look at conflict resolution, Chapters 3 to 6 focus on four methods of conflict resolution: negotiation, mediation, group facilitation, and advocacy. These methods have been selected because they represent some of the most common conflict resolution methods used by helping professionals. Chapter 7, a new chapter for this second edition, includes additional methods of conflict resolution: fact finding, trust building, peacebuilding, parenting coordination, family group conferencing, and spiritual healing. Some instructors may design courses that focus on just one or two conflict resolution methods, while others will cover the entire spectrum (see the *Instructor's Manual* for specific suggestions on how to design courses based on this text). Chapter 8 concludes with ways that helping professionals can support the growth and development of conflict resolution within their agencies and communities.

Since the first edition of this text was published in 2000, many advances have been made in the field of conflict resolution. Because several approaches to conflict resolution were still in their infancy, recent theoretical development and research have helped clarify the conceptual bases of these approaches, as well as provide empirical support for their effectiveness and appropriateness for particular types of conflicts. This second edition reflects these changes, including updated references throughout. In particular, Chapter 4 provides greater clarification concerning the process of transformative mediation and Chapter 5 clarifies the distinction between mediation and facilitation. This text also incorporates feedback from professors and students, who suggested that the first edition did not include enough content on theories of conflict, creativity, and spirituality in conflict resolution. If you are familiar with the first edition, you will notice a number of significant changes made in order to address these concerns. The theoretical basis in Chapter 1 has been expanded to provide greater background on the nature of conflict. Whereas the original Chapter 2 focused on reflective practice as the intentional use of theory, skills, and values to guide practice, the new Chapter 2 adds the importance of creativity and imagination into the mix. This does not mean that professionals should merely rely on chance creativity or blind imagination, but that they should balance the use techniques and reasoned choices with the strategic and artistic use of spontaneity, vision, and inventiveness. As existing methods of conflict resolution evolve and new ones emerge, this text will also need to keep pace with progress. For updated references and information, or to provide feedback for future editions, please feel free to write Dr. Allan Barsky at Florida Atlantic University, School of Social Work, HEC 1008T, Fort Lauderdale, FL, USA 33301-2206 or barsky@barsky.org.

On any given day, helping professionals may be faced with an array of difficult conflict situations—angry clients, power struggles within the agency, cross-cultural misunderstandings, fights over limited resources, and so on. This book does not try to provide all the answers; however, it does present several foundations that offer helping professionals secure and inspirational places to start.

ACKNOWLEDGMENTS

This book originated from courses and materials I developed for Ryerson University in Toronto and The University of Calgary in Alberta, Canada. When I began teaching conflict resolution in 1992, there were few educational materials designed specifically for helping professionals. Although many helping professionals contributed to this field through research, training, and practice, most of their writings were restricted to particular areas of practice—for example, family mediation or victim-offender reconciliation programs. As I began to build a set of learning materials based on a more comprehensive approach to conflict resolution, I was fortunate to work with many talented and insightful students in Toronto, Calgary, and, most recently, Florida Atlantic University in Fort Lauderdale and Boca Raton. I thank these students for experimenting along with me and providing constructive feedback as we learned together.

I extend my gratitude to Alma Dea Michelena, Trudy Brown, and others at Brooks/Cole Publishing for their ongoing support through both editions of this book. Many thanks to Jill Traut, Laura Larson, and the other staff at Interactive Composition for their professional and thoughtful editing process. I am also indebted to the following conflict resolution educators and practitioners, who reviewed this text and offered their insightful feedback: Lorraine Schaffer of the University of London, Julianna Padgett of Southern University in New Orleans, William Hargett of Oklahoma State University, Winston Burt of the University of Northern Iowa, Michelle

LeBaron of the University of British Columbia Program on Dispute Resolution, and other anonymous reviewers.

Finally, I must acknowledge the support from those closest to me: my husband Greg, my 3-year-old daughter Adelle, and my mother Edith. Not only have they supplied me with love, hugs, and encouragement, but they have also provided me with lots of everyday conflict! They keep me humble about my sense of expertise in conflict resolution and offer me lots of opportunities to continue learning.

—Allan Edward Barsky

About the Author

Allan Edward Barsky, J.D., M.S.W., Ph.D., is a professor of social work at Florida Atlantic University in Fort Lauderdale. He has a combined background in social work, law, and conflict resolution, with particular experience in the areas of divorce, child welfare, and community mediation. Dr. Barsky's book authorships include *Successful Social Work Education: A Student's Manual*; *Alcohol, Other Drugs, and Addictions*; *Interprofessional Practice with Diverse Populations*; and *Clinicians in Court*. He has also authored numerous articles in the *Conflict Resolution Quarterly*, the *Negotiation Journal*, the *Family Courts Review*, and other scholarly journals and textbooks. Dr. Barsky is a regular lecturer and consultant on mediation and cultural diversity issues at professional conferences and educational institutions, having presented workshops and courses in Canada, Finland, Israel, the Netherlands, the United Kingdom, and the United States. He is a past president of the Ontario Association for Family Mediation, a former national board member of Conflict Resolution Network—Canada, and a Distinguished Teacher of the Year (2005) at Florida Atlantic University College of Architecture, Urban, and Public Affairs.

About the Cover

The drawing on the front cover of the first edition of this book is "The Challenge," by artist Doris Cyrette. The drawing depicts a conflict between two figures of different size and power. This conflict represents a challenge between the figures, as well as a challenge to helping professionals wanting to help them with their conflict. In contrast, the image on this edition is entitled "Harmony." Here, Cyrette portrays a state of love and serenity among three figures, as well as synchronicity between these figures and their environment. Although the field of conflict resolution still faces many challenges, it has developed substantially since the first edition was published. Enhanced conflict resolution theory, models, skills, and research offer renewed hope for harmony, peace, and justice, even when significant challenges arise and conflict seems intractable.

Introduction

A 14-year-old girl named Pawn has just been convicted for theft of a car. The judge requests a psychosocial assessment to help decide an appropriate sentence—perhaps probation with some type of voluntary counseling. Pawn is subjected to a battery of tests and interviews by a range of helping professionals. The professionals meet for a case conference.

A Freudian psychoanalyst[1] concludes, "Pawn's antisocial behavior derives from deep-rooted conflict between an overactive id and a defective ego; Pawn requires at least 2 years of psychoanalysis."

A cognitive therapist counters, "That's nonsense! Pawn has distorted thought patterns which tell her that she can only expect positive attention when she acts out; Pawn requires 6 months of therapy based on cognitive restructuring."

A systems counselor[2] chuckles and suggests, "The real issue lies in the scapegoat role that Pawn plays in her family in order to deflect attention away from her alcoholic father; Pawn and her parents must attend 3 weeks of structured family therapy."

The conflict resolution professional finally responds, "Great! Then we all agree. . . . There is a problem . . . we each have different perspectives on Pawn's situation . . . and we have several possible solutions to consider."

One client. Many points of view. Difference of opinion is just one of many types of conflict that helping professionals encounter in their everyday practice. The vignette highlights the polarization of professionals based on divergent theoretical perspectives. But is it only the conflict resolution expert who can see the common threads and work toward joint problem solving? In fact, all helping professionals are conflict resolution practitioners. Some of us just don't know it yet.

This text provides a comprehensive set of educational materials, designed for helping professionals interested in the theory and practice of conflict resolution. Although you may be studying conflict resolution from the perspective of a particular

---

[1]Freudian psychoanalysis focuses on helping people by dealing with intrapsychic conflicts or subconscious issues (Freud, 1963).

[2]A systems counselor helps clients by focusing on the interactions between the client and other systems, such as families, peer groups, education systems, work systems, healthcare systems, and religious institutions.

profession—nursing, psychology, social work, education, community development, pastoral counseling, corrections, or child and youth work—the essential aspects of conflict resolution extend across professions. The advantage of an interdisciplinary text is that you will be challenged to look at conflict situations from diverse points of view. Ideally, the composition of your class will include people from a broad range of backgrounds and perspectives. Expressing your different values, attitudes, and opinions will stimulate conflict and enrich your learning experience.

In this chapter, we begin with an introduction to social conflict, its sources, and different ways that conflict can be understood. In order to determine the best way to deal with conflict, we must first understand how it typically arises and progresses. The following section builds on this discussion of social conflict by introducing a range of roles that helping professionals can play in helping people handle conflict more effectively. The next section provides an overview of conflict resolution theory, including its roots in specific disciplines. Given this basis, I explain the structure of this text and offer suggestions on how to use it most effectively. The final sections provide a set of discussion questions and class exercises, as well as a detailed case study ("Conflictia") that forms the basis for certain exercises used throughout the text.

CONFLICT RESOLUTION ROLES AND DEFINITIONS

Deliberate choice of language is crucial to effective conflict resolution. Many conflicts arise because of miscommunication. Perhaps the speaker was unclear, or the listener made an error in processing the message. Alternatively, neither is to blame. Rather than look for responsibility, the conflict may be resolved by rectifying the parties' understandings of one another and moving on. Better yet, consider whether the conflict could have been **pre-empted**.[3]

I have already used a number of terms having technical meanings and usage. To clarify these and to pre-empt any further misunderstandings, I want to ensure that we have common interpretations of these terms, as well as others that will be used throughout the course of this text.

Conflict resolution (or CR) refers to the various ways in which people or organizations deal with social conflict. **Social conflict** exists when two or more parties have differences in beliefs, values, positions, or interests, whether the divergence is real or perceived.[4] If Chris thinks the world is round, and Isabel thinks the world is flat, they have a difference in beliefs. If Jane wants her agency to focus on the mental health of clients, and Mary wants the agency to focus on their social welfare, they have a conflict based on different values. If Jane wants Dick to work overtime, but Dick wants to go home early, they have a difference in positions. If the psychiatric department of a hospital needs more beds for suicidal clients, and the cardiology

---

[3]*Pre-empting* and other "professional jargon" shown in boldface throughout the text are defined in the glossary.

[4]When some helping professionals hear the term *conflict resolution*, they wonder whether it is related to "intrapsychic" or "subconscious" conflicts. Although psychodynamic theory may help CR practitioners understand how individuals behave (Weinhold & Weinhold, 2000), conflict resolution is directed toward social conflict (conflict between people) rather than conflict within one person's psyche.

department needs more operating space for surgery, they have a difference of interests. If Will assumes Grace is angry at him for buying an expensive car, they have a conflict based on a perceived difference, even if Grace is actually pleased with Will's purchase. By assessing and understanding the nature of a particular conflict, professionals tailor their interventions to deal most effectively with the conflict (Menkel-Meadow, Love, Schneider, & Sternlight, 2005).

Although many people assume conflict is harmful, conflict in and of itself is neither good nor bad (Wilmot & Hocker, 2007). Rather, the manner in which we deal with conflict determines whether it is constructive or destructive. In a school situation, teachers and counselors may have different views on how to allocate resources in the school's budget. Teachers want greater funding for books and educational supplies, for instance, whereas counselors want more funding for psychosocial testing and services. If these differences escalate into hostile relations, the result will be destructive. If these differences spur both groups of helping professionals to work together for a creative solution, the result will be positive. Conflict can be viewed as an opportunity and motivation for change. In fact, the ability to express conflicting values and beliefs advances two values held by most helping professionals: freedom of expression and respect for diversity among individuals and groups.

Different theorists, cultural groups, families, and individuals have different views on the nature of conflict—an exchange of resources, an adventure, a struggle, a balancing act, a game, an expression of disrespect, or a breakdown in communication (Wilmot & Hocker, 2007). How people perceive conflict will affect the ways they try to handle it. People can respond to conflict in a variety of manners, ranging from avoidance and withdrawal, to collaboration and problem solving, to litigation and fighting. Some responses may be helpful; others, counterproductive. Often, it depends on the nature of the conflict and the goals of the people faced with the conflict.

Consider a case manager, Cameron, who asks his boss for a raise in salary. The boss, Bruce, originally rejects Cameron's request. If Cameron views this conflict as an exchange of resources, he could point out all his contributions to the agency and how his salary should reflect these contributions. He might also look for other jobs, with pay that better reflects the quality of services he provides. If Cameron views conflict as an adventure, he could treat Bruce's initial rejection as an invitation to try new and creative approaches to work through the conflict (e.g., brainstorming new ideas, developing innovative arguments to persuade Bruce). If Bruce views this conflict as a struggle, he may see it as a battle or trial requiring him to stand firm and use whatever power he can muster to thwart Cameron's attack. If Bruce sees the conflict as a balancing act, he may deal with Cameron more delicately. On one hand, he notes his agency cannot afford to give raises; on the other hand, he wants to keep his employees, including Cameron, happy. He may try to find benefits to offer Cameron that will not put the agency's budget in jeopardy. If Cameron views the conflict as a game, he may explore different strategies to see which is most likely to help him win; for instance, will Bruce be swayed more effectively by crying, making threats, "sucking up,"[5] or being honest and direct? If Cameron perceives the conflict as an expression

---

[5]Using flattery to win favor.

of disrespect, he may feel hurt and respond either by withdrawing in order to avoid further hurt or by verbally attacking Bruce to defend his honor. If Cameron views the conflict as a problem in communication, he may review what he said with Bruce and develop a clearer explanation of why he deserves a raise. In some situations, people involved in conflict have similar views of its nature and will dance the same dance; often, people have different views of conflict and will unwittingly adopt strategies that clash.

Helping professionals can assume a myriad of *roles* in order to assist individuals, families, groups, organizations, and communities with conflict situations: negotiator, mediator, advocate, facilitator, healer, expert/consultant, arbitrator, administrator, buffer, and penalizer (Chetkow-Yanoov, 1997).[6] Within each role, professionals can draw from a range of approaches to practice. *Approaches to practice (sometimes called theories or models of practice)[7] suggest the specific goals, strategies, and skill sets to guide practitioners within each role.* I will cover various approaches to practice in Chapters 3 to 6, in relation to specific CR roles. At this point, I will provide just an overview of the roles helping professionals can play.

To simplify the discussion of CR roles, consider a two-party conflict: A husband and wife are in the middle of a divorce. One issue is how to divide their family property. The term *party,* adopted in CR from legal jargon, refers to any individual,

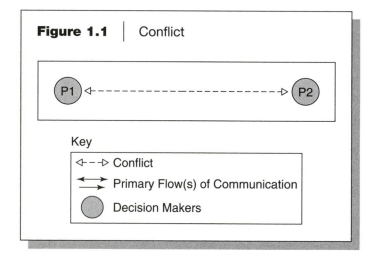

Figure 1.1 | Conflict

Key

◁– –▷ Conflict

Primary Flow(s) of Communication

⬤ Decision Makers

---

[6]Other conflict resolution roles include ombudsperson, investigator, and hybrids of other roles (e.g., med-arbitrator; parenting coordinator, or mediative evaluator; see Shienvold, 2004). See the glossary for definitions of these.

[7]Although some practitioners use the terms *theories* or *models* of practice, there is still debate about what constitutes a theory or model, and which approaches satisfy these requirements. Furlong (2005) suggests that *theories* are abstract principles or explanations of physical or psychosocial phenomena developed to provide explanations that can be tested for their validity through research, whereas *models* are structures or representations that are developed to help guide practice. Ideally, models are based on clearly articulated theories and sound research. Many approaches to CR are still emerging, meaning that it will take some time for their theoretical bases to be clarified and for research to substantiate their validity and effectiveness.

group, or corporate entity (e.g., a social agency, a government, or a business enterprise). An **interested party** is a party who has a direct interest (or stake) in how a conflict is resolved. In the example, the husband and wife are the interested parties. Each has a direct stake in how their property is divided. The husband suggests, "I've worked hard to earn a living and pay for this house. You're not entitled to 20 percent, never mind half." In defense, his wife responds, "You're the one who ran off with another woman. As far as I'm concerned, that means the house is mine." If we designate the husband and wife as Party 1 (P1) and Party 2 (P2) respectively, we can represent the conflict as in Figure 1.1. *The dashed line indicates the parties directly involved in the conflict.*

Broadly speaking, **negotiation** refers to any manner in which two or more parties interact with each other in order to deal with a conflict situation. The husband and wife could sit down at the kitchen table and calmly discuss how to divide their property. They could become embroiled in a heated argument. They could try to manipulate each another by threatening to destroy property, changing locks on the door, or lying about the true value of their retirement investments. These actions are different means of negotiation. In a simple negotiation, the conflict and the communication both flow directly between the parties to the conflict, as illustrated in Figure 1.2. *Whereas the dashed line indicates the parties involved in the primary conflict, the solid line depicts which parties are communicating directly as part of the conflict resolution process (in this case, negotiation). The circles identify the decision makers in the negotiation, P1 and P2.*

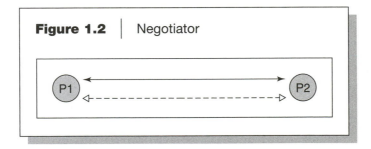

Figure 1.2 | Negotiator

Negotiation occurs not only between clients but between coprofessionals, as demonstrated in the case conference scenario described at the beginning of this chapter. *Negotiation* and *bargaining* are often used interchangeably. Some writers refer to negotiation to describe interest-based CR, in order to distinguish it from the notion of positional bargaining (Chapter 3 explains positional and interest-based negotiation in further detail). I avoid use of the term *bargaining*, because of its pejorative connotations in common parlance (i.e., trying to get something cheap; trying to gain something at another party's expense). Instead, I refer to several different approaches to negotiation.

An **advocate** is a person who acts in support of an interested party during negotiation, litigation, or another conflict resolution process. In the divorce situation, one or both spouses may have their own advocates. The wife hires a lawyer to help her win possession of the matrimonial home. She asks the lawyer to take her lecherous husband to court. The lawyer encourages her to consider negotiation, where the lawyer will meet with the husband's lawyer to try to work out a reasonable settlement. Assuming each spouse has an advocate (AD1 and AD2), the situation appears as in Figure 1.3.

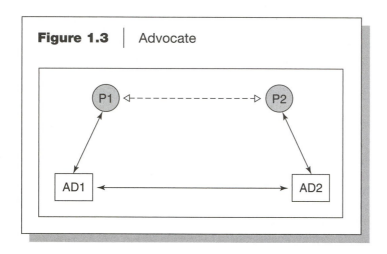

Figure 1.3 | Advocate

Note that the dashed line represents the primary conflict, which still occurs between P1 and P2. The flows of communication for the purposes of conflict resolution, however, extend between each advocate and his or her client, as well as between the two advocates. In this advocacy model, no direct communication takes place between P1 and P2. The ultimate decision makers (as identified by the circles) are P1 and P2, even though they rely on their advocates for representation and advice.

In legal situations, such as divorce, we often think of lawyers as advocates. However, a vast range of helping professionals can and do assume advocacy roles. A professor can advocate for a mature student to be accepted into a university program in spite of low grades. A discharge planner in a hospital can advocate for a patient who wants to remain in the hospital until home support systems are in place. A feminist counselor can advocate for subsidized child care for single-parent families. A probation officer can advocate for vocational upgrading support for a client on probation.

As you will see further in Chapter 6, an advocate affects the balance of power between parties by providing one party with information, conflict resolution skills, or other resources. Advocates are particularly useful, even necessary, when one party is at a power disadvantage in relation to the other party (Ellis & Stuckless, 1996). When one party hires an advocate, however, the other often responds by hiring its own advocate.

Some literature refers to "advocating for oneself." Given the definitions described here, this is negotiation rather than advocacy. Advocates and the other CR helping roles described later can be referred to as "third parties." **Third parties** play a role in the CR process, but they do not have a direct interest in the specific resolution of the conflict. AD1 is a partisan who desires a positive result for the husband, but AD1 will not have to live with the ultimate division of property in the same way as the divorced spouses will.

An **expert/consultant** is a professional who provides information, expertise, or advice to one or both interested parties to help them resolve a conflict. The expert/consultant does not facilitate communication or direct the process of conflict resolution between the parties. Consultation is a form of education. For example, the husband or wife may agree to go to a psychoeducational group to learn about the process and stages of dealing with separation. The group counselor plays the role of expert when she provides information and suggestions about how to deal with one's former spouse. If the former spouses have children, they will learn how to deal with their mutual anger and distrust, so their children do not get caught in the crossfire. In this scenario (Figure 1.4), the wife's expert is providing suggestions to her, but the husband and wife still communicate directly with each other in order to resolve their differences. The circles show that P1 and P2 are the primary decision makers, even though P2 is relying on her expert for advice.

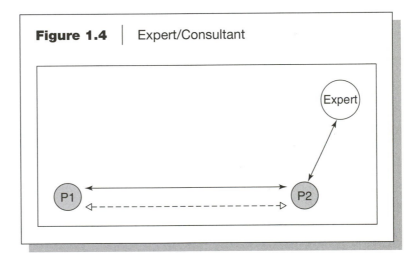

Figure 1.4 | Expert/Consultant

Other examples of expert/consultants include supervisors and pastoral counselors. Human service professionals, for instance, may go to their supervisors to obtain advice about how to deal with a conflict between them. Pastoral counselors may provide spiritual or moral guidance to clients who are struggling with interpersonal conflicts.

An **evaluator** is another expert role that helping professionals frequently assume. If the wife and husband agree to submit to a custody evaluation, the clinician will assess both parents' abilities to parent their children. The clinician will make recommendations about the best interests of the children: where the children should reside; how they should spend time with both parents; what parenting responsibilities should fall on which parent (Gould, 2004). The older child has been wetting her bed since her parents separated; accordingly, the evaluator recommends that both parents follow a certain bedtime regimen in order to support the daughter through this difficult time. The parties are not necessarily bound by the recommendations; however, they will tend to heed the recommendations because they are coming from an independent third party with expertise in child custody. If the husband and wife were in court, the judge may ask them to go for a custody evaluation. The evaluator will make recommendations to the judge, but the judge will have ultimate authority to decide the parenting plan (e.g., which parent will have custody and how visitation with the children will be arranged). The situation with a judge and expert evaluator would present as in Figure 1.5.

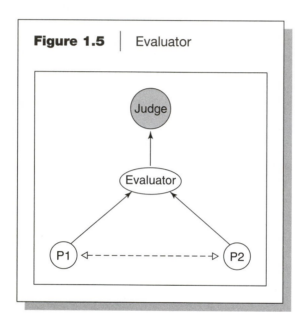

Figure 1.5 | Evaluator

Note that the judge is now the decision maker, as indicated by the circle. As the solid lines indicate, both parties provide information to the evaluator, who makes a recommendation to the judge. The judge then imposes a decision on the parties. This CR model does not provide for any direct communication between the husband and wife.

A **facilitator** is a professional who assists with communication between parties to a conflict.[8] Facilitation functions include bringing the parties together, providing a space for discussion, clarifying misunderstandings, encouraging joint problem solving, and assisting each party to hear the others (Eller, 2004). A facilitator could work directly with the interested parties or with their advocates. A teacher notices that a student's schoolwork has been deteriorating since his parents' separation. The teacher decides to assume the role of facilitator and calls both parents for a meeting. The teacher helps them discuss how their son is falling behind in class. To deal with this problem, the parents decide to spend more time helping their son

---

[8]*Parties to a conflict* is legalese for "interested parties" or individuals who are directly involved in the conflict. Some CR literature refers to parties as "conflictants" or "disputants," but these terms reinforce adversarial feelings between the parties.

with his homework. Assuming that P1 and P2 do not have advocates, the situation presents as in Figure 1.6.

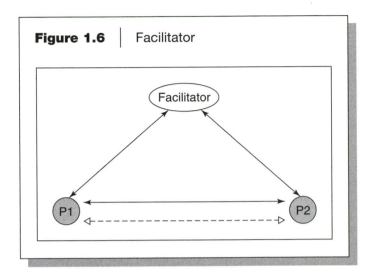

Figure 1.6 | Facilitator

The communication flows back and forth among all three individuals, as indicated by the solid lines. P1 and P2 remain the decision makers.

A **mediator** is a third party who assists interested parties in negotiating a conflict. A mediator controls the mediation process but does not have authority to decide the outcome for the parties. In other words, a mediator is a type of facilitator who follows a particular model of intervention, using specific skills and strategies. The mediator coaches the parties on how to deal with conflict constructively and, conversely, moves parties away from dysfunctional patterns of interaction. More detailed definitions, including whether a mediator must be neutral or impartial, are analyzed in Chapter 4. Figure 1.7 shows that the mediator facilitates communication between the

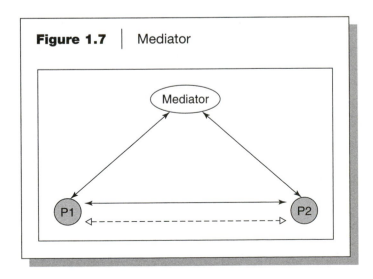

Figure 1.7 | Mediator

wife and husband (as indicated by the solid lines), but the wife and husband retain ultimate decision-making power over how to divide their property (as indicated by the
circles). Advocates or other helping professionals can also participate in mediation.

Some people use the terms *mediation* and *conciliation* interchangeably. Others
distinguish conciliation as a process that is outcome oriented (to facilitate settlement), whereas mediation is more process oriented (to facilitate better relationships
and deal with underlying psychosocial issues). According to this dichotomy, conciliation generally requires only one or two sessions, whereas mediation may take four
to eight sessions. Conciliators tend to be more interventionist than mediators, offering suggestions and directing the parties toward specific options for settlement. In the
1970s and 1980s, the term *conciliation* was used most frequently to refer to services
that were attached to courts, tribunals, or other mandated government agencies
(Noone, 1996).

In this text, I talk about various approaches to mediation, but avoid use of the
term *conciliation*. People tend to confuse conciliation with reconciliation. Reconciliation suggests the aim of the CR process is to return the parties to a previous
form of relationship—for example, to work out an arrangement for separated
spouses to move back together, as an intact family. Although some mediation
clients choose to reconcile, this may not be their goal. Divorce mediation is designed to help former spouses redefine their roles so that they can live peacefully,
but separately and apart. If separated spouses want to reconcile, then family counseling would be more appropriate to help them with this transition. This topic is
raised again when we get into the debate on the difference between mediation and
therapy.

A **healer** is a facilitator who helps parties work through the underlying causes
of a conflict. Psychotherapists, clergy, and elders within certain cultures often assume the role of healer (Pranis, 2005). Whereas the mediation field is still debating the extent to which mediation involves therapeutic processes (if at all), healers
specifically focus on underlying psychosocial and spiritual issues. Techniques for
healing include helping parties listen sensitively to one another, explore taboo
ideas, overcome historical hatreds, depart from traditional customs, discontinue
behavior that victimizes other groups, improve self-understanding, accept responsibility, provide apologies, and reconcile previous relationships (Chetkow-
Yanoov, 1997; Montville, 1993). Many models of psychological intervention
clearly place the therapist in a healing role: for example, Rogerian-humanistic
therapy, psychoanalysis, narrative therapy, and cognitive restructuring (Pro-
chaska & Norcross, 2003). Traditional healing processes also exist within many
ethnic communities: *ho'opononopono* among native Hawaiians, family group
conferencing among New Zealand's Maori people, *fa'amanata'anga* among the
Kwar'ae of the Solomon Islands, and healing circles among Native North Americans, to name a few (Hudson, Morris, Maxwell, & Galaway, 1996; Tannen, 1998;
Wilmot & Hocker, 2007). In our diagrams, the role of a healer appears very similar to that of a mediator or facilitator. Figure 1.8 could represent a couples counselor, clergy person, or elder who is helping both the husband and wife reconcile
their marriage (Picard & Melchin, 1988).

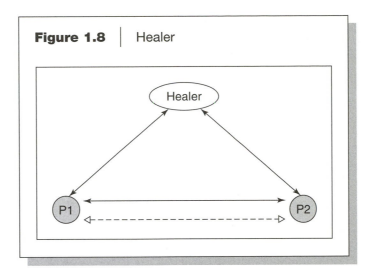

Figure 1.8 | Healer

The solid lines show communication flowing between all three parties, with the circles indicating that P1 and P2 make the ultimate decisions. Unlike a mediator, a healer could work with just one of the parties—for instance, helping a woman come to terms with her partner's having an affair with a younger woman.

An **arbitrator** (Figure 1.9) is an independent third party who hears evidence from the conflicting parties and determines an appropriate resolution for them (American Arbitration Association, n.d.). A judge is a type of arbitrator, imposed on parties who are involved in court proceedings. Labor laws and other forms of legislation sometimes impose specialized arbitrators on conflicting parties. In other situations, parties choose arbitration on a voluntary basis. When arbitration is legislatively mandated, the rules of the arbitration process are predetermined for the parties. If arbitration is voluntary, the parties can select their own arbitrator and establish the rules of arbitration by agreement.

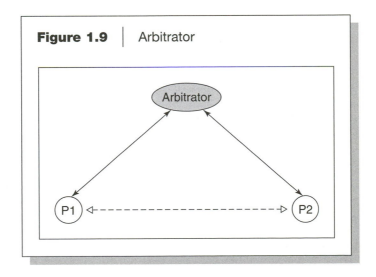

Figure 1.9 | Arbitrator

Note that there is little or no communication between the parties during arbitration. As the solid lines show, the primary flows of communication are between each party and the arbitrator. The arbitrator makes the decision, as indicated by the circle.

If the parties were represented by advocates, then the advocates would communicate with the arbitrator. In our divorce situation, the spouses direct their lawyers about how to represent them, but the arbitrator and lawyers control the process and communication once in the arbitration hearing. If the spouses came to you in your capacity as a helping professional to arbitrate a dispute, would you accept this role? Consider whether arbitration is consistent with the ethics of client self-determination (Rave & Larson, 1995).

For most helping professionals, an administrator is someone who manages the employees and resources of an organization. In a conflict resolution context, an **administrator** is a professional who assists with *implementation* of the resolution of a conflict (Figure 1.10).

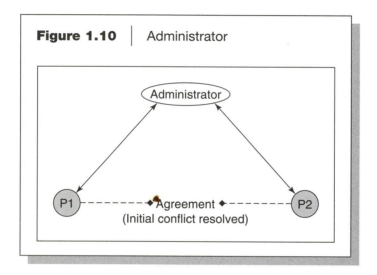

Figure 1.10 | Administrator

As the circles indicate, the P1 and P2 are the decision makers regarding how the conflict was initially resolved, but the administrator takes a decision-making role regarding implementation. In our divorce mediation, for example, the former spouses agree that the husband will pay monthly child support. An administrator could be involved as a monitoring agent, to ensure the husband pays support as agreed (e.g., at an agency that enforces child and spousal support agreements). In addition to a monitoring role, administrators operationalize agreements by encouraging compliance, facilitating ongoing communication between the parties, providing interpretation of disputed clauses, and identifying potential trouble spots early on (Chetkow-Yanoov, 1997). The role of an administrator looks similar to that of a mediator or facilitator, but the administrator generally gets involved only after another third party has facilitated the basic agreement. The role of parenting coordinator, described in Chapter 7, is another example of an administrator.

A **buffer** (Figure 1.11) is an individual or agency that separates conflicting parties during an intense, destructive phase of conflict.

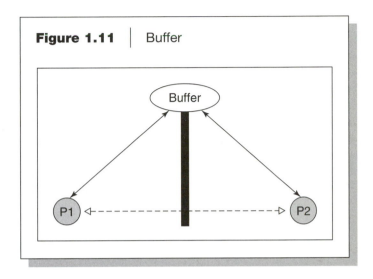

Figure 1.11 | Buffer

As the wide bar indicates, the buffer separates the parties and stops direct communication between them. Each party may communicate separately with the buffer, as indicated by the solid lines. The role of United Nations peacekeepers is a prime example of the buffer role (Chetkow-Yanoov, 1997). Peacekeepers provide a physical barrier between two warring factions in order to stabilize a situation. The buffer role is temporary. It is designed to allow time for other conflict resolution processes to work out a more permanent solution (Lederach, 2005). Peacekeeping is a bit of a misnomer. Peacekeeping may ensure an absence of war, but absence of war is not the same as peace. Peacemaking or peacebuilding, terms adopted by some mediators, goes beyond peacekeeping (see Chapter 7 for further detail). True peace requires mutual understanding and respect, ongoing constructive communication, and a relationship that can deal well with differences (Barash & Webel, 2002). A truce enforced by buffers hopefully provides an opportunity for peacemakers to help the parties bring about a full and lasting peace.

Supervised access is an example of the buffer role in our divorce situation. If our wife and husband are hostile toward one another, a buffer may be necessary to safeguard the spouses and the child. Some social agencies offer supervised access. Typically, supervised access involves the custodial spouse bringing the child to the agency so that the noncustodial spouse can meet the child there. The agency may simply supervise the transfer of the child from one parent to the other, or it may supervise the entire visitation. In families with a history of violence, the agency can make arrangements so that no contact exists between the former spouses. In contrast to a facilitator, a buffer blocks direct communication between the parties, and communication is primarily top-down from the buffer to each party.

A **penalizer** (Figure 1.12) is an individual or agency with the power to impose sanctions on parties for misconduct.

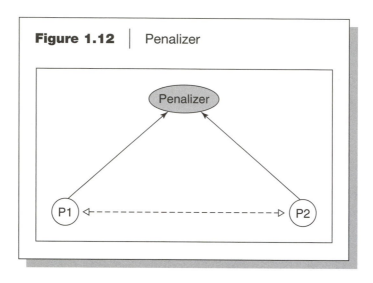

Figure 1.12 | Penalizer

Note that the parties communicate with the penalizer rather than with each other, as indicated by the solid lines. The primary decision maker is the penalizer, as indicated by the circle. Criminal law courts impose sanctions such as fines and incarceration. Some clergy teach that a divine power will punish those who act in an evil manner. Teachers sanction certain types of student behavior through grading, granting privileges, and withdrawing them. Social workers, psychologists, and other mental health professionals may frown on using sanctions as means of social control. Still, there are many examples where such helping professionals do make use of sanctions. A divorce counselor, for instance, may discontinue services to a spouse who becomes abusive. Some helping professionals justify the use of sanctions to promote constructive conflict resolution behavior. In jurisdictions with "mandatory mediation," conflicting parties are required to try mediation before they can have access to the public court system. Police sometimes drop charges when parties agree to go to a community dispute resolution center. Parole officers advise parolees that they will be returned to jail if they breach conditions of parole. Are these examples of undue coercion or creative use of authority? Ethically, one must consider whether the ends justify the means (Dolgoff, Loewenberg, & Harrington, 2005). Whereas most helping professionals feel comfortable in facilitative roles, they are likely to experience an internal values conflict if they are pressed into the role of penalizer. The penalizer's decisions are top-down, and the parties are not encouraged to communicate with one another. Although there are legitimate roles for penalizers, this book focuses on noncoercive conflict resolution.

Interventions that employ the 11 roles just described are sometimes called *conflict management, dispute resolution,* or **alternative dispute resolution** (ADR). These terms are related, but entail conceptual differences. Conflicts range from mild differences, to disagreements, to campaigns, to litigation and fighting (Wilmot & Hocker, 2007).

Disputes fall within the latter, more intense part of this range.[9] **Dispute resolution** refers to formal institutions that provide conflict resolution services, particularly within law-related systems. The "alternative" in ADR refers to alternatives to court processes. First popularized in the 1970s, ADR was seen as a way to divert cases from an expensive, formal, and adversarial court system, to cheaper and more informal ADR programs (Bush & Folger, 2005). ADR could mean any alternative to court, including negotiation, arbitration, healing, and assessments (Roth, Wulff, & Cooper, 1993). Some practitioners use *ADR* to refer specifically to mediation, given that court-affiliated mediation programs are the most popular type of ADR program. The term *ADR* seems to suggest that court is the pre-eminent form of conflict resolution. In order to avoid the notion that mediation and other forms of CR are simply alternatives to court, some CR professionals have reframed ADR to mean "appropriate dispute resolution."

CR professionals may also reframe "dispute" to "conflict" in order to focus clients on the positive aspects of conflict. The presence of conflict means there is energy that can be utilized to produce change. Permission to express differences is vital to the operation of a free and democratic society. For many people, even the term *conflict* feels uncomfortable. Their experience suggests that conflict is fighting, wars, violence, exploitation, rivalry, or humiliation (Chetkow-Yanoov, 1997). Perceptions of conflict are culture bound. Some cultures place a high value on harmony and cooperation; others place a high value on competition and individuality (Barsky, Este, & Collins, 1996; LeBaron, n.d.; Wilmot & Hocker, 2007). CR professionals need to respect people's experience and culture, but they must also help people explore new ways of viewing and dealing with conflict.

On its face, the term *conflict resolution* implies that the purpose of intervention is to resolve or end the conflict. Some professionals prefer the term *conflict management* because it suggests that conflict is an ongoing phenomenon to be dealt with in a strategic manner. For others, *conflict management* suggests that conflict is dealt with in a top-down manner, by people who have the power to control or suppress conflict. In contrast, the term *conflict transformation* has been used to describe processes that focus people on more constructive ways of dealing with conflict in their relationships. Another term that has recently emerged is *conflict engagement*, which suggests that the purpose of intervention is to engage people in conflict more effectively (Mayer, 2004b). This book adopts the more popular term, *conflict resolution*, with the understanding that the purpose of intervention is to resolve the parties' *underlying* concerns, whether that means ending the conflict, improving their relationship, learning how to deal with conflict in more constructive ways, using conflict to foster social justice, or instilling spirituality or greater meaning into their lives.

THEORETICAL CONTEXT

In order to trace the roots of conflict resolution, we need to consider whether we are talking about CR as a theory, discipline, or technique of practice. The formalized study of CR in the field of collective bargaining and labor relations began in the early 1900s

---

[9]Some theorists distinguish conflicts from disputes by suggesting that social conflict exists whenever there is a difference of interests, beliefs, values, et cetera, between people, whether or not the parties express their differences to one another. Conflict only becomes a dispute once one or both express their differences or act on them (Menkel-Meadow et al., 2005).

(National Institute for Dispute Resolution, 1987). In the helping professions, mediation and other collaborative forms of CR began to emerge as distinct models of practice in the 1970s; however, the use of CR techniques and strategies in the helping professions extends back much earlier (Deutsch, 1973; Zastrow, 2003). This text covers both "emergent" and "contractual" CR. *Contractual* CR refers to models of practice in which the professional is specifically hired as a CR practitioner—for example, a separating couple that agrees to hire a family mediator. The spouses sign an agreement to mediate, which establishes the role of the mediator and makes the terms of the mediation process explicit. In contrast, *emergent* CR occurs when a helping professional uses skills and strategies of CR but is not specifically hired as a CR specialist. The CR role emerges out of another form of relationship—for instance, a teacher who mediates an argument between students, a nurse who facilitates a tumultuous case conference, a probation officer who negotiates a contract for work with a client, or a clergy who arbitrates a dispute between parishioners. Because these practitioners do not have an explicit agreement with the conflicting parties to assume a CR role, their functions are likely to differ from those of a contractual CR professional. In some situations, a practitioner's prior role allows him or her to move into a CR role; in other situations, the prior role inhibits such a transition. CR theory and literature extend across both contractual and emergent CR (Pruitt & Carnevale, 1993).[10]

CR draws from a broad range of disciplines, including psychology, business administration, law, education, social work, political science, strategic studies, and radicalism. Ironically, turf wars are not uncommon among CR professionals from different disciplines. Which theory or theories drive CR? What are the values and ethical bases that underlie CR? What professional background do you need, if any, to be certified as a CR professional? Can just anyone hang up a shingle and practice? Some arguments about restricting CR practice to certain professions are raised under the guise of ensuring competence and accountability. CR does not fall under the natural domain of any single discipline, though different disciplines may fit best with certain types of conflict situations.[11] My own view is that diversity among CR professionals should be encouraged rather than stifled. The following sections provide a brief sampling of how different disciplines contribute to our understanding of conflict and conflict resolution.

1. Psychology

Psychology provides many theories on the etiology of conflict: personality theories, communications theories, behavioral theories, decision-making theory, cognitive theory, attribution theory, reactive devaluation, systems theories, sociocultural theories, problem solving, and developmental theories (Weinhold & Weinhold, 2000).

---

[10]People who take courses in mediation or other models of CR often do so with the intention of developing a practice in contractual CR. Although good opportunities exist in this growing field, there are still far more uses of CR on an emergent basis, as part of one's other professional roles. Another wonderful facet of emergent CR is that many CR strategies and techniques can be used in your personal life as well as in your professional life.

[11]For example, medical practitioners for situations that require medical expertise or teachers where educational expertise is required. Some CR roles do not depend on substantive knowledge of the dispute. Mediators, for example, are experts in process. Advocates with substantive expertise, on the other hand, may be required to assist a party with weak knowledge in a particular area.

Personality theories suggest that people have persistent characteristic traits that affect how they deal with conflict. These traits may be inborn, learned, or developed in response to earlier life experiences (e.g., rigid parenting , childhood sexual abuse, or other traumatic events). People with carefree, easygoing personalities may be more amenable to working through problems without a high level of conflict. Conversely, people with certain personality disorders (narcissistic, borderline, or obsessive-compulsive) are prone to high-conflict relationships and experiences. People with narcissistic personality disorder, for instance, are so centered their own needs and wishes that they have a sense of entitlement. They do not acknowledge the needs and perspectives of others, denying responsibility for their problems and chronically blaming others (Eddy, 2003). The literature is mixed on what types of therapy are effective in curing or controlling personality disorders. Regardless, CR professionals must find ways to take personalities into account when determining what types of conflict resolution strategies will be most effective with a particular person. When dealing with people with low self-esteem, for example, even mild confrontation may be too much for them to handle. The CR professional may find it best to avoid direct criticism, given how these individuals tend to internalize disapproval and withdraw. Helping them identify their strengths can help them become more assertive. Consider a person who grew up in a home with alcoholism. This person may have learned that yelling is an appropriate way of responding to conflict. Merely asking the person not to yell may not be sufficient; the person's yelling response may be so deeply ingrained that it is not completely voluntary. Alternatively, consider a person who is naturally shy. Because this person may have trouble speaking up in public, a CR professional might want to offer another method of addressing conflict (e.g., online conflict resolution where people interact over the Internet rather than face-to-face; Raines, 2005; Syme, 2006).

Communications theory teaches us about functional and dysfunctional ways in which people impart and receive messages (Ivey & Ivey, 2007; Nicoterra, 1995; Oetzel & Ting-Toomey, 2006). Consider a simple question from Sally to Gil: "Do you want to go to the movies?" Simple? Perhaps not. When the process of communication is broken down into components, we see ample room for misunderstandings. Before asking the question, Sally formulates her thoughts: "I want to go to a movie with Gil." She then puts these thoughts into words or codes. Wanting to avoid sounding too direct, Sally chooses not to make a statement but instead to ask Gil whether he wants to go. Gil hears the question and must interpret it. Assuming that he has no problems with his hearing, proficiency in English, or cognitive abilities, Gil still has a number of choices for interpretation. He concludes that this is an open question, not thinking that Sally really does want to go to a movie. He was not thinking about going to a movie, so he says, "Not really."

One role for CR professionals is to facilitate more effective communication. If we know how communication is coded, transferred, and uncoded, we can teach, model, and facilitate more effective communication. Microskills training and interviewing courses are based on communication theory (Ivey & Ivey, 2007). Basic listening skills such as paraphrasing, reflection of feelings, and summarization are crucial to conflict resolution. Reflective listening allows the listener to check back with the speaker to ensure that the message intended was the message received (see Chapter 2). Furthermore, use of reflective skills helps build a trusting relationship, because the listener demonstrates empathy with the speaker. Consider the last verbal argument you witnessed. Both parties were talking, perhaps even talking loudly. Was anybody really listening?

Behavioral theories (classical conditioning, operant conditioning, and social learning) suggest that the manner in which people react to conflict is a learned response (Furlong, 2005). According to classical conditioning, certain behaviors are triggered by stimuli that the person associates with particular types of responses. Assume that Barney responds to fear by withdrawing. If Barney learns to associate being in a crowded room with fear, then being in a crowded room will tend to trigger Barney's fear response, withdrawal. If a CR professional wants to help Barney respond more constructively, the CR professional could help Barney with strategies on how to avoid the problematic trigger or help Barney find new ways to respond to the trigger. According to operant conditioning, people tend to repeat behaviors that are rewarded and tend not to repeat behaviors that are not rewarded. Consider a toddler who throws a tantrum, and his parents respond by making a big fuss. If the toddler enjoys the attention, the toddler is more likely to throw tantrums in the future. A CR professional could teach the parents how to manage their response to the tantrums in a manner that does not reinforce the tantrum behavior. According to social learning theory, people tend to model or follow the behavior of people who are significant in their lives. If you grew up with parents who used problem-solving approaches to resolve conflict, you are more likely to use them yourself. CR professionals often use modeling by demonstrating constructive responses to dealing with conflict (e.g., modeling listening and assertiveness skills for clients).

Decision-making theory looks at various factors that affect people's choices and behaviors. For instance, do they operate on egocentric interpretations of fairness, do they have overconfidence about the likelihood of attaining favorable outcomes, do they rigidly adhere to a commitment even if it is no longer in their best interests, and do they assume that conflict is a win-lose proposition rather than look for opportunities for win-win solutions (Bazerman & Shonk, 2005)? Decision-making theory combines research and knowledge from economics, psychology, strategic studies,[12] game theory,[13] and even mathematics (Barash & Webel, 2002; Menkel-Meadow et al., 2005; Yilmaz, 1997; Young, 1961). In order to help two or more people make joint decisions, CR professionals can use decision-making theory to assess how different individuals may be making their decisions. If you were thinking about asking your boss for a raise, what factors would influence your decision? Would your decision be based on a rational cost-benefit analysis, taking into account the risk that your boss might fire you? Would emotions such as pride, frustration, or hope affect your decision? Would past experiences shape your choice? Would your choice be a conscious decision, or would subconscious processes affect your behavior? How can you ensure that your cognitions or thought processes are not distorted? (See Appendix 1 for Decision Tree Analysis, one method for helping people make reasoned decisions).

---

[12]Studies for military strategy and national defense.

[13]Game theory is an approach to determining how parties will act and respond to one another under specific circumstances, using mathematical models. Many of the models assume that participants will act rationally, meaning that they will try to minimize risks and maximize gains to themselves.

Cognitive theories describe how distorted thought processes develop and affect the choices people make in their lives (Furlong, 2005; Mayer, 2000). One cognitive distortion that is particularly pertinent in conflict situations is the belief that there is always someone who is right and someone who is wrong. This is called *dualistic thinking*. CR professionals can help people with dualistic thinking understand that conflict situations may be more complex. Sometimes, there can be more than one person who is right, more than one person who is wrong, or various levels of innocence and guilt. Another type of cognitive distortion relates to the effects of precedents on people's expectations. If you had never owned a sport-utility vehicle (SUV), and the government said that you cannot have one because of SUVs' impact on the environment, you might not be too upset. If you owned an SUV and the government said you could not have one, you would probably be more upset. Knowing that people's expectations are often based on precedent, CR professionals can help people frame changes as adding to, rather than subtracting from, what people have. Rather than tell people you are going to take away their SUVs, for instance, the government could offer people alternatives that will help them save gas and money, as well as contribute to cleaner air (Hackley, Bazerman, Ross, & Shapiro, 2005). Other common cognitive biases that CR practitioners need to consider are

1. The assumption that negotiations are necessarily fixed-sum, which leads negotiators to miss opportunities for mutually beneficial trade-offs;
2. Self-serving or egocentric interpretations of fairness;
3. Overconfidence about the likelihood of attaining a favorable outcome;
4. Escalation of commitment to a previously selected course of action, when it is no longer the best alternative; and
5. Overlooking the value of considering the cognitive perspective of one's counterpart (Bazerman & Shonk, 2005, p. 53).

Attribution theory, a subset of cognitive theory, suggests that people attach different meanings to past, current, or future events, depending on their beliefs, attitudes, and past experiences (Wilmot & Hocker, 2007). When individuals are hurt or negatively affected by an event, for instance, they try to make sense of it by ascribing its cause to someone or something. Most people prefer to see themselves in a positive light, so they assign blame to a situation or to others (Furlong, 2005). Ascribing innocence to ourselves means we do not have to confront the fact that we may have been lazy, negligent, lacking information, or mean. Ascribing negative intentions or blame to others ("She ran over my bike on purpose") makes it hard for people to trust one another and work through conflicts collaboratively. Accordingly, attribution theory helps explain certain stereotypes, particularly when we use them to blame or scapegoat others for social problems such as unemployment and violence (Ting-Toomey & Oetzel, 2001). By understanding attribution processes, CR professionals can strategize ways to help people reconsider their assumptions or beliefs. They can also use confidence-building strategies (Chapter 7) to help people establish greater trust and overcome stereotypes or other misperceptions. In the situation where a car driver ran over a bicycle, the cyclist might label the driver as evil or intentionally hostile. By helping the cyclist consider whether this event was just an accident or some other explanation, the helping professional can help the cyclist and driver develop more accurate understandings of what actually happened, including each other's motivations. In metaphoric terms, a CR professional helps people with clouded or distorted vision by asking them to try wearing different lenses. These lenses may help people see things more clearly, in greater detail, with higher acuity, or from a different perspective.

Reactive devaluation, another offshoot of cognitive theory, refers to the way people often respond suspiciously to offers made by others who are seen as the enemy. If someone you dislike proposes a solution, you might reject it simply because you do not trust the other person. If the same proposal came from a friend or even a neutral person, you might be willing to accept it (Dubler & Liebman, 2004). CR professionals can use the converse of reactive devaluation to help people resolve conflict—for instance, acting as neutrals themselves and offering suggestions for solution. Alternatively, they could bring others into the conflict resolution process whom the distrustful parties might be able to trust (e.g., friends, admired elders, or independent professionals).

Systems theories teach us that a relationship between individuals or groups is not simply the sum of the parts. Interactions are dynamic processes. Components of a system are interdependent. The actions of each individual in a system affect the actions of each other individual (Kirst-Ashman & Hull, 2005). CR specialists can help clients understand that they can really only control their own behavior; however, they can try to behave in ways that are more likely to bring about positive responses in the other. Systems tend to work toward a certain homeostasis or equilibrium, making it hard for people to move away from ingrained patterns of interaction, either straying from their expected roles or bending the rules of behavior that govern the system (Wilmot & Hocker, 2007). Your boss always puts on a tough face, making it difficult to approach him; as a result, you usually avoid confronting him. How can you change your pattern of interaction, not knowing whether your boss will respond in kind? Systems theory also teaches CR professionals to look beyond the immediate disputants when helping them resolve conflict. Conflict exists within all social systems, including social, political, religious, and economic systems. If the primary conflictants are feeling stress from employers, family members, neighbors, healthcare professionals, clergy, bankers, or other systems in their social environments, the CR professional may need to focus part of the CR process on work with these systems (Mayer, 2004).

Sociocultural theories view conflict in relation to diverse aspects of cultural and social interaction, including differences in language, communication styles, role expectations, conceptions of time, values, beliefs, norms, and rituals. Sociocultural diversity may be based on ethnicity, race, culture, sexual orientation, gender, age, political affiliation, socioeconomic status, ability/disability, or other group identifications. Understanding sociocultural diversity is important to ensuring that CR processes are effective, whether the conflict is among members of the same group or between people from different groups (Oetzel & Ting-Toomey, 2006). In patriarchal cultures, for instance, men have greater political clout than women (Miller, 2001). If a CR practitioner is mandated to advocate on behalf of women, the practitioner could benefit from knowing ways in which women from that culture can exert power and influence, notwithstanding the overall system of patriarchy. CR practitioners must also be aware that people from different cultures have different perceptions of time. People who have a flexible view of time, for instance, may run into conflict with people who expect them to adhere to rigid time schedules (e.g., "The meeting starts promptly at 8:30 A.M." or "The client will complete her goals by March 15"). Likewise, people who prefer a slow or natural pace may find it difficult to participate in a CR process that moves forward quickly or according to artificial deadlines (Macduff, 2006).

Many CR models build on a generic problem-solving approach, common to most helping professions. *The traditional problem-solving approach is a staged model, which directs the professional to proceed through a prescribed sequence of steps; for example, (1) identify the problem or issues; (2) identify the underlying concerns, needs, and interests of the parties; (3) generate options; (4) build agreement; and (5) implement and monitor the decision* (Fisher, Ury, & Patton, 1997; Kruk, 1997; Hoefer, 2006). During implementation and monitoring, other problems may be identified, sending the parties back to the first step. Anthropologists note that while linear models fit well with Western cultures, other cultures are more comfortable with circular models (Wilmot & Hocker, 2007). Rather than asking the parties to move through steps sequentially, circularity suggests that there is no fixed beginning or end, with iterations back and forth through various stages. How the problem is seen, for instance, depends on what is happening at other points of the process. One might have to revisit problem definition while working on agreement building or implementation. None of the stages are fixed at just one point in time.

Developmental theories predict a series of tasks and challenges that people tend to experience as they progress through various life stages. Developmental theories, such as Erikson's (1950) psychosocial stages of human development, can help CR professionals helping clients with family-based conflict. Parent-youth conflict, for instance, may be explained by the transitions that a family experiences when a youth moves from childhood to adulthood. As adolescents strive for autonomy and identity development, their parents may have difficulty with challenges to their authority. Knowledge of developmental stages allows the CR practitioner to help both parents and youths view conflict as part of the family life cycle and redefine their roles in relationship to one another.

Another branch of developmental theory that has specific interest to CR professionals is the process of dealing with loss. Kübler-Ross (1997) identifies five stages that people go through when they face their own mortality: denial, anger, depression, bargaining, and acceptance. These stages apply well to various sorts of loss issues. Conflict often occurs around loss: loss of a relationship (such as a job or marriage); loss of physical abilities (perhaps from a car accident), loss of property (resulting from theft or other crime), or loss of independence (from illness, aging, etc.). When people are in early stages of dealing with loss, they have difficulty acting in "rational" manners. Denial may mean they refuse to acknowledge that conflict exists. Anger may cause them to desire retaliation rather than constructive resolution. Depression may sap their motivation and energy to deal with conflict. If CR practitioners can identify the stages affecting a particular individual, they can help that person move on (Furlong, 2005). They can also help the other parties empathize with the grieving individual.

Some models of CR are based on very specific psychosocial theories and models of intervention (Weinhold & Weinhold, 2000). For example, family mediation models have been developed based on strategic and structural family therapy (Aponte, 1991; Irving & Benjamin, 1995), narrative therapy (Winslade & Monk, 2000), and existential theory (Gaynier, 2005). Other models are less specific about their theoretical premises, allowing the CR professionals to do their own interpretations. The risk of using CR strategies without a theoretical or empirical foundation is that we have no premise to say what will be effective, what will not be effective, and why. Still, many models of CR are in the early stages of developing a comprehensive, evidence-based theory of practice (MacFarlane & Mayer, 2005).

2. Business Administration

Business administration has contributed to conflict resolution in a number of ways. First, compared with other disciplines, business has a long history of using mediation and arbitration (Douglas, 1962; Kauffman, 1991). Both forms of CR are built into management-labor relations, including collective bargaining processes and grievance procedures for employees. Second, the role of management is basically one of conflict resolution: how to manage people and how to manage other resources of the enterprise (Elangovan, 1995). Organizational behavior theory helps us understand the operations of power and politics in business settings, as well as in not-for-profit agencies (Robbins, 1998). Perhaps surprising to some helping professionals, management has been a leader in analysis of cross-cultural conflict; with globalization of business, management has explored differences in management styles and negotiation styles between people from different countries (Rahim & Blum, 1994). Finally, business schools have been leaders in development of negotiation theory (Lewicki, Litterer, Minton, & Saunders, 1998). While one might assume that negotiation theory from business is all about how to win in a competitive, capitalist environment, business and workplace literature since the 1980s contains numerous examples of CR models that focus on process, relationships, and collaboration (Bush & Folger, 2004; Dana, 1996).

3. Law

Traditionally, the Anglo-American legal system was based on an adversarial model of conflict resolution (Bossy, 2003), with justice based on an analysis of the rights of individuals (Dworkin, 1977; Rawls, 1971). Under this model, conflicting parties could bring their conflicts to court for a determination of rights and resolution prescribed by a judge (Barsky & Gould, 2002). The adversarial system provides a fixed procedure designed to give conflicting parties equal opportunity to present their arguments before an impartial judge or panel of judges. The adversarial process may provide "just solutions," but often at the expense of the relationship between the conflicting parties (Conley & Barr, 1990). Although many of us still think of courts as the ultimate forum for legal disputes, only a small percentage of lawyers do courtroom work. Most lawyers help clients by negotiating contracts or other legal agreements in order to prevent potential conflicts or to resolve disputes once they have arisen. Even among cases that get filed in court, fewer than 10 percent are actually resolved by a full trial of the issues. Most cases are resolved by negotiations, between the parties or between their lawyers. Trials are like the tip of the iceberg: the most visible part. The bulk of the iceberg sits below the water's surface, highlighting the fact that we are not even aware of most disputes, because they are resolved informally and in private.

Until the 1980s, few law schools provided skills or training in CR processes other than trial advocacy. Since then, negotiation, collaborative law, settlement conferences, mediation, and other forms of CR have become much more popular. Indeed, some helping professionals have complained that lawyers have become too dominant in the field of CR. Research has identified different approaches to CR between lawyers and therapists who become CR professionals (State Justice Institute, 1998). Lawyers tend to focus more on rights and settlement of overt legal issues; therapists and other helping professionals tend to focus on process and establishment of a positive relationship between parties (Marlow, 1987). However, these trends are just generalizations. Many legal theorists have challenged traditional legal approaches to CR, encouraging lawyers and other CR professionals to focus more on process, underlying interests, and relationships between the parties (Fisher et al., 1997; Marlow, 1997; Menkel-Meadow et al., 2005).

In criminology and law, the concept of restorative justice has also gained popularity since the 1980s. Whereas traditional forms of *retributive justice* require that people be punished for committing crimes or hurting others, *restorative justice* emphasizes repairing damages and relationships, making things "right" between people who cause or are affected by the commission of a crime. Mediation (Chapter 4) and family group conferencing (Chapter 7) are two of the more prevalent examples of CR processes that embrace restorative justice. Both offer perpetrators, victims, and other community members an opportunity to create solutions that repair the harm caused by the crime (Bazemore & Umbreit, 2001).

4. Education

Education does not have a definitive theory of CR, though it has been a leader in development of educational materials and models of peer mediation[14] (Association for Conflict Resolution, Education Section, n.d.; Safe Schools Ambassadors, n.d.). Many components from CR theory can be traced to constructs in education. Since the 1940s, various models of education have been designed to instill cooperation and conflict management skills in children (Maryama, 1992). One of the unique contributions that education has brought to CR concerns translating abstract theory and complicated processes into terms that can be easily understood by children as young as 3 or 4 years old (Kraybill, 1985). In fact, you might say CR experts could have learned all they needed to know from their kindergarten teachers: Be nice to

---

[14]Peer mediation in schools generally refers to mediation between students, with a student mediator. Teachers and school counselors provide training and support for the student mediators.

others; clean up after yourself; don't fight; if you make a mistake, say you are sorry; if you want something, ask nicely; and when someone else is speaking, be quiet (Fulghum, 2003). Although these teachings are often presented as universal rules of etiquette, they are steeped in cultural assumptions that do not apply across all groups. What is considered a polite request within one group, for instance, might be considered rude or inappropriate in another.

I have had students complain that some conflict resolution readings I provide are too elementary for university students to be studying.[15] In fact, some of the most practical CR materials do sound basic. The challenge comes when you have to put them into practice, at the moment of heated conflict. Think back to the last time you were involved in an argument. How many of the golden rules did you break? Working with some of the brightest and most skilled helping professionals, I have often had to remind them of the basic tenets for constructive interaction. Well-adjusted adults sometimes lapse into making faces and hurling insults when they feel angry, hurt, or simply tired. As I often say to students or clients, "If you catch me breaking any of the ground rules for peaceful dialogue, please let me know."

There is a growing literature on conflict in educational institutions (Barsky & Wood, 2005; Phelan, Barlow, Myrick, Rogers, & Sawa, 2003). Ironically, many of the same institutions that study and teach conflict resolution are fraught with conflict problems themselves. Universities and similar institutions are supposed to promote excellence, independent thought, and academic freedom, while constrained by limited resources, departmental politics, and convoluted bureaucracies: a perfect combination if you want to foster conflict. Consider your experiences in your place of learning: what types of conflict occur, and how are they handled?

5. Social Work and Related Professions

Social work is similar to education in that it plays an important role in CR but borrows from many other disciplines (Barsky, 2006b; Kruk, 1997; Mayer, 2000). Some of the primary contributions of social work come from the field of community development. Social workers have been at the forefront of coalition building, interdisciplinary cooperation, and strategic alliances to advance the causes of disadvantaged groups in society (Bratton, 1997; Zastrow, 2003). Social psychologists have also contributed to community-based conflict resolution. Kurt Lewin's 1940s theories of majority-minority relations, for example, have been used to develop workshops and exercises to build better relationships between ethnic groups with deep-rooted histories of conflict (Bargal & Bar, 1992). Volunteers and other laypeople provide some of the most crucial community work in CR. Unfortunately, their work often goes unnoticed because of inadequate documentation in research or other professional literature.[16]

---

[15]In Israel, kindergarten teachers respond to disruptive students by saying, "Don't act like Members of the Knesset [Parliament]."

[16]Bargal and Bar (1992) suggest the use of participatory action research as a way to wed research and provision of services. Nonprofessionals are more inclined to participate in this form of research, because they can use the research information during the process of intervention.

6. Political Science and Strategic Studies

Political science and strategic studies analyze how governments, nations, social movements, and other political institutions respond to conflict. Helping professionals who work with individuals, families, and small groups may wonder about the relevance of conflict resolution at international and other macro levels.[17] However, the Harvard Program on Negotiation and many other CR institutes often draw parallels between conflicts at these different levels (Fisher & Brown, 1994; also see, in general, the *Negotiation Journal*). International conflicts in the Middle East, Bosnia, Burundi, Northern Ireland, and elsewhere have surprising similarities with conflicts occurring in families, schools, neighborhoods, and workplaces. Conflicts at all of these levels often entail strong emotions (anger, mistrust, fear), blocked communication, and unmet needs or wishes. Strategies that work at one level can often be transferred to the other.

Tension often exists between "strategic studies" and "peace and conflict studies." Both are legitimate areas of conflict resolution. However, as with the lawyer-therapist dichotomy, the orientations of these studies vary significantly. Strategic studies look at how to prevent war, how to win war, and how to encourage states to resolve problems through political processes (negotiation) rather than through force.[18] Peace and conflict studies focus on nonviolent, collaborative means of conflict resolution. Although both branches prefer not to use force, strategic studies are generally more willing to consider the threat and use of force as valid alternatives. As a helping professional, you will have to gauge for yourself whether you are willing to use force or power. You likely place a high value on peace and client self-determination. When, if ever, is the use of force justified? To defend a client from physical harm? To defend a client from emotional harm? To defend a client from social harm?[19] Does it depend on the type of force—physical, psychological, economic, political?

People who use violence typically feel that their violence is justified. They may claim that others have mistreated them or denied them of their basic physical, psychological, social, or spiritual needs (e.g., "They took our land," "They made fun of me," "They destroyed our family," or "They won't let us practice our religion"). When people feel they have been unjustly treated, they often believe that violence is required in order to reclaim their rights and resources or to save face in a humiliating situation (Schirch, 2004). Conflict resolution professionals can make use of peace and conflict theory to help people understand the relationship between perceived injustice and violence, as well as what types of nonviolent responses are effective in redressing perceived injustice.

7. Radical Perspectives

Radical helping professionals may be familiar with a conflict model of practice (Gould, 1987; Rossides, 1998). According to this model, the practitioner's role is to agitate

---

[17]A *macro level* of professional practice refers to community development, public policy development, or other interventions with systems larger than individuals, families, and small groups (i.e., micropractice).

[18]In the *Journal of Strategic Studies*, Miller (1997) defines *peacemaking* as "[a] strategy pursued by an external power, based mainly on diplomatic, although possibly on economic and military measures, designed to promote conflict resolution" (p. 106).

[19]Examples of social harm include unemployment, poverty, discrimination, and inadequate education.

conflict in order to stimulate social change. Marxist, structuralist, and other radical practitioners view oppression in society as a dominant factor in their work (Alinsky, 2001; Carniol, 2005; Freire, 1994; Lundy, 2004; Marx, 1964; Sandole & van der Merwe, 1993). Acting on behalf of certain minorities—for example, women, people of color, gays and lesbians, or people with disabilities—these practitioners use strategies such as protests, strikes, boycotts, and civil disobedience to fight for social improvement. Rather than work on a consensual basis with existing social institutions, they apply the conflict model, using short-term social disorder to transform society.

The premises behind the conflict model are significantly different from those behind most conflict resolution models. The term *conflict resolution* is broad enough to include all means of dealing with conflict, but most professionals in the conflict resolution movement strive toward collaborative problem solving. Some radical professionals question or even reject mainstream conflict resolution, suggesting that it ignores the power differentials between privileged and oppressed groups in society. According to this view, models that promote peace and harmony suppress conflict and permit continued oppression of disadvantaged groups (Nader, 1992). How can oppressed groups in society expect to be dealt with fairly if they rely solely on collaborative processes and the goodwill of their oppressors? This type of question needs to be taken seriously, regardless of whether you see yourself as a radical professional.

My own bias is that both collaborative and radical conflict processes have legitimate roles. In fact, they are not mutually exclusive. One may need to use them in combination. A client may need to initiate conflict with a welfare worker in order to upset the status quo. Following this confrontation, negotiation may be useful in coming to a new understanding. This book focuses on collaborative processes, but the limitations of collaborative processes and alternative conflict responses will be raised for discussion throughout the text. For radical professionals, collaborative conflict resolution may not fit with certain aspects of your work—challenging societal institutions and people in power; upsetting the status quo. However, you may find collaborative CR applicable for work within a particular group—for example, building coalitions and alliances, working with colleagues within an agency, and helping clients handle conflict with others who have similar power or status in society.

8. Eclectic and Integrative Approaches

For all CR professionals, as you read on and work through the exercises, consider whether collaborative CR can work fairly if there is a significant power differential between the parties. What is your role, if any, with regard to redistributing power? If collaborative CR is not appropriate for a particular situation, then is a better alternative possible? CR is about selecting the best means of conflict resolution. Unfortunately, some mediators and other CR professionals fall into the trap of becoming so enamored with one mode of CR that they promote it to the exclusion of all other modes.

Two possible directions are to take an eclectic or an integrative approach. By using an eclectic approach, the practitioner assesses the situation and selects theories or models of CR that best fit the situation. By using an integrative approach, the practitioner looks for ways to integrate or combine the best features of various approaches (Corey & Corey, 2006). For learning purposes, you may want to focus on one approach at a time. As you become familiar and comfortable with various approaches, consider how you can match approaches with various situations or combine aspects of various approaches.

SAFE CLASSROOM AND CONSTRUCTIVE FEEDBACK

Now that we have considered various types of theory that inform conflict resolution, it is time to put theory into practice. This section provides specific suggestions on how to ensure that you contribute to a positive teaching and learning environment in your conflict resolution class. In order for everyone to get the most out of the discussions, role-plays, and other exercises in this book, participants must have a safe atmosphere for taking risks, opportunities to individualize learning activities, and room for the learners to take responsibility for their own learning. Although the style of the instructor contributes or detracts from these factors, everyone in the class plays a key role. After all, there are far more learners than instructors in the class.

To foster a safe atmosphere in the classroom, offer your colleagues unconditional respect[20] and constructive feedback. Giving and receiving feedback are skills that are useful in CR practice, as well as in learning situations. *Giving feedback* means sharing your thoughts about another person's behavior, enabling the other person to reflect on whether the information is helpful and whether to try to make changes based on the feedback. In order to provide constructive, nonthreatening feedback, consider the following guidelines:[21]

GUIDELINE	EXAMPLE
1. Focus on *behavior* rather than on *person*.	"The pace of questioning was very fast," rather than "You were very fast."
2. Focus on direct *observations* rather than on *inferences*.	"Your voice was raised," rather than "You sounded angry."
3. Focus on *description* rather than *judgment*.	"Your reframing allowed the client to see things from your perspective," rather than "Your use of reframing was good [or bad]."
4. Focus on *here and now* or in *future*, rather than on *there and then*.	"The next time a client confronts you like that, you could try an empathy statement," rather than "You missed a good opportunity to use an empathy statement."

---

[20]Chapter 3 describes how to "separate the person from the problem." A person might vehemently disagree with another individual's beliefs or values but still demonstrate respect for the individual.

[21]These tips on feedback are derived from a flyer entitled "Constructive Feedback." Unfortunately, the flyer did not provide information about the author.

GUIDELINE	EXAMPLE
5. Focus on *behavior* in terms of *more or less*.	"To make your point more dramatically, you could use larger hand gestures," rather than "I didn't like your hand gestures."
6. Focus on *sharing ideas* rather than *giving advice*.	"One alternative would be to terminate the meeting," rather than, "You should have terminated the meeting."
7. Focus on the *value* it has to the receiver.	"Your arguments were direct and assertive, two skills that you said you wanted to improve."
8. Give feedback in *small amounts*.	Select one or two good points, rather than flood the person with feedback.
9. Focus on what the person can *use*.	Avoid making suggestions about things the recipient cannot change (e.g., "The problem is you are too tall").
10. Be aware of appropriate *time and place* for giving it.	Sometimes feedback about sensitive issues should be left for a private exchange, rather than in front of others.
11. Use *clear and concrete* examples.	"The mood in the room cheered up when you told the Sherpa anecdote," rather than "Your story thing was nice."
12. Use I statements rather than "you" or "we."	"I try to be very assertive in similar situations," rather than "You need to be more assertive."

The recipient of feedback also plays an active role in the exchange of feedback. Strategies for *receiving feedback* include the following:

- Hear and understand what has been said to you—reflect back what you have heard; clarify and ask for more information to ensure that you have understood the message intended.
- Check out feedback with others.
- Give yourself time to reflect on feedback.
- Decide what you will do with the feedback. You may decide to validate what the other person said and try to incorporate the feedback in the future. Alternatively, after deliberation, you may decide for yourself that no change is necessary at this time.
- Offer thanks for feedback in order to acknowledge the other person's honest attempts to offer constructive feedback.

Ideally, feedback for learning purposes is separated from sanctions, such as grades or remuneration. Some CR courses are offered on a pass-fail basis in order to reduce student anxiety about grades. Some CR professors allow students to negotiate their grades. I avoid giving grades for role-plays, to encourage students to take risks and feel less inhibited about showing themselves making "mistakes" (how else can we learn?). Instead, I ask students to provide process recordings[22] or detailed analyses of their role-plays. Grades are based on the students' analysis of the process rather than the performance itself.

In addition to giving and receiving feedback, you can use the exercises in this book to practice facilitating the feedback process. For each small-group exercise, designate a facilitator to help the group provide feedback to one another. The facilitator should use questions that fit with the suggestions for feedback provided earlier—for instance, asking about behaviors rather than asking whether the performance was good or bad, and inviting people to focus on positive skills demonstrated in the role-plays. Use the *debriefing* questions provided after each role-play to assist with facilitating feedback, but feel free to add your own questions to go over the main points of the exercise (McGuire & Inlow, 2005). Do not be surprised if conflicts arise during debriefing. Use the CR skills you are learning to help you deal with them.

USING THIS TEXT TO MAXIMIZE LEARNING

I would like to say this text is prepared in a way that allows you to select chapters of interest and read them in any order. Unfortunately, I cannot. The topics presented build on one another in the sequence presented, particularly the first three chapters. Chapter 1 has provided an overview of conflict resolution, including definitions, roles, and theories that inform CR practice. Chapter 2 describes the nature of a reflective practitioner in CR practice, including issues related to professional awareness and artistic use of self. Being aware of your feelings, values, and beliefs will help ensure that you respond to conflict situations in a deliberate, effective, and creative manner. Reflective practice is crucial regardless of the method of CR that you are learning or using. Chapters 3 to 6 illustrate how helping professionals can use four specific methods of CR: negotiation, mediation, group facilitation, and advocacy. Within each CR method, practitioners can apply different theories and approaches. The theories and approaches presented in the negotiation chapter provide a basis for understanding the theories and approaches that can be used for mediation, group facilitation, and advocacy, because these are basically forms of assisted negotiation. Chapter 7 introduces additional CR methods in which helping professionals can assume the role of a third-party practitioner: fact finding, trust building, peace building, parenting coordination, family group conferencing, intergroup encounters, and spiritual healing. This chapter highlights the breadth of methods that helping professionals can use to help people affected by conflict. Chapter 8 provides concluding suggestions about CR for helping professionals, including ways that you can participate in the growth and development of the CR movement, in your workplace, in your community, nationally, and internationally. Appendix 1 describes Decision Tree Analysis, a method for helping people make reasoned decisions about how to respond to a conflict situation. Trees provide graphic representations of decision choices and potential outcomes, allowing rational analysis of the risks and benefits of various courses of action. Appendix 2 provides a sample process recording, which is a method of analyzing CR processes and role-plays for the major assignments. Appendix 3 demonstrates how metaphors

---

[22] An example of a process recording is provided in Appendix 2.

(symbolic language) can be used in CR to help people view issues from different per-spectives. Appendix 4 lists resources for further information and research, including videos, professional associations, and databases. If you happen to skip a section and come across a strange term, you can find easy access to a definition in the Glossary. The References lists all the resources cited throughout the text.

I have attempted to structure this text based on the tenets of andragogy—that is, adult learning (Knowles, Holton, & Swanson, 1998). Adults come into the class with significant life experience and knowledge that can be used to enrich the class. Adults have the capacity for self-directed learning, based on internal motivations. The role of the educator is to provide a safe environment for learning and to offer support (MacKearcher, 1997). The materials provided are not intended to be pre-scriptive. I present a range of CR approaches for you to explore and experiment with. Ultimately, you will have to decide which ones to integrate into your practice. Often, the most successful exercises and assignments are those initiated by students themselves—be imaginative and creative.

Different people learn best in different ways—through reading, discussing, observing others, or doing it themselves (Kolb, 1974; Lewicki, 1997). Accord-ingly, each chapter contains theoretical abstractions, discussion questions, and class exercises that you can observe or experience firsthand. Professors often ask students to prepare for classes by reading the material ahead of time; this ap-proach makes sense, for professors, since most of them are abstract conceptualiz-ers. Although this ordering works for some students, others learn best by doing first and then going back to the theory. Throughout the text, I emphasize the value of preparing for any CR intervention. If you decide to "wing it" for class exercises, you may find yourself at a disadvantage compared with others who read the materials and prepare in advance. However, as long as you reflect back on the experiential exercises and go back to the theory, you can effectively inte-grate theory and practice. Am I condoning procrastination and cramming at the end of the course? You can certainly choose the best way for you to learn with-out me telling you (Barsky, 2006b).

Throughout the text, I provide self-inventories to help you reflect on your progress and focus your learning. Some inventories are designed to help you clarify your value orientations and preferred styles of conflict resolution. Others help you identify your CR strengths and learning needs. I have included more exercises than you could possibly complete in one course, so pick and choose exercises that best meet your professional development goals. Some jurisdictions have moved toward competency-based accreditation for CR professionals; that is, in order to obtain a license or certification to practice CR, you will be required to demonstrate specific skills and knowledge. The inventories in this text can help you prepare for these re-quirements. If you intend to apply for a particular form of accreditation, contact your local CR associations in order to determine their specific requirements (for further information, see Professional Associations in Appendix 4).

The exercises at the end of each chapter include conflict situations from a broad spectrum of contexts: family counseling, child welfare, mental and physical health, education, professional ethics, gerontology, social assistance, criminal justice, interdis-ciplinary practice, anti-oppression, human services, and pastoral counseling. Feel free to alter certain case facts to bring the exercise closer to your own preferred area of practice. However, students often find it exciting to play roles that are new or unfamiliar.

KEY POINTS

- Social conflict exists when two or more parties express differences in beliefs, values, or interests, whether the divergence is real or perceived.

- *Conflict resolution* refers to any means of dealing with conflict, including negotiation, mediation, and advocacy.

- Alternative methods of CR can be differentiated by who has decision-making power, what is the role of the third-party intervenor (if any), whether communication flows between conflicting parties directly or indirectly, and whether the process is adversarial or collaborative.

- Helping professionals can use elements of CR within their traditional helping roles (emergent CR). Alternatively, helping professionals can undertake explicit CR roles (contractual CR).

- CR draws on a range of theoretical perspectives in order to analyze conflict and develop models of intervention.

- The classroom experience can be used as a laboratory for learning how to deal with conflict, particularly when providing, receiving, or facilitating feedback during class exercises.

DISCUSSION QUESTIONS AND EXERCISES

1. WARM-UP EXERCISE: "How Long Is this Class, Anyway?" Before the class gets started, we need to decide how long the class is and how we are going to spend this time: lecture, theoretical discussion, practice role-plays, videotapes, and so forth. Let's make this a class decision. Your mission, should you choose to accept it, is to discuss these issues and present your instructor with the decisions. You have 15 minutes.

   Debriefing: Ask one person to facilitate discussion of the following debriefing questions:

   - What strikes you most about how people dealt with this conflict?
   - What roles did various people in the class play?
   - What skills techniques did different people use?
   - What made dealing with this conflict more difficult than you might have originally thought?
   - What did you learn about how you deal with this type of conflict?

2. MEANING OF CONFLICT: This is an exercise in "free association." When you hear the word *conflict*, what are the first images that come to mind? Write down three or four words that came to mind, to be shared with the class.

   Debriefing: After you have composed a list of words from the whole class, consider the following questions:

   - Which of the words have positive connotations? Negative connotations?

- How do you personally feel about dealing with these different types of conflict?
- What is the relationship between diversity and conflict?

3. ROLES AND NEUTRALITY: Identify your role as a helping professional (e.g., teacher, therapist, vocational counselor). In the course of your work, does neutrality play a role? If so, what is this role? Does neutrality depend on your model of practice (e.g., solution focused, behavioral, ecosystems)? Your professional values? What does your profession's code of ethics say about neutrality (McCorkle, 2005)?

4. MAPPING CR: During a Parent-Teacher Association meeting, two parents, Ms. Jones and Mr. Singh, complain that a boy named Kyle Bragin is bullying their children. Kyle's parents become defensive and say that little Bonnie Jones and Rajib Singh must be lying to their parents; Kyle is a good son. As the arguments escalate, Kyle's teacher tries to separate everyone. Once tempers cool down, the school guidance counselor, Mrs. Finch, asks to meet all four parents in her office to see whether there is some way they can work out this problem together. Describe the role that each person in this scenario is playing. Draw a diagram, indicating the directions of the conflicts and flows of communication between all of the parties.

5. CAT AND DOG, PART I: How do you stop a cat and a dog from fighting?

6. CAT AND DOG, PART II: In a cat and dog fight, which animal has more power? Why? Will the one with more power win the fight?

7. GOLDEN RULE: The Golden Rule says, "Do unto others as you would have them do unto you." How is this lesson helpful in conflict situations? How might this lesson be problematic? Under what circumstances would it be better to use the Platinum Rule, "Do unto others as they would like done unto them"?

8. UNDERLYING THEORY: Identify a theoretical perspective you are familiar with from your previous education or practice (e.g., existential theory, organizational theory, social construction theory, psychoanalytic theory, attachment theory). List the key elements of this theory, including its assumptions, descriptors, and predictions about human behavior. How does this theory help you understand the nature of social conflict and how you could intervene in a constructive manner?

9. ETHICS OF VIOLENCE: When, if ever, can a helping professional justify use of violence to resolve conflict? Consider the code of ethics of your own profession and various models of practice within it. Try to come up with an ethical rule that is based on your values. Give examples to illustrate the limits of your rule (i.e., when violence is justified and when it is not justified).

10. STINKING THINKING: Assume you have a car that you take to a garage for service. Consider each of the following scenarios. Write down your answer to (a) before reading (b).

   a. The service manager says that her mechanics can make your brakes 20 percent safer than they are. How much would you pay to have your brakes made 20 percent safer?

   b. Assume instead that the service manager says that they can make your brakes 20 percent less safe and that she will pay you to allow them to make your brakes less safe. How much money would she have to pay you in order to allow them to make your brakes 20 percent less safe?

Now, compare what you wrote for (a) and (b). Which amount is greater? Most people say they are willing to pay less to improve their brakes than the amount they will demand to allow the garage to make their brakes less safe. Is this rational? Which theory in this chapter helps explain the difference between (a) and (b)? How could the service manager reframe the offer in (b) in order to make you more likely to accept it (Hackley et al., 2005)?

11. PERSONAL CONFLICT RESPONSES: Assume that one of your coworkers, Zoë, is lazy and unreliable. When Zoë misses work or falls behind, Zoë's work falls into your lap. Your supervisor, Jamna, knows what is going on but has done nothing about it.[23] Your natural reaction would be to

    a. Do Zoë's work and avoid getting into any conflicts.
    b. Confront Zoë and Jamna in an assertive manner.
    c. Get angry and blow off steam.
    d. Bring Zoë and Jamna together to problem solve with you.
    e. Make a deal with Zoë that if she does half her work, you'll pick up the other half.
    f. Other (specify) _____

    • What are the positive aspects of your natural response?
    • What are the potential risks or problems with your natural response?
    • Which of the other responses would you like to learn to do more effectively?
    • If you approached Zoë to negotiate a solution, would you see Zoë as
      _____ a friend? _____ an adversary? _____ a professional colleague?
      _____ the cause of the problem
      _____ other? (specify) _____
    • Is your primary goal
      _____ not doing Zoë's work? _____ getting Zoë to do her fair share?
      _____ reaching agreement? _____ reducing your anger?
      _____ developing a better relationship with Zoë?
      _____ improving the way in which you handle conflict with Zoë?
      _____ connecting with Zoë in a more spiritual manner?
      _____ Other? (specify) _____
    • If you decide to meet with Zoë, how would you begin?
      _____ Tell her you will not do her work?
      _____ Suggest a fair solution?
      _____ Say a prayer or opening meditation?
      _____ Tell her what you'll do if she doesn't agree?
      _____ Demonstrate care and understanding for her situation?
      _____ Tell her you will go to your supervisor if she does not agree?
      _____ Take the most comfortable chair?
      _____ Therapize or counsel her?
      _____ Other? (specify) _____
    • What is your basic strategy?
    • What do you find to be the most persuasive way of influencing people like Zoë?

---

[23]Some of the questions below are derived from Ertel (1991).

CONFLICTIA

The following case study provides a context for selected exercises throughout the text. The details in this case are meant to enrich the exercises and provide a real-life flavor. If you prefer to set the role-plays in your own community, develop a background information sheet that can be shared with the other students you are working with.

Conflictia is a city-state, established in the year 2007 by the League of Collaborative Nations as a pilot site for a new society in which various helping professionals have been provided with special training and expertise in conflict resolution. Conflictia is neither a Garden of Eden nor a Paradise Island. The city is populated with people who have real problems, diverse needs, and limited resources.

Approximately 600,000 people live in Conflictia. The demographics of Conflictia's population include the following:

Economic Level	Ethnic Background	Religion	Educational Level of Adults	Employment Status
8% wealthy	28% Asian (including Pacific Islands)	25% Muslim	10% less than high school (grade 12)	8% unemployed, looking for work
15% upper-middle economic class	10% South American	20% Buddhist	55% high school graduates	22% unpaid, work in home
42% middle economic class	15% North American	15% Catholic	30% university degree or college diploma	16% employed in financial and service industries
25% marginal income and wealth	16% European	10% Protestant	5% more than one university degree	9% employed in agriculture
10% live below poverty line	12% African	15% Hindu	**Age Distribution**	16% employed in high technology
	5% Middle Eastern	2% Jewish	23% under 18	12% self-employed (business)
	14% mixed	9% atheist	27% from 18 to 30	15% employed in manufacturing
		3% agnostic	32% from 31 to 65	12% employed in helping professions
			18% over 65	

Politically, Conflictia operates under a parliamentary democracy with a single Council of Representatives. Three parties currently hold seats in the government: (1) the Right of Center (ROC) Party, (2) the Left of Center (LOC) Party, and (3) the Somewhere in the Middle (SIM) Party. ROC's leader, Mr. Alby Wright, is head of state, by virtue of his party's majority vote in the last election. Dr. N. D. Sisive is party leader for the SIMs. Ms. Sasha Lizte leads the LOCs.

Diversity Plus is the largest mental health and social service agency in Conflictia. This agency provides services to adults, children, families, and groups with problems ranging from mental illness to conflict with the law, immigration, domestic violence, drug abuse, and family planning. Diversity Plus hires a broad range of helping professionals, including psychologists, social workers, family therapists, nurses, pastoral counselors, human service workers, criminologists, and youth care providers. Some services are publicly funded, based on a means test.[24] Others charge a fee for service.

The largest hospital in Conflictia, Conflictia Hope, has 280 beds. Conflictia Hope is a general hospital, but it has special units for people with cancer, AIDS, and heart disease. Conflictia Hope employs medical doctors, nurses, psychologists, and social workers.

Two schools in the city's downtown core are Conflictia High School (grades 9 to 12) and Conflictia Elementary School (kindergarten to grade 8). Both schools employ teachers and guidance counselors. Conflictia Elementary offers special programs for children with emotional problems, learning disabilities, and cognitive impairments.

Conflictia Justice Center includes a variety of services for people who have breached the criminal laws of Conflictia. It employs judges, lawyers, probation officers, and other counselors. The Justice Center is mandated to promote "restorative justice," meaning that it encourages offenders to rectify damages they have caused and repair relationships with those they have hurt.

ROLE-PLAY 1.1: "SUFFER THE BUFFER"

There is trouble in the cardiac ward of Conflictia Hope Hospital. Two patients in a shared room are fighting over whether to turn the television on or off. Plato is bored and wants to turn the television on in order to watch a soap opera. Phineas has a headache and hates soap operas. He wants the television off. Nyron[25] is a nurse who hears them arguing and comes into the room. To prepare for this role-play, each person should only read the **confidential facts** for his or her own role.

Confidential Facts for Plato and Phineas

Plato is particularly upset that Phineas is objecting to his watching soaps, because Plato pays a daily fee to rent the television. Phineas receives public assistance and cannot afford to pay for his own television. Both are recovering from triple bypass

---

[24]To be eligible for publicly funded services, family income must fall below the poverty line established by the government on an annual basis.

[25]Role-play names can be changed to match the genders of the people playing various roles. Often, I use names beginning with the same initial as the role, in order to help you remember who is playing which role (e.g., Nyron—Nurse).

surgery, and their doctors have told them to reduce their stress. Before starting the role-play, think about the role you are playing and how you will portray it. Write down a few notes to focus your thoughts. What are your reasons for being in the hospital? What are your possible arguments for how to deal with the conflict over the television? Why has this conflict escalated into a fight? How will you respond to the nurse if the nurse acts authoritatively, meekly, and so forth?

Confidential facts for Nyron

You are going to take on two CR roles, buffer and arbitrator. Refresh your memory about these roles, if need be, by rereading the sections on buffers and arbitrators. Write down some of your strategies and sample sentences that you might use. Do not try to memorize them. Do not bring your notes when you go into role. The notes are just a tool for preparation and reflection.

Confidential facts for Observers

As you watch the role-play, try to identify at least three strategies that Nyron uses in handling this conflict. How did the parties respond to each strategy?

Debriefing: After the role-play, have one of the observers facilitate debriefing, using the following questions:

- What did Nyron do that contributed positively to the process?
- What did Plato and Phineas appreciate about the way Nyron handled the conflict?
- What other CR approaches could a nurse use in a similar conflict situation?
- If the conflict escalated into a fight, how would (or should) a police officer respond?

If you have a conflict, make sure it's big enough to matter, and small enough to do something about it.

—**Anonymous**

The Reflective CR Practitioner

The key distinction between helping professionals and lay helpers is that professionals make deliberate choices about how to intervene, based on their discipline's knowledge and value bases. This applies equally for conflict resolution. Conflict is pervasive in human interaction; thus, everyone is constantly involved in conflict resolution. Some people have a natural aptitude for CR; others learn their CR skills through normal socialization processes (e.g., following family and cultural norms; learning how to behave within the school system). Because CR professionals are not unique in their use of CR, their advantage (if any)[1] lies in their ability to use themselves consciously, learning from each situation and strategically drawing from CR theory, skills, and values (Furlong, 2005).

In this chapter, I focus on the process of reflection that professionals use to integrate theory, skills, and values with practice (Figure 2.1) (Kolb, 1974; McGuire & Inlow, 2005). The first section, "Personal and Professional Awareness," explores ways in which you can become more conscious about how you respond to conflict situations. "Value Base" highlights the common values among CR professionals and identifies areas of disagreement among CR professionals. "Conflict Styles" provides a framework for analyzing your predominant orientation toward dealing with conflict. "Basic Skills" provides definitions of communication skills that are fundamental to all modes of CR: listening, questioning, and making statements. These skills are common to all helping professions, but the examples provided are specific to conflict situations. Your challenge is to integrate these values and skills with the theory presented throughout this text. As you read on and participate in the exercises, leave yourself time to reflect back on what you have learned and to relate it to your outside experiences.

---

[1]Be careful about assuming that a professional is the best one to intervene in a conflict situation. In many circumstances, the parties do not trust professionals as much as others in their social systems (friends, family members, neighbors, etc.). Although this text focuses on roles of professional helpers, community developers and educators may be interested in how to instill conflict resolution skills and principles within a community context (Chetkow-Yanoov, 1997; Kirst-Ashman & Hull, 2005).

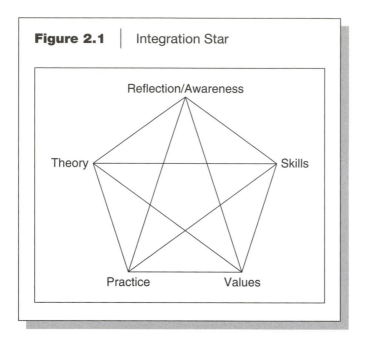

Figure 2.1 | Integration Star

Reflection/Awareness

Theory

Skills

Practice

Values

PERSONAL AND PROFESSIONAL AWARENESS

Reflection in professional practice is like looking in a mirror, except the reflection goes beyond one's physical appearance. When practitioners reflect on themselves, they strive to become mindful of how they present themselves (the behavioral domain), what thoughts are going on in their mind (the cognitive domain), and what feelings are being evoked (the affective domain). Ideally, practitioners have a high level of self-awareness during their interventions (reflection in action). Because we are all in the process of developing greater self-awareness in the moment, we can all benefit from deliberating before an intervention and reflecting back afterward (Lang, 2004). This process may be as simple as taking a few moments before and after an intervention to mull over thoughts and feelings in your head. Prior to an important meeting, you can use more methodical techniques, such as meditation, breathing exercises, or positive self-messages to center yourself, becoming calm, focused, and free from distraction (Chodron, 2001). Writing journal entries or brief descriptions after your meetings can be used to heighten your awareness of your responses to particular situations, while providing a record that will enable you to review your progress over time. Peer consultation or clinical supervision can also support your reflective efforts. Consultants or supervisors help you identify underlying thoughts and feelings. They ask questions to raise insights and encourage you to explore areas that you might have missed. In other words, they assist with reflection by holding a mirror so you can look more closely at yourself (Kadushin, 2002). Finally, you can use the discussions, inventories, and exercises in a conflict resolution course for interactive reflection. View your teachers and colleagues as a community of teachers and learners who help one another through giving and receiving feedback. You can facilitate greater self-awareness and new insights by sharing experiences and asking each other questions (McGuire & Inlow, 2005).

When conflict arises, emotions are apt to mount: anger, fear, frustration, excitement, despair, vengeance. Different people respond differently. CR professionals need to be aware of their emotions—not to squelch them, but to ensure these feelings do not impair their ability to deal with conflict effectively. Reflection helps practitioners identify their natural emotional responses to various types of conflict, particularly what "pushes their buttons." Once awareness is raised, practitioners can strategize how to deal with difficult situations (Noonan, 1998), rather than simply lay blame or respond out of defensiveness. Reflection is also part of self-care for a professional. By attending to your own feelings, you can ensure that you do not become overstressed, disillusioned, or consumed by the conflicts you are working with (Grellert, 1991).

1. Emotions

In order to help others respond effectively to conflict, professionals must begin with themselves (Chodron, 2001; Hunt, 1987). We use ourselves as a guide—if a situation makes you mildly angry and your client furious, you can begin to question what has caused the difference in your responses. Are you acting on different information; are your perceptions different? Are you affected by the same conflict in a different manner? Given these differences, an intervention that works for you may not work for the client. Emotions affect how you think, how you behave, and even how you respond physically (e.g., blood pressure rises when feeling stressed). All emotions have the ability to help or inhibit your ability to deal with conflict. This section explores three examples—liking, disliking, and anger—to show why it is important to continually strive for mindfulness of your emotions.

Feelings of liking and disliking can affect your responses to conflict in many ways. If you like one client more than another, for instance, you might unconsciously show favoritism to the one you like. If you strongly dislike a coworker, you might automatically discount that person's suggestions, even when the suggestions are reasonable. If you are very fond of your neighbors, you might be naturally inclined to acquiesce to their requests, even when they are unreasonable. By continually observing your feelings of liking and disliking, you can choose more deliberately how to respond (Fisher, Alol, & Wingate, 2005).

Anger is one of the most pervasive emotions in conflict situations. Depending on how we use anger, it can energize us toward either constructive or destructive responses. If we try to hold anger in, it will tend to build inside and come out in ways that we have no control over—for example, headaches or other somatic responses, passive-aggressive behavior, clouded thinking, or conflict avoidance. Conversely, if we ventilate or dump our anger on another person, then we are likely to exacerbate the conflict. If we can learn to channel our anger toward dealing with the rudimental problems, then it acts as a positive force. Self-awareness helps us avoid even subtle responses that may be perceived negatively by others. When we feel contempt, for instance, we tend to smile with one side of our mouth (Freshman, 2005). By avoiding this type of half-smile, we can project more constructive messages through our body language.

If you are angry about something, consider the underlying source of the anger. Anger is a secondary emotion (Picard, 2002). For example, your anger at a client may be rooted in frustration with the client's lack of progress in therapy. Your anger at a supervisor may be derived from fear that the supervisor will chastise you for making a mistake. Your anger at colleagues who are leaving your agency may be caused by feeling hurt or abandoned. Once you identify the underlying emotion, you can begin to process it. This could mean letting a client know you feel frustrated by the lack of progress made in therapy, asking your supervisor for support rather than censure, or letting your colleagues know that you will miss them. This allows you to take responsibility for your own anger, while communicating your underlying feelings in a nonthreatening manner.

Display of emotions varies depending on the model of intervention. A psychoanalyst presents with little emotion, allowing clients to open up and transfer their feelings onto an empathic, nonjudgmental listener. A motivational educator, in contrast, presents with excitement and dramatic techniques in order to sell the message. Similarly, different models of CR work best with different types of emotional expression. Mediators who want to demonstrate impartiality avoid displaying pleasure or displeasure with one party or the other. Advocates who want to persuade decision makers might use emotional displays to win sympathy. Negotiators who prefer not to tip their hand (e.g., disclose their bottom line) mute their expressions of emotion. Certainly, different situations call for differential use of self. As you develop your own style of CR, remember to build on your strengths. Some negotiators are more effective when they approach conflict calmly and rationally. Others are more effective when they express their exuberance, umbrage, or fear. How you display emotions should also take the other person's cultural norms into account.

2. Cultural Awareness

Because culture affects the way people understand and respond to conflict, CR professionals must become aware of their cultural predilections. Rather than prescribing a singular approach to CR, this text presents an array of approaches. This allows practitioners to select CR approaches that are consonant with their own cultural attitudes and norms. Cultural awareness also helps practitioners select CR approaches that are culturally appropriate for the people they are dealing with.

As a Canadian, I know that my country of origin values "peace, order, and good government." These terms are written into the constitution and form the basis for Canada's justice system. When working with CR practitioners in Israel, I became keenly aware of how my personal identity as a Canadian set me apart from most Israelis. On the surface, Israeli responses to conflict seemed argumentative, confrontational, and chaotic. Conversely, many Israelis saw me as nice and even-tempered, but too naïve and indirect. I had to learn how to interpret Israeli interactions from their cultural perspectives and how to adapt CR approaches to fit with the cultural common sense in Israel. As an Israeli colleague noted after one of my workshops:

> When I hear you talk about conflict resolution, it all seems to make so much sense. But when I try to translate it in my head from English to Hebrew, it doesn't seem to work. I can't just translate it word for word.

I had to help Israeli colleagues interpret CR theory and skills to fit with their cultural frames. I also had to learn not to judge Israeli culture or take on airs of cultural superiority. It is not that Israelis have disdain for peace, order, or good government; however, they tend to have different patterns of interacting and implementing these constructs. By reflecting on my experiences, I was able to identify areas of similarity, as well as areas of difference. In the process of learning about other cultures, I became more conscious of my own.

One's personal identity can be comprised of various factors, including ethnicity, culture, gender, age, sexual orientation, and political affiliation. Identity affects one's ways of viewing the world as well as one's emotional and verbal responses (Freshman, 2005). By becoming more mindful of one's identity(ies), one can act more deliberately in conflict situations.

Some aspects of cultural diversity that are of particular significance in conflict situations include power distance, collectivism versus individualism, and uncertainty avoidance (Ting-Toomey & Oetzel, 2001; Wanis–St. John, 2005). *Power distance* refers to cultural expectations about respect or deference to people in positions of authority, such as parents, elders, or professionals. For instance, do you prefer to call your instructor Professor, Dr., Mr., Mrs., or Ms., or do you use the instructor's first name? Regardless of your preference, how does your instructor prefer to be addressed? When people have higher levels of power distance, they may tend to defer to those in positions of authority rather than challenge or confront them.

The *collectivism-individualism continuum* refers to the extent to which a culture prioritizes individual needs over group needs (Weinbold & Weinbold, 2000). In your family of origin, for instance, were you encouraged to put family needs above your own, yielding to your parents' wishes, or were you encouraged to develop your own unique identity, speaking up for yourself even if it meant disagreeing with your parents? People from collectivist cultures tend to resolve conflict based on the needs of their family or community rather than their individual needs or interests.

Uncertainty avoidance refers to the degree to which a culture embraces or steers clear of ambiguity. Do you (and other members of your cultural group) prefer to have clear, specific plans at the start of a meeting or when you set off on a vacation, or do you feel comfortable with an open-ended agenda that may lead who knows where (Macduff, 2006)?

Although characteristics such as uncertainty avoidance and power distance are affected by culture, there are also individual differences within each cultural group. As you strive to gain awareness of your predilections, consider how they may affect you in various types of conflict resolution roles and situations.

3. Conscious and Artistic Use of Self

Many models of CR, including some presented in this text, provide practitioners with explicit stages, strategies, and techniques for intervention. These guidelines provide a secure framework and manageable steps for developing professionals. Still, CR is not simply the rigid application of a script or technical intervention. Professionals need artistry to implement CR in creative and flexible manners (Picard, Bishop, Ramkay, & Sargent, 2004). Whereas some writers argue that artistic ability is an innate talent, I believe that artistry can also be developed through reflective processes. Through self-reflection, CR practitioners learn to intervene in conflict consciously and deliberately. Conflict happens in the moment. Rather than merely "talking about" conflict in the past or in the abstract, CR professionals have the most profound impact by responding spontaneously but elegantly as conflict arises. Although preparation for conflict resolution is important, CR professionals must be also mindful of the moment, listening carefully to others and improvising according to what is happening around them (Balachandra, Bordone, Menkel-Meadow, Ringstrom, & Sarath, 2005). The magic of CR occurs when practitioners go beyond the mechanical repetition of certain techniques and discover inspired interventions befitting the unique conflict situation.

Although art and elegant CR processes happen in the moment, CR professionals should not simply rely on chance opportunities or subconscious responses to conflict. CR professionals can use a number of strategies to stimulate imaginative, visionary CR processes and to remain open for serendipitous opportunities for creative CR processes to occur. First, CR professionals can envision their work not only as a job or career but as a vocation. A *vocation* is a calling or endeavor that a person assumes with a passion. The passion may come from one's core values, morals, religious beliefs, or spiritual drives.

Second, CR professionals can use their passion and commitment to inspire others—helping them move past base desires or drives, such as violence or revenge, to higher ideals such as peace and social justice. This requires both optimism and naïveté. Whereas people embroiled in long-term, violent conflict might see no reason to trust or hope, CR professionals can help them see a spark of hope that might initiate something much grander than they ever imagined. Initially, CR professionals might merely ask others to dream. "If you could wave a magic wand and things would be better, what would better look like?" Without high goals and aspirations, people will not be inspired to reach beyond what seems pragmatic, to what could be. Help people find the beauty and opportunity in what surrounds them. Show them how they can take a problem-saturated story of their past experiences and develop a more positive narrative to guide them into the future.

Third, CR professionals can inspire themselves and others to take risks:

- When you feel denigrated, offer respect.
- In the face of fear, offer your vulnerability.
- When division and hate is all around you, build solidarity with those close at hand and then reach for others as far as you can touch.
- When overwhelmed by complexity, seek the elegant essence that holds it together (Lederach, 2005).

Giving peace a chance is risky, but if we do not give peace a chance, then we are destined to further violence. Consider not only the risks of taking the next step toward peace, but also the risks of not taking the next step.

Fourth, CR professionals can respect the natural and traditional CR processes that already exist within a family, community, or culture. Some CR professionals are too quick to impose their own processes on clients. When CR professionals engage and get to know clients, they should be open to building on client strengths, including their own knowledge of what works or could work for them (Lederach, 2005).

If you think I am dreaming in Technicolor, I am. But I am also dreaming in high definition and wide screen. Some people criticize peaceniks as being soft, naïve, or cowardly. Effective peacebuilders are anything but. They require confidence, assertiveness, practical knowledge, and courage. Faith, hope, and imagination do not mean being foolhardy. There are many positive examples of people who have used moral imagination to inspire others toward peace and social justice. When Martin Luther King enlisted African Americans to use nonviolence and civil disobedience to challenge racial segregation, can you imagine their initial responses? "Whites control government, police, and the courts . . . and you want me to violate the law by going into a Whites-only establishment? Are you crazy?" Similarly, who would have thought prior to the 1990s that apartheid in South Africa would end without a civil war or that the Irish Republican Army would renounce all forms of terrorism? It is easy for people to feel jaded or pessimistic in the face of Al Qaeda's campaign of terror, or a nasty divorce, or even a political campaign plagued by mudslinging. CR professionals, however, can play a vital role in inspiring hope and creating a time and space for people to engage in imaginative dialogue, problem solving, and peace building (Lederach, 2005; Mayer, 2004a).

VALUE BASE

Values are priorities. They indicate our preferences about what is good or important to us. As CR professionals, values guide both our goals and the means to those goals. Who you are on the inside determines much of how you will implement skills and intervene in conflict. If you value peace, then the model of practice you select will be directed to meet this goal. Ideally, the model uses peaceful means to bring about peace. If not, can you justify using nonpeaceful means, fighting, to bring about peace (Corey, Corey, & Callanan, 2003; Dolgoff et al., 2005)? CR theory and practice must be predicated on values and not simply on what research proves to be effective.

1. In Search of Common Values

Given the breadth of CR models and the range of backgrounds among CR professionals, it would be misleading to say there is a common value base of CR. A common value base does exist among practitioners who favor collaborative, nonviolent conflict resolution. These professionals are guided by the values of peace, respect for diversity, consensus building, and community (MacFarlane, 1999). Some people find professionals of this ilk to be optimistic, perhaps even naïvely so. However, a good part of CR is selling the process to conflicting parties. When conveyed in a genuine manner, the confidence and idealism of CR professionals inspire clients to strive for similar ideals.

An elderly man is mugged by a young thug. The man feels violated, humiliated, dismayed, and vengeful. The last thing on his mind is to have a chance to meet face-to-face with the thug and talk things out. What can a CR practitioner offer the man?

> People are basically good. Right now you are wondering how I could possibly say this about the youth who mugged you. Perhaps you are right. But what do you really know about him? What does he know about you? Would you like the opportunity to tell him who you are and how you feel about what he has done? Do you think he would have mugged you if he knew who you were?

It would be hypocritical for CR practitioners to say that all CR professionals must have the same values—if we respect diversity, then this includes diversity within the field. In fact, there are significant debates within CR about a number of values, including privacy, satisfaction, social justice, empowerment, and recognition. Most helping professionals ascribe to the ethic of confidentiality—that is, a professional who learns personal information from a client will keep that information private, unless the client consents to release such information. Many CR professionals argue that one of the advantages of mediation and negotiation is that they are confidential processes. This allows parties to work out their differences in a safe environment, without having to worry about how others will respond. Some CR professionals, however, raise concerns that conflicts should remain in the public domain. Court, for example, is open to the public in order to ensure open accountability. In addition, decisions made in one case can be used as precedents to support decisions in similar cases in the future. Under this concept of justice, fairness is achieved when like cases are decided alike. When negotiations, mediation, or other CR processes are closed to the public, accountability is more difficult to gauge and precedent cases are not made known to society (Freshman, 1997). When you are deciding whether your CR process should be open or closed to the public, the extent to which you value client privacy must be factored in.

2. Satisfaction, Social Justice, and Transformation

Bush and Folger (2005) suggest that there are three different value orientations for mediation: satisfaction, social justice, and transformation.[2] The Satisfaction Story is predicated on the belief that mediation satisfies people's needs and interests. Through mediation, people are able to resolve their differences informally, amicably, and in a manner that produces mutually agreeable solutions. The Social Justice Story is based on the notion that mediation organizes individuals around common issues and promotes stronger social ties. This provides the community with an opportunity to organize disadvantaged groups in order to challenge the power brokers and promote social justice. The Transformation Story suggests that the promise of mediation is its capacity to transform the manner in which conflicting parties deal with conflict. Bush and Folger identify two components of transformation: empowerment and recognition. **Empowerment** refers to the ability of mediation to promote client self-determination, choice, and autonomy. **Recognition** refers to the ability of mediation

---

[2]Bush and Folger also identify a fourth orientation, oppression, which suggests that mediation is not a valid means of CR. The oppression perspective is described in Chapter 1 in relation to radical practitioners.

to enhance interpersonal communication and empathic understanding among conflicting parties. Depending on which orientation you accept, your choice of models of CR will vary significantly.

When you approach a conflict, what do you value? What is your ultimate goal for the process? Any resolution of the conflict? A fair solution? An efficient solution? Social harmony? An enduring solution? In case you have not noticed, I have avoided presenting a definitive answer. As you work through the readings and exercises, you will clarify your own value base for CR.

3. Attitude toward Power

Although most helping professions believe in a client's right to self-determination, various professionals have different attitudes toward the use of power in their work. At one extreme, some professionals see themselves as impartial facilitators—that is, professionals who support clients to fulfill their goals in a nondirective manner. In contrast, other professionals believe that they are justified and perhaps required to use their power to influence the way clients and others make decisions.

A professional's attitude toward the use of power may depend on the situation. For example, a child protection worker will remove a child from a family if it poses an immediate risk to the child's welfare. If, however, the child's immediate safety is assured, then the worker will try to work with the family on a voluntary basis. Reflect on your own attitudes toward the use of power in your type of work. When are you more likely to exert your influence? When are you less likely to do so?

Understanding your attitudes toward power will help you decide the types of CR roles and models of intervention that you will use. For example, a liberal-minded family therapist is more likely to encourage family members to come up with their own solutions to family conflicts. A radical feminist therapist is more likely to influence decisions by altering the power balance in the family to give the women more power. An administrator with an egalitarian style is likely to share power with others in the organization. An authoritarian administrator will use decision-making power without inviting input from others. As you explore various approaches to CR, consider the role of power and how it fits with your own attitude toward power.

4. Professional Ethics

Professional values are often expressed in professional codes of ethics. The same is true in many areas of CR. There is not one code for all CR or even for any branch of CR, such as negotiation or mediation. If you are practicing CR as part of your other professional identification (e.g., youth worker, psychologist, teacher), you are bound by the code of ethics of that profession, if any. Some professions, including social work, have articulated specific policies for members who practice CR (National Association of Social Workers [NASW], 1999). In certain realms of CR practice such as family mediation, CR associations have developed their own codes of ethics (Association of Family and Conciliation Courts, 2000; Family Mediation Canada, n.d.).

In most jurisdictions, membership in a CR association and adherence to its code of ethics is voluntary. This means that CR professionals who wish to operate on a different set of standards and values do not have to belong to any association. No wonder that you will find CR professionals with very different values.

For sample codes of ethics, see the websites listed in Appendix 4. Note the differences and similarities between the codes of ethics from various CR associations. Note, too, how many values questions are open for interpretation.

5. Values Clarification

Even with the guidance of professional codes of ethics, CR practitioners face many situations where there is no clear guidance on how to act. A code may say, for instance, that a professional must act honestly and respect the rights of others. Does this mean that professionals must disclose their bottom lines when they are negotiating with others? What circumstances, if any, permit professionals to use deceitful or coercive tactics in trying to achieve justice for their clients? In order to determine not only how to *behave* but also how to *be* as a conflict resolution professional, we must be mindful of the values that are inherent in the strategies we use and the conflict resolution roles that we assume.

CONFLICT STYLES

Conflict style refers to one's preferred response or natural inclination when faced with conflict. Certainly, people respond differently to different types of conflict situations; however, people do have general tendencies to respond to conflict in

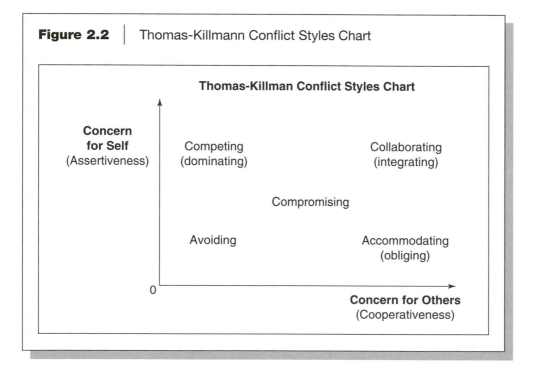

Figure 2.2 | Thomas-Killmann Conflict Styles Chart

particular manners. The Thomas-Kilmann Conflict Mode Instrument (Thomas & Kilmann, 1974)[3] helps CR professionals determine their own preferences, as well as those of others they are working with (for an updated version that includes cultural perspectives, see Kraybill, 2005c). By assessing your own conflict style, you can develop greater control over how you respond to particular conflict situations. By assessing others' conflict styles, you can determine appropriate interventions (e.g., how to persuade them; how to encourage them to use different approaches to conflict).

The Thomas-Kilmann Instrument begins with the proposition that there are two primary orientations toward conflict resolution, assertiveness and cooperativeness. Figure 2.2 describes these dimensions as concern for self (assertiveness) and concern for others (cooperativeness).

1. Avoiders

The bottom-left quadrant of the diagram describes avoiders, people who are low on concern for self and low on concern for others. Avoiders may deny that conflict exists, consciously or nonconsciously. Alternatively, they acknowledge that conflict exists but do what they can to avert or withdraw from conflict. By avoiding conflict, they tend to satisfy neither their own needs nor the needs of others. I forgot to write a letter of reference for a student. When the student calls, I do not answer and do not call back. I avoid having any conflict with the student (at least for now), but I really do not satisfy either of our needs. Avoidance of overt conflict may be useful when the conflict is merely the symptom of a separate underlying problem; for instance, when a child is acting out, you might try to deal with the underlying issues and avoid dealing directly with the acting-out behaviors. If a child whines because he is hungry, the parent might offer the child food rather than reprimand the child for whining. Teaching the child alternatives to whining may be more effective when the child is not hungry.

2. Accommodators

The bottom-right quadrant, accommodators, denotes people who have low concern for their own needs and high concern for the needs of others. Accommodators value positive relationships with others. They go out of their way to please others, even at the expense of their own needs. My boss asks me to stay late to complete a work plan and budget for a project. I am tired but agree to stay late tonight and even offer to work through the weekend. My boss will be happy, but I'll be exhausted. Accommodation may be useful when people acknowledge they are wrong and want to demonstrate reasonableness, or when they want to help others save face in a potentially embarrassing conflict (Wilmot & Hocker, 2007).

---

[3]The Thomas-Kilmann Instrument is one of the more popular frameworks among CR professionals for analyzing conflict styles, but it is certainly not the only one. The Myers-Briggs Scale (Myers, 1987), for example, is an interpersonal styles inventory commonly used in business settings. Taxonomies of management styles also provide frameworks to analyze interactions with people who have different preferred modes of operating: Introverts—Extroverts, Sensors—Intuitives, Thinkers—Feelers, and Judging—Perceiving (see http://www.cpp.com to order copies of either of these instruments).

3. Competitors

The top-left quadrant, competitors, characterizes people who are low on concern for the needs of others but high on concern for their own needs. Competitors are out to win. They exert power to influence others or impose their will. Personal success is important. Amicable relations with others are not. A professional colleague disagrees with my assessment of a client. I respond by pointing out all the errors in my colleague's thinking. Even if I am right, consider the cost to my colleague and our relationship. Whereas some competitors use tactics that are aggressive, violent, or unethical, competitors can also use tactics that are assertive, constructive, and ethical (e.g., using one's personal charisma to help persuade a colleague to support a particular position in an upcoming staff meeting). Successful competitors select strategies that they know will be effective: if they are more likely to win by being nice than by being nasty, they will be nice.

4. Compromisers

The middle section of the diagram, compromisers, demonstrates people who pay some attention to the needs of others and some attention to their own needs. They opt for solutions that are partial wins, for themselves and for others. Unfortunately, compromises are also partial losses for themselves and for the others. The solutions may be fair, but nobody is completely satisfied. I want government to provide full public funding for mediation services. Government balks. I suggest a compromise that government subsidizes up to half of the cost for people whose income is below the poverty line. If government accepts, at least I have achieved part of what I set out to accomplish. Compromise tends to foster better relationships than competition, but not as well as collaboration. In some instances, compromises can be formulated in ways that maximize wins and minimize losses (constructive trade-offs) or ways that offer quick, short-term solutions (Wilmot & Hocker, 2007).

5. Collaborators

The final quadrant, collaborators, illustrates people who have high concern for their own needs, as well as for the needs for others. They seek out solutions that are "win-win" (i.e., mutually beneficial). Collaborators encourage joint problem solving. A client claims that I have breached my obligation to keep information confidential. I invite the client to discuss these concerns and to see whether we can work things out in an amicable fashion. Collaborators use cooperative strategies such as jointly analyzing problems, self-disclosing, demonstrating respect, validating the other's views, offering suggestions designed to meet both parties' interests, and accepting responsibility for the conflict, where appropriate.[4] Collaboration is particularly important when you need consensus in order to implement a decision or when the issues are too important to fight or compromise over.

---

[4]When working with clients, be careful about using the term *collaborators*. For some, this term has negative connotations as it was used to describe people who collaborated with the Nazis during World War II. Terms such as *team members*, *joint problem solvers*, *colleagues*, *allies*, and *mutual support systems* can be used to avoid this trouble.

6. Selective Use of Styles

Given the structure of this model, you might conclude that we should all be striving toward collaboration. However, different conflict styles are useful for different purposes. Avoidance, at first glance, seems to satisfy nobody's needs. Yet many of us use, and could use, avoidance strategies in certain situations. A member of a therapy group is whispering to a neighbor. The whispering is disruptive, but you decide to ignore it because it is not important enough to confront at this time. Pick your fights, as well as your efforts at collaboration. Collaboration has its costs: time, energy, mental fatigue. Sometimes, avoidance is just easier than dealing with the conflict.

Accommodation is useful when the relationship is more important than the particular dispute. An involuntary client[5] comes in for the first time and demands a break for a cigarette. You are very busy, but you accommodate the client. Confronting the client now may be counterproductive until you have built some rapport. Accommodation can be used as a strategy—if you accommodate someone now, that person may feel more obliged to accommodate you later. Of course, accommodation can lead the other person to continue to expect accommodations. Accommodation is particularly useful when the issue is much more important to the other person than it is to you (e.g., your partner is Muslim and maintains Halal dietary laws; although you would like a ham sandwich, you agree to go to a Halal restaurant because your partner's religious beliefs are more important than your inclination for ham).

Competition may be required to protect oneself from immediate dangers (self-defense) and to respond to others who are competitive. A landowner is planning to demolish a building, leaving your clients homeless. You have offered to meet with the landlord and clients to work things out, but the landlord does not respond. You refer the clients to a lawyer to help them with a court action to stop the demolition. Unfortunately, people often resign themselves to competition without giving the other alternatives a sufficient chance to work. As you will see in later chapters, there are many strategies to move people from competitive styles to more collaborative ones. If competitors can see that they lose nothing through collaboration, they may be persuaded to try it.

To some extent, conflict styles are culturally determined. For example, Americans tend to have a higher degree of competing style; traditional Asians tend to have a higher degree of avoiding and obliging styles. Whereas Western cultures place high value on individual rights and freedoms, Asian culture places high value on harmony and community. Avoidance demonstrates sensitivity to others and respect for the existing social hierarchy. In Asian societies, when someone avoids confronting conflict directly, others will help with healing wounds or resolving the conflict in indirect ways (Wilmot & Hocker, 2007). In other words, what Americans might term avoidance could be considered "saving face" by dealing with conflict indirectly, rather than confronting in a disrespectful manner (Ting-Toomey & Oetzel, 2001). Within Western cultures, women tend to be more accommodating than men

---

[5]An *involuntary client* is a client who is required to attend counseling or other helping services—for example, someone convicted of a criminal offense or suspected of child abuse who must go for counseling services. The client would not have sought services unless there were legal consequences or other sanctions.

(Kolb & Williams, 2003; Miller, 2001). This results from socialization processes, in which women are encouraged to care for their families and men are encouraged to be successful in competitive work environments. CR practitioners need to be able to recognize these types of cultural and gender differences, as well as within-group variations. For instance, when people who tend toward accommodation are placed in a conflict with people who are competitive, do you encourage them to use their traditional styles? If not, are you showing disrespect for their traditional norms and values?

Some theorists question whether conflict styles are fixed personality types or predispositions that vary depending on the situation (Nicoterra, 1995). Most CR models of intervention assume that conflict styles are not fixed, although they may be deep-rooted. CR professionals can use different styles depending on the needs of the situation; they can also encourage others to move from one conflict style to another.

BASIC SKILLS

Skills are the doing part of CR: how you behave, how you communicate, how you interact with others in the conflict. Skills translate your theoretical knowledge and value base into what you do in practice. All conflict interventions are based on how you present yourself, verbally, physically, emotionally, and spiritually. In this section, I introduce communication skills that are basic to virtually all forms of CR.[6] In the chapters on negotiation, mediation, facilitation, and advocacy, I describe how to use these skills with particular CR models and identify other skills that are specific to each model. The fundamental communication skills are listening, questioning, and making statements. I also touch on special issues for written communication in CR.

1. Listening

Active listening refers to the intentional use of self in order to demonstrate to a speaker that you have heard and understood what the speaker has said. If you listen passively, you may have heard and understood the speaker, but the speaker has no way of knowing this. Empathic listening can be demonstrated through the use of attending, paraphrasing, reflecting feelings, and summarizing (Evans, Hearn, Uhlemann, & Ivey, 2004; Ivey & Ivey, 2007).

Attending refers to being present with others, demonstrating that you are with them in mind as well as in body. Attending requires focusing on others, rather than daydreaming or focusing on your own thoughts and feelings. Attending skills comprise behavioral, nonverbal responses to indicate listening and understanding: leaning forward, maintaining regular eye contact, nodding one's head, constructive use of silence, and so forth. Facial expressions should be consonant with the messages that are being conveyed (e.g., smiling at good news). Utterances, such as "uh-huh" and "mm-hmm" are attending skills, but these can be distracting. Accordingly, utterances should be used sparingly, if at all. Vocal qualities, such as the pitch, pace, and fluidity, can also be used to demonstrate interest and understanding in what is being said.

Some people find intentional use of silence to be the most difficult skill, particularly in conflict situations. To novice practitioners, silence feels like a nonresponse.

---

[6]For more detailed explanations of communication skills, see Ivey and Ivey (2007).

However, silence is a very powerful tool. Silence breaks up the flow of communication. In the heat of the moment, people may need time for feelings to de-escalate. Silence demonstrates that you are taking time to think. It also gives the other person time to think about what he or she has said. Cooler heads may prevail. Within some cultures, silence also demonstrates respect.

Attending behaviors are particularly important in CR, because people often mirror the expressions and behaviors of those around them. "Smile and the whole world smiles with you," goes the cliché. Though this is far from an absolute truth, you can either escalate or de-escalate conflict through the use of particular attending behaviors. If someone starts to yell, rather than raise your voice, try speaking softly. Besides catching the other person off guard, you are modeling the type of behavior you hope the other will adopt. If people are flailing their arms in anger, restrain your own gestures.

Although attending skills are important, nonverbal cues are often difficult to interpret. Verbal listening skills provide the speaker with explicit feedback about how you are receiving his or her messages. *Paraphrasing* refers to restating what the speaker has said. A paraphrase can be constructed with words that are similar to those used by the speaker or with words that are quite different but still convey the same message. The following exchange between an addictions counselor (Agnes) and her client (Clara) demonstrates how Agnes can use both types of paraphrasing.

CLARA: *Don't tell me that I have to stop drinking.*

AGNES: *You don't want me to tell you that you have to stop drinking.*

CLARA: *Darn right! You think it's easy just to get up one morning and never pick up a bottle again.*

AGNES: *I guess you're telling me that I do not know how hard giving up alcohol would be for you.*

Paraphrasing shows people you understand what they think and believe. Reflecting feelings is similar to paraphrasing but indicates you understand the person's affect or emotions. You can reflect feelings that are explicit in the person's statement or ones that can be implied from the way the person presents the message.

CLARA: *When I come to see you, I just get more depressed.*

AGNES: *You feel discouraged when you come here.*

CLARA [sobbing]: *I don't know what else you want from me.*

AGNES: *I can see how sad you feel right now.*

Whereas paraphrasing restates what someone has just completed saying, the skill of *summarizing* refers to a condensed restatement of what the person has said over a longer time frame. To summarize, highlight the key messages presented by the person throughout that period.

AGNES: *Let me see if I understand what you've been telling me, Clara. You don't think that I should be telling you to stop drinking, because I do not know how hard that would really be. I haven't been very helpful. In fact, you feel more depressed since you've been coming to see me. Anything else you want to add?*

In addition to summarizing the content of what others have said, you can also summarize areas of agreement, areas of disagreement, and how the process has been going (Kraybill, 2005a). Summarizing, reflecting, and paraphrasing let people know how accurately, or inaccurately, you have understood them. The tone and wording of your questions should invite the person to give you feedback and correct any inaccuracies. You are not telling the person what she thinks or feels. You are asking (explicitly or implicitly) whether you understand how she thinks or feels. This clarifies communication, pre-empting further conflict.

Effective listening requires accurate observation and interpretation skills. Remember that a simple message goes through a series of stages before you can respond to it. When you hear someone speak, you need to determine what the speaker means. Pay attention to verbal as well as nonverbal cues. A client may call you a wonderful helping professional. Depending on the client's tone of voice and facial expressions, you may take this as a compliment (the client is being genuine) or as an insult (the client is being sarcastic). To become more deliberate about this decoding process, try to separate your direct observations from possible interpretations.[7] The Chinese word for "listen," *tip*, means "attend delicately with our ears, eyes, and a focused heart" (Ting-Toomey & Oetzel, 2001, p. 181). When you observe a particular behavior, first try to describe it in specific, concrete terms (e.g., the client is smiling). Consider multiple possible interpretations (e.g., the client is happy, nervous, or hiding something). At this point, you must suspend ethnocentric evaluation. Reflect on the meaning by looking at the situation from different cultural lenses or frames. You might even check with the other person to help you interpret his or her response (e.g., "So would you say that you're feeling more content, anxious, or guarded?").

Effective listening is absolutely crucial to CR. When faced with conflict, people often become defensive. They feel the need to refute the message they received and tell their own story. This exacerbates the problem, because the other side now feels defensive and responds in kind, perhaps even more forcefully. Consider the following sequence between two children playing in a sandbox:

CHUCKIE: *Hey, you threw sand in my face!*

CHELSEA: *No, I didn't.*

CHUCKIE: *Yes, you did!*

CHELSEA: *No, I didn't!*

CHUCKIE: *Yes, you did!*

What could be better than a strong argument to win a debate? Ironically, one of the most persuasive techniques for persuading others is to listen to them. Active listening demonstrates to others that you have truly heard them. People who feel they have been heard are more apt to listen to you. When faced with a conflict, show

---

[7]The process recordings for major assignments in this text will help you with this process, asking you to identify both observations and possible interpretations.

the others that you understand "(a) that they feel strongly, (b) what they feel strongly about, and (c) why they feel strongly about it" (Gould & Gould, 1988).[8] Note what happens if Chelsea listens rather than fights back:

CHELSEA: *Hold on a minute. You're very angry.*

CHUCKIE: *Yes, you're mean.*

CHELSEA: *You're very angry at me.*

CHUCKIE: *Of course, I'm angry.*

CHELSEA: *You're angry because you think I threw sand at you on purpose.*

CHUCKIE: *Well, didn't you?*

You may think this example is too contrived; however, a little active listening can move conflict a long way toward peaceful resolution.

Remember the cultural components to communication. Words, vocal qualities, gestures, and facial expressions have different meanings among different cultures. Familiarity with the other person's culture will help you interpret his language and nonverbal behavior so that you can convey messages in culturally appropriate manners (LeBaron Duryea, n.d.). For example, active listening may be inappropriate in certain cultural contexts. If status and hierarchy are the norm within a culture,[9] a subordinate may offend a supervisor by using paraphrase and reflection of feeling. Rather, the subordinate can demonstrate interest and respect by listening silently and using appropriate nonverbal responses (e.g., head nods, restrained eye contact). Once again, the point of this discussion is not to prescribe a particular type of interaction but to make practitioners aware of the choice of skills and how they can influence dealing with conflict.

2. Questioning

Questions are useful for finding out others' thoughts and feelings, as well as inviting their participation in a dialogue ("What do you think?"). If you are gathering information for an assessment or evaluation, remember to cover the five Ws: who, what, where, when, and why. Remember, however, that questions can be intrusive. Think how you feel when someone peppers you with a series of questions. Novice interviewers tend to overuse questions, rather than engage people in a more natural conversation. You can encourage people to open up and be frank through active listening skills much more readily than through a succession of questions.

Questions can be either open or closed. *Open* questions encourage respondents to answer in their own words, without limiting their choices. *Closed* questions give

---

[8]The power of effective listening is beautifully demonstrated in a videotape, Gould and Gould's (1988) *From No to Yes*. This film is part of an entertaining series of management education videotapes by John Cleese. Although the context is business, the lessons are directly relevant to the helping professionals.

[9]As discussed earlier for cultures with high power distance.

respondents a limited choice of answers, such as yes or no. Compare the following examples:

1. Closed: *Do you support the prochoice stance on abortion*
   Open: *What are your views about the prochoice stance on abortion?*
2. Closed: *Which value is more important, individual freedom or safety?*
   Open: *How do you prioritize values such as freedom and safety?*

Closed questions are useful when you want to know specific information or when you want to encourage the respondent to provide a brief answer. Open questions are useful when you want to encourage the respondent to open up and when you do not want to limit the range of possible answers. In the first example, the closed question suggests that there are only two possible positions: supporting the prochoice stance and opposing it. In fact, the respondent may have an alternate position (e.g., conditional support or support for a stance that neither opposes nor accepts the prochoice position). The open form of the question does not box the respondent into an artificial choice. Dichotomies tend to reinforce argument and lock people into sides. Inviting discussion about many points of view tends to open up dialogue.

In CR, the clarity of questions is vital. People with opposing views often misinterpret one another, imputing false motivations on one another. If a patient advocate asks a nurse, "When can the patient return home?" the nurse could interpret this question in two ways: what needs to happen before the patient is discharged, or on what day and at what time will the patient be discharged? If the nurse assumes the advocate is asking for a specific date and he does not know the date, then he may think the request is unreasonable. If the advocate wanted to know "What needs to happen before discharge?" then a more specific request would ease communication.

Questions should be worded in a nonjudgmental manner so clients do not feel that they are being challenged or blamed. If you ask a new client, "Why were you late for your appointment?" the client may interpret this as a personal affront. To avoid putting the client on the defensive, you could try "Did you have any trouble finding our office?"

Finally, statements should not be disguised as questions. If I ask a student whether she would like to present her assignment to the class, this suggests that I am giving her an option to say yes or no. If I want her to present her assignment, I should say so directly. People who are conflict avoiders or accommodators tend to use questions rather than state opinions or make direct requests. In order to be more assertive, they need to let the other person know what they really think or want. Being assertive does not mean being aggressive or insulting.

3. Making Statements

Statements are used to provide facts or opinions. Facts connote objective truth, whereas opinions connote an individual's subjective reality. Without getting into a philosophical debate about truth and reality, people often state personal opinions as if they were universally accepted facts. In CR, separating facts and opinions can be used to deconstruct conflicts. If I say, "This student has a severe learning disability,"

I am presenting it as fact. If you have a contrary assessment, I have just insulted you because I have suggested that you don't know simple truth. If I state my assessment as an opinion, I can acknowledge that your opinion is different but not necessarily wrong. Once we acknowledge a legitimate difference of professional opinions, we can work together in a more collegial fashion (Fisher & Brown, 1988).

As with questions, statements should be clear and nonjudgmental. If you want the other person to accept the truth in what you are saying, say it in terms that are easy for the other person to understand and accept. Assume Lionel is a liberal psychiatrist speaking with Cassie, a conservative community worker. If Lionel speaks in the language of a liberal psychiatrist, his message may be doomed to failure. Consider the following example:

LIONEL: *We need to establish affirmative action programs for people with major disorders on the first DSM axis in order to provide them with equal access to job opportunities.*

First, the community worker may not be familiar with "major disorders on the first DSM axis." Cassie is more likely to understand "mental illness." As someone who identifies as a conservative, Cassie is also likely to reject anything related to "affirmative action." To Cassie, this sounds like reverse discrimination. If Lionel uses terminology that is familiar to Cassie, the probability of her hearing and accepting his message increases. Lionel can refer back to points that Cassie has made, showing that he has heard her and is building on her perspectives (Gould & Gould, 1988), as follows:

LIONEL: *You seem to be concerned about the fairness of requiring businesses to hire people with mental illness. On the other hand, I don't think you're saying that these people should not be working. I'm wondering if we can figure out ways to improve access to jobs for people with mental illness, without imposing unfair restrictions on businesses.*

The trick is to learn how to speak persuasively and assertively, without coming across as combative or presumptuous. Use *I statements* to explain your thoughts and feelings: "I feel incensed about . . ." or "I believe the problem resulted from . . . ." These types of statements let people know where you are coming from, without imposing your thoughts or feelings on others. When you offer ideas or opinions, explain the facts on which they were based. If there is disagreement, you do not have to back down. You can make your points firmly but stay respectful and amicable (Gould & Gould, 1988). Avoid blatant rejections of the other person's ideas. Rather than "That's ludicrous," try "I look at the problem from a different perspective."

When people want to persuade others, they tend to use contention or assertions to state what they want. Although people often rely on contention, acknowledgment and inquiry tend to be more effective methods of persuasion (Stone, Patton, & Heen, 2000). You can acknowledge the other's perspective by using active listening skills, as described earlier. Active listening encourages the speaker to trust you and open up to your ideas. Questions can be used to facilitate insights. Rather than tell a client to leave an abusive relationship, ask the client questions about the patterns of abuse and whether the client thinks the abuse will stop. Even though you are encouraging the client to leave, you are respecting the client's right to decide whether and when to leave.

When in doubt about what to say next during a conflict situation, use listening skills (including silence). Asking questions and making statements are more risky.

4. Written Communication

Although general writing skills are important in CR, they really go beyond the scope of this book. For classic texts on effective writing, consider Strunk and White (2000), Williams (2005), and the publication manual of the American Psychological Association (2001). In this section, I highlight concerns related to CR strategies. In later chapters, I describe writing skills that are required for certain models of CR—for example, using neutral language as a mediator; using persuasive language as an advocate (Kaminski & Walmsley, 1995).

Some people are more comfortable with oral communication, others with written. Oral communication is generally more informal, flexible, and timely. Written communication provides the writer with more time to think about what to say and how to say it; the reader also has more time to read and interpret it.[10] In CR situations, your choice of written, oral, or combined forms of communication should be made with strategic purposes in mind.

With written communication, the writer has the benefit of more time to ensure that the messages are conveyed clearly, concisely, and nonjudgmentally. The reader can deliberate over the message before responding. Written communication also makes it easier for both parties to use advocates or consultants to help them interpret and respond to messages.

Because the reader retains a record of the communication, writing can have a powerful effect on the reader. This can be a plus or a minus. If you make a mistake while talking, the mistake may be passed by or easily forgotten. If you make a mistake in writing, the problem takes on a higher level of significance. Documentation provides a fixed record of communication that can be used as (1) a framework for implementation of agreements or (2) evidence in procedures to resolve future conflicts.

Technological advancements—including fax, email, and the Internet—have meant that people can communicate through writing instantaneously, cheaply, and to broad audiences. Since the 1990s, a number of online CR programs have even been developed specifically to take advantage of these benefits (Raines, 2005; Syme, 2006). Advancements in web-based communication can also enhance CR in terms of providing new channels for sharing ideas, exchanging information, and promoting causes. Unfortunately, many conflicts have been exacerbated by miscommunications made through these technologies—for example, confidential email messages being sent to people by mistake, hurtful messages sent in the heat of anger, and messages that are easily misinterpreted because the sender was more concerned about sending the message quickly than accurately. Using communication technology tends to be more impersonal than face-to-face exchanges. People sometimes convey insulting messages through technology that they would never dream of conveying in person. In addition, written communication does not convey emotions in the same manner as oral communication (Tannen, 1998). Consider a counselor who has just had a

---

[10]Levels of formality and pacing do vary. In some cases—such as court trials—oral communication is very formal. With email and other technologies, written communication is often informal and instantaneous.

difficult interview and emails her supervisor, "This client is crazy and should be locked up." If this message were conveyed in person, the supervisor might realize that the counselor is joking and blowing off steam. Although the oral statement may come across as judgmental, it looks even worse when it is transmitted via email. Email does not convey the worker's sense of frustration or intention to be funny. Because of the potential for miscommunication, be particularly cautious with humor in written communication.

All communication skills require deliberate choices about how to present yourself, orally, behaviorally, and in writing. Although professionals try to minimize miscommunications, errors are apt to happen, and further conflict may result. Remember that communication is not just a onetime event; it is ongoing. If miscommunication occurs, bring the parties together to clarify everyone's understandings. As noted earlier, blaming one side or another for miscommunication does little to resolve it. The focuses need to be on how to fix the problem and how to prevent it from reoccurring.

KEY POINTS

- Reflective conflict resolution professionals are defined by their ability to integrate CR theory, values, and skills with their practice.
- *Reflection* refers to the process of becoming aware of one's use of self, including thoughts, feelings, and behaviors presented during an intervention.
- Reflection includes developing awareness of one's own culture, enabling the practitioner to recognize differences with clients or others, so that responses to conflict can be adapted for diverse cultural contexts.
- Although each CR model provides practitioners with specific techniques and steps to follow, CR practitioners should also use artistic strategies to stimulate imaginative, visionary thinking and take advantage of serendipitous opportunities that arise within each conflict situation.
- Choice of models of CR depends on one's value base, the goals one aspires to as a professional.
- A practitioner's attitude toward power will determine how facilitative or how directive that practitioner will be when intervening in conflict situations.
- Although CR does not have a value base common to all practitioners, collaborative, nonviolent CR is based on the values of peace, respect for diversity, consensus building, and community.
- Individuals tend to favor one of five conflict styles: avoiding, accommodating, competing, compromising, or collaborating.
- Different situations require CR professionals to adopt different conflict styles.
- Effective communication skills are integral to all CR processes.
- Listening skills are particularly important in CR to demonstrate understanding to other parties and to clarify any misunderstandings.
- Clear, concise, and nonjudgmental language pre-empts conflict and fosters effective communication.

DISCUSSION QUESTIONS AND EXERCISES

1. WATCH AND SEE: Observe a segment of a movie or television program that features a conflict. Ensure that you watch the process leading up to the conflict, as well as what follows the conflict. Identify the sequence of nonverbal communication between the parties. (a) What are your direct observations? (b) How do you interpret them? (c) What are some other possible interpretations for the observations that you made? (d) How did the other party interpret this communication?

    Use the following example for your format:

    • OBSERVATION 1: A vein was pulsing on Kelly's left temple.
    • INTERPRETATION: Kelly was angry at Maude.
    • ALTERNATE INTERPRETATION: Kelly was hyped up from having just run upstairs.
    • OTHER PARTY: Maude did not seem to notice.

2. PERSONAL VALUES INVENTORY: Consider the following list of values:

    • Peace
    • Respect for other people
    • Life
    • Mental health
    • Wisdom
    • Family
    • Work
    • Spirituality/religion
    • Amicable relationships
    • Education

    • Harmony
    • Personal privacy
    • Personal security
    • Physical health
    • Mutual understanding
    • Financial success
    • Winning
    • Law and order
    • Community welfare
    • Other (specify) _____

    Rate each value by marking it as VH (value highly), VM (value moderately), or VL (value little). Within the VH group, rank-order each value, with 1 being the highest value, 2 the next highest, and so on.

    After you have completed this exercise individually, try to come up with a rank ordering that represents the class's highest five values. First, divide the class into small groups (three to five per group), and have each group come up with its own list. When each group has reached a consensus, have one representative from each group get together and work out a list of values that represents the whole class. At each stage, try to work on a consensus basis (i.e., try to build agreement among all participants). If after 15 minutes agreement does not look possible, use majority votes to settle differences.

Debriefing: What were the most difficult parts of this exercise? Did any of your personal rankings change as you moved into group decision making? If so, what led to these changes?

Diarizing: Mark two dates in your calendar, one near the middle of this course and one near the end. On each of these dates, reflect back to your values list. Consider whether any of your values have changed, and keep track of these changes by updating the chart.

3. CULTURAL AWARENESS: Identify three cultural groups to which you belong (e.g., by nationality, ethnic background, race, religion, gender, sexual orientation, or political affiliation). Analyze how each of these three groups deals with various issues raised in this chapter: anger, display of emotions, power, time, and use of various communication skills. How do you think your culture affects the way you deal with conflict? If you are not sure about your culture's attitudes toward some of these issues, interview relatives or others from your cultural group. For further information, conduct a literature search on your particular cultural groups (LeBaron, 1997; Wanis–St. John, 2005).

4. CONFLICT STYLES IDENTIFICATION: This exercise is designed to help you identify your predominant style(s) of handling conflict. Identify three situations in which you have been faced with a conflict: one with a family member, one with a coworker or classmate, and one with a client. Before reading on, write down a brief description of what happened in each situation.

   In each of the three situations, identify the manner in which you dealt with the conflict: avoidance, accommodation, competition, compromise, or collaboration.

   Are there any patterns in the way that you deal with conflict? Does it depend on the situation? Does it matter if the other person is in a subordinate or superior position to your own? Which conflict styles give you the greatest difficulty? Refer back to your answers to Exercise 10 in Chapter 1—are the conflict styles identified in that exercise consistent with the ones you have identified in this exercise? If there are differences, how do you explain them?

5. CONFLICT STYLES SCENARIOS: For each of the following scenarios, select the most appropriate conflict style, and provide reasons for selecting that type of response.

   a. You are the administrator of a social agency and need to decide how much money should be spent on paperclips. Some employees want fancy gold paper clips, and some want the cheapest clips possible.

   b. A client threatens to commit suicide. You are a psychotherapist who has a professional obligation to protect clients from life-threatening situations.

   c. A colleague at work wants to go to a family member's wedding and asks you to take his shift. You want to go to a movie that night.

   d. You and a colleague are having a case conference about a terminally ill client who wants to have her life supports removed (e.g., a ventilator and feeding tube). You support a client's right to choose passive euthanasia. A colleague says she opposes passive euthanasia.

   e. You are supervising a field practicum student who you believe dresses inappropriately. The student believes that he should be able to come to work dressed as he pleases.

   f. Your professional association says that a client has raised a complaint against you for malpractice. You believe that you are innocent and that the client's allegations are unreasonable.

   g. When you referred a client for HIV testing, you told her that testing is done on an anonymous basis. After the client has gone for the test, you find out that the test is not truly anonymous. You wonder whether to tell the client because you know the client will be furious with you.

h. The agency that funds your services tells you it is cutting your budget by 5 percent. You don't think your budget should be cut. You need to decide whether and how you will respond to the agency.

i. You are facilitating a therapy group. One group member is constantly late, and another says the late person should be thrown out of the group.

6. WORLD'S WORST CR: This is your opportunity to show how bad a CR professional you can be. Write down five things that you think run counter to everything you know so far about good conflict resolution skills. Designate one person to play a helping professional, working with a couple of newlyweds. The couple is arguing about whether to keep the toilet seat up or down after use. The helping professional will intervene using the list of five rotten CR skills as much as possible. Observers should take note of what strategies and techniques the helping professional uses. Have fun with the role-play (about 5 minutes of role-playing).

Debriefing: Refer back to the section on feedback in Chapter 1 to refresh your memory about giving and receiving feedback. (a) Helping professional, what horrible techniques did you try to use, and how did the couple respond to them? (b) Couple, how did you feel when the helping professional . . . ? (c) Observers, in spite of your colleague's best attempts at being horrible, what effective CR skills did your colleague demonstrate? Repeat the exercise with a new person taking on the helping role.

7. LISTENING: For each of the following client statements, provide an example of reflection of feeling or paraphrase:

a. The police just barged into my apartment and started going through all of my personal stuff. I was so scared, I couldn't say anything.

b. My son tells me that you're always picking on him in class. He never had problems with any of his other teachers.

c. The doctor said my tumor is malignant. Now you're telling me that I shouldn't worry!

d. I've been waiting to see you for over an hour. Don't you think I've got better things to do than waste my time hanging around your waiting room?

e. When I received your bill, I could not believe how much you are charging. There's no way I'm going to pay such an outrageous fee.

8. MIRRORING: In order to develop greater control over nonverbal skills, you need to be able to see yourself in action. Practice in front of a mirror or on videotape. Without using any words, try to convey a range of messages: satisfied, agree, disagree, concern, interest, hope, surprise. How do you use your hands, facial expressions, and body to convey different messages? Ask a colleague to give you feedback to see whether the colleague interprets your messages as you intended to convey them. To see how different people interpret different facial expressions, write down the feelings you believe are being conveyed by each of the following emoticons:

Ask a colleague to do the same and then compare your answers. If there are differences in your interpretations, share your reasons for why each of you interpreted the feelings in a particular way. See if you can sort out your differences (gaining an understanding of each other's perceptions, rather than trying to convince your colleague that you are right).

9. I STATEMENTS: For each of the following statements, identify the underlying message and reframe it into an *I statement:*

a.   You are making me nervous.
b.   You need to be more careful.
c.   The problem with your idea is that you aren't looking into the future.
d.   If you cannot be reasonable, then there's no use talking to you.
e.   The best solution is to divide it in half.

10. COMPLIMENTARY CIRCLE: Giving and receiving positive feedback are underused skills in CR. It is easy to take people for granted and embarrassing for a humble helping professional to receive compliments. This exercise provides an opportunity to show your colleagues how much you appreciate them. Everyone in the room gets into a circle. In turn, give the person to your right a piece of positive feedback. Use the sentence stem "What I appreciate about _____ is _____ ." Recipients of compliments respond by thanking the previous speaker. The instructor goes first.

11. TOUGH TALK: Identify and briefly describe an issue that you have wanted to discuss with a friend, family member, or coworker but have avoided discussing. What are your reasons for wanting to have this discussion? Why have you been reluctant to actually have the discussion (what are your fears or concerns)? What are the costs of not having this discussion? Which suggestions in this chapter could you use to help you engage the person in this difficult conversation (Stone et al., 2000)?

12. INSPIRED RESPONSE: This exercise is intended to help you develop imaginative responses to difficult conflict situations. Consider the following scenario:

You are working in an agency that has a strict policy on client confidentiality. You are having lunch with your supervisor, Shantell. Shantell starts sharing a story about a client. You think the story is hilarious but inappropriate, given that you're in a public place and everyone in the restaurant can hear her. You want to confront your supervisor, but you're scared because Shantell has a reputation for being vindictive to those who criticize her.

a.   How would you ordinarily respond in this situation?
b.   What is a response that is opposite to how you would respond?
c.   Think of a teacher whom you admire. How would this person respond?
d.   Think of a comedian who you think is funny (e.g., Jerry Seinfeld, Ellen DeGeneres, Chris Rock). What type of humorous response might this person create for a comedy sketch?
e.   Looking back on each of your responses, can you think of other creative ways to respond to this conflict?

Figure 2.3 | Communication Skills Inventory

This inventory lists the key skills identified in this chapter. You can use this inventory to monitor your progress and to focus your professional development. For each skill, circle the letter that signifies the level where you believe you are today. Place a check mark (√) where you plan to be at the end of the course. This will help you prioritize your learning. Mark your diary to remind yourself to come back to this inventory halfway through the course and at the end of the course. Underline where your progress is at the midway point of the course. Put an asterisk where you are at the end of the course.

    You can also use these inventories for feedback from others. When you are participating in a role-play or assignment, provide a blank copy of the inventory to a colleague, and ask for specific feedback on the criteria that you are trying to improve upon. Focus on no more than four skills at a time.

    Coding: a—needs improvement; b—competent; c—very good; d—outstanding

ORAL SKILLS

Attending (nonverbal listening)	a	b	c	d
Constructive use of silence	a	b	c	d
Paraphrasing	a	b	c	d
Reflection of feeling	a	b	c	d
Summarization	a	b	c	d
Open question	a	b	c	d
Closed question	a	b	c	d
Appropriate pacing	a	b	c	d
Nonjudgmental questions and statements	a	b	c	d
Clear questions and statements	a	b	c	d
Concise questions and statements	a	b	c	d
Statements are assertive but not aggressive	a	b	c	d
Culturally appropriate language	a	b	c	d
Other: _____	a	b	c	d

WRITING

Nonjudgmental	a	b	c	d
Clear	a	b	c	d
Concise	a	b	c	d
Assertive but not aggressive	a	b	c	d
Culturally appropriate language	a	b	c	d
Other: _____	a	b	c	d

ROLE-PLAY 2.1: "LISTENING TO ANGER"

There is trouble in Conflictia. People from Asia are very angry that they have been left out of the power structures in Conflictia. Asians are underrepresented in government, education, and professional roles. Asians tend to support the SIM Party, but the ROC Party always seems to be in power.

The two role-players for this exercise are Amal (a person of Asian descent who has a degree in education) and Verna (a vocational counselor with Diversity Plus). Amal has come to Diversity Plus to help him find a job. Amal is very frustrated, believing that he has been discriminated against by prospective employers. During this role-play, Amal will direct his anger at Verna. Verna will use listening skills to demonstrate empathy—for instance, acknowledging Amal's feelings and clarifying the behaviors or experiences behind these feelings. In order to prepare for the role-play, Amal can list examples of bigotry he has experienced and how he can convey his anger (through facial expressions, voice, and choice of words). Verna can prepare by reviewing the section on listening skills. Observers should keep track of the skills used by Verna, using the Communications Skills Inventory. After your first role-play of this situation, change roles. Have the new person playing Verna prepare by meditating,[11] using breathing techniques,[12] taking a moment for self-reflection, or using other centering techniques prior to the role-play.

Debriefing: What emotions did Amal display? How were these emotions displayed? Give examples of listening skills that Verna used effectively. How did Amal respond to each of these skills? If you were Amal, what could you do (on your own) to manage or transform your anger, prior to meeting with Verna?[13] How did the use of centering techniques affect Verna's ability to listen to Amal in the role-play?

ROLE-PLAY 2.2: "POLICIES FOR DIVERSITY PLUS"

Being a new agency, Diversity Plus needs to develop its policies and standards of practice. An interdisciplinary team has been appointed to identify the key values to which Diversity Plus aspires. All future policies will be based on this list.

The interdisciplinary team consists of Sarit (a social worker), Yota (a youth counselor), Penelope (a pastoral counselor), and Nicolai (a nurse). Before going into role, all role-players should prepare a list of values based on their ascribed roles.

---

[11]For examples of meditation techniques, see http://www.meditationsociety.com.

[12]One breathing technique is to alternate breathing through each nostril. First, hold your right nostril closed using your index finger, breathe in slowly through your left nostril, hold your breath for a brief time, and then exhale. Repeat, using each of your fingers to hold your nostril. Then, switch to holding your left nostril and breathe through your right nostril, using the same sequence of fingers. You can repeat this process two or three times, helping you feel more still and in touch with your breathing and the rest of your body (Kestner, 2005).

[13]For example, avoid stimulants, forgive, become more spiritual, focus on your fear rather than anger (Wilmot & Hocker, 2007), or ventilate with a friend rather than with Verna.

Think about what your profession stands for. Also, consider your vision for the agency. What ideals would make Diversity Plus an inspired place for you to work? (If the specified roles are not familiar to you, you can change the professions to ones that are more familiar to you).

Yota will take the lead in facilitating the discussion. Begin by creating a comprehensive list of values on a chalkboard or flipchart. Let everyone have an open discussion about the values (15 minutes). To close the discussion, ask everyone to mark asterisks (**) next to the items they value most. Each person is entitled to put up seven asterisks and can distribute these asterisks in any combination (e.g., one asterisk for one value, six for another). When each person has had a chance to mark seven asterisks, count the asterisks for each value. The values with the most asterisks will represent the values with the highest priorities. Save the results of this exercise to refer back to them for exercises later in the course.

Debriefing: What were the sources of the values that you identified during the role-play? Your family? A specific culture? Broader society? Your profession? What types of conflict resolution are most consistent with the list of values generated by your list of values? What types of conflict resolution would not fit? How did you decide to distribute your asterisks? What were advantages of using the asterisk process for decision making in this case? What was problematic about it?

"Negotiation" is derived from the Latin neg (not) and otium (leisure or ease). Hence, the word negotiation reflects the inherent tension (not leisure) within the activity.

—Jonathan Cohen (2003, p. 436)

Negotiation

Recall from Chapter 1 that we defined *negotiation* as any interactions between two or more parties involved in a conflict. Negotiation includes formal negotiation, in which the conflicting parties get together explicitly for the purposes of bargaining or resolving a specific dispute. However, it also includes emergent negotiation, in which conflicting parties have not expressly declared their intentions to negotiate (Fisher & Brown, 1988). Because of the pervasiveness of conflict in social interaction, virtually all interactions between individuals or groups could be viewed from the perspective of negotiation. As people work through their differences, negotiation presents opportunities for fights, oppression, and violence but also opportunities for creative problem solving, deeper understanding, social justice, reduced tensions, and enhanced relationships.

In this chapter, I focus on negotiation between parties who are directly involved in a conflict, such as negotiations between helping professionals and clients, between coprofessionals, or between client systems (Shulman, 2006). Chapters 4 through 7 build on the theories and approaches described in this chapter, because each of them show how helping professionals can assist others involved in negotiation. In other words, mediation, facilitation, advocacy, and so on, can be viewed as different methods of helping people negotiate. As you work through this chapter, think about the challenges faced by people who are struggling to negotiate conflict on their own. In later chapters, you can use these insights to consider how helping professionals might be able to help negotiators overcome these challenges.

The following section describes clinical and legal issues pertaining to negotiations and contracting. I devote the largest part of the chapter to a comparison of four approaches to negotiation: power, rights, interests, and transformation. These approaches are integrated in a Negotiation Preparation Tool that provides a strategic approach to analyzing conflict situations in order to prepare for negotiation. The discussion questions and experiential assignments at the end of this chapter will help you compare and contrast how various approaches to negotiation can be put into practice.

CONTRACTING

Most helping professionals are familiar with negotiating, though they generally use different terminology. For instance, helping professionals "contract" with clients in the early stages of a problem-solving process (Shulman, 2006). In the process of contracting, they try to come to an agreement about the problem for work, the professional's roles and obligations, and the client's roles and obligations (Rothman, 1998). Although helping professionals ascribe to the principle of client self-determination, they often unwittingly impose terms on their clients. Consider the following example of a professional's explanation of client confidentiality, its extents, and limitations.

> Everything we discuss in our sessions remains confidential. In other words, I will respect your right to privacy. I will not tell anyone about what you say, unless I have your express written permission. There are a few exceptions. For instance, if anything raises concerns that a child or other person may be put at risk of harm, I have a professional obligation to take steps to help that person avoid the harm. . . .

Here, the professional is telling the client what confidentiality means, rather than negotiating it. The professional may ask the client to agree, but even then, the terms of the contract for confidentiality are all or nothing. Genuine negotiation with the client would allow the client and professional to discuss all the terms of the contract and develop individualized provisions that meet the needs of this client. Consider a client who does not want confidentiality. This client might negotiate an agreement where the professional is not bound to keep anything confidential— the client may even ask the professional to broadcast information about the client. In other words, free and informed negotiation enhances a client's right to self-determination.[1]

Literature on work with involuntary clients, in particular, views clients and clinicians as having conflicting interests (Dolgoff et al., 2005). In child protection cases, for example, social workers are mandated to investigate allegations of child abuse and neglect. Parents suspected of abuse are interested in privacy and autonomy. The workers are interested in ensuring the safety of the child. In order to engage parents on a voluntary basis, the worker tries to negotiate terms of a working arrangement that satisfy the interests of the parents and the worker. Ideally, the parents and worker turn an involuntary relationship into a purely voluntary one, in which both the parents and worker agree to a certain working relationship. If the worker is unable to secure the child's welfare needs through voluntary interventions, the worker can impose the authority of the child protection system (e.g., by initiating court proceedings). In between these extremes, the worker can use various levels of bargaining and persuasion in order to fulfill the child protection mandate (Murdach, 1980; Tjaden, 1994).

---

[1]In legal literature, contracting between individuals is called *private ordering*. This term suggests that the parties to the contract are free to negotiate or arrange their affairs as they see fit, without state intervention or limits. Capitalism and free markets are based on the principle of private ordering. Socialism puts constraints on private ordering. The rights of the community, in certain circumstances, will supersede the rights of individuals to private ordering.

When negotiations lead to an agreement, the agreement might be a legally binding contract. *Contracts* are essentially promises that each party makes to the other. Contracts can be enforceable even if they are not drafted by lawyers or signed and witnessed. Legally drafted agreements are easier to prove in court. However, oral and implied contracts are also enforceable. An *oral* contract is a verbal agreement. An *implied* contract exists where the parties do not explicitly say they are entering an agreement; however, an agreement can be inferred from the pattern of behaviors that existed between the parties. For instance, even if you do not verbally promise confidentiality to a client, you may imply such a promise indirectly: you meet with the client in a private office, the certificate on your wall says you are a licensed professional, and you encourage the client to trust you and share personal information. Although verbal and implied contracts are enforceable, written contracts have a number of advantages.

- Both parties are clear about whether they have entered into a contract.
- The terms can be spelled out specifically, to ensure that both parties have the same understandings.
- Written contracts tend to solidify the commitment of both parties.
- Before the contract is signed, lawyers, supervisors, or others can review it in order to provide legal or other professional advice.
- If disputes arise in the future, then the document can serve as evidence of the parties' agreement.
- Terms of the written agreement can be modified with subsequent written agreements, providing a paper trail of the sequence of events.

Oral agreements tend to be less formal and take less time to produce. People often use oral agreements when they assume there will be no problem with enforcement. Implied contracts are problematic because neither party can be sure if they have entered a contract and if so, what the precise terms of the contract are. As a helping professional, preferred practice suggests that you be deliberate about entering contracts and explicit about their terms, whether the contract is oral or written.

Written contracts are particularly important when the subject of the conflict has serious legal ramifications (e.g., criminal behavior, child abuse or neglect, physical injuries, monetary losses). Many agreements do not have legal ramifications and may not even be intended to be legally enforceable. In family therapy, a counselor may help family members negotiate a "family contract." The contract may specify the roles, privileges, and obligations of each parent and child in the family. The contract encourages each party to fulfill a certain set of obligations. However, the family members do not intend it to be a legally enforceable contract. In other words, if one family member does not live up to the terms of the agreement, the others cannot go to court to make that person comply.

In most jurisdictions, drafting formal contracts is a function restricted to licensed lawyers. If a nonlawyer drafts a formal contract, that person may be subject to criminal charges for "unauthorized practice of law." The role of a helping professional in writing informal agreements with clients is to help them articulate their wishes and expectations for one another. When preparing informal agreements, helping professionals should advise the clients that they are not providing legal advice and are not drafting legally binding contracts. They should also ensure that their informal agreements avoid the trappings of a legally binding contract:

- Use a title for the document such as "Memorandum of Understanding," "Unofficial Peace Treaty," or "Nonbinding Family Agreement," rather than "Contract" or "Agreement."
- Do not have the clients or witnesses sign the document.
- Use plain language, rather than technical, legal language.
- Include a sentence that states the document is not intended to be a legally binding agreement.

These points will make it clear to clients that the agreement is, in fact, an informal one. In some situations, a helping professional will help clients come to a general understanding and then ask the clients' lawyers to draft the general understanding into a legally binding contract. This ensures that the clients have an opportunity to obtain independent legal advice[2] before they sign the contract and make it enforceable. If you are concerned about the legal ramifications of negotiations and contracting, ensure that you obtain your own legal advice. You may also have an ethical obligation to ensure that clients have an opportunity to consult with a lawyer to ensure they are apprised of their legal rights.

APPROACHES TO NEGOTIATION

Negotiation theory can be categorized in a number of different manners: contractual versus emergent (Pruitt & Carnevale, 1993); positional versus principled (Fisher et al., 1997); exchange of discourse versus exchange of resources (Isenhart & Spangle, 2000; Rifkin, Millen, & Cobb, 1991). Although I cannot describe all theories of negotiation in one chapter, I try to capture the breadth of theories and models by focusing on four approaches (or orientations) to negotiation: power, rights, interests, and transformation (Furlong, 2005; Hermann, Hollett, Eaker, & Gale, 2003).[3] As Figure 3.1 demonstrates, each approach can be applied separately, as well as in combination.

The power approach to negotiation views parties as competitors. Each party uses its power to try to influence the other and gain advantage. Conflicts are resolved by who is strongest—for instance, the party with the greatest physical strength, the best weapons, the most political clout, the highest intelligence, or the largest financial resources. In the purest form of power-based negotiations, there are no rules of

---

[2]*Independent* legal advice refers to separate legal advice for each party. One lawyer cannot advise all parties to an agreement because there may be a conflict of interest between the parties.

[3]Van Es (1996) uses four categories, attributing each to a particular era: (a) the "warrior" concept, dating back to the Byzantine Empire; (b) the "mercantile" concept, dating to the Renaissance; (c) the "civil" concept, attributed to the Enlightenment; and (d) the constructive concept, attributed to the 20th century.

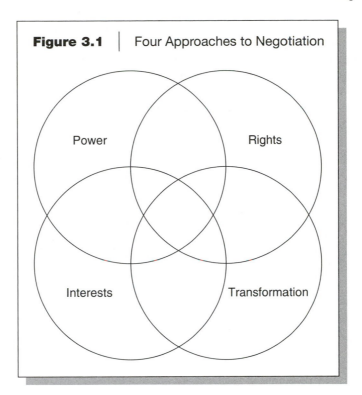

Figure 3.1 | Four Approaches to Negotiation

Power

Rights

Interests

Transformation

fair play.[4] Parties can lie, cheat, bludgeon, or commit other savage acts on one another. Winning is the highest value.[5]

The rights approach was intended to be an "enlightened response" to the injustice and barbarism of the power approach by imposing rules of fair play. Rather than presume that "might is right," the rights approach suggests that "right is right." Under the rights approach, the legal system creates a set of procedures and rules designed to treat people fairly, regardless of their position of power or powerlessness (Bossy, 2003). The rule of law suggests that laws rather than force govern people. Laws dictate who is entitled to what and under what circumstances. If parties are uncertain about who is right or what is right, they can go to court for a determination by an impartial judge.[6] To the extent that the law is clear, parties need not go to court. They can negotiate based on their rights. Rights-based conflict arises when

---

[4]In many forms of power-based conflict, there are rules of fair play; for instance, the Geneva Convention describes fair treatment for prisoners of war. This is just one example of how power-based and rights-based conflict approaches overlap.

[5]Although using power may include the use of violence and extreme coercion, people can use power in a nonviolent and ethical manner.

[6]They could also go to arbitration, which is a rights-based process similar to court, but with a private judge.

people have conflicting rights or when one party believes that another has violated his or her rights but is not accepting responsibility. In either case, a judge can resolve matters for the parties by applying relevant laws. While the rights perspective encourages greater civility, legal battles are still "civil wars" (i.e., the process is adversarial).

The interests approach,[7] popularized in the 1980s by the Harvard Negotiation Project (Fisher et al., 1997), *shifts the focus of negotiation from adversarial conflict resolution to joint problem solving based on trying to satisfy one another's interests.* Interests are the parties' underlying concerns, what they really want to achieve. In its purest form, parties try to resolve conflicts by identifying mutual interests and ways of satisfying one another's interests, regardless of their rights or power. Interest-based negotiation asks parties to focus on negotiating what is truly important to them, rather than trying to win by achieving a solution that fits with their original positions. When the interest approach is implemented effectively, collaboration replaces competition. The quality of the ongoing relationship between the parties is more important than determination of their legal rights. Interest-based negotiators reframe "opposing parties" into "partners" or "counterparts" (Cohen, 2003).

The transformative approach suggests the primary purposes of negotiation and other forms of CR are to change the way people view conflict and improve how they interact in response to the conflict. According to Bush and Folger (2005), the basis of problematic conflict is not a difference of rights or contradictory interests, but rather the destabilizing effect that it has on the people involved in the conflict. Conflict tends to make each person feel more vulnerable and more self-absorbed, leading the interaction to become more destructive, alienating, and dehumanizing. Bush and Folger suggest that interpersonal conflict can be transformed through the processes of empowerment and recognition. *Empowerment* refers to restoring each party's sense of his or her own value, strength, and capacity to handle life's problems. *Recognition* refers to each person acknowledging and demonstrating empathy for the situation and problem of the other (Institute for the Study of Conflict Transformation, n.d.). While the other approaches focus on how to resolve conflict, transformation focuses on the moral and personal growth of the parties. The actual conflict need not be resolved. Accordingly, transformative negotiation is oriented toward individual and relational processes, rather than producing specific outcomes. The exchange of communication between parties is more important than how resources are distributed between them.

Lederach (2005) defines *conflict transformation* as "envision[ing] and respond[ing] to the ebb and flow of social conflict as life-giving opportunities for creating constructive changes processes that reduce violence, increase justice in direct interaction and social structures, and respond to real-life problems in human relationships" (p. 14). This definition emphasizes that conflict, peace, and social justice are ongoing processes. *Conflict transformation* refers to changing the way we view and respond to conflict in order to promote positive change: "From the transformational perspective, conflict is the tension between what is and what could be. Conflict

---

[7]The interests paradigm is the cornerstone of Fisher et al.'s (1997) model of "principled negotiation."

forces parties to deal with deeper issues and thus serves as a constructive social process" (Isenhart & Spangle, 2000, p. 9).

The following sections provide more detailed descriptions of these models. First, however, I want to illustrate how these contrasting CR approaches relate to practice. Consider a conflict involving sex discrimination: women in the community earn only 70 percent of what men do for work of equal value. You are working with a group that wants to rectify the problem. You can approach this case from any of the four approaches.

From a power perspective, the cause of this conflict is based on the imbalance of power between men and women; for example, men hold the greatest number of managerial positions, where salary decisions are made. In order to address this imbalance, your strategy may depend on placing more women in management (positions of power). Men will become relatively less powerful.

In contrast, a rights approach starts with the premise that men and women have equal rights. This includes the rights of women to equal pay for work of equal value. The fact that women are earning 30 percent less than men means that these rights have been violated. Your strategy may begin with informing employers about equality rights and negotiating ways to implement them. If employers do not agree to abide by these rights, you may decide to go to court or a human rights tribunal for a judicial determination and enforcement.

Using an interest-based approach, you need to assess the underlying interests of the parties. Women want equal pay for work of equal value. Their underlying concerns include fairness and respect. Businesses and managers want to minimize their expenses in order to maximize profits. However, they can also agree that workers should be treated with fairness and respect. Your approach would be to engage the parties in a joint problem-solving process, so that each of their interests can be satisfied. Ultimately, this will result in better working relationships and mutual benefits.

The transformative approach suggests that the conflicting parties need to gain (a) a better understanding on one another's situation, and (b) a stronger sense of control over their own destinies. For businesses, this means learning about the impact of discrimination on women and acknowledging the validity of women's feelings. For women, this means learning and acknowledging the pressures on businesses and managers. Neither party has to agree with the other. However, your intervention ought to help each party take greater control over their roles in the conflict. Both parties can be transformed, regardless of whether the specific conflict about equal pay is resolved to both parties' satisfaction. Even if the women do not obtain full parity in salaries, their participation in a constructive CR process provides them with a greater sense of pride and purpose. They may also develop new and deeper understandings that may help them deal with the conflict in a more constructive way in the future (Lederach, 2003).

Although the issues have been simplified, this scenario highlights some of the key differences in applying different models. As you work through the various approaches to negotiation in more detail, consider the assumptions of each and how each approach views success.

POWER-BASED NEGOTIATION

This section begins with a definition of interpersonal power, followed by a description of a power-based approach to negotiations.

Interpersonal power refers to the capacity of individuals or groups to influence one another (Pinderhughes, 1989). **Power** is a dynamic process because it occurs in interactions between people. One person may have more power or influence over another in some situations, but less power over the other in different situations. Consider, for instance, a clinical supervisor's power in relation to a clinician. The supervisor has the authority of the agency to direct the clinician about how to intervene with particular clients. The clinician is likely to heed the supervisor's advice even if the clinician disagrees, provided that the advice is about professional matters within the agency's mandate. The clinician is less likely to heed the supervisor's directives about matters that the clinician believes are personal or beyond the agency's mandate. Furthermore, the clinician is more likely to rebel if the supervisor uses power to dictate on repeated occasions. Accordingly, after a person exercises power over another, that person will have less power to influence the other in the future.

Power-based negotiation is a distributive process in which each party tries to exert influence on the other in order to achieve a solution that meets his or her preferred outcomes or self-interests. This approach is sometimes called *distributive negotiation*, because it focuses on dividing existing resources rather than creating new resources or seeking mutually acceptable solutions (Wilmot & Hocker, 2007). Power-based negotiations are essentially competitive interactions. Because the primary goal of the interaction is to maximize personal gain, parties using this perspective may adopt whatever strategies they can to influence the other side (Druckman, 1993). These strategies include positional negotiating, intransigence, secretiveness, bluffing, threats, and use of force.

In *positional negotiations*, each party takes a stance and argues in favor of that stance. Rather than start with problem definition, each party starts by offering a solution.

PHYSICIAN: *This client needs to go on a diet to lose weight.*

FEMINIST THERAPIST: *This client needs an opportunity to explore her body image and the unrealistic expectations society places on women.*

Once a party offers a solution, backing down becomes difficult. Neither party wants to look weak or lose face. Because both parties are reluctant to move from their original positions, deadlocks are not uncommon. The question becomes "Who is right, the physician or the feminist therapist?" In power negotiations, might is right. If the physician has greater status in the agency, the position of the physician may prevail. Alternatively, the therapist might find allies in the agency to support her stance and win the debate.[8] Regardless, positional negotiations set up at least one party to be the "loser."

---

[8]Debating and alternatives to debating are described in greater detail in Chapter 5.

When positional negotiations are headed toward an impasse, parties often agree to compromise. In other words, both parties give in, at least partially. Each saves face, knowing that the other side is also reducing its demands. Still, both parties are generally reluctant to make concessions, because one party's loss is the other's gain (i.e., the parties are playing a zero-sum game). The need to appear tough leads to further intransigence on both sides.

Positional negotiations encourage parties to use the following strategies:

- **Tilt the process in your favor.** To gain a competitive advantage, positional negotiators arrange for negotiations to take place on their own turf, a setting where the other party has a psychological or tactical disadvantage (e.g., the home team controls access to facilities such as restrooms, kitchens, telephones, and computers). Other ways to slant the process include outnumbering the other side at the negotiation table, scheduling negotiation times that are disadvantageous to the other side, or designating some of your demands as preconditions to negotiating (Menkel-Meadow & Wheeler, 2004).

- **Make as extreme an offer as is tenable.** If both parties know they will need to compromise, their initial positions will not reflect what they really want or what they view as a reasonable solution. By inflating initial offers to settle, there is "room to negotiate." Neither party wants to make too extreme an offer, to ensure that they do not put off the other. The first offer must be sufficiently reasonable to demonstrate seriousness about the negotiations. The parties will go through a series of offers and counteroffers, eventually communicating more realistic goals and expectations (Ellis & Stuckless, 1996).[9]

- **Let the other side make the first offer.** The first party to make an offer is placed at a strategic disadvantage. Not knowing how the second party will respond, you do not know how extreme an offer to make. If your offer is close to your bottom line and the counteroffer is extreme, you leave little room to maneuver in negotiations. If your offer is too extreme, the other party will refuse to negotiate with you.

- **Be secretive.** Because the object is to win, information becomes a valued commodity. Parties do not want to share information—particularly their bottom lines. Unfortunately, neither party can make an informed decision if the other party is holding back relevant information.

- **Bluff.** Bluffing is a form of deceit, though the term *bluffing* tends to carry fewer negative connotations (Menkel-Meadow & Wheeler, 2004). Bluffing is related to secretiveness but goes further. Rather than simply withhold information, you intentionally provide misinformation. An example of bluffing in poker is to pretend that you have a better hand than you actually have. The appearance of strength influences others, even if you do not have the actual strength (cards) to back up the appearances. Bluffing has three downsides: the ethics of bluffing are

---

[9]Ellis and Stuckless refer to this process as a "convergence-concession" approach.

questionable,[10] the other side might call your bluff, and people may not want to deal with you if they know you are a bluffer.

- **Be patient in negotiations.** If you look anxious to settle quickly, you weaken your bargaining position. The other side knows you are more likely to make compromises. Accordingly, the incentive in positional bargaining is to draw things out, to show that you can withstand conflict over a long duration. Delay tactics may also be a sign that the other party has no real interest in resolving the conflict. If the status quo gives one party an advantageous position, that party has no incentive to bargain in good faith (Pruitt & Carnevale, 1993).
- **If you make compromises, make small concessions.** Neither party wants to give up more than they have to, so any concessions tend to be small.
- **Play tit-for-tat.** This strategy suggests that you should respond to an opposing party in the same manner that the party treats you. If the other party is cooperative, you will reciprocate by being cooperative. If the other party becomes competitive, you will become competitive (Rapoport, 1974). Ideally, this approach encourages both parties to cooperate. Unfortunately, tit-for-tat often turns into a game of chicken. One party makes a threat, and the other party responds in kind. The threats escalate, and it becomes difficult for either party to back down.
- **Threaten.** Threats are commitments to punish the other side if it does not accept your position. Threats are more likely to persuade the other side if the proposed sanctions are large and the threats are credible. Credibility depends on whether it seems reasonable that the threats can and will be carried out. Threats and similar exercise of force may produce compliance in the short term. However, they may also generate resentment, resistance, and withdrawal. Under certain circumstances, threats may be viewed as legitimate. For example, the criminal justice system is essentially a system of threats: laws are established; if people break the law, they can expect to be punished. This type of threat has legitimacy because it has the general support of society and because the nature of the punishment fits the crime.
- **Harass.** *Harassment* refers to punishing the other side until it gives in to your demands. As with threats, punishment may produce compliance, but it harms the relationship between the parties. When people are harassed unjustly, they will eventually rebel (Pruitt & Carnevale, 1993).
- **Make your adversary feel good.** Often, negotiators will win more in their self-interest by being nice than by being mean. Power-based negotiators may stroke the other party's ego, show respect, and act humbly, not out of altruistic beliefs but because they can achieve more favorable terms (Menkel-Meadow & Wheeler, 2004).

---

[10]Helping professionals generally agree that intentional deceit is unethical; however, some might argue that the ends justify the means. In other words, if a person needs to bluff in order to achieve something of higher moral value, then deceit is justified. Others suggest that certain forms of deceit, such as misrepresenting your bottom line, are part of the accepted game of negotiations. Consider which of the following schools of thought fit with your view on honesty in negotiations: utopian (an idealist who is always open and honest with others, even if it hurts), metopian (an individualist who is self-absorbed and does not care about the impact on others), or pragmatist (a realist who decides what is best in each circumstance, knowing that sometimes it is best to be honest because "what goes around, comes around") (Menkel-Meadow & Wheeler, 2004).

If both sides use adversarial strategies, then negotiations become protracted and agreement becomes difficult. Even when agreement is reached, parties are often dissatisfied. Often, the solution is a compromise, and the relationship between the parties becomes antagonistic.

As these examples suggest, positional negotiations present many problems, particularly for helping professionals. Still, it is important to understand the nature of positional negotiations in order to learn how to respond to others who approach negotiation from this perspective. You can either play the game with them or encourage them to play a different type of game, based on one of the other approaches to CR.

In extreme cases, the only rule in power negotiations is that the party with the greater power wins. In most interactions, however, the parties have a tacit understanding about the rules of the game: you can use conventional weapons, but not nuclear weapons; you can punch the head, but not below the belt; you can use harsh words, but not any physical violence. Although these rules of the game put certain limits on the types of power that can be used, the ultimate goal is still personal victory.

Power does exist in relationships, so, at the very least, it must be acknowledged. Certainly, there are times when use of power is justifiable, even necessary. The most common example cited is self-defense, when the person is being attacked. This appears to be a zero-sum game: either the attacker suffers, or the person attacked suffers. Too often, however, people assume use of power is required when there are other alternatives. If you are being attacked, use of force may incite the other to use even greater force. In aikido and other martial arts, for instance, you learn to move with force rather than against it. If someone charges at you and you ready yourself by planting your feet, force will meet force. Both of you will suffer from the impact. Alternatively, you could use the momentum of your charging opponent to your advantage; that is, move with the force rather than against it (Edelman & Crain, 1993). The interest-based approach, described later, demonstrates how helping professionals can apply this strategy in various social conflicts.

Helping professionals frequently work on behalf of disadvantaged individuals or groups. The "disadvantage" often relates to negotiation power. Helping professionals can help disadvantaged people gain negotiation power through advocacy techniques, described in Chapter 6. Power, however, may not be a critical problem if the helping professional can engage the parties in one of the nonpower approaches of negotiation. Rather than having one party try to use its power over the other party, for instance, parties can join forces to work toward mutually acceptable goals (Wilmot & Hocker, 2007). Using *power with* another person rather than *power over* another person fits with the interest-based and transformative approaches to negotiation, described later.

RIGHTS-BASED NEGOTIATION

Rights-based negotiation is premised on what the relevant laws prescribe. Negotiators argue their positions based on their respective rights or entitlements. Whereas power-based negotiators try to influence the other side by exerting various forms of influence, rights-based negotiation comes down to which party has the better legal arguments.

If you are negligent in your professional practice and a client suffers as a result, your client could sue you for compensation. If you know the client would win in court, there is no need to actually proceed through a trial. You could negotiate compensation based on your projection of what a court would award, "bargaining in the shadow of the law" (Mnookin & Kornhauser, 1979). A client who is denied welfare could initiate a case with the welfare appeals tribunal. However, the welfare worker could negotiate with the client based on what they believe the tribunal would decide. In both cases, the parties save the costs and aggravation of going through adversarial hearings.

Clear laws make it easier for parties to negotiate their rights. If the law is hazy or uncertain, the parties do not know which way a judge might decide. In conflict situations, parties have a tendency to view conflicts from their own perspectives, often reckoning that a judge would decide in their favor. "I'm right, so you must be wrong." If neither party is willing to budge from this position, they may need to go to a judge or other arbitrator to decide which one really is right. Even when laws are clear, they may be open to different interpretations and judicial comment. Because parties have little control over how rights are established or interpreted, rights-based negotiations can be frustrating.

The rights approach is most easily recognized in terms of public laws and legal disputes. However, this approach also applies with regard to rules in families, communities, social agencies, and other organizations. Community norms and ethics, for example, prescribe appropriate types of behaviors. Your sense of right and wrong may tell you that divorce is a valid option for couples with irreconcilable differences. A colleague may believe that marriages are sacrosanct. Your sense of right comes from certain cultural values—namely, autonomy and freedom. Your colleague's beliefs come from a particular religious perspective. Negotiation based on rights is problematic because there is no universal agreement on what actually is right. Neither side has room for compromise unless someone gives up a fundamental belief.

Agency policies create rules for clients and helping professionals. Some agencies, for example, restrict services to clients who are national citizens or immigrants with appropriate visas or legal status. How would you respond to an undocumented alien in need of your services? If you resort to a rights perspective, you must refuse the client. The client and you cannot negotiate away the rules of the agency. If you agree to provide services, you are contravening policy and putting yourself in conflict with the agency. If you believe that serving undocumented aliens is morally right, you could advocate within your agency to change the rules (i.e., recognize a different set of rights).

Communities and organizations establish rules to create a sense of order. At its best, a rights approach prevents conflict because everyone knows his or her respective rights. Little time and energy is spent negotiating. For the most part, people comply with the laws tacitly. Accordingly, clear and fair laws promote efficient transactions between people. Rights also temper illegitimate use of power. Laws prohibit certain types of violence, coercion, and exploitation. Laws also encourage games of fair play: negotiating in good faith, arbitration, court trial, due process, and so on.

On the downside, a rights orientation favors rules over relationships (Conley & O'Barr, 1990). Although the rights approach places limits on the illegitimate use of power, the process to resolve disputes is adversarial: my rights versus yours. One side wins; the other loses. The system does not encourage parties to look for creative solutions for their mutual benefit. If a case has to be decided by a judge or arbitrator, the emotional and financial costs are highly taxing on the parties. Parties also lose the ability make decisions for themselves.

A primary concern about the rights perspective is determining who establishes rights in the first place. In democratic societies, elected governments are given the primary responsibility for making laws and initiating law reform. Elections and political processes tend to be adversarial. Again, there are winners and losers. Minority views and people without representation lose out. Those with political power ultimately determine how rights are allocated in society. Similarly, rights in communities and organizations are determined by those with power. Minority rights may be protected by constitutions or other laws; however, laws can also be used for social control or imposing prejudicial rules.

Given the limitations of the rights approach, what are the alternatives? How can we have justice without law (Auerbach, 1984)? What is the basis for negotiation if we do not rely on a base of rules (Conley & O'Barr, 1990)?

INTEREST-BASED NEGOTIATION

Interest-based negotiation (IBN) *refers to a joint problem-solving process in which the parties strive to resolve their mutual interests rather than advance their individual rights or positions.* Some authors call this *principled negotiation*[11] (Fisher et al., 1997) or an *integrative approach*[12] (Ellis & Stuckless, 1996). In terms of conflict styles, IBN favors collaboration. It draws theoretical support from game theory. Positional and rights orientations view conflict as zero-sum games: if one party gets more, then the other party will get proportionally less. In contrast, IBN encourages parties to play cooperative games and seek out win-win solutions. In many cases, fighting over resources leads to losses by both parties (e.g., the cost of hiring lawyers, time and energy devoted to fighting, and destruction of one another's resources). If people problem-solve cooperatively and find common ground, they can actually create and share new resources (Menkel-Meadow et al., 2005). Whereas power-based negotiation is distributive because it focuses on how to divide resources, IBN is integrative because it focuses on how to build a solution that meets everyone's needs, interests, and goals.[13] Accordingly, IBN encourages trust and amicable relationships between the parties. If the parties can truly collaborate for their mutual interests, the relative balance of power between them becomes a nonissue. They use *power with* each other, rather than *power over* one another.

---

[11]The principles provide a framework for the parties to follow in order for negotiation to be constructive for both parties.

[12]The approach is integrative by focusing on the interests of both parties, rather than one party's interests versus the other's. Furthermore, integrative negotiation encourages the parties to satisfy their interests in terms of both process and outcome (e.g., to develop a fair process as well as a fair outcome).

[13]In metaphoric terms, this is the difference between *dividing the pie* and *expanding the pie*, or perhaps finding a completely new pie.

The Harvard Negotiation Project suggests a seven-part framework for negotiation:

1. Focus on interests, not positions.
2. Invent options for mutual gain.
3. Apply objective criteria.
4. Improve communication.
5. Build a positive negotiating relationship.
6. Consider alternatives.
7. Obtain commitments (Fisher et al., 1997).

These components do not represent a sequence of steps, but rather strategies to be used in various combinations. When problems arise in negotiation, these points can be used as a diagnostic checklist to determine the nature of the difficulties and strategies to employ to move negotiation forward. The relative importance of a particular component depends on the particular situation.

1. Focus on Interests, Not Positions

The central tenet of IBN is that negotiators should avoid positional bargaining and work on satisfying their interests. But what exactly are interests, and how do they differ from rights or positions? *Positions* are strategic stances or demands of the parties. *Interests* refer to their underlying needs, values, concerns, or desires. In order to identify interests, ask the parties why they are pursuing certain positions or demands. Find out what is truly important to them, at a fundamental level. Consider the following scenario:

> Ferdinand has a 12-year-old daughter, Demi. A child protection worker, Whoopi, has been asked to investigate Ferdinand for possible child abuse. Upon meeting with family members, Whoopi is concerned for Demi's safety and decides to place Demi in temporary foster care. Ferdinand contests this decision. He has used corporal punishment with Demi but does not believe that this practice constitutes abuse.

Whoopi's position is that Demi must be removed from her family home. Ferdinand's position is that Demi should remain with him. If they pursue a power or rights perspective, both will become entrenched in their positions. They will tend to restrict their vision of possible solutions to Whoopi's position or Ferdinand's position.

In contrast, if they pursue an interest-based perspective, they will try to understand one another's interests and look for creative solutions that are satisfactory to both of them. If Ferdinand asked Whoopi, "Why do you want Demi placed in foster care? What are you really concerned about?" Whoopi would say that she is interested in Demi's safety, ensuring that she is not abused and that her psychosocial concerns are being met. If Whoopi were to ask Ferdinand about his underlying interests ("What are your reasons for wanting Demi to stay home with you?"), he would say that he loves Demi and is interested in her welfare. Both Whoopi and Ferdinand could agree they were interested in Demi's welfare. They have different understandings about what this means or requires. However, they have a common goal and can engage in a joint problem-solving process to resolve their differences. Their selection of possible solutions opens up.

- Arrange for an independent helping professional from the community to conduct a family assessment and suggest services, if needed.
- Have a relative move into the family home to assist with parenting.
- Develop an agreement about what types of punishment are appropriate and what types are inappropriate.
- Ensure that Demi has a counselor or support person to confide with.
- Refer Ferdinand to parenting skills training.
- Provide Ferdinand with liberal access while Demi is in foster care.

Ferdinand does not want Whoopi making life difficult for him. Whoopi does not want to make life difficult for him, either. They could agree to work out a plan to resolve their differences as quickly and amicably as possible, so Ferdinand's family can get on with life without interference from Whoopi.

In order to prepare for negotiation, identify the other parties' interests, as well as your own. The natural tendency is to see conflict from one's own perspective. Try to put yourself in the others' shoes. Why are they advocating a particular position? What are their underlying concerns, hopes, expectations, aspirations, or preferences?[14] Consider the use of role reversal to help you understand the motivation and viewpoints of other parties. Role reversal is a type of role-play in which you assume another party's role and have a colleague assume your role. By taking on the other party's role, you gain an experiential understanding of that party's interests.

If conflicting parties have similar interests, they can easily agree to a common goal. If the parties' interests conflict, they may be able to identify common goals by exploring deeper levels of underlying interests (Pruitt & Carnevale, 1993). The hierarchy of interests includes desires, values, and basic needs (Warfield, 1993). I will use a brief case to illustrate.

> Dorothy, aged 52, lives with her 82-year-old mother, Miranda. Miranda's health has been deteriorating. After Miranda fell in the bathtub, Dorothy decided that Miranda should move into a specialized nursing home. Miranda wants to stay at home. Their counselor wants to help them identify common interests in order to engage them in joint problem solving.

- **Desires or wants are based on cognitive decision-making processes and emotional reactions.** Miranda says she wants to live at home because that is where she has lived all her life. She has never lived in an institution and would not know how to adapt to all of the changes. She is afraid to go to a nursing home, because she believes that is where people go to die. Dorothy wants Miranda to go to a nursing home because a nursing home can provide better care for Miranda. Each person has a valid argument, based on her own reasoning. Unfortunately, their desires conflict.
- **Values are nonreasoned choices that define a person's core convictions about what is important.** Underneath Miranda's desire to remain at home lies her value

---

[14]To help you remember each of these terms, you can use the mnemonic CHEAP.

for independence. Moving into a nursing home would mean giving up her independence. In contrast, Dorothy's original position is based on her value for health. Miranda and Dorothy might agree to negotiate based on two principles: independence and health. This would provide a basis for joint problem solving. However, if they do not agree on these principles, the counselor can ask them what underlies their stated values.

- **Needs are more basic requirements than values.** *Physical* requirements include food, water, sleep, shelter, and safety from bodily harm. *Psychosocial* needs include security, identity, recognition, respect, status, and self-actualization (Chetkow-Yanoov, 1997; Maslow, 1987). Miranda's value for independence may be based on her need for survival. She does not believe that she can survive without independence. Similarly, Dorothy's value for health may also lie in her need for Miranda's survival. Accordingly, both can agree to work toward a common goal. The focus of the problem is what it will take to ensure Dorothy's survival. If they cannot agree on a common goal at this level, the counselor can help them explore even deeper levels of interests.

As the parties move from positions to desires, values, and needs, they tend to move from the specific to the general. If parties cannot agree on specific goals, they may find it easier to agree on more general principles. Once general principles are in place, the parties can work out more of the specifics.

2. Invent Options for Mutual Gain

Options are possible solutions or outcomes of the CR process. When people become entrenched in conflict, their initially perceived choice set tends to be narrow. Remind yourself and the parties you are negotiating with that it is important to keep an open mind, to be creative.

Once both parties have agreed on general principles, they can work together to invent possible solutions. In order to become creative, parties need to suspend judgments. For example, brainstorm as many ideas as you can. Do not worry if they are reasonable or viable. A free-flowing dialogue fosters creativity. Do not have concern about whether the ideas are better for one party or another. Just raise as many ideas as possible. As you brainstorm, list all the ideas on a flipchart or chalkboard. Even ridiculous ideas can spawn constructive options. If you are not sure what options are available, gather information from friends, professionals, or other resources in the community.

In Dorothy and Miranda's situation, they might brainstorm the following options: Let Miranda stay home and put Dorothy in the nursing home; hire a home aide to help with Miranda's care; put off the decision until the next crisis; have Miranda spend time with different family members in order to give Dorothy respite; don't allow Miranda to take baths; look for a supportive housing arrangement that provides more independence than the nursing home; turn Dorothy's house into a nursing home and take in more patients.

Avoid making decisions about whether options are worth considering until all your ideas are exhausted. When one person puts forward an idea, it is very easy for the others to reject it. If each successive idea is rejected, then no options will be left. If you list all the options first, then the choice is not *yes* or *no* but which of the options is best (or, in some cases, least harmful). Parents can use this strategy with children. If a parent asks, "Would you like a tuna sandwich for lunch?" the child can reject this suggestion, hoping the parent will present a better offer. If the parent says, "Would you prefer tuna or peanut butter?" the child cannot simply say no. If the child knows there are only two choices, the child will choose between them (or so the parent hopes!).

People tend to be more creative under certain conditions: when they are at ease, when stress levels are low, and when they are motivated by positive goals (Pruitt & Carnevale, 1983). Accordingly, try to establish an environment conducive to these conditions. Use humor to lighten the mood. Develop a positive working relationship and goals for work before moving into option generation and problem solving. Choose a convenient time and tranquil place for negotiating. In positional negotiations, parties often use time as a pressure tactic. For instance, serious negotiations are left until the eleventh hour, just before a crisis point (e.g., the strike deadline, the court date, the straw that breaks the camel's back). Another positional strategy is to start negotiations late in the day, just before the weekend. Parties do not want to give up their Friday evening or weekend, so they pressure themselves into settling as soon as possible. In IBN, parties need ample time to work through problems and develop creative solutions. The parties may establish time lines for decisions, but these should be based on identified interests rather than pressure tactics.

Other methods of spurring creativity (thinking without borders) include wordplay, hat-switching, and flipping (Menkel-Meadow et al., 2005):

- *Wordplay* **refers to switching or deleting certain words or adding different types of emphasis to different words in a sentence or suggestion.** If Miranda suggests that Dorothy *quit her job*, Dorothy could ask, "Rather than quitting, how do you think I could *expand my job*?" This might encourage Miranda to offer, "Perhaps you could take a job in a nursing home, so taking care of me would be part of your job."
- *Flipping* **refers to reversing an option so that it applies to the other party.** If Dorothy suggested putting Miranda in a nursing home, Miranda could flip this by joking, "Perhaps we could put you in a special nursing home." This could help them think about the possibility of moving into a specialized facility where both could live together, providing supportive care for Miranda without taking away all her privacy and autonomy.
- *Hat-switching* **refers to asking people to view the situation from different perspectives.** For instance, Dorothy could ask, "What do you think your doctor might suggest?" Other possible views include those of a social worker, clergy person, elder, child, police officer, respected celebrity, or even a nasty celebrity. If Miranda were viewing the issue from her grandchild's view, she might offer, "Let's all go for ice cream. I can think better with ice cream." Sometimes, viewing things from the vantage of people who lack formal education, worldly experience, or moral direction can lead to some of the most creative thinking.

Ideally, the parties invent an *elegant option*, a win-win solution that resolves the conflict to everyone's satisfaction. It is creative, ingenious, and often quite simple, at least in hindsight. When parties are unable to identify an elegant solution, they may have to select between less-than-perfect solutions.

3. Apply Objective Criteria

Once an exhaustive list of options has been created, the parties need a way to choose between them. Rather than argue about which options are best, begin by seeking agreement to the general principle that decisions will be made on the basis of criteria that are fair and legitimate. Once you have agreement on this principle, you can start identifying objective criteria. *Make the choice of criteria a joint decision rather than have each party come up with his or her own criteria.* Explore various sources for objective criteria: What standards would a neutral third person suggest? What principles would experts in the field suggest? What precedents have been used in similar situations? When suggesting criteria, consider ones that will appeal to the other party. If your suggestions appear self-serving or illegitimate, the other party will reject them.

Dorothy and Miranda might defer to the expertise of a gerontologist: How do other families make decisions about the care of elder parents? If a choice has to be made between independence and physical healthcare, what principles or criteria should be used to make the decision? They might explore empirical research and literature to see what has been written about the issues. The gerontologist or the literature does not make the decision for Dorothy and Miranda. They just use these resources for ideas. Ultimately, they have to decide on the criteria and apply them (Menkel-Meadow et al., 2005).

4. Improve Communication

In Chapter 2, I described the importance of communication skills in conflict resolution. Active listening skills are particularly important for building positive relationships between parties. *To be effective, you must not only listen but ensure that the other parties know you are listening and understanding them. Demonstrate that you are a reasonable person, open to persuasion.* Admit areas of ignorance and use questions to become more informed. Ensure that your statements are clear, nonthreatening, and assertive. Determine whether there are particular problems in communication—for example, lack of opportunities for communication, misinformation, or mistrust. Where these problems exist, how can you rectify them? Remember that what others say is not necessarily how they truly feel or think. Use nonthreatening questions and active listening skills to check your interpretations of what you have heard.

Many conflicts are aggravated because the parties never make opportunities to communicate. If one party is a conflict avoider, demonstrate that communication is in both parties' best interests. Find out what they fear (Adler, Rosen, & Silverstein, 1998). If they fear rejection, yelling, or physical violence, establish ground rules to make the interaction safe. In Dorothy's case, she may have been scared to talk to her mother about the nursing home because of feelings of guilt. By putting off the discussion until a crisis occurred, neither side has had an opportunity to process her ideas and feelings with the other.

Ideally, establish face-to-face communication in an amicable environment. Distance technologies may be more convenient, even necessary in some situations. However, in-person communication tends to be more humanizing. You can see one another's expressions and interact spontaneously. If you need to use distance technologies, videoconferencing and telephone conference calls are the most humanizing. Fax, email, and regular mail tend to be more formalized and disengaged. They also require a lapse of time as communications are transferred back and forth. In some circumstances, formalizing and drawing out communication can be advantageous (e.g., to allow heads to cool).

If conflict is aggravated by misinformation, provide opportunities for full and frank disclosure. If parties are positional, they tend to guard their own information and treat the other person's information with mistrust. By moving into joint problem solving, exchange of information becomes reciprocal.

When areas of mistrust persist, construct alternatives that are not dependent on trusting one another. Discussing sexually transmitted diseases with a new partner, for example, is very difficult. If you ask your partner about past sexual and drug use behavior, the partner may question your love and trust. You want to trust your partner, but with fatal diseases like AIDS, trust is difficult. In order to move beyond the area of mistrust, the partners can agree to be tested for sexually transmitted diseases together. They depend on an independent source of information—the health practitioner who tests them. In addition to providing HIV information and testing, the health professional can provide guidance on how to discuss HIV issues in a constructive manner.

5. Build a Positive Negotiating Relationship

A key difference between interest-based and positional or rights-oriented negotiation is the emphasis that IBN places on relationships. *Parties negotiate to improve interactions, not simply to solve a particular problem.*

Game theory illustrates that parties are more likely to cooperate when an ongoing relationship exists between the parties (Rapoport, 1974). If two strangers are involved in a onetime conflict knowing that they will never see each other again, they have no incentive to make amicable relations one of their goals. Family members, coworkers, neighbors, and friends have ongoing relationships. If negotiations are adversarial, one party might win the immediate battle but lose out in the bigger picture. An employer, for example, may have greater bargaining power than employees. If the employer simply coerces employees into submission, however, the employees will become angered and resistant. Both sides will eventually lose out. In order to encourage conflicting parties to build a positive negotiating relationship with you, help them understand your interdependence and the prospects for conflict over the long run.

One of the key principles suggested by Fisher and colleagues (1997) is to "separate the people from the problem" (p. 17). In other words, the focus of negotiations should be to resolve the problem. Express strong views about a problem, asserting your position passionately but without attacking the person. You are more likely to persuade a person who you have treated with respect than one whom you have offended.

You do not need to like a person in order to negotiate effectively with that person. Helping professionals often work with "repugnant clients"—that is, clients with attributes the professional finds offensive. Clients may express racist views, smell from stale cigarettes, spit when they talk, or speak in condescending tones. Still, helping professionals abide by the ethic that everyone deserves respect. They must find ways to work with the client, in spite of these concerns. Treat the person with respect.

Deal directly with the problem. If the problem is related to the relationship, raise that as an issue. If someone is "pushing your buttons," take time out to reflect on why this is happening. Ask a supervisor or peer to help you debrief.

IBN encourages parties to consult with one another rather than make unilateral decisions. If Dorothy tells Miranda that she has found a nursing home for her, Dorothy has left Miranda out of the decision-making process. Instead of presenting Miranda with a fait accompli, Dorothy should discuss the concerns and try to come up with a joint decision.

Fisher and Brown (1988) suggest that a positive negotiating relationship is one that can deal effectively with differences. Parties need not agree with one another in order to have a good relationship. I have had some of my most heated and contentious discussions with people I love dearly. Disagreeing does not mean rejection. People can have positive rapport even if they have different values, attitudes, and beliefs. They must simply respect diversity.

For certain people and within certain cultures, however, disagreement does have negative connotations. Consider, for instance, individuals with a poor self-image or weak interpersonal boundaries. Disagreement comes across as personal rejection. When negotiating with someone with low self-esteem, be particularly careful to separate the person from the problem. Give the person ample positive feedback. Reaffirm that you are not attacking the person when you are disagreeing. Build on positives.

Consider Chinese and other Eastern cultures where communal harmony and congeniality are highly valued (Wilmot & Hocker, 2007; LeBaron, n.d.). The concept of a relationship that deals well with differences fits better with an individualistic society. Within communitarian cultures, people are more concerned about group needs and interests. When negotiating with someone from a communitarian culture, focus on fostering peace and congenial relations. If possible, work toward common goals rather than trying to satisfy each party's separate ones.

Fisher and Brown (1988) identify six unconditionally constructive strategies for building positive negotiation relationships:

- **Rationality**—even if they are acting emotionally, balance emotions with reason.[15]
- **Understanding**—even if they misunderstand us, try to understand them.
- **Communication**—even if they are not listening to us, consult them before making decisions on matters that affect them.
- **Reliability**—even if they are trying to deceive us, neither trust them nor deceive them; be reliable.
- **Noncoercive modes of influence**—even if they are trying to coerce us, neither yield to that coercion nor try to coerce them; be open to persuasion and try to persuade them.
- **Acceptance**—even if they reject us and our concerns as unworthy of their consideration, accept them as worthy of our consideration, care about them, and be open to learning from them. (p. 38)

---

[15]Adler, Rosen, and Silverstein (1998) provide a useful framework for how to manage feelings such as fear and anger in negotiations.

These principles encourage negotiators to act in ways that promote a positive relationship, regardless of whether the other party reciprocates. Negotiating morally is valued in and of itself (Van Es, 1996). The six principles apply to formal negotiations as well as informal or emergent ones.

Many people question the wisdom of Fisher and Brown's guidelines. "Sounds great from an ideological perspective, but won't they allow people to walk all over you?" Actually, it is great ideologically. The six guidelines correspond with professional ethics such as unconditional positive regard, respect for all people, client self-determination, and being nonjudgmental. As for the pragmatic concern, these principles do not suggest that you go soft and allow people to take advantage of you. They support the notion of being respectful of others while being assertive with your interests. If you are being attacked, confront the problem rather than the person. Identify ways to confront that do not put the other person on the defensive. Remain open to working together for an amicable solution. If you are unable to arrive at a reasonable solution, you do not need to come to any agreement.

Radical professionals may still see this approach as being soft: If individuals or groups are being oppressed, they have the right to fight back. Does oppression justify the use of deception or coercive modes of influence? Must people offer respect or acceptance to those who oppress them? As you go through the experiential exercises, try different approaches. Consider what methods are most effective in dealing with oppressive parties. Return to the values you identified in Chapter 2 in order to see whether these are consistent with your experiential understandings.

6. Consider Alternatives

Whereas options are possible solutions (outcomes), **alternatives** *are possible CR processes (actions).* Negotiation is one method of CR, but many others are possible: avoiding, fighting, mediating, litigating, flipping a coin, and so on. When a party decides to engage in a CR process, the result is not certain. In order to map out various alternatives and their likely outcomes, one could draw a decision tree (see Appendix 1; Aaron, 2005). Given a particular conflict situation, consider what attributes you are looking for in a CR process: cost-effectiveness, timeliness, fairness, affability, mutual satisfaction, and so on. Once you have identified your goals, select a process that is most likely to satisfy these goals.

The term **BATNA** *refers to a party's best alternative to negotiated agreement* (Fisher et al., 1997). By considering one's own BATNA, a party can decide whether it is better to negotiate or to select another alternative. In Dorothy and Miranda's conflict, Dorothy's alternatives include taking some sort of unilateral action, such as refusing to care for Miranda or going to court to have her mother declared mentally incompetent. Neither of these is very appealing to Dorothy. She loves her mother. Working things out on an amicable basis is important to her. If Dorothy and Miranda cannot negotiate a resolution on their own, Dorothy's BATNA is to try to resolve the conflict with the aid of their counselor. Because Miranda also wants an amicable settlement, she may be persuaded to try this alternative.

To some extent, the use of BATNAs falls into the power approach to negotiation rather than interest based. The stronger your BATNA, the stronger your bargaining power. If your agency fires you for breaching client confidentiality, your alternatives include negotiating, walking away, looking for another job, and suing for damages. If you have a strong case based on your legal rights, your BATNA may be going to court. Because your BATNA is strong, the agency will be willing to negotiate a favorable severance package. The agency will want to avoid court. Although you are the more powerful party, you do not have to use your power coercively. You can choose to negotiate using the interest-based approach.

In contrast, consider a situation in which you are in a less powerful position: The government decides to deregulate your profession, believing that money can be saved by hiring nonprofessionals and by closing down your regulatory body. Assume that government has support of the general electorate. What are your alternatives to negotiation with government? Your profession could initiate a strike, but public support would not be with you. You could go to court, but there is no basis in law to reinstate your professional status if the government decides to deregulate. You could mediate, but government has shown no willingness to cooperate. Because your BATNA is weak, the government can take unilateral action, with little concern for your interests.

Using a power approach, you could take steps to strengthen your BATNA. For example, create a public awareness campaign to educate the electorate about the advantages of licensing in your profession. With public support, the potential effectiveness of a strike improves. By gaining relative power, you may be able to bring the government to an interest-based negotiating table. Alternatively, you could take steps to weaken the government's BATNA. The government's BATNA is taking unilateral action to deregulate the profession. Governments obtain their legitimacy through democratic processes. Although the government was elected and has the legislative authority to pass such laws, changing laws without consultation puts their legitimacy into question. By questioning the morality of the government's process, you weaken its BATNA and encourage it to engage in public consultation (a form of negotiation). Chapter 6 provides a more detailed description of how to use various sources of power. At this point, I want to focus on IBN.

Rather than negotiate specific outcomes, you could negotiate a process. Processes can be designed to be expedient, fair, or just. Some situations call for quick resolution. You and a colleague are deciding where to go for lunch. If you take the time to go through the steps of IBN, your lunch hour may be over before you have a decision. Consider a quick alternative: each person gives one suggestion, and you flip a coin to decide which of the two suggestions to follow. If there are more than two people, put all of the suggestions in a hat and draw one. The process is fair, and you still have time for lunch.

If parties have tried IBN but reached a stalemate, they could decide to negotiate a process, giving an impartial third party the responsibility for making the decision. Divorcing parents who are contesting where a child should live, for instance, could agree to have an independent family evaluation (Gould, 2004). The evaluator[16]

---

[16]An *evaluator* is a professional with expertise in making certain types of assessment. The recommendations of the evaluator can be binding or nonbinding, depending on the prior agreement of the parties. If the recommendations are nonbinding, one or both parties may disregard them. If the evaluator is a trusted expert and conducts the assessment fairly, the parties are more likely to follow the recommendations.

would conduct home visits with both parents and observe the child in each home. The parents would agree to abide by the recommendations of the evaluator. The evaluator would make the decision based on a professional assessment of the best interests of the child.

Impasse during IBN often occurs when there is a zero-sum game—that is, when a fixed pool of resources has to be divided. For distributive decisions, many techniques are available for creating a fair process.

- **Taking turns**—If there are a number of objects to be divided, each person can take a turn selecting an object. To reduce the advantage of going first, you can adjust the order of selections. Person A selects first. Person B gets the next two selections. Person A gets the next two selections, and so on.
- **Separating who makes the division and who chooses**—Person A divides the resources into two pools. Person B selects which pool to take. Person A will have an incentive to make the pools equally attractive.
- **Using buy-sell agreements**[17]—Person A sets a price for the entire property in dispute. Person B can buy out Person A according to the price provided. If Person B chooses not to buy at that price, then Person A buys out Person B at the same price.

These examples demonstrate how IBN is not a mutually exclusive process. Through IBN, parties can agree to participate in other processes in order to determine all or some of their outstanding conflicts. Different processes have different advantages and disadvantages. By matching the appropriate process with the goals of the parties in a particular situation, parties are able to satisfy their mutual interests.

7. Obtain Commitments

Parties who reach their own decisions about how to resolve a conflict are more likely to follow through on their decisions than decisions imposed by a third party (e.g., a judge in court or a supervisor in an agency). Parties tend to be more committed to their negotiated solutions because they have agreed to the terms. In contrast, imposed decisions may be disappointing to one or both parties. Dissatisfied parties frequently try to thwart implementation.

That said, negotiators must ensure that they have true commitments from one another. Some parties give the appearance of acquiescence without really giving a commitment to follow through. Others do not like confrontation, so they say they are agreeing, without having any intention of implementing the decisions.

In order to ensure that commitments are genuine, check out how the other party plans to implement the decisions. Are the plans realistic? Do you detect any hesitance? Have you allowed the other parties to say they really are not satisfied with the agreement? Let them know that you do not want just any agreement but one that both sides can live with and will be able to follow. Railroading people into agreements does not work if you are depending on each other to implement the decisions.

---

[17]Also called "shotgun agreements," although this term has obvious connotations of violence.

In Dorothy and Miranda's situation, Miranda may be worried that Dorothy will reject her if they do not come to an agreement. Accordingly, Miranda might agree to a plan that she is not really happy with, just to appease Dorothy. In the excitement of coming to an agreement, Dorothy may not be aware of Miranda's concerns. If these concerns are not raised, Miranda will have trouble following through. To encourage Miranda to raise her concerns, Dorothy might say, "Before we say this is a done deal, let's review the plan. What do you like about it? What concerns do you still have?" This allows Miranda to raise her concerns without feeling defensive.

Help the other party make commitments. Implementation may require assistance from other people. "Great, we've come to an agreement between us. But how do I explain this to my family and to my neighbors?" The conflict does not end when parties reach an agreement. Accordingly, both parties have an interest in helping one another with implementation.

Consider a conflict between supervisors and counselors about the agency's overtime policy. The supervisor and counselors might agree that counselors can take time off on Fridays in lieu of overtime pay. This may suit their interests, but how does the supervisor sell this plan to the program director or other agency powers? The counselors do not want to give the supervisor a problem, because the supervisor's problem is their problem, too. How can the counselors help their supervisor explain their solution to the program director? If the supervisor cannot follow through on the agreement, how can you alter the agreement to make it more feasible? IBN is about working together, giving each other workable solutions.

8. Limitations of Interest-Based Negotiation

Since the 1980s, IBN has become one of the most popular models of negotiation among CR professionals. Proponents of IBN maintain that the model promotes joint decision making, so both parties are satisfied with the resolution. The model works particularly well when (a) the parties are flexible, (b) they are able to suspend their individual ambitions, (c) they have faith in their own abilities to negotiate, and (d) they have had prior success in resolving some issues (Pruitt & Carnevale, 1993).

In spite of the advantages of IBN, it does have limitations. One or more parties may be reluctant to engage in IBN because of lack of trust, anger, or other strong emotions. As game theory demonstrates, mistrust and anger promote competition rather than collaboration (Rapoport, 1974). Roger Fisher, one the key theorists who popularized IBN in the 1980s and 1990s, has recognized that his original framework for IBN did not sufficiently take emotions into account (Fisher & Shapiro, 2005). Negotiators can enhance the primarily rational problem-solving process of IBN by learning how to assess and respond to emotions such as anger, fear, hope, anxiety, sadness, pride, and embarrassment—whether these emotions exist in oneself or the other person (Jameson, Bodtker, & Jones, 2006; Ryan, 2006).

IBN is also difficult to implement when the conflict comes down to a difference between strong principles. On the one hand, if a conflict is based on a difference of positions, the parties can look underneath the positions to see whether they have common underlying interests. On the other hand, if the conflict is based on a fundamental difference between the parties' core values, there may be no middle ground and no opportunity for reaching a mutually satisfying agreement.

IBN may also be inappropriate when an expedient, authoritative decision is needed. If many parties are involved and a decision is needed quickly, IBN may take too much time. Furthermore, if the decision is relatively unimportant, investing an inordinate amount of time in the decision-making process is counterproductive (Pruitt & Carnevale, 1993).

IBN entails a number of cultural biases, including rationality and individuality, as described earlier. This approach also fits best with cultures that value disclosure and direct confrontation of conflict. IBN may be less appropriate in cultures that value face-saving and indirect methods of CR over disclosure and confrontation (Ting-Toomey & Oetzel, 2001). As you work through the materials and exercises, consider whether and how IBN could be reconstructed in order to deal more effectively with such cultural differences.

Finally, IBN may be inappropriate if your goal is not to reach a mutually satisfying agreement. If you are being exploited by a more powerful party, using the power approach may be necessary. If your objective is to obtain a just solution, the rights approach may be more appropriate. If your aim is more visionary, to construct a higher order of relations between individuals and groups, consider the transformative approach.

TRANSFORMATIVE NEGOTIATION

Bush and Folger (2005) define *transformative mediation* as *a conflict resolution approach in which a third-party facilitator promotes empowerment and recognition between the parties*. In this section, I provide a brief overview of how transformation can be applied in a negotiation context, without the aid of a third party. Chapter 4 provides a more detailed analysis of this approach in the context of mediation.

To illustrate the transformative approach, consider the following scenario:

> Humphrey is a human service professional working in a government-mandated workfare program. Humphrey's client, Camilla, is 23 years old, unemployed, and educated to a Grade 10 equivalence. She has few job skills and sparse job experience. Humphrey offers her a workfare position, doing physical work in the city's parks at minimum wage. Camilla refuses this position. She wants to go to college to learn computer skills so that she can work her way to a better-paying career. Humphrey has seen her vocational test results, and they indicate that she has poor aptitude for this type of work. She insists that she wants to learn computer skills. Humphrey cannot force her to work, but if she does not agree to a plan with Humphrey, she will lose all social assistance benefits.

If you view this situation from a problem-solving approach, you could employ the IBN framework and try to work out a mutually agreeable solution with the client. On the other hand, the transformative approach suggests that the object of your efforts is to work toward empowerment and recognition.

1. Empowerment

Empowerment refers to any process in which individuals or groups gain greater control over matters that affect them. At a psychological level, empowerment is marked by enhancement of one's self-esteem, confidence, and perception of self-efficacy. At a social level, empowerment involves gaining power through education, politicization, and collective action (Freire, 1994; Torré, 1986). Bush and Folger (2005) suggest that parties are empowered when

- they realize more clearly what their goals and interests are and why they are important;
- they become more aware of the options available to them (what choices are available and that they have control over them);
- they improve their conflict resolution skills, including their ability to listen, communicate, organize and analyze issues, present arguments, brainstorm, and evaluate alternative solutions;
- they gain awareness of resources already in their possession or available to them to achieve their goals and objectives; and
- they reflect, deliberate, and make conscious decisions for themselves about what they want, and they are able to analyze the strengths and weaknesses of various choices before making decisions.

Humphrey can empower Camilla by applying these principles in his interaction with her. First, he can help Camilla identify her goals and interests. Initially, she says that she wants a career in computer programming. Humphrey probes deeper: "Why do you want to be a computer programmer?" Camilla acknowledges that she has to find a job that meets her basic needs (food and housing), but she is also interested in a career that makes her feel proud.

In terms of options, Humphrey has access to information that Camilla does not know. His agency has lists of job opportunities. He can also help Camilla locate alternate sources of funding if she wants to return to school rather than join the workfare program.

Camilla's communication and problem-solving skills are limited. If Humphrey negotiates without empowering Camilla, she will have trouble articulating her concerns and coming up with reasonable options. Instead, Humphrey asks Camilla whether she would be willing to learn some basic conflict resolution skills. She agrees. They set aside a session where he teaches her about basic listening skills and assertiveness skills (similar to those described in Chapter 2). They role-play so Camilla can practice her new skills. She can use these skills to negotiate with Humphrey and also apply them in other aspects of her life.

Camilla has had difficult experiences in school and work. Most feedback from her teachers and employers has been negative. Accordingly, Camilla has little self-confidence when it comes to working. Humphrey can help Camilla build her self-confidence by asking her to identify her strengths. Although she initially reported having no job skills, Humphrey helps her identify that she is reliable, friendly, and honest. She also helped raise two younger siblings while her parents were away at work. From this experience, she has learned time management skills, cooking, and conflict resolution.

One of Camilla's best friends got a job in computer programming and really likes it. Camilla thought it would be a good job for her, but she really has not thought about it very much. Humphrey helps Camilla reflect on her life goals, including what she wants from a career. He asks her to complete a three-question homework assignment. What type of job would you like to see yourself in 5 years from now? Which of your personal strengths will help you achieve this type of goal? What are three or four of the greatest challenges that you think you will face? They agree to discuss the answers at their next session.

Camilla and Humphrey may or may not come to an agreement about a job or work placement. However, Camilla will be empowered whether or not they resolve the conflict to their mutual satisfaction.

Helping professionals usually see themselves as the ones who facilitate the empowerment of clients; however, helping professionals can also use Bush and Folger's framework to empower themselves. Humphrey, for example, can reflect on his own goals and interests. Although his initial position is that Camilla should go on workfare, his underlying interests are to foster Camilla's self-determination and to fulfill his agency's mandate. If these interests conflict, he will have to choose between them. However, working through the other steps, he may be able to come up with options that he did not originally identify. Helping professionals are in an ongoing process of professional development. By reflecting on their conflict resolution skills and experiences, they can improve their practice and empower themselves. In turn, empowered professionals are better able to empower and recognize their clients (Pinderhughes, 1989).

2. Recognition

Recognition is comparable to the Rogerian therapy concept of demonstrating empathy—that is, demonstrating you understand another person's world from that person's frame of reference. Rogers (1957) identifies empathy as one of the core conditions[18] for developing a positive counseling relationship. Counselors can demonstrate empathy through the listening skills described in Chapter 2: attending, paraphrasing, reflecting feelings, and summarizing.

According to Ivey and Ivey (2007), demonstrating empathy is most effective when the counselor's feedback is concrete, immediate, nonjudgmental, respectful, and authentic. However, a counselor must also ensure that empathy is conveyed in a manner that is culturally appropriate. Within some groups, for instance, listening in silence is more appropriate than using paraphrasing and reflecting back. Although recognition and empathy share some similarities, recognition entails techniques designed specifically for dealing with conflict.

In conflict situations, people (including helping professionals) often become angry or defensive. This creates a tendency to become wrapped up in one's own interests and problems, to the neglect of the other party's. Bush and Folger (2005) use the term *recognition* to remind conflicting parties to avoid becoming self-absorbed but rather recognize the other party's situation: Recognition occurs when

---

[18]The other core conditions are genuineness and unconditional positive regard. Other literature refers to these as conditions for "therapeutic alliance."

parties choose to become more open, attentive, sympathetic, and responsive to the situation of the person they are negotiating with.

A party can provide recognition to others through thoughts, words, and actions:

- By reflecting on the others' situation out of a general concern for their predicament
- By consciously letting go of one's own viewpoint in order to open up to seeing the others in a different, more positive light
- By trying to understand how what seemed to be a hurtful or irrational act by the others might be the product of the other parties' reasonable response to stresses they have been enduring
- By openly acknowledging one's changed understanding of the others
- By apologizing for having "thought the worst" about the other party or for past "retaliatory conduct"
- By changing one's behavior to accommodate the other's interests, in light of the new understanding (Folger & Bush, 2005)

The experience of recognition means giving recognition, rather than receiving recognition. However, there is an interactive effect between recognition and empowerment. When a party receives recognition, the validation is empowering. Conversely, an empowered party is more confident and self-assured, making it easier for that person to offer recognition to the other.

In Camilla's case, Humphrey can offer recognition by trying to gain a better understanding of where she is coming from. It would be easy for him to get wrapped up in his own job: he has made an assessment, offered Camilla a suitable position, and wants to wrap up this case so he can get on to his next client. Work is piling up. If Camilla will not be reasonable, then he is wasting time with her. To recognize Camilla, Humphrey begins by reflecting on his role as a workfare counselor. He sees himself not only as an agent of the workfare program but as a human service professional who has a genuine interest in helping clients help themselves. He must start where the client is. He realizes he has not been seeing things from Camilla's perspective and decides to try to suspend his initial assessments and judgments. He thinks, "If I were in Camilla's shoes. . . ." He begins to see Camilla in a different light—not as a resistant client but as a client who is advancing her own interests. She has probably had negative experiences with other bureaucracies, so her anger is not aimed at him personally. She has said that she wants to be a computer programmer; from her perspective, maybe that is reasonable. Humphrey shares his understandings with Camilla and asks her whether he is understanding her more accurately. She corrects him on a few points, and he remains supportive. He apologizes for sounding as if he knew what was best for her. He offers to work together with her to develop a career plan that meets her needs.

Offering recognition often leads the other party to offer recognition in return. Camilla says that she understands that Humphrey was trying to help her and was just trying to do his job. Humphrey is caught off guard by her level of insight and recognition. As a helping professional, his focus is to help his client, but Camilla's words do make him feel appreciated.

Transformation can be viewed as a means to move the parties toward interest-based negotiation. If the parties are empowered and recognize one another, they are better able to work together and resolve differences to their mutual satisfaction. Bush and Folger, however, purport that transformation is an end in and of itself. Successful negotiation results from empowerment and recognition, regardless of whether the parties come to an interest-based agreement. Through transformation, people have a greater understanding and appreciation of one another. They also have a more positive sense of themselves and their capabilities. Agreement is not necessarily the ultimate goal. People can come away from a conflict disagreeing with one another but still having grown from the experience.

Given the transformative approach, you may be wondering what the difference is between transformative negotiation and therapy. How would Humphrey's intervention differ if he decided to intervene based on systems theory? Feminist theory? Psychodynamic theory? Humanistic theory? I leave these questions for you to consider as you work through the exercises. Similar questions are raised in Chapter 4 but in relation to transformative mediation.

3. Limitations of Transformation

In one sense, asking about the limitations of transformation is the wrong question. Transformation is about changing the way that individuals, organizations, cultures, and the world manage conflict. It is a movement based on high ideals and visions. How can one speak of limitations when the movement is based on high ideals and visions for humanity? Success or failure is not based on the results of a single conflict or interaction but on whether society becomes more decent and moral through fundamental changes in the way that people deal with conflict.

Because research into the effectiveness of transformative CR is only beginning to emerge, strengths and limitations of the approach are difficult to gauge. Proponents have strong convictions in its effectiveness (Bush & Folger, 2005). Questions for further study include the following: When does transformative negotiation work? What factors contribute to its effectiveness? How well does this model work when a significant power imbalance exists between the parties? To what extent does transformative mediation between a small number of individuals have an impact on the way that their families, schools, workplaces, or communities deal with conflict?

On its own terms, the goal of transformation is neither winning, settlement, fairness, nor justice. Parties seeking these goals are likely to opt for other processes. For instance, parties embroiled in conflict are often angry with one another. They want to fight it out, take revenge, or give the other side its just desserts. If they are not motivated to engage in transformative negotiation, they will tend to resist the process.

Although transformative negotiation is arguably most effective when both parties are motivated toward transformation, the approach can be employed by a single party whether or not the other party follows suit. One party can offer empowerment and recognition to the other, regardless of whether the other returns the same. In fact, the approach is based on the premise of offering empowerment and recognition because they are inherently good, not because you expect reciprocity. "I will act morally, regardless of the actions of the other parties." When evaluating negotiation for success, the important question is "How well did *I* follow the principles of transformation?"

CULTURAL DIVERSITY ISSUES

Culture refers to shared beliefs, values, language, and behavioral norms that occur among groups with common experiences. Such groups can be defined by ethnic background, nationality, religion, gender, sexual orientation, socioeconomic status, education, and disability (LeBaron, 1997). Diversity issues are pervasive in negotiation. For helping professionals, diversity issues arise in a number of realms.

- Various professions are reaching out to diverse communities in order to provide better services. Existing models of practice and system requirements may not meet their needs.
- As recent immigrants work their way through employment services, health services, welfare programs, schools, and other bureaucracies, they often come into conflict with helping professionals who are the gatekeepers and service providers in these systems.
- Disadvantaged groups are becoming more organized, so that they are better prepared to negotiate for social justice and confront systems where helping professionals work.
- As diverse groups move into helping professions (including conflict resolution), older professional values and cultural norms are being challenged.
- In many jurisdictions, courts and legislatures are recognizing freedom from discrimination for people from diverse backgrounds; helping professionals are often responsible for implementing these rights (e.g., access to employment, school, or social services).
- Conflicts also arise within diversity groups. Although some cultures prefer to resolve intracultural conflict on their own, others welcome the assistance of helping professionals from outside of the community (LeBaron Duryea & Grundison, 1992).

Cross-cultural conflicts arise at various levels: misunderstandings due to differences in language or cultural interpretations, disputes over allocation of resources between majority and minority groups, conflicting values, and mistrust from previous experiences of oppression or exploitation. Although it is important to recognize cultural components to disputes, be careful about stereotyping or blaming a particular diversity group for causing conflict. If this is a two-party conflict, both cultures play a role in the development of the conflict and its resolution (Ting-Toomey & Oetzel, 2001).

Each negotiation approach has different implications for conflict and culture issues. Consider a conflict between a client (Clarence) from a disadvantaged group and a therapist (Thelma) from an advantaged group in the community. During a session, Clarence yells:

> You pretend like you care about me, Thelma, but that's only for an hour. Then you go home to your nice house in your nice neighborhood with your nice family.

From a power perspective, Clarence perceives that Thelma comes from a position of greater power and influence. He is a client from a background of poverty, low education, and social discrimination. Thelma has a good job, educational background, and home. Clarence also sees her as a person with authority. As a helping professional, Thelma does not want to exploit Clarence with her power. If she wanted to use her power with good intentions, she might employ her authority and expertise to give Clarence advice on how to behave.

> You are getting angry. Why don't we try to calm down and talk to each other like civil adults?

The reason Clarence verbally attacked Thelma may be seen as a way for him to exert power. By asking him to calm down, she may be trying to take away his power. Clarence may respond by becoming even angrier. Conflict will escalate unless Thelma can find a way to diffuse it.

If Thelma uses a transformative approach, she will demonstrate empathy with his frustration. She will also try to understand his cultural background. Rather than becoming defensive, she will try to offer him support. Rather than quell his power, she will try to empower him.

> You don't think I really care about you. This seems to be affecting our working relationship. Please tell me more about how you would like to see my role.

In addition, Thelma might explore Clarence's cultural background by speaking with other helping professionals from his culture (Barsky, Este, & Collins, 1996). She may learn, for instance, that her sense of professional boundaries is perceived as a lack of caring within Clarence's culture.

From an interest-based perspective, Thelma would encourage Clarence to engage in joint problem solving with her. Her strategies could include "separating the person from the problem" and "balancing reason with emotions." Within certain cultures, these presumably positive suggestions could be detrimental. Separating the person from the problem could be seen as insensitive. For some groups, a positive relationship with the person is inseparable from being able to work together on problems (LeBaron, 1997). Clarence has already indicated that Thelma is emotionally detached from him. He is more accustomed to sharing details of his private life with a person he knows more personally.

In terms of balancing reason with emotions, Thelma might run into trouble once again. Emotions are expressed differently among different cultures. The fact that Clarence raised his voice may be an expression of anger. However, his culture may have a different sense of what type of voice levels are appropriate in a given context. For Thelma to respond in a calm, rational tone, Clarence might interpret this as further evidence that Thelma does not care about him. Accordingly, emotional expression must be construed within a cultural context. Vivid display of emotions does not necessarily mean a lack of rationality. On the other hand, some people demonstrate little emotion even though, underneath, their feelings are affecting their ability to make reasoned decisions.

These examples just touch the surface of issues related to culture and conflict. Consider literature and research on specific cultures and conflict when you are working with people from a particular culture (Brett et al., 1998; Irving & Benjamin, 1995; LeBaron, n.d.; Ting-Toomey & Oetzel, 2001). More cultural issues are discussed in Chapters 4 and 5.

PREPARATION FOR NEGOTIATION

Given the four approaches to negotiation, you may decide that one is most consonant with your own personal and professional values. If so, that approach may become your predominant framework for negotiating. Otherwise, you may decide that different approaches are required for different types of circumstances. In any event, preparing yourself is vital for effective negotiation. The Negotiation Preparation Tool (Figure 3.2) is designed to help you assess a conflict situation and devise an appropriate plan for negotiation, regardless of your chosen approach.

The Negotiation Preparation Tool is not a fixed recipe to be followed step-by-step. It is designed to help you analyze conflicts and frame them in a way that helps you decide how to respond to them. Apply the framework loosely; that is, feel free to use various parts of the tool without following all of its suggestions. Different conflict scenarios will call for emphasizing different parts of the tool.[19] Return to the tool at various stages of negotiation to reevaluate your strategies. Initially, for example, you might decide to use rights-based strategies. Later, you might choose to move from contention to interest-based cooperation. This tool is divided into four sections: analysis, strategies, skills, and evaluation.

Figure 3.2 | Negotiation Preparation Tool

1. ANALYSIS
   a. Define the issue under dispute. How did each of the parties become aware of the conflict? On the surface, what is the conflict about (see Lewicki, 1997)?
   b. What is the nature of the difference underlying the conflict?

   - *Difference of interests or needs?*
     A difference of interests often comes down to the problem of how to distribute limited resources (including tangibles, such as money and property, or intangibles, such as time, emotional energy, and status). Distribution can be based on the parties' relative power, rights, or joint interests. Can the pool of resources be expanded before distribution is made? Can parties focus on mutual interests rather than divisive ones? Sometimes, parties can prioritize their interests and ensure that fundamental needs (e.g., food, shelter, and security) are satisfied before trying to meet other needs or interests.
   - *Difference of understandings?*
     A difference in understandings can be based on differences in the parties' thought processes, perceptions, memories, beliefs, and interpretations, or differences in the information they are relying on (e.g., different research, rumors, assumptions, or personal observations). To resolve differences in understandings, see 2d, Communication Strategies.

---

[19]This tool draws from Lewicki (1997), Fisher and Urtel (1995), Bush and Folger (2005), and Furlong (2005).

- *Differences of values, ideologies, or attitudes?*
  Values, ideologies, and attitudes (VIAs) form during childhood and generally remain stable throughout adulthood. When a conflict is based on a difference in VIAs, trying to change the other party's VIAs is difficult, if not impossible.[20] Rather than try to change someone's VIAs, you could focus your negotiation on exploring differences and validating one another's perspectives (see transformative approach). Another alternative is to separate VIAs from interests: Agree to disagree on VIAs, and then negotiate other issues based on one of the other approaches. A third alternative is to try to identify a higher-order value that both parties can agree on (Druckman, 1993; Menkel-Meadow et al., 2005). Conflicts are often multidimensional. If the conflict is based on more than one type of difference, identify each of these, and assess which aspect is the primary cause of the conflict or which can be addressed within a reasonable time frame and cost constraints.
- *Differences of social status*
  Social status may include identities in relation to culture, ethnicity, gender, religion, sexual orientation, and other aspects of human diversity, as well as status within organizations (e.g., manager vs. front-line worker). If a conflict is caused or exacerbated by stereotypes or bigotry, what types of strategies can you use to diffuse these? If you feel your own social identity is being attacked, what can you do to ensure that you do not act solely out of defensiveness, anger, or fear? (Identity-based CR will be discussed further in Chapter 5.)

c. What additional theories of psychology or social systems help you understand the conflict between the parties (e.g., game theory, conflict styles, systems analysis, personality theories, developmental theory, feminist analysis, attribution theory, sociocultural theories)? How do your chosen theories help you interpret the situation?

d. What is your overall goal for negotiation (win, win-win, transform the conflict, build a better relationship, reconcile, develop a socially just solution, etc.)?

e. Based on your goal, what are your specific objectives? How will you know you are successful? (Consider process objectives as well as outcome objectives.)

f. What approach(es) have you and the other party tried in the past to handle your conflict? What was helpful and unhelpful about these approaches? What patterns of interaction from the past require change?

g. Which approach(es) are most likely to help you achieve your overall goal?

2. STRATEGIES
   Use the information from your analysis to help you select strategies. Focus on the sections related to the approach(es) you identified in 1g. The four approaches are power, rights, interests, and transformation. Communication is separated out as its own category, because it overlaps with various approaches.

(continued)

---

[20]Short-term strategies may help people negotiate solutions to specific disputes, but it is unlikely they will have much impact on core values, ideologies, or attitudes. In order to help people modify their VIAs, one must look at long-term strategies.

Figure 3.2 | *Continued*

a. *Power-Based Strategies*

    i. What is your original position? Have you already disclosed this? If not, how will you disclose it?

    ii. What is the other party's original position?

    iii. What concessions are you willing to make? Under what circumstances will you compromise?

    iv. What is your bottom line for negotiation?

    v. What is your best estimate about the other party's bottom line?

    vi. What information will you share with the other party?

    vii. What information will you not share?

    viii. What information do you hope to obtain from the other party?

    ix. What strategies will you use in negotiations (e.g., debate, play tit-for-tat, be intransigent, bluff, sand-bag, distort facts, passively mislead, threaten, use force, make extreme first offer, make small concessions, etc.)? For each tactic that you intend to use, identify the reasons for using it and the risks involved. Consider clinical and ethical issues, including effectiveness, competence, honesty, integrity, and whether the means justify the ends in both the short term and the long term (Menkel-Meadow & Wheeler, 2004).[21]

    x. How can you ensure that you have assessed the other's power accurately (neither underestimating nor overestimating it)?

    xi. How can you improve your relative power (see Chapter 6 for sources of power and additional strategies to improve them)?
(Also, consider use of BATNA as described in Item 2c.)

b. *Rights-Based Strategies*

    i. What laws, policies, or other rules are relevant to the present conflict?

    ii. What do these laws, policies, or rules say about your rights?

    iii. What do these laws, policies, or rules say about the other's rights?

    iv. Are the rights of any third parties relevant (e.g., the community's rights, a child's rights)?

    v. What arguments support your rights?

    vi. What arguments support the other's rights?

    vii. How can you counter the other party's arguments?

    viii. If the laws, policies, or rules do not favor your rights, how can you change them (e.g., initiate law reform processes, advocate changes in agency policy, develop community support to change rules)?

    ix. What is the most effective way to communicate your rights to the other party (e.g., informal dialogue, formal face-to-face negotiations, exchange of letters)? What are the advantages and risks of this form of communication?

    x. If you and the other party cannot agree on whose rights prevail, what processes can you use to obtain a determination of rights (e.g., court,

---

[21]Consider, for instance, rapport building with involuntary clients, such as parents accused of child abuse. Is it ethical to feign interest in the clients' welfare in order to foster a positive relationship with them? If you are honest with the clients about your dislike for them, how can you develop a positive working relationship for the sake of the client and their children?

administrative appeal, arbitration)? (Consider mapping out your alternatives and choices using a decision tree similar to those presented in Appendix 1; Aaron, 2005).

    xi. Would legal advice or legal representation assist your case?

    xii. What other resources can you use to help assert your rights (e.g., investigator, ombuds, police, community leaders, state officials)?

  c. *Interest-Based Strategies*

    The following questions and strategies are based on Fisher et al.'s (1997) seven-point framework:

      i. **Focus on interests, not positions.** What are your interests? What are the other's interests? Which interests do you have in common? Which interests conflict? Are these conflicting interests based on any deeper interests that you do share (e.g., underlying desires, values, needs, hopes, or fears)?

      ii. **Invent options for mutual gain.** Identify all possible options for solution. Is it better to brainstorm individually or together? What other sources of information can you access to help you invent options? Do not evaluate the options until you have finished identifying them.

      iii. **Apply objective criteria.** What principles or standards can be used to assess the options? What sources can you explore that might help you identify objective criteria (e.g., experts in the field, literature, precedent cases; principles that operationalized fairness for a particular situation)?

      iv. **Improve communication.** See (d).

      v. **Build a positive negotiating relationship.** Consider use of unconditionally constructive strategies: rationality, understanding, consultation, reliability, noncoercive modes of influence, and acceptance. What makes employing these strategies difficult in the present conflict (e.g., past negative experiences, stereotypes, mistrust, displaced emotions, stress that is not directly related to the conflict, rigid or unclear organizational structures or chains of command)? How can you try to overcome these challenges? How can you encourage collaboration (e.g., focusing on the future and joint interests; accommodating the other in a strategic fashion; using confidence-building measures, [22] procedural trust,[23] and attributional retraining[24])?

      vi. **Consider alternatives.** What are your alternatives to a negotiated agreement? Which of these is your BATNA? What are the other party's

(continued)

---

[22]For example, one party takes unilateral steps to show good faith and to see if the other will respond in good faith; parties work on minor issues first and when they see each other acting in good faith, they can move onto more important issues (Furlong, 2005; see also Chapter 7 on trust building).

[23]Use processes that are intrinsically fair and do not require high degrees of interpersonal trust (e.g., flip a coin to make a decision rather than ask parties to just sit down and talk through a solution).

[24]Attributional retraining refers to uncovering and *gently* challenging one the other person's assumptions by raising questions to facilitate insight, raising doubts, and offering new information to consider (Furlong, 2005).

Figure 3.2 | *Continued*

alternatives? Which one is the other's BATNA? (Consider using decision trees to identify alternatives and BATNAs from each party's perspective; see Appendix 1.) How will you know when it is best to terminate negotiation and move to another alternative? What are the advantages and risks of your BATNA? If the other party has a strong BATNA, what incentives can you use to encourage that party to negotiate? Rather than negotiate for a specific solution, would it be useful to negotiate a process designed to produce a fair result? How can you improve your BATNA? How can you worsen the other's BATNA? (Note that these last two strategies are power-based rather than interest-based strategies.)

vii. **Obtain commitments.** What commitments do you need in order to make an agreement work? What commitments are you prepared to make? What commitments is the other party prepared to make? Are these commitments feasible? How can you solidify the commitments? How can you help the other party make commitments? What strategies can you use to ensure that commitments are followed by all parties? If not everyone affected by implementation is at the table, how do you plan to secure their commitment (if needed)?

d. *Communication Strategies*

i. What past problems, if any, stem from miscommunication? How can you rectify these problems? (E.g., if the conflict is caused by the parties' relying on different information, then sharing information is important; if the parties have different interpretations of the information, then they can explain these differences to one another; if parties cannot understand one another, consider the use of an interpreter;[25] if a party is making false assumptions, surface those assumptions and share new information.)

ii. What communication problems do you foresee in upcoming negotiations? How can you pre-empt these?

iii. What is your purpose for communication (e.g., to demonstrate that you hear and understand the other party, to persuade, to build trust, to share information, to reach an agreement)?

iv. Given your purpose for communication, what is the best forum for negotiation (e.g., face-to-face, electronic mail, telephone)?

v. How can you tailor the forum for negotiation so that it promotes constructive communication (e.g., sufficient time, good working space, low stress, few distractions)?

vi. If direct communication is problematic, what type of facilitator(s) might help the process (e.g., representatives for each party, mediator, supervisor)?

e. *Transformative Strategies*

The transformative approach is based on the following strategies:

i. **Empowerment:** How can you empower yourself (e.g., envisioning conflict as an opportunity for constructive growth rather than a stressful event,

---

[25]An interpreter is not only someone who can translate from one language to another but one who can explain different constructions of language that arise from different cultural experiences.

taking responsibility for decisions rather than blaming others or hiring experts to represent you; improving your communication skills)? How can you empower the other party (e.g., giving the other time and space to think constructively, offering to share power rather than use power against the other, focusing on higher purposes for the negotiation)? What are the potential barriers to empowering yourself or the other party? How can you resolve these barriers (Bush & Folger, 2005; Lederach, 2005)?

ii. **Recognition**: What reflective processes will help you think about and understand the other's situation (e.g., journaling, speaking with a supervisor, reading literature, using role-reversal techniques, engaging in active listening with the other party)? How can you offer recognition through words? How can you offer recognition through your actions? What will make offering recognition difficult? How can you address these challenges (Lederach, 2005)?

3. SKILLS

Once you have identified your primary strategies, consider which of the following skills are required in order to implement these strategies.

a. Uses basic communication skills (e.g., listens effectively to the other side, asks questions to gain information and assure better understanding, and makes statements assertively without becoming aggressive; refer to Chapter 2 for more details).

b. Demonstrates Roger's core conditions:

- Empathic understanding
- Unconditional positive regard (respect, care, and concern)
- Genuineness

c. Demonstrates rationality—balances emotions with reason

d. Demonstrates reliability (honest, open, credible)

e. Demonstrates openness to persuasion and creative ideas

f. Separates the person from the problem

g. Focuses on joint problem solving

h. Demonstrates acceptance—even if the other party rejects you or your concerns

i. Obtains agreement to follow an agenda (organizing issues to be negotiated)

j. Establishes constructive rules for interaction (e.g., information will be shared; neither party will threaten force; time lines for negotiations)

k. Acknowledges power issues

l. Uses persuading skills:

   i. Demonstrates having heard the other side, before actively trying to persuade

   ii. Articulates own position, rights, interests, or beliefs (depending on the approach used)

   iii. Uses "I" statements to express personal feelings, values, or ideologies

   iv. Builds on the other's ideas, values, or interests

   v. Uses language the other party can accept

   vi. Asserts positions or interests without becoming harassing, threatening, or manipulative (unless these are consciously selected strategies)

   vii. Backs up opinions with objective facts or information

(continued)

Figure 3.2 | *Continued*

      viii. Uses appropriate emotional displays to support statements, without detracting from them (e.g., expressing strong convictions, hope, sadness)
      ix. Deals directly with arguments from the other party rather than ignoring, discounting, or side-stepping around them
  m. Paces communication effectively (balances processing of information with moving the negotiation process ahead)
  n. Analyzes the total pool of shared information so as to understand areas of agreement and disagreement
  o. Creatively brainstorms and invents options
  p. Uses flipcharts or other notes to maintain records and provide visual cues for negotiators
  q. Builds on the positives (e.g., constructive moves of the other party; areas of commonality)
  r. Respects other party's freedom to agree or disagree
  s. Articulates and records terms of agreement, if any
  t. Refers back to negotiation preparation tools for assessment, strategies, and skills
  u. Provides authentic apology (see Chapter 7)
  v. Accepts apology graciously
  w. Inspires self and others to higher ideals, spiritual meaning, or moral imagination

4. PITFALLS TO AVOID
  a. Assumes one knows the whole story
  b. Tries repeatedly to convince the other
  c. Assumes one knows the other person's intentions
  d. Holds the other person responsible for fixing the problem
  e. Proceeds only on the basis of rational decision-making (ignoring emotions)
  f. Declares the other person as ethically questionable or immoral
  g. Uses anger or sarcasm as a coercive threat
  h. Ignores the roles of people outside the immediate conflict (e.g., possible support people or people who impose stress and make it difficult for the other party to negotiate amicably and reasonably)
  i. Ignores one's own emotions (rather than using them consciously)
  j. Proceeds in the heat of anger if and when a time-out might be useful
    (Back & Arnold, 2005)

5. IMPLEMENTATION AND EVALUATION
Planning, implementation, and evaluation of negotiation are iterative processes. Although this tool is presented in sequential form, you can move back and forth through various sections as you negotiate. In order to move from planning to implementing, jot down a few notes to remind you of your primary assessments, key strategies, and skills. Keep these as a checklist to help you focus and troubleshoot while you are in negotiation. During the process, remain open to new understandings of the dynamics and the need to alter your strategies accordingly.
  a. What was my original understanding of the nature of the conflict? How is my interaction with the other person affecting my views of the conflict?

b. Do our strategies seem to be working? Are we moving toward my stated goals and objectives? If not, why? Consider process objectives, relationship objectives, and outcome objectives.

c. What are the strengths and limitations of the strategies I have been using? What other strategies would be useful at this point?

d. What are the strategies of the other party? What are the strengths and limitations of these strategies? How can I best respond to these strategies?

e. If difficulties exist, would it be useful to bring in help (e.g., a consultant, an advocate, a mediator, a buffer, an arbitrator)?

f. What ethical dilemmas or values issues need to be considered (Menkel-Meadow & Wheeler, 2004)?

Videotaping or audiotaping sessions provides an excellent means of reviewing your use of skills and strategies. You can review these on your own or with the help of a peer, supervisor, or teacher. Compare how you planned to proceed with what actually took place. Look for crisis points, critical incidents, and factors that moved the negotiations forward. Formal research into your negotiations can make use of various methods: single-system design, quantitative evaluation, naturalistic inquiry, and action research. Although this book is not a research text, the value of various types of research requires at least some mention. Single–case study design can help you monitor the effectiveness of your negotiation interventions on a case-by-case basis. Quantitative program evaluations are useful for determining the effectiveness of a program that uses a particular model of negotiation on a regular basis (Grinnell & Unrau, 2005). Naturalistic inquiry is particularly useful for gaining an understanding of the negotiation process from the parties' perspectives (Denzin & Lincoln, 2005). Action research is similar to program evaluation, but it combines simultaneous research, evaluation, and program development (Herr & Anderson, 2005). Often, the research is conducted by practitioners themselves rather than outside research consultants. This allows practitioners greater control over how research is conducted and provides them with ongoing research results rather than one report at the end of the evaluation process (Lewin, 1948). Informal evaluation, as described earlier, may be sufficient for your individual purposes. Formal evaluation is more costly. However, the results of formal evaluation can be published so that others can also learn from your negotiation experiences.

KEY POINTS

- Helping professionals can approach negotiation from one of four approaches, separately or in combination: power, rights, interests, and transformation.

- According to the power approach, each party exerts its influence on the other in order to maximize its personal gain, often to the detriment of the relationship between the parties.

- The rights approach suggests that conflicts be resolved in accordance with rights as established by public laws, organizational rules, or community norms.

- Interest-based negotiation is a joint problem-solving process in which parties strive to satisfy their mutual interests, including the opportunity to build a more positive relationship.

- Transformative negotiation is a process designed to provide parties with empowerment and recognition. Empowerment occurs when parties gain a greater sense of self-determination, choice, and autonomy. Recognition occurs when a party gains a better understanding of the other's situation and demonstrates this newfound empathy to the other through words or deeds.

- When negotiating with people from diverse cultures, helping professionals must deconstruct the assumptions underlying various theories and strategies in order to assure that their interventions are culturally appropriate.

- Preparation for negotiation is an iterative process in which helping professionals reflect on negotiation theory, assessment, strategies, and skills at various points throughout the negotiation process.

DISCUSSION QUESTIONS AND EXERCISES

1. CONTRACTING: You are working with a psychiatric patient, Pat, who is at risk of committing suicide. Your suicide prevention model suggests that you negotiate a "safety plan" with the client (e.g., Pat will stay with a friend overnight; you will contact the friend by phone to provide the friend with instruction about what to do in case of emergency, Pat will call the 24-hour crisis line if Pat starts to think about committing suicide; Pat will meet with you tomorrow to make further plans). Should this agreement be implicit, explicit and oral, or written? What are the advantages and disadvantages of each type of agreement? Do you or Pat require legal advice before finalizing this agreement? Why or why not? Is this agreement a legally binding agreement? What are the consequences if either one of you breaks the agreement?

2. NEGOTIATION SUCCESS: Select on of the four negotiation approaches described in this chapter: power, rights, interests, transformation. Which of the following definitions of success fit best for a negotiator using this approach?
   I believe that negotiation is successful if

- I win (maximize gain for me).
- both of us win (maximize joint gain).
- we satisfy our underlying interests.
- the process is efficient (save money and other resources).
- the process is fair (equal bargaining power, neutrality, or impartiality in the process).
- we achieve a fair outcome (equitable distribution of resources—consider, who decides what is fair?).
- I showed compassion, kindness, honesty, and respect.
- we develop a better relationship (harmonious, amicable, able to deal with differences).
- the process leads to retributive justice (appropriate consequences hold people accountable for their misdeeds).

- the process leads to restorative justice (restitution or compensation).
- we avoid court (e.g., conflicts are settled informally, in negotiation or mediation).
- we achieve durable solutions (solutions that last, without new conflict arising).
- we develop more effective conflict resolution skills.
- we become more empowered.
- we give and receive recognition (through words and actions to each other).
- we achieve better decisions (how do you judge what is "better?").
- we enhance the community (better off than prior to the intervention).
- we promote diversity.
- we promote social control (enforcement of societal norms).
- we diffuse anger
- Other: _____

  If you were to design a research project to evaluate success of a CR program, how would you measure success? How would you decide what to measure?

3. POSITIONAL STRATEGIES: Read through the following dialogue between Theodore, a therapist, and Clarabelle, his client. Identify the positional negotiation strategies that they use. How does this interaction display the power approach? How could Theodore approach this conflict from an interest-based approach?

   THEODORE: *After last week's session, I started to think that there's a problem we have to discuss.*

   CLARABELLE: *I don't know what you mean. Let's just forget it.*

   THEODORE: *No, I really think that we have to talk about it. What do you think the problem is?*

   CLARABELLE: *What do you think the problem is?*

   THEODORE: *This therapy is about you. It's important to explore your feelings.*

   CLARABELLE: *Well, if you really want to know, I think that you're always trying to lay a guilt trip on me.*

   THEODORE: *I'd never do that. I respect you, as I do all my clients.*

   CLARABELLE: *Well, you asked, and I told you.*

   THEODORE: *Perhaps you are feeling frustrated about your lack of progress.*

   CLARABELLE: *What do you mean? After all I've been through? There you go again, making me feel guilty.*

   THEODORE: *Then maybe we should just terminate our relationship.*

   CLARABELLE: *I'm not saying that. I just think there has to be more give and take.*

   THEODORE: *So, what exactly do you want me to do?*

4. POWER AND ETHICS: In negotiations with a client, when, if ever, is use of power by a helping professional justified? Necessary? Consider your profession's code of ethics, including concepts such as self-determination, respect, safety, compliance with the law, and imposition of values.

5. DEALING WITH THREATS: You are working with a drug-abusing client, Dora. Dora is desperate to get into a drug abuse treatment program. You tell her that there is a waiting list of 3 weeks. Dora threatens to blow up your agency if you

cannot get her in the program within 2 days. You believe that the threats are real and that Dora has the ability to follow through. How will you negotiate with Dora? Consider the four approaches to negotiation and strategies within each approach.

6. RIGHTS AND RELATIONSHIPS: You are working for a gay, lesbian, and bisexual community center. The local government offers funding for programs for street youth. You submit a proposal on behalf of your agency. The government says that it cannot accept your proposal because it does not want to promote sexual deviance among street youth. You consider your alternatives: assert the rights of the group you represent by challenging the government's decision in a court case (judicial review); assert their rights through demonstrations; try to develop a better relationship with members of government. What are the advantages and disadvantages of each of these alternatives? What other alternatives should be considered? Which alternative is best? Why? (Consider use of Decision Tree Analysis.)

7. SMOKING POSITIONS, RULES, AND INTERESTS: You are working with a client, Cleo, who asks whether she can smoke. You tell Cleo that the office building has a "no smoking" rule. The two of you get into an argument about whether she has the right to smoke. What are each of your positions? If you bargain from a positional orientation, what range of outcomes might you consider? What type of compromise might you reach?

Now, analyze the case from an interest-based approach. What are Cleo's underlying interests? What are your interests? Brainstorm 10 to 15 options that might satisfy these interests. How does this interest-based approach differ from the positional approach (Fisher et al., 1997)?

8. A SLICE OF EVENING PIE: Your supervisor announces that your agency is extending its hours so it can serve clients on evenings and weekends. She suggests that you and three colleagues alternate each week, taking either a weekend or evening shift each week. You have a child who is in school from 9 A.M. to 4 P.M. every weekday. Jules has no children. His commute to the agency takes over an hour, each way. Selma lives close to the agency. She has a physical condition that makes her tire easily, so she needs lots of rest and a regular routine. Whitney wants to go to grad school and work part-time. None of you like the idea of alternating shifts. What options can you generate for mutual gain? How can the expanded schedule become an advantage rather than a problem?

9. COLD OFFICE: You and a colleague share an office. You find the office hot and stuffy, so you turn on the air conditioner. Your colleague finds the office too cold and wants to turn on the heat. You suggest a compromise, leaving both the air conditioning and the heat off. Your colleague asks whether there isn't a better solution. What is the nature of this conflict? How else can you resolve this conflict (Fisher et al., 1997)?

10. CLASS COMPETITION AND COOPERATION: You are in a class where the term project is a paper requiring library research. During the ninth class, the professor will provide the specific research topics. You fear that everyone will rush to the library after that class to take out all of the books. If one or two

people horde most of the books, others will suffer. What CR theories can you use to analyzing this situation? What are the incentives favoring competition between students? What are the incentives favoring cooperation? How would you approach negotiations with your classmates?

11. SHARING A DRINK: Have someone bring a bottle of a drink that most people enjoy. Select five people in the class, and give them each a glass. The mission for these five people is to identify a method of dividing the drink. All five people would like as much of the drink as possible. The parties agree to following principles for division: fair, practical, and enforceable. Brainstorm alternatives. Once you have an exhaustive list, apply the principles for selection and negotiate an agreement about the process for division. Implement the decision. Evaluate the process and implementation according to the suggestions earlier in this chapter.

12. ROLE REVERSAL: You are working with a client who has a mental illness and is putting others at risk of serious harm. Your supervisor suggests the client be given sedatives, even though the client does not want them. What is your view on using medication to sedate this client? Write down your reasons. In order to gain a better understanding of someone with a different view, find a partner in the class to do a role reversal. Your partner will play your role in a discussion about this issue. In order to understand your perspective, provide your partner with your list of reasons. You will argue the other person's point of view.

Debriefing: What made it difficult for you to assume the other person's role? What did you learn by taking on this role? How might this knowledge help you negotiate about the issue of involuntary use of medication?

13. POWER AND JOINT PROBLEM SOLVING: You are working with an agency that serves youth in conflict with the law. The agency receives referrals from probation officers. Your role is to negotiate a plan with a youth and the youth's parents to deal with underlying problems and to prevent the youth from reoffending. If the youth does not agree to a plan, then the youth will have to return to court to face charges. Consider the ethics of this model. Is it ethically appropriate to use power to push clients into a joint problem-solving process? Is this constructive use of power or an insidious form of social control? How can you construct your negotiation process with the youth in order to minimize the ethical concerns (Menkel-Meadow & Wheeler, 2004; Tjaden, 1994)?

14. PRESSURE TO AGREE: You have been looking for a job for 3 months and have just received your first offer. You like the agency and the type of work that the agency offers. Unfortunately, the salary is substantially below your expectations. The agency's position regarding salary is "take it or leave it." Use the Negotiation Preparation Tool to analyze this conflict and to strategize how to approach negotiations. What type of conflict is this? What is your preferred approach? How will you know whether your negotiations are successful? Can negotiations be "successful" even if you do not reach an agreement with the agency?

15. NEGOTIATING CONCEPTS OF TIME: You are working with a Native American community. In your culture, as well as that of your agency, people set appointments

for meetings and conduct meetings in offices. The beginning and end times are fixed, with about 5 minutes of flexibility for lateness or running overtime. Most people from the community you are working with have a different sense of time. People meet when needed and when the time is appropriate, rather than at an artificially predetermined time. Meetings are often held out in the community or in someone's home rather than in an office building. Meetings seem informal to you, with no clear boundary between when the meeting begins and ends. What are the implications of these cultural differences for negotiations between you and members of the community? How do you negotiate a set of norms for meetings that are acceptable to both you and members of the community (Macduff, 2006)?

16. DECONSTRUCTING INTEREST-BASED NEGOTIATION: Review the key components of interest-based negotiation (Fisher et al., 1997). Identify the underlying assumptions of this approach, and deconstruct it using a postmodern, feminist analysis. For suggestions on how to deconstruct a model of intervention, see Culler (1982), Lederach (1986), or Pennell and Ristock (1997).

17. TRANSFORMATIVE VERSUS INTEREST-BASED NEGOTIATION: Assume that you adopt the transformative approach to negotiation. Accordingly, you view success as empowerment and recognition. Assume further that your client views success as satisfaction of interests. Are your respective perspectives at cross-purposes? In negotiating with this client, whose perspective will prevail?

18. POLITICAL CORRECTNESS: You work on a committee for advancement of rights of people with disabilities. During a public meeting, a city official refers to people with disabilities as "gimps." The official thinks it is just a joke, but you find the term offensive. What is the nature of this type of conflict? What are your primary goals in negotiating with the official? How can you best achieve them?

19. STEREOTYPES: Faith is a White woman of Scottish decent. She is negotiating with Carlos, a Latin American. Faith views Latin men as macho, impractical, disorganized, and stubborn. How will these stereotypes affect how she acts as a negotiator? What can Carlos do to respond to these stereotypes (Menkel-Meadow et al., 2005)?

20. LEARNING NEEDS: Review the Negotiation Preparation Tool. Identify five or six skills or strategies that you want to focus on for professional development. These could be areas that you want to explore even though they do not seem to fit with your preferred approach. Alternatively, identify skills and strategies that you believe will be most important for your specific areas of practice. As you work through the role-plays and exercises, remember to practice your chosen skills and strategies.

ROLE-PLAY 3.1: "CONTRACTING WITH CLEM"

This is a role-play between a psychologist, Sylvie, and a client, Clem. Sylvie works for Diversity Plus, specializing in work with men who have been physically abusive with their partners. Clem was referred by his probation officer, following charges of assault against his partner. Clem's probation officer wants to know whether Clem is cooperating with the psychologist, one of the conditions of his probation.

The purpose of this role-play is to practice contracting with clients. Because this is the first session between Sylvie and Clem, they need to negotiate the terms of confidentiality and exceptions to it. In order to prepare for this role-play, Sylvie should jot down notes for herself about what issues are negotiable and what issues are not negotiable. Clem should consider, from a client's perspective, what terms would be agreeable to him. He is not familiar with the concept of confidentiality, so Sylvie will need to be able to explain what it means, including different options.

During the role-play, first work toward an oral agreement. Once an oral agreement is reached, prepare a written agreement that reflects what you agreed to orally. This role-play takes 15 to 25 minutes.

Debriefing: What unexpected issues arose in the role-play? What did Sylvie do that helped make contracting more effective? If Sylvie could do the role-play over again, what would she do differently? Does the confidentiality contract between Sylvie and Clem satisfy the needs and expectations of third parties (e.g., the agency, probation, Sylvie's profession, Clem's partner)? If not, what else should be considered? Does either party in this scenario require legal advice before signing the contract? Is this contract a legally binding agreement? If either party breaks the agreement, what are the legal consequences, if any?

ROLE-PLAY 3.2: "NEGOTIATING FOR GRADES"—FOUR APPROACHES

This role-play has two roles: a university professor, Dr. Proulx, and a student, Sandy Simms. Dr. Proulx has given Sandy a grade of 78 percent for her final term paper. Sandy needed at least 81 percent in order to achieve an A for the course. Ordinarily, Sandy would not complain. However, if she gets an A in this course, then she is eligible for a scholarship that will enable her to do research in conflict resolution for her graduate program. Dr. Proulx believes that 78 percent was a fair grade.

Divide the class into pairs. Each pair will select a different approach for negotiating between Dr. Proulx and Sandy. If possible, have each pair videotape their role-play, so the class can review the role-plays together and analyze the different dynamics that occur depending on the approaches of the parties.

In order to prepare for this role-play, use parts of the Negotiation Preparation Tool that are appropriate to your chosen approach. Add facts where needed (e.g., the university requires a class average of 70 percent; students have a right to appeal their grades to an appeals committee in the faculty). Remember that one of the best ways to prepare for negotiations is role reversal—put yourself in the other person's shoes in order to identify his or her positions, rights, interests, and values, as well as how he or she might be persuaded in negotiation. Set aside at least 40 minutes for this exercise.

Debriefing: If you have ever approached a professor in the past to challenge a grade, what strategies did you use? How were these strategies different from those you used in the role-play? What approaches proved to be most effective? If you were a professor, which approach to negotiation would be most appropriate for this type of conflict? Why?

ROLE-PLAY 3.3: "EXTERNAL EVALUATION CONFLICT"— CONFLICT STYLES AND INTEREST-BASED NEGOTIATION

Rajib works as a researcher who evaluates the effectiveness of publicly funded social services. Ellen is the executive director of the Conflictia Immigration Program (CIP), a branch of Diversity Plus. CIP helps immigrants find housing, training, and employment, as well as develop social supports and other settlement needs. CIP has recently incurred a 20 percent cutback in funding. This has had a negative impact on morale, as the number of clients is rising and the number of staff has been decreasing. The last thing Ellen needs is an "egghead" researcher who knows nothing about immigration services to start interfering with clients and staff. Given the cutback in program funding, spending more money on useless research seems ridiculous.

Rajib is not thrilled with this project, having no prior experience in immigration work. He would rather spend more time on a gerontology project he has been doing. Rajib has already picked up on bad vibes from the agency. He is well grounded in evaluative research and takes great pride in his work. Ellen and Rajib have scheduled a meeting in Ellen's office for 9 o'clock Monday morning. The ostensible purpose for this meeting is to establish some sort of understanding about how they are going to work together, but Ellen's real purpose is to make Rajib disappear.

In order to analyzing the impact of different conflict styles, consider the following questions:

- How would Ellen respond if her preferred style is competitive? Compromising? How should Rajib respond to each of these scenarios? How can he try to move Ellen toward collaboration (if that is desirable)?
- How would Rajib respond if his preferred style is accommodating? Avoiding? How should Ellen respond to each of these scenarios?

In the actual role-play, Ellen will play competitive. She can use the first question above to prepare for the role-play. Rajib will encourage collaboration. Rajib should use the following questions to prepare:

a. What should Rajib do in advance of the meeting in order to raise chances for an effective negotiation (consider the timing, place, setup, and premeeting communication)?

b. What must Rajib watch for in order to separate the people from the problem? (Think of specific comments that he can use to address this issue.)

c. How important is a trusting relationship? If important, what can Rajib do about this?

d. What are Ellen and Rajib's original positions (i.e., what are they each trying to achieve)?

e. What are the interests underlying these positions?

f. What are their mutual interests?

g. What are the possible options?

h. What are the possible advantages and disadvantages for each of these options? (Would a decision tree or other preparation tool be helpful?)

i. How do you evaluate the options (i.e., what criteria/general principles could be used)?
j. What is Ellen's BATNA?
k. What is Rajib's BATNA?
l. What can each do to improve his or her BATNA?
m. What might block an agreement?

Discuss these questions in small groups. Identify key strategies that you want to test or practice. Role-play the situation using these strategies.

Debriefing: What strategies seemed to be effective? What strategies seemed ineffective? What did you learn for future negotiations?

ROLE-PLAY 3.4: "JOINT COUNSELING DEBATE"—SKILLS DEVELOPMENT

Chris and Sanchez are two of the clinical supervisors at Diversity Plus. The agency has asked them to develop an agency policy about domestic violence, particularly wife abuse. They have run into a conflict about whether to see male and female partners together when there has been a history of abuse. In this exercise, they will debate this issue starting from the following perspectives.

* Chris believes that the only way for couples counseling to be effective is to see both members of the couple together. Chris thinks that safeguards can be put into place to ensure that abuse does not take place during the process of counseling, and that the couples should have the ultimate say in terms of whether they should be seen together.
* Sanchez believes that where there is a history of spousal abuse, the two partners should not be seen together. He also thinks there is no way for the worker to ensure safety if both partners are seen together. Sanchez refutes the argument that the couple should have the final say, because it is the counselor who is responsible for ensuring that counseling is safe and effective.

Use the Negotiation Preparation Tool to prepare for this role-play. Identify two strategies that you want to focus upon for this exercise. Consider which skills are needed in order to implement these strategies. The purpose of this exercise is to focus on skill development. Do not be too concerned about your choice of approaches and strategies. Give yourselves at least an hour for this role-play, with frequent breaks to debrief. Let the others in your group know which skills you want to focus upon. Ask for suggestions before going into role.

Directions for Observers: As you observe the role-play, write down at least three key exchanges between Chris and Sanchez (exactly what one person said and how the other person responded). For each exchange, write down whether the response was an acknowledgment (paraphrase, summary, or reflection of feeling), inquiry (question exploring the other's thoughts, perceptions, or feelings), or counterstatement.

Following the role-play, give the negotiators feedback on how frequently they used each type of response and give examples of which responses tended to be most effective.

Debriefing: Have the facilitator ask each role-player, "Which negotiation skills did you use effectively?" and "Which skills would you like to improve upon?" Ask observers to provide examples of how certain skills were used effectively. Feel free to go back over the same stages of negotiation for practice rather than complete each negotiation role-play from beginning to end.

ROLE-PLAY 3.5: "WHAT DO I GET FOR ROLE-PLAYING?"— NEGOTIATING CLOSE TO HOME

The question of who participates in role-plays can raise conflicts between students in a class. The following role-play may or may not be close to issues that have arisen in your group. Play the roles as written. When you debrief, consider how similar issues have been dealt with in your group. Remember—separate the person from the problem.

Out of 12 students in the class, only 7 have participated in role-plays. Different students have different excuses for why they have not participated.

The class needs to decide what, if anything, should happen about the fact that 5 students have not participated. Consider whether this should be decided by consensus, by one person in the class, by majority vote, or by some other alternative.

The reasons given by the students for not participating are as follows:

- KAREN: My turn to role-play doesn't come up until next week.
- KOBY: I was sick on the day I was supposed to role-play.
- KELLY: I don't like role-plays, so I decided not to come to class.
- KATE: I haven't done role-plays before.
- KYLE: I had to finish writing a paper for the same day as the role-play.

Some of the opinions expressed by other people in the class were:

- BARB: That's not fair.
- BOB: It's their loss.
- BRURIA: Why should I have to do it if they don't?
- BETTY: I don't care one way or another.
- BILLIE: What about the so-called standards of our profession?
- BRAD: I like having more time to role-play rather than watching others.
- BUNNIE: They should not be able to pass this course unless they role-play.

Assign each of these roles to 12 people in the class. Use the Negotiation Preparation Tool to prepare, and allot 30 to 40 minutes for this role-play.

Debriefing: What types of preparation helped the most? What, if anything, moved each person from his or her original position? How was negotiating between twelve people different from negotiating between two?

MAJOR ASSIGNMENTS

The following role-plays may be used for major assignments in the course. Each assignment calls for a written analysis of a conflict resolution exercise in which you participated. Include the following content areas for your analysis:

1. **Heading**—Indicate the assignment name and number, student(s) submitting this paper, professor's name, course name, educational institution, and the date submitted.

2. **Introduction**—Briefly describe the context of the role-play (what was the conflict about). Define three or four of your educational objectives for the assignment. What did *you* want to learn? Focus on your own objectives as a developing CR professional, rather than the particular details of the substantive conflict. For example, "My first learning objective for this assignment was to develop a practical understanding of how game theory (Rapoport, 1974) can be applied in the context of a conflict between professionals in a social agency," not "The purpose of the assignment was to get Pam to stop calling Arnie a wimp and to get Arnie to promise not to slash Pam's tires every time he was mad at her." [1 paragraph]

3. **Preparation**—Describe the steps that you and the other parties took to prepare for this exercise—for example, reflection or mental preparation; use of instruments to aid in preparation; theory and approaches from your readings that you planned to apply; steps taken to set up the meeting; issues you expected to deal with; and strategies you prepared. Include brief descriptions of key concepts from your readings (you should use 3 to 10 scholarly books or articles in addition to this textbook). If you used any preparation instruments, you can attach these as an appendix or simply summarize how you used them. If you decided to enter the role-play with little or no preparation, indicate this, but also note what types of preparation might have been useful in retrospect. [1 to 3 pages]

4. **Overview of the Intervention**—Briefly describe the overall process of the conflict resolution interaction. Write this narrative in either third person or first person, depending on which you believe will be more clear and concise. [2 to 3 pages]

5. **Process Recording**—Use the following table format to develop a process recording that provides a detailed analysis of key interactions during the role-play. The left column includes a word-for-word transcript of what the parties said during these key interactions. You do not need to transcribe the whole role-play, just the key interactions. Audiotaping your role-play can be helpful for transcribing; otherwise, use your memory. Start a new row each time a new client or professional speaks, so the comments across each row relate to just one person's response. The second column describes what you observed about the client(s) or other parties during that segment of the role-play (e.g., "The client was smiling from ear to ear"; "The client raised her voice"). Also, include different interpretations of what you observed ("The raised voice may have indicated she was either nervous or angry"). The third column indicates the thoughts or feelings of the work at that point in the interaction (e.g., "I thought she was angry at me, so I felt defensive"). The right column indicates skills and theory that either were

used or could be used by the professional at this point (e.g., "Hatley's (2007) anger theory suggests that anger often masks feelings of insecurity; Power-based CR suggests that I could play on the client's insecurity in order to put her on the defensive"). [5 to 8 pages]

NARRATIVE (Verbatim)	OBSERVATIONS OF CLIENT AND POSSIBLE INTERPRETATIONS	REFLECTIONS (Thoughts and Feelings of the Professional[s])	SKILLS, THEORY, AND ALTERNATIVES

6. **Critique**—Provide an overall critique analysis of what worked well, what did not work well, and why. Be sure to use nonjudgmental, positive, future-focused language. Rather than "My pathetic attempt to use structured role reversal really sucked," try "I was trying to use role reversal so that Mabel could gain an insight into Garnet's concerns. Mabel was not ready to engage in a role reversal, because I had not dealt with her anger (Sibyl, 2006). If I were to be faced with this type of conflict in the future, I would try. . . ." Your critique may also include any ethical, cultural, or practical issues that arose in trying to apply certain theories in your role-play. [3 to 6 pages]
7. **Conclusion**—Describe any follow-up that you would suggest for dealing with the conflict in the exercise. Identify your key learnings from this exercise, including how the role-play and analysis may have added to your understanding of what you have read and discussed in class. Was there anything that you learned that went beyond what was covered in class and in your readings? [1 to 3 paragraphs]

Use the American Psychological Association (2001) manual to format this paper (15 to 20 pages, double-spaced except for the process recording, which is single-spaced; no abstract or separate title page is needed; 5 to 10 scholarly references). *I have provided a sample assignment and process recording in Appendix 2 to illustrate how to carry out this analysis.*

Grading will be based on your ability to synthesize material from the class and your readings with the exercise. Try to integrate skills, theory, values, and reflection as specifically and accurately as possible. This will show that you know how to apply your CR knowledge in a practice situation, as well as how to critique the CR approaches that you used. You will not be graded on your actual performance in the exercise but on your analysis of the exercise. For example, even if you did not use a certain strategy effectively in the exercise, you can demonstrate in the analysis that you know how it could have been applied.

You may write up assignments individually or as a small group (2 to 4 people). If you hand in an assignment as a group, then everyone in the group will be assigned the same grade. You do not need to hand in your audiotapes or videos, but you should hold onto them until you have received your final grade at the end of the term. Both parties should read the common facts, but the *confidential facts should be read only by the designated party*.

ASSIGNMENT 3A: PHYLLIS'S CASE

Phyllis has recently been admitted to the Conflictia Hope Hospital. She was having auditory hallucinations that caused her to destroy most of the furniture in her apartment. She was seen by a psychiatrist, Dr. Nguyen, who wanted Phyllis to be admitted on an involuntary basis because she was a danger to herself and others. Previously, Phyllis has been diagnosed as having schizophrenia. She has been able to function well when she stays on her medication. However, she does not always take her medication as prescribed.

Sandy is a systems counselor who has been working with Phyllis in the community. Phyllis wants to get out of the hospital right away and has been uncooperative with hospital staff. The hospital has contacted Sandy and asked her to meet with Phyllis, because Sandy has developed a positive relationship with Phyllis.

Sandy's Confidential Facts (not to be read by Phyllis)

You do not work for the hospital, and you need to define what your role will be in meeting with Phyllis. You believe she can be returned to the community, but you do not have the power to decide this. You also believe that Phyllis does need some type of monitoring to ensure that she is safe. If she does not follow through on her medication, then she is likely to continue to have more problems. Try to work out a contract with Phyllis to deal with the conflict.

Phyllis's Confidential Facts (not to be read by Sandy)

When Sandy arrives, you are quite angry with her. You think she is teaming up with the hospital against you. You hate the psychiatric ward at the hospital, because you don't think of yourself as crazy or sick. You acknowledge that things got out of control at home, but you believe this will not be a problem in the future. You went off your meds for a few days because you thought they were turning you into a zombie—you've been feeling lethargic and unmotivated. You also feel embarrassed about the nervous twitches that you have developed from the meds. You are scared about having hallucinations again, but the hospital also scares you. Your mother was admitted to a mental hospital when you were 12, and she never got out.

Your main goals are to get out of the hospital and to be left alone. You want Sandy to promise to get you a discharge from the hospital. You want to be treated like an adult and a human being. In order to prepare for this meeting, think about how Phyllis would present herself and what questions that you might expect from Sandy. You do not have to show great insight into your issues, unless Sandy draws these out during your meeting.

ASSIGNMENT 3B: METHADONE MAINTENANCE CASE

You're Off Drugs and Alcohol (YODA) is a substance abuse treatment program at Diversity Plus. Due to concerns about the spread of HIV and AIDS among intravenous drug abusers—through sharing unclean needles—YODA has decided to open up a methadone maintenance clinic in the Huntington Community of Conflictia. Methadone maintenance is a chemical therapy used for people addicted to heroin. Methadone is a synthetic opiate that is used to prevent heroin users from going through withdrawal. Studies show that methadone maintenance is related to improved social functioning in the family, at work, and so forth. Darth is the director at YODA. One of Darth's roles is to maintain positive relations within the community.

Not In My Backyard (NIMBY) is a community group in Huntington that opposes the plans for the methadone program. NIMBY believes the program will attract undesirables to their neighborhood, particularly minorities such as North Americans and Buddhists. NIMBY fears the clinic will put their children at risk. It believes the clinic will lead to increased crime and violence. NIMBY is also opposed to the concept of taxpayers spending money on giving drugs to drug addicts, even if it is methadone. Sidney is the spokesperson for NIMBY. Sidney's position is that YODA must not be allowed to open any type of methadone maintenance clinic.

NIMBY has threatened to go to court for an injunction to prevent YODA from opening its program in its neighborhood. In response, Darth called Sidney for a private meeting in order to try to settle things out of court.

Darth's Confidential Facts

You see NIMBY as a group of rednecks, for whom you have little patience. You find Sidney particularly shallow and abrasive. However, you are responsible for ensuring the best possible services for YODA's target population. That means that you may have to work out an amicable arrangement with NIMBY. You could go ahead with the plans without consulting NIMBY, but at what costs?

Conflictia has no other methadone maintenance program, and three of your clients have tested HIV-positive in the last 2 months (one woman and two men). Methadone maintenance is not a cure-all. There is actually a low level of success in terms of detoxification from methadone and all other drugs. However, methadone does work as a means to stopping intravenous drug use, and it fits with your agency's philosophy of "harm reduction," as opposed to abstinence. The only other location that would be suitable for the program would be the Bridal Path Community. Bridal Path has a sister organization to NIMBY called NOTE (Not Over There Either), and there would be even fiercer resistance if YODA tried to set up a methadone program there. Accordingly, you see Bridal Path as a nonstarter. Huntington is the only location that will work. It is accessible via public transit and you already have land where you can build a clinic.

Sidney's Confidential Facts

You represent a group of upstanding citizens in the Huntington community. You want to ensure that the streets are safe from drug users and traffickers. The proposed methadone maintenance program was initiated without any consultation with the community. Accordingly, you believe that YODA does not care to hear your views. Darth appears to show concern, but you think Darth is just a "bleeding heart liberal." There are two schools and a daycare program within three blocks of the proposed clinic. However, you do not believe that there is any good place for it. You do not agree with the idea of handing out free drugs to anyone. It just encourages more drug use and crime, and does nothing to prevent AIDS. If people are concerned about stopping the transmission of AIDS, then they would be well advised to get off all drugs. You have seen news reports from Zurich where they allowed needle use in a public park, and it attracted drug users from all over Europe. You do not want Huntington to become a magnet for those types of people. One possibility for the clinic would be to place it in the Bridal Path Neighborhood. This is not your first choice, since you oppose any distribution of methadone or other opiates, but at least the Bridal Path is far from your neighborhood.

You are not sure what will happen if the case goes to court. There are 60–40 odds that you can get temporary injunction, and only a 20 percent chance of gaining a permanent injunction. The costs may be prohibitive, but you may be able to scare off YODA by initiating a court proceeding (even if you have no intention of going through with a full trial). You may also try to solicit political pressure from your local member of the legislative assembly, who happens to be leader of the ROC Party, Mr. Alby Wright.

*Take the first step in faith. You don't have to see the whole
staircase, just take the first step.*

—Martin Luther King, Jr.

4 CHAPTER | Mediation

Chapter 1 defines *mediation* as assisted negotiation. Two or more people involved in a conflict sit down with someone they trust to talk about their differences. This broad definition encompasses a wide range of possible interventions. Although programs, practitioners, and research studies have produced more specific definitions of mediation (Milne, Folberg, & Salem, 2004), these definitions are really describing specific models or approaches to mediation. Because there is no universally accepted explication of mediation, it is often difficult to discern what people are talking about when they say they are mediating. Mediation has been defined differently for different times, cultures, and contexts of conflict.

Although CR literature frequently describes mediation as a new alternative, the mediation role has existed throughout history and in a variety of forms. Mediation is a natural way in which people help others deal with problems. Friends, neighbors, elders, clergy, parents, or community leaders have traditionally assumed the role of mediator on an informal basis. Virtually every society has had some form of mediation. Anthropological research on mediation in different societies ranges from modern Liberia to sixth-century Gaul, thirteenth-century France, early China, contemporary Singapore, and the Kalahari Desert among the bush people (Bossy, 2003; Cappelletti, 1979; Chia, Lee-Partridge, & Chong, 2004; Noone, 1996). Mediation as a distinct profession and as an institutionalized alternative to court and other dispute resolution systems is relatively new. For example, the first court-based family mediation service began in 1961 at the Los Angeles County Conciliation Court. California became the first state to mandate family mediation in 1989 (Milne et al., 2004). Licensure and accreditation for family mediators began in the 1980s, as did development of professional mediation courses and academic programs. While many mediation programs and associations have focused on developing professional standards and models of practice for mediators, other proponents of mediation have been looking at how to support mediation as a skill set or approach to conflict that can be used by everyone, regardless of professional status.

This chapter begins with an overview of four of the more popular approaches to mediation: settlement focused, interest based, therapeutic, and transformative. The next section explores how helping professionals can use mediation in a range of contexts. A case study illustrates the seven phases of the mediation process, high-lighting the similarities and differences in how mediation is implemented with each of the four approaches. The following section contrasts mediation with interventions of other types of helping professionals. The next section explores how mediators need to take culture and diversity into account. The role-plays at the end of this chapter provide opportunities to practice each of the seven phases of mediation. Each role-play includes an inventory of skills and activities that can be used for each phase. As you develop your own model of mediation practice, you can draw from these inventories and identify which skills and activities to emphasize.

APPROACHES TO MEDIATION

As the profession of mediation evolves, different approaches to mediation have developed. These approaches continue to be refined, critiqued, and evaluated for effectiveness. This chapter focuses on four of the more popular approaches to medi-ation: settlement-focused mediation, interest-based mediation, therapeutic media-tion, and transformative mediation. This section begins with an overview of these approaches, followed by analysis of six key components and assumptions about the mediation process.

Settlement-focused mediation[1] *focuses on how to help people terminate conflict by bringing them to agreement in an expeditious manner.* Settlement-focused medi-ation (SFM) is related to the rights-based approach to negotiation, as the mediator encourages parties to solve their differences according to pre-existing rules and laws (Coogler, 1978; State Justice Institute, 1998). Under SFM, mediators are task ori-ented and interventionist. They keep the parties focused on the key issues in dispute and do not delve into underlying issues such as emotions, relationships, and the his-tory of the dispute. SFM is often used by judges in pre-trial settlement conferences and by mediators helping clients with financial or business disputes (Noone, 1996). Government officials who are mandated by legislation to resolve certain types of disputes in accordance with the law may also adopt this approach.[2] The primary advantage of SFM is efficiency, as matters can typically be settled in just one or two sessions. This may save time, emotional energy, and financial costs (including the costs of lawyers who may attend mediation with their clients). SFM may also be popular among people who do not want to delve into relational or emotional issues, perhaps because of cultural reasons or perhaps because they believe that doing so will just stir up more controversy.

Some mediators use an approach related to settlement-focused mediation called *evaluative mediation.* Evaluative mediators make assessments about the conflict and the best ways to resolve the conflict. Evaluative mediators communicate these assessments to the parties in order to encourage settlements of their disputes. There are many risks in evaluative mediation: (a) the mediator's assessment may be wrong,

---

[1]Sometimes called *rule-based* or *structured mediation.*

[2]Such officials are often called *conciliators* rather than mediators. Conciliation may be used by human rights commissions, labor relations boards, and welfare review tribunals.

(b) the parties may surrender their self-determination and simply acquiesce with the mediator's assessment, (c) the parties may abandon any attempt at collaboration in order to sway the evaluator's assessment in their own favor, and (d) the parties may become confused about whether the role of the mediator is more like that of a facilitator or a judge. Proponents of evaluative mediation suggest that it is a more efficient way of mediating, given higher rates of settlement, less time to reach solutions, and use of the mediator's expertise to bring the parties to solution (rather than having to refer the parties to additional professionals for assessments) (Lowry, 2004). I use the term *settlement-focused mediation* in this book because, although it can include a mediator providing evaluations to parties, the focus is on fostering settlements, rather than providing evaluations. Providing evaluations is just one possible strategy that settlement-focused mediators can use to bring parties to settlement.

Interest-based mediation encourages parties to resolve underlying interests rather than just their overt conflict. Interest-based mediators help parties move away from positional bargaining, selling the merits of a win-win, cooperative approach (Mayer, 2004b).[3] The role of the mediator is basically to facilitate interest-based negotiation. Among helping professionals, interest-based mediation is more popular than settlement-focused mediation because it attends more to relationship issues and encourages parties to make self-determined choices about how to resolve their conflicts.

Therapeutic mediation is designed to help parties deal with psychological and social issues that have contributed to their conflict and have blocked their ability to resolve it. Therapeutic mediators help parties restructure their relationships, enhance communication and problem-solving skills, and deal with underlying emotional issues (Irving & Benjamin, 2002; Pruitt & Johnston, 2004). This model draws extensively from communication theory, ecosystems theory, insight-oriented cognitive therapy, structured family therapy, and strategic family therapy. Although therapeutic mediation has therapeutic aspects, it is not therapy per se. The focus of mediation is still to resolve specific conflicts that the parties bring to mediation.

Although therapeutic aspects occur throughout mediation, key differences from interest-based mediation occur at the beginning and end of the process. In the initial phases, therapeutic mediators conduct an assessment and premediation preparation in order to ensure that the clients are psychologically ready to participate constructively in mediation. After mediation, therapeutic mediators conduct follow-up sessions to see how the agreement has been working, including its impacts on the parties' relationships with each other and other social systems in their environment. Therapeutic mediation was developed for family conflicts, specifically in separation and divorce situations. It can be particularly useful in work with high-conflict parents, where the premediation interventions can help parents work through emotional challenges and develop insights into how to past interactive patterns were problematic and require change.

Transformative mediation promotes empowerment and recognition between the conflicting parties. This approach is designed to transform the way people deal

---

[3]Some mediators call this approach *facilitative mediation, integrative mediation,* or *principled mediation.*

with conflict by helping them develop mutual understanding and self-efficacy. It downplays the importance of settling specific issues in dispute (Bush & Folger, 2005; Gaynier, 2005). Transformation is a humanistic, healing process. Ideally, transformation transcends the immediate parties involved in the conflict. It engenders a philosophy that fosters social harmony and humanism (Bush & Pope, 2004). Agreement is not the goal of transformative mediation, though agreement may be a by-product.

* * *

One of the more common definitions of mediation suggests that mediation is a voluntary, confidential, nonadversarial CR process in which a neutral third party, the mediator, assists clients of relatively equal bargaining power reach a mutually satisfying agreement (Ellis & Stuckless, 1996). This definition underscores a number of assumptions:

- Mediation is voluntary.
- Mediation is confidential.
- Mediation is a nonadversarial process.
- Mediation is facilitated by a neutral third party.
- Mediation requires that the parties have equal bargaining power.
- The function of the mediator is to help the parties reach a mutually satisfying agreement.

On the surface, these assumptions may appear valid, even obvious. However, each has led to significant debate among proponents of mediation. I will review each of these assumptions in light of the four approaches to mediation.

1. Voluntary

To say that "mediation is a voluntary process" suggests that it is not imposed on people. If they mediate, it is through free and informed choice. Although this may be true in some contexts, mandatory and coerced mediation have been used in various circumstances. In some jurisdictions, parties must try mediation before they have access to a court trial. In others, parties are encouraged to go to mediation in order to avoid negative sanctions—for instance, police who advise citizens to go to community mediation or victim-offender mediation in order to avoid criminal charges (Umbreit, Coates, & Vos, 2005) or educators who ask misbehaving students to try **peer mediation** rather than receive detention or suspension (Crawford & Bodine, 2005).

Those who advocate for mandatory or coerced mediation suggest that people embroiled in disputes need an incentive to try mediation, particularly if they have had no prior experience with it. If they do not like the way mediation progresses, they can terminate the process without coming to an agreement. Mandatory or coerced mediation fits best with settlement-focused or interest-based mediation. Both approaches view dispute settlement as a primary function of mediation. They also allow the mediator to use some authority or pressure to move the parties toward settlement. In contrast, therapeutic and transformative mediation place more emphasis on empowering the parties to make their own decisions, including the right to reject mediation.

One aspect of mediation where consensus exists is that mediators do not decide the outcome for the parties. Rather, they encourage clients to take responsibility for making their own decisions about how to handle their conflict. Mediators do not try to suppress or eliminate conflict. Instead, they help parties deal with conflict deliberately, consciously, and constructively (Milne et al., 2004).

The assumption of voluntariness raises two important questions for helping professionals: (1) Is it ethical to send people to mediation against their will? (2) Is it effective, or will people simply resist the process (Ricci, 2004)?

2. Confidential

One of the advantages of mediation often cited by proponents is that it is a confidential or private process. Whereas court proceedings are open to the public, matters discussed within mediation are generally supposed to "stay in the room." Mediators offer clients confidentiality in order to encourage them to trust the process and open up, even if the discussions turn to topics that may potentially be embarrassing. In order to protect the confidential nature of mediation, many jurisdictions have passed laws that provide mediation the protections of privilege. *Privilege* means that neither the mediator nor the parties can be subpoenaed and compelled to testify in court about what was said in mediation. Similar to confidentiality, privilege encourages parties to communicate openly in mediation without fearing that what they say might be used against them in a subsequent proceeding (Association of Family and Conciliation Courts, 2000; Family Mediation Canada, n.d.; Uniform Mediation Act, 2003).

Although many mediators view confidentiality as vital to an effective mediation process, there are many exceptions to both confidentiality and privilege. Information about child abuse, elder abuse, or abuse of people with disabilities, for instance, may be subject to mandatory reporting requirements. Furthermore, confidentiality and privilege do not apply for court or disciplinary proceedings concerning allegations against a mediator for professional misconduct or malpractice. Some laws also allow courts to compel mediators or parties to testify in matters related to criminal acts (e.g., if one client threatened to kill the other) or matters of national security (e.g., under the Patriot Act).

Some mediators offer clients a mediation process that is neither confidential nor privileged. Mediation must be open to the public, for instance, if it pertains to a policy issue for a governmental organization that is subject to laws requiring all meetings to be open. Some mediators offer "open," "recommending," or "nonconfidential" mediation to parties as part of hybrid mediation processes such as **mediation-arbitration (med-arb)** or mediation-evaluation (Ricci, 2004). Initially, the mediator tries to help the parties negotiate their own agreement. If the parties cannot come to agreement on their own, then the mediator changes hats (or roles) and becomes an arbitrator or evaluator. A med-arbiter uses information from the mediation stage to help inform the arbitrated decision. A med-evaluator[4] uses information from the

---

[4]Often, the professional is simply referred to as an evaluator, rather than a med-evaluator, even though the professional's role includes both mediative and evaluative functions.

mediation to help inform his or her evaluation and recommendations, which the med-evaluator may provide to court. Whereas some mediators believe that hybrid roles are effective and ethical processes, others question whether these hybrid roles actually defeat the purpose of mediation (Love, 1997; Shienvold, 2004). In terms of confidentiality, mediators must consider whether parties will be able to openly discuss all their concerns and all the possible solutions, if they know that their communications may be disclosed in court or other forums.

Settlement-focused mediation fits best with hybrid models such as med-arb, in which information from the mediation can be used in later processes. During the mediation stage, parties are not expected to discuss relational or emotional issues. Accordingly, they will not be as concerned about information from mediation being used at a follow-up hearing. Their main goal is to settle the dispute, whether in mediation or in the follow-up process. The other approaches to mediation invite parties to disclose various levels of personal information related to emotions and relationships. Offering confidentiality and privilege in these processes is important if the mediator wants to encourage parties to trust the process and open up. Even when mediators offer confidentiality, however, absolute confidentiality cannot be assured.

3. Nonadversarial

Mediation is frequently viewed as an alternative to adversarial processes such as court, arbitration, and adjudicative grievance procedures. This perspective suggests the mediator's role is to encourage the parties to cooperate rather than compete. If the parties adopt power or rights-based approaches, the mediator may have difficulty moving them away from adversarial positions and tactics. However, the mediator may be able to help them work toward settlement in spite of their adversarial relations. Settlement-focused mediation would view settlement as success. The other models, however, suggest that the mediators must also resolve underlying issues or foster more positive relations between the parties.

Historically, some cultures viewed **reconciliation** (restoring relationships) as the ultimate goal of mediative processes (Bossy, 2003). The predominant view in professional literature suggests that success in mediation does not require reconciliation, although it might include fostering better relations. Paradoxically, mediation and reconciliation sometimes work in opposite directions. For instance, when a separated couple is involved in mediation over child custody and visitation issues, the purpose of mediation is to come to an amicable resolution whereby parents remain separated from each other. In contrast, reconciliation counseling is designed to help bring parents back together as a couple and as a reunited family. Some writers suggest that mediation is better suited to conflicts requiring some type of ongoing relationship, rather than when there is no prospect of a future relationship (Stulberg & Keating, 1983). Mediation can be used to help the parties renegotiate their roles into a different form of relationship instead of reconciling into the pre-existing one (Emery, 1994).

Consider: Is it necessary for mediators to help parties move toward more amicable relations, or is settlement of the immediate issues in dispute sufficient? Will settlements endure if the parties have not resolved their relational problems? Is reconciliation the ultimate goal of mediation?

4. Neutral Third Party

Most mediation literature and codes of ethics suggest that mediators must be independent, neutral, or impartial. However, the authorities differ as to which terms to use and what each of these terms mean (Mayer, 2004a; Taylor, 1997).

Independence suggests that the mediator has no economic, emotional, psychological, or authoritative affiliations with any party involved in the conflict. If the mediator is related to one party—for example, as a therapist, parent, lawyer, or teacher—then the other party might have concerns that the mediator will be biased. If the mediator discloses any affiliations to the parties, the parties have the option of accepting or rejecting the mediator.

Some authors equate neutrality with independence, but others go further. *In order to be **neutral**, the mediator must have no pre-existing biases, no decision-making authority, and no stake in a specific type of outcome. In addition, the mediator must not demonstrate bias toward one side or the other.* Each of these aspects of neutrality poses certain difficulties.

First, all mediators have pre-existing biases (Beck, Sales, & Emery, 2004). At the very least, aren't all mediators interested in helping the parties resolve their conflicts—amicably, constructively, efficiently, fairly, or effectively? Don't all people carry certain values and biases? One response to these concerns suggests that mediators must conduct a self-assessment of their biases. For some biases, a mediator can try to suspend them, so that they do not impose them on the parties. For example, a mediator who believes that religion is important must recognize that clients have a right to make their own decisions about religion. Biases that the mediator intends to bring into the mediation process should be disclosed. During the initial phases of mediation, for instance, mediators describe their approach to mediation. If the mediator values promotion of amicable relations, the parties will know this from the start and will have an opportunity to accept or reject services from this mediator.

In terms of no decision-making authority, most mediators would agree that they cannot mediate if they also have the ability to impose decisions on the parties. However, some conflict resolution practitioners use med-arb, a hybrid process in which they begin the process as mediators. If the parties do not come to a resolution in mediation, then the CR practitioner becomes an arbitrator and makes a decision for the parties (Shienvold, 2004). Similarly, a judge in a pre-trial conference uses mediative strategies to try to bring the parties to a settlement. If the parties do not settle, then the judge hears the case and makes a decision for the parties. In most jurisdictions, the judge who conducts the pre-trial does not hear the case if it goes to trial. If conflicting parties know that their mediator may become their judge or arbitrator, they may act differently in the mediation process. During mediation, a mediator wants the parties to feel free to disclose information, even if it might be embarrassing. If the information may be used in arbitration or court, the parties may be less willing to divulge information.

Although all four contemporary approaches to mediation say that the parties have a right to make their own decisions, some approaches allow for greater mediator influence than others. Settlement-focused mediators are most likely to use directive techniques in mediation in order to bring about a settlement. Interest-based and therapeutic mediators are less directive but still adopt strategies where the mediator encourages amicable solutions. Transformative mediators are the least directive mediators. They focus on facilitating communication and understanding rather than facilitating settlements. Still, they cannot deny that they have an influence on how settlements are reached.

The third aspect of neutrality, having no stake in a particular outcome, suggests that the parties are free to make their own decisions about how to resolve their conflicts. Whereas traditional mediators such as clergy and elders were able to influence people to conform to religious or community norms, most contemporary, professional mediators would not find this acceptable.[5] Still, mediators are subject to constraints and incentives created by the systems they work for. For example, if success in mediation is measured by what percentage of cases settle, then mediators may be enticed to pressure parties into settling. If a mediator receives funding from a body with a particular political viewpoint, then the mediator may feel pressure to guide the parties to solutions that fit this view.

The final aspect of neutrality is not siding with one party or another. This ensures that the process is fair and perceived by the parties to be fair. In some cases, this means treating everyone equally: giving both parties equal time to speak, ensuring that both parties feel heard, and providing negotiation support to both parties. One of the biggest controversies in mediation concerns how to handle an imbalance of bargaining power between the parties (described later). If the mediator intervenes to redistribute bargaining power, then is the mediator being neutral? If the mediator does not intervene, then is the process fair?

Consider the place of neutrality in bioethics mediation. In bioethics mediation, the mediator helps healthcare providers work through ethical conflicts with patients and family members concerning the care of the patient (e.g., the family of an unconscious patient want to keep the patient in intensive care, but the doctor views this as futile because the patient is going to die, and the hospital can use the intensive care bed for another person who has a greater chance of living). Bioethics mediators are usually employed by the hospital. Although the patient and family might have initial concerns that the hospital's mediator will side with the healthcare staff, there are benefits to having an in-house mediator. First, an in-house mediator is available to handle urgent situations. There may not be time to hire an outsider. Second, an in-house mediator has specialized knowledge of medical ethics, laws and policies governing what can and cannot be done, and mediation processes that fit best with this type of situation (Dubler & Liebman, 2004). In order for the family to trust the mediator, the mediator needs to establish neutrality by the way he or she responds to

---

[5]Whereas traditional mediators were often chosen because of their position and what they represented in the community, professional mediators are usually chosen because they are viewed to be neutral. They emphasize the rights of the parties to resolve disputes according to their own values and interests. Still, some mediators are chosen not because of professional mediation training but because of knowledge, status, and experience in a particular field relevant to the type of conflict. Lawyers for legal matters; accountants for financial issues; helping professionals for psychosocial, family, and community conflicts; business managers for organizational matters; and former heads of state for international conflicts are some examples.

the parties. Also, the hospital must be supportive of the mediator being neutral rather than supportive of staff positions and preferences.

Some writers suggest that mediators need to be impartial rather than neutral. *Impartiality refers to absence of bias or favoritism to either party.* The mediator must not side with one party or the other. Furthermore, the mediator must not be seen to side for one party or the other. The mediator's background is not relevant as long as the mediator can show by word and by deed that the mediator is not biased. Although this concept deals with some of the issues around neutrality, the question still arises about what it means to be impartial when there is an imbalance of power between the parties. Rifkin, Millen, and Cobb (1991) suggest that a mediator needs to demonstrate "equidistance" as well as impartiality. *Equidistance refers to the ability of the mediator to assist all parties express their "sides."* Equidistance allows the mediator to align temporarily with each party, so long as the mediator eventually assists all parties equally (Beck et al., 2004).

Must a mediator be independent, neutral, equidistant, or impartial? Why are these qualities important? Are they values that are inherent to all forms mediation? Are they simply means to an end? Can mediation be effective if mediators are not independent, neutral, equidistant, or impartial?

5. Equal Bargaining Power

Power imbalances occur when one party has more information, better negotiation skills, greater resources, or more strength than the other party. *Power balancing refers to mediation strategies aimed at rectifying power imbalances in order to promote productive and effective negotiations* (Lang, 2004). Power-balancing strategies include ensuring that the disadvantaged party has access to information, time to reflect before making decisions, opportunities to enhance negotiation skills, or support from others to counter the greater strength or resources of the advantaged party.

The issue of bargaining power raises important concerns for both proponents and critics of mediation. Basically, four views exist: (a) Mediators should only mediate if there is relatively equal bargaining power between the parties; (b) mediators should only mediate if there is equal bargaining power between the parties or if they can balance bargaining power through their interventions; (c) mediators should mediate regardless of bargaining power between the parties and have no obligation to rebalance power when an imbalance exists; and (d) mediators should never mediate, because they cannot properly assess for power imbalances and because they cannot properly redress power imbalances when they do exist. My own view is "It depends." Therapeutic mediators[6] are most likely to view power balancing as an integral role of the mediation process (Irving & Benjamin, 2002). Therapeutic mediators often deal with family disputes rather than commercial or public policy disputes. In family disputes, therapeutic mediators are aware that power imbalances frequently exist between spouses, as well as between parents and children. Balancing power is necessary in order to protect spouses or children from coercion, exploitation, and abuse. Accordingly, family mediators must be knowledgeable about how to deal with issues

---

[6]Particularly feminist-informed therapeutic mediators.

related to safety and power imbalance (Charbonneau, 1994; Flynn, 2005). Challenging power imbalances may also be necessary in conflicts involving social injustices (McCormick, 1997), such as racism, homophobia, and discrimination against people with disabilities.

Those mediators who do not view power balancing as legitimate often specialize in mediating commercial disputes. Although power imbalances exist in commercial relationships, businesses operate in a capitalistic, competitive environment. If the parties do not use a mediator, they would still negotiate under the dynamics of a power imbalance. Many commercial mediators believe that they should not interfere with the parties' relative strength in negotiating with one another. According to this view, power balancing is contrary to neutrality and impartiality. Why would a more powerful party submit to mediation if it knows the mediator will power balance in favor of the weaker party?

Transformative mediators also view power balancing as inappropriate. They emphasize the rights of the parties to make self-determined choices. This includes the right of the parties to choose whether to participate in mediation. If a weaker party believes that mediation will not be fair, then that party can refuse to participate in mediation. Transformative mediators do support the use of empowerment interventions, but differentiate these from power rebalancing. The purpose of power balancing is to redistribute power to the weaker party in order to ensure that the mediation process is fair. The purpose of empowerment is to provide both parties with skills and support to enable them to make self-determined, conscious choices (Bush & Folger, 2005). This still raises the ethical dilemma of the mediator's role when self-determination, fairness, and impartiality conflict (Menkel-Meadow & Wheeler, 2004; Ricci, 2004).

The settlement-focused and interest-based models of mediation do not specifically indicate how mediators should deal with power imbalances. It may depend on the context of mediation or the values of the particular mediator.

Some feminist critiques suggest that mediation between men and women is inherently unfair given the systemic disadvantages of women in society. Some are concerned that mediators are incapable of assessing for power imbalances, particularly woman abuse. Others believe that mediators are not able to power balance and assure the safety of women, even if mediators were able to assess for such problems (Girdner, 1990; Pearson, 1997). During the 1990s, feminist-informed models began to develop in order to respond to these concerns. Feminist-informed mediators conduct more thorough assessments for power imbalances and abuse. They establish firm ground rules to minimize the risk of exploitation or abuse. They are also very interventionist when abuse or power imbalance issues do arise (Flynn, 2005; Milne, 2004).

6. Mutually Satisfying Agreement

Although most definitions of mediation suggest that one of the mediator's functions is to help the parties reach a mutually satisfying agreement, this description fits best with the settlement-focused and interest-based paradigms of mediation. On the surface, this role seems obvious. Why would parties go to a mediator if not to get help to settle their dispute? If a mediator adopts a transformative approach, however, the role is to facilitate empowerment and recognition. Likewise, if a mediator adopts a therapeutic approach, then reaching a mutually satisfying agreement is not the only role. Therapeutic mediators foster more positive communication and relationships between the parties, as well as help them resolve underlying issues.

Although many mediators view agreement as a central goal for mediation, mediators must ask whether any agreement is sufficient. Must the agreement be fair? Durable? Reasonable? Legal? If the parties are satisfied with an agreement, then why should a mediator question their decision?

* * *

In summary, various mediation approaches lend themselves to different ways of handling cases. Further research is needed to answer questions about which approaches are most effective and for what purposes (Beck et al., 2004). Mediators tend to have different orientations depending on their professional backgrounds (Kruk, 1997). Mediators with mental health backgrounds tend to focus on family systems, affective issues, needs, and subjective criteria for fairness; mediators with legal backgrounds tend to emphasize the contract, cognitive negotiation, rights, and objective criteria for fairness (Hermann et al., 2003). Professional background may affect one's approach to mediation. However, the field of mediation has encouraged cross-fertilization between professions, in which people of different professional backgrounds are learning mediation from each other and blurring boundaries traditionally associated with their professional backgrounds.

Individual mediators and programs must determine which approaches to adopt. As you work through this chapter, consider how you will determine your model of practice. Will it depend on your values, the agency context, the clients' request, or which approach has proven clinically to be most effective?

WAYS HELPING PROFESSIONALS CAN USE MEDIATION

One area of talent that helping professionals bring to mediation is their ability to deal with process—for instance, facilitation skills, active listening, and helping people express feelings. Helping professionals also have content knowledge and expertise that are advantageous for mediating in specific contexts: divorce and separation, intergenerational family disputes, child abuse and neglect, community conflict, teacher-student conflict, altercations in healthcare and residential treatment settings, social policy development, workplace harassment, cross-cultural disputes, and criminal justice (Center for Social Gerontology, 1997; Cummings & Davies, 1994; Kruk, 1997; Wilhelmus, 1998). Some helping professionals focus on mediation between individuals. Others mediate primarily between groups and larger social systems (Kirst-Ashman & Hull, 2005; Zastrow, 2003). The following two sections illustrate informal and formal roles for helping professionals as mediators.

1. Emergent Mediation

Helping professionals are involved in both contractual and emergent mediation. Although the field of contractual mediation is growing, emergent mediation is still far more pervasive in practice. In emergent mediation, helping professionals retain their primary professional identification (e.g., as a psychologist, teacher, social worker, therapist, or counselor). They do not become mediators as such, and they do not even identify themselves as mediators. However, they can draw from a broad range of mediative techniques without becoming a formal mediator. Consider the following examples:

- Two professional colleagues are debating the ethics of a particular intervention. You offer to help them work through the problem. They see you as a professional peer rather than a mediator, though you are using a mediative approach.
- You are a community development worker. Your community is split about its goals. You use mediative techniques to help them build consensus.
- You are a physician who has an elder patient with advanced dementia and is seriously ill. During the course of treatment, family members disagree about the use of a feeding tube. As a physician, you have a professional opinion on this matter, but you also want to help family members reach agreement about how to proceed. You decide to assume a role as informal mediator (Back & Arnold, 2005).
- You are working with a family in which the teenager has rejected the parents' religion. In your role as therapist, you employ mediative strategies to help them come to a mutual understanding (Favaloro, 1998).

Professional codes of ethics for mediators (including rules related to competence, confidentiality, dual roles, and informed consent) do not specifically apply to emergent mediators. When acting as an emergent mediator, the professional is guided by the codes of ethics of his or her primary role (e.g., nurse, psychologist, teacher, parole officer).

2. Contractual Mediation

Unlike an emergent mediator, a contractual mediator is hired specifically to mediate. The process typically begins with an explicit Agreement to Mediate. The Agreement to Mediate, sometimes called a *retainer,* specifies the roles of the parties, the role of the mediator, and the parameters of the mediation process. Contractual mediators typically subscribe to a code of ethics for mediators. When a helping professional assumes the role of a contractual mediator, for example, it is generally inappropriate to carry on a dual role. Accordingly, it is important to consider whether a conflict of interest exists between your usual helping role and your potential role as a mediator. The following cases illustrate possible conflicts of interest:

- Priscilla is a psychologist who has conducted a battery of psychological tests with a client named Clint. Clint is going through a divorce and asks Priscilla to mediate. If Priscilla accepts the mediation role, what happens to the information from the psychological tests? Can Priscilla use this information in mediation? Does Clint's former spouse have access to this information?
- Charles and Chester are child protection workers. Chester is having a dispute with a family that is upset that Chester has put their children into foster care. If Charles offers to mediate this dispute, what concerns might the family have (Thoennes, 1991)?

- Alex is an antipoverty advocate. A government official asks Alex to mediate a dispute between two agencies that serve unemployed individuals. If Alex accepts this role, must he relinquish his advocacy role (Noble, Dizgun, & Emond, 1998)?
- Stephanie is a student who has been suspended from school. Her teacher, Tony, is also the chief mediator in the school's conflict resolution program. If Tony were involved in the original suspension, how could he act as a neutral or impartial mediator in Stephanie's case?

Conflict of interest is particularly problematic in small, isolated communities. In small communities, it is virtually impossible for mediators to have no prior relationships with the parties. While bringing a mediator from outside the community may be the answer, this is not always practical or desirable. Aside from the costs of bringing in a mediator, local mediators have the advantage of understanding the local culture and context of the dispute (LeBaron, n.d.).

Although some helping professionals work exclusively as mediators, most mediate as just one part of their practice. Social agencies and court-affiliated services are able to hire full-time mediators if they have sufficient referrals. Mediators in private practice, however, need to build referral sources over time in order to be able to generate sufficient cases to support a practice. In most jurisdictions, mediators cannot expect to simply hang up a shingle and wait for cases to show up at the door (Mayer, 2004a). Mediators need to become known in their communities, educating potential referral sources about mediation, generally, and their own services, in particular.

MEDIATION BETWEEN INDIVIDUALS: A CASE ILLUSTRATION

Rather than present a single model of mediation, the following description provides a comparative analysis that incorporates skills and strategies from the four approaches to mediation presented above. By reviewing an integrated framework, you can see how each approach handles similar issues. When you are mediating a particular conflict, you will want to assess the needs of the clients and make deliberate decisions about which approaches to mediation to apply.

The basic mediation framework consists of seven phases: preparation, orientation to mediation, issue definition, exploring interests and needs, negotiation and problem solving, finalizing an agreement, and follow-up. Settlement-focused and interest-based mediators are more likely to follow these phases in sequence, because one of their primary interests is directing parties toward agreement. Therapeutic and transformative mediators are more likely to use the phases flexibly, because their approaches are more facilitative and less directive. Although each approach to mediation entails certain core principles and strategies, each approach also allows for considerable variability.

Consider the following scenario:

Elvis and Englebert are two employees at Conflictia Software Enterprises (C-Soft). Elvis is 28 years old and has been with the company for 5 years. He is considered a senior employee in this young, progressive company. Englebert is 22, fresh out of college. In the 2 months

Englebert has been working for C-Soft, Elvis has subjected Englebert to a series of hazing rituals—shaving his head, putting tacky messages on the screen saver of his computer, and filling his mouse with blue pudding.

The next seven sections demonstrate how each phase of mediation could be approached by mediators with various perspectives. Toward the end of this chapter are seven role-play exercises, each focusing on one of the seven phases. Each role-play also includes an inventory of skills and activities to be considered at each phase of mediation.

1. Preparation

Cases can find their way into mediation through various avenues: self-referral, referral by third parties, or imposition by third parties. Englebert might request mediation, Englebert's friend might suggest mediation and contact a mediator, or Englebert and Elvis's supervisor might demand that they go to mediation.

The supervisor might decide to mediate the conflict personally, as an emergent mediator. One of the roles of a supervisor is to deal with relations between employees. Emergent mediation is less formal than contractual mediation. The supervisor would abbreviate, omit, and combine many of the skills and activities of mediation. For example, there would be no formal Agreement to Mediate and limited introductions, because the parties already have a relationship with their supervisor.

If the parties go to a contractual mediator, this could be someone who works for the agency (e.g., in their human resources department[7] or employee assistance program[8]). Alternatively, the mediator could be from outside of the agency (e.g., a private mediator, a mediator who works for a human rights tribunal, or a mediator who works for a service that receives cases diverted from court).

Assume that Englebert goes to his supervisor, Sheryl, to file a formal harassment complaint about Elvis. Sheryl suggests that they use the services of a human resources counselor to mediate their dispute. Neither Elvis nor Englebert knows anything about mediation. Englebert says, "You can't force me to go to meditation . . . medication . . . whatever." Sheryl suggests that they each meet individually with the mediator, so they can make informed choices. Contractual mediation does not formally begin until the parties have signed or orally committed to an Agreement to Mediate. Sheryl believes that mediation should be voluntary, so she says that there will be no negative consequences from C-Soft if they decide not to mediate.

The mediator, Medina, receives the mediation referral from Sheryl. *The mediator accepts basic information about the conflict from the referral source: who is involved, how can they be contacted, and whether the case includes any special concerns, such as a risk of violence.* Medina does not want to gather too much information at this stage so that the parties can present the information themselves. If Medina accepts

---

[7]Sometimes called a *personnel department*.

[8]Employee assistance programs traditionally provide counseling, vocational, and therapeutic services. However, some employers now offer mediation services as part of their employee assistance programs, harassment committees, or legal assistance programs.

more information from the referral source, she risks having the parties believe that she has pre-existing biases when they enter the process.

In order to prepare for mediation, the mediator contacts the parties, conducts preliminary assessments to ensure that the case is appropriate for mediation, arranges for interaction between the parties, and strategizes how to begin the mediation process. Because Medina knows this case includes a claim about workplace harassment, she inquires whether there are any safety issues: (a) Is the harassment ongoing? (b) Are the parties continuing to go to work during mediation? and (c) Has either party's employment been suspended? Sheryl says that both parties are continuing to work, but they have been placed in separate departments. She does not believe there are any safety issues. Medina asks whether either party has an uncontrolled substance abuse problem, mental illness, or other concerns that might hinder their ability to mediate (Barsky, 1997b). Sheryl says she does not know of any problems in these areas.

Medina contacts each party by telephone to arrange for the first mediation session. Settlement-focused mediators generally use this phase to schedule meetings, without further assessments. Other mediators, particularly therapeutic ones, assess the parties' willingness and ability to negotiate more thoroughly. Elvis indicates reluctance to mediate. He does not think he did anything wrong, so why should he be punished? Medina assures him that she is not there to judge or punish him. She has no power to judge or sanction either party. Englebert hints that he feels intimidated by Elvis but says he does not fear face-to-face contact with him.

To ensure that both parties can negotiate fairly, Medina decides to meet with both parties individually before bringing them together. If Medina took a settlement-focused approach, she would prefer to meet with both parties together right from the start. However, interest-based, therapeutic, and transformative mediators are likely to meet individually first if they are concerned about safety issues.

Medina considers possible legal issues that might arise in this case. Neither party has a lawyer. However, if harassment were proven, C-Soft could fire or discipline Elvis; Englebert could also sue Elvis for damages. Medina informs the parties about the benefits of obtaining independent legal advice and ensures that they have access to legal advice, should they be concerned about their rights or other legal issues. Both parties decline legal advice at this phase. Mediators from all perspectives need to consider whether legal advice is important. The extent to which they encourage or direct parties to obtain legal advice depends more on the nature of the legal issues than their approach to mediation. Still, settlement-focused mediators tend to be most directive about legal advice because they view the dispute as based in rights. Transformative mediators tend to be least directive, because empowerment includes the right to reject legal advice.

The mediator considers who should be included in the mediation process: Englebert and Elvis, Sheryl, witnesses, people who have participated in other hazing rituals, and support persons for both parties. She decides to begin with Elvis and Englebert, the two people directly involved in the conflict. Settlement-focused and interest-based mediators tend to limit the number of people in order to keep the process simple. Therapeutic mediators are more likely to involve support persons or others who are indirectly affected by the conflict. For instance, if Elvis had low self-esteem and was overly dependent on his mother for advice, the mediator might bring his mother into a premediation meeting to help Elvis work through these issues. Transformative mediators tend to give the parties more say about who to include in the mediation sessions. Bringing in additional parties is generally easier than asking parties to leave mediation. Accordingly, mediators can limit the number of people involved at the beginning and bring in others on an as-needed basis—for example, to balance power, to offer suggestions, or to help implement decisions made in mediation. If attorneys or interpreters are needed, they should be included from the start.

Medina arranges appointments with each party in her office. *The office is arranged in a manner that is conducive to mediation: private, quiet, impartial, and comfortable.* The room has a round table, enabling parties to sit around it and take notes. The light and color schemes are soft. Ventilation is good. The office is housed in the same building where Elvis and Englebert work. This presents two potential problems. First, others in C-Soft can see when they come to mediation, partially infringing Elvis and Englebert's right to confidentiality. Second, the office is affiliated with C-Soft, giving the impression that Medina might use the authority of the employer to influence the outcome of mediation (e.g., pressuring the parties to agree to terms that reflect the norms and policies of C-Soft). Settlement-focused mediators are less concerned about this type of issue than other mediators. However, Medina can raise this issue to see whether the parties are really concerned about Medina's affiliation with C-Soft.

2. Orientation to Mediation

The orientation phase begins with the first meeting with the parties, either jointly or individually, and ends with the parties agreeing to mediate. The primary purposes of this phase are to help the parties understand mediation and to obtain their commitment to a particular process. The mediator tries to establish norms that will ensure that the parties participate constructively.

As Medina goes to the reception area, she conducts a preliminary assessment based on a visual scan (Leviton & Greenstone, 1997). She notes that Englebert and Elvis are sitting at opposite ends of the reception area. They are giving each other no eye contact. They appear uncomfortable even being in the same room as each other. Englebert is nervously tapping his hand on his leg. Elvis is humming to himself, perhaps trying to imagine he is somewhere else. Elvis's clothes are immaculate, whereas Englebert looks a bit disheveled. Medina wonders whether this could indicate Elvis is more organized and perhaps more powerful in negotiating. She notes that these assessments are tentative and that she must be careful to avoid stereotypes.

Medina welcomes Elvis and Englebert by name, shakes their hands, and invites them into her office. As they walk back to her office, she reviews key points that she wants to cover in the opening of her session. She notes that it is important to model effective communication skills and encourage the parties to follow suit. She also wants to build trust by demonstrating impartiality. For settlement-focused mediators, the orientation phase is relatively short. The mediator provides an introductory statement that explains the goals of mediation, the role of the mediator, confidentiality, what happens if the parties come to an agreement, and what happens if they do not.[9] Each mediator personalizes the opening statement, so that it feels comfortable to the mediator and so that it is tailored to the needs of the parties. In this case, Medina might begin with the following statement:

My name is Medina, and your supervisor has asked me to help you resolve a conflict that has arisen in recent weeks. Sheryl has not given me the details of your concerns except to say that both of you are considering whether you can work things out in mediation. At this point, all you have committed to is today's session. If both of you agree to mediate, I will ask you to sign the Agreement to Mediate [Medina provides copies to the parties].

As a mediator, my job is to help you talk about your concerns and work out a solution that both of you can agree on. I am not a judge, and I am not going to make decisions for you. I may be able to make suggestions, but it is up to the two of you to decide what you want to do. I will do my best to remain impartial. In other words, I will not take sides with either one of you. If you have any concerns about my ability to be impartial, please feel free to raise these so that we can discuss them. Mediation does not work unless you believe that I am impartial. [Medina pauses to see whether the parties have any questions and to check what their body language may be saying.]

If you are able to come to an agreement, then we will work out ways to ensure that both of you are able to follow up on your commitments. This may mean having lawyers draft a legally binding agreement. Most of the time, these types of disputes can be worked out informally and we simply write a letter of understanding. This letter states your expectations, but it is not a legal document. I understand that you do not want legal advice at this time, but we will talk about it again if any legal issues arise.

If you are not able to reach an agreement, then we can discuss other alternatives. I understand there is a possibility that this conflict could go to the Harassment Committee at C-Soft. However, the Agreement to Mediate that I will ask you to sign says that mediation is confidential and privileged. I will not pass on any information to the Harassment Committee, your supervisor, or anyone else at C-Soft. At the end of mediation, you may agree to share certain information in order to implement the decision. C-Soft has assured me that it will honor your right to confidentiality in mediation. The main exception to confidentiality is when someone may be put at risk of physical harm. I have a professional obligation to take reasonable steps to help prevent the harm from occurring. Even if this comes up, I will try to obtain your consent to disclose information before taking further steps.

You probably have some questions about mediation and some of the things I have just said. . . .

Other issues that can be included are the credentials of the mediator, the length of time the parties can expect to spend in mediation, and ground rules for the process (e.g., one person speaks at a time; everyone will use respectful language; no smoking during mediation sessions; everyone will turn off cell phones). Some mediators are directive about the ground rules, indicating that the mediator is in control of the process. Other mediators have the parties suggest ground rules, supporting the

---

[9]In some jurisdictions, the laws dictate specifically what court-appointed mediators must include in their opening statements.

clients' ownership of the process. If there is a high level of conflict at the outset, the parties may be unable to negotiate ground rules. Accordingly, the mediator may be wise to provide at least basic ground rules at this phase.

Mediators select language that is neutral, positive, and future focused. For example, the introductory statement speaks of "concerns" rather than problems or disputes. The focus is on working out concerns and coming to agreement, rather than finding out what has happened or determining who is to blame. The introductory statement can be broken down into components to allow the parties to ask questions as the mediator explains various aspects of mediation. Each introductory statement needs to be tailored to the particular situation, including the nature of the dispute, the agency's policies, the clients' level of language, and the mediator's model of mediation. If either party is not fluent in the same language as the mediator, an interpreter should be used from the outset. The interpreter should be independent. Having one party interpret for the other creates a conflict of interest.

Interest-based mediators provide similar information in their introductions. However, they also describe the basics of interest-based negotiation and place more emphasis on collaboration.

> Mediation is a nonadversarial process. In other words, I will encourage you to problem solve together. I will begin by asking each of you, "What are your primary concerns?" As you explain where you are coming from, I'll make sure that we are all on the same page by asking clarifying questions and summarizing your concerns. We will then take this information to develop a list of issues to work on. I will help you prioritize which issues to work on first. For each issue that we address, I'll help you identify *common interests*. These are concerns or hopes that both of you share. We will then work on how to resolve these concerns. What types of solutions can we find where both of you are satisfied with the results? There are no winners and losers. Both of you need to be satisfied in order for us to come to an agreement.

Interest-based mediators are less directive than settlement-focused mediators. Interest-based mediators emphasize the parties' ownership of the dispute and any agreements they conclude. Interest-based mediators often highlight the advantages of mediation over adjudication.

> Mediation is less formal than the hearings conducted by the Harassment Committee. Mediation allows you to come to your own decisions rather than have someone impose them on you. You are the best judges of how to resolve your concerns. If you are happy with the solution, you are more likely to follow through than if the decision is imposed by a third party, such as the Harassment Committee.

Therapeutic mediators begin premediation with individual meetings, so they do not necessarily use a formal opening statement. Instead, *therapeutic mediators engage each party with a brief introduction and thorough assessment process.* They may explain the general goals and format of mediation, including the premediation phase, but they tend to use premediation to focus on assessment and preparation of the parties for the joint mediation sessions. Because the therapeutic model was developed specifically for family mediation, adaptations must be made for mediation in other contexts. Generally speaking, the mediator assesses the following areas:

- The ability of each party to communicate with the others
- The intensity of the conflict and how the parties seek to resolve differences
- The nature and extent of any violence between the parties
- The extent to which the parties trust or mistrust one another
- The degree to which each party exhibits flexibility
- The patterns of interaction between the parties and relevant systems (including social supports and sources of stress)
- The level of dependence or attachment between the parties in their relationship
- Whether the parties want to continue or terminate their former relationship
- The extent to which the parties can focus on the future
- The overall cognitive functioning of the parties (including how this may be affected by memory impairments, substance abuse, mental illness, or personality disorders)
- The ability of each party to carry out social functions relevant to the dispute (e.g., parenting, work)
- The financial, social, and emotional resources of each party
- Ethnocultural issues that are relevant to the issues in conflict
- Critical incidents that lead the parties to their current situation and request for mediation
- Potential conflicts with third parties that may impinge on the mediation process (Irving & Benjamin, 2002)

In order to conduct this type of assessment, Medina meets separately and then together with the parties. The individual meetings allow each party to ventilate their feelings and tell their stories without escalating conflict with the other party.[10] These meetings also give the mediator an opportunity to offer individualized support. Medina gives Englebert and Elvis some leeway to talk about the history of their relationship, but she focuses them on the present context of the conflict. She uses her active listening skills to confirm that she is hearing their perspectives, but she is careful to avoid responses indicating that she agrees or sides with either one.

In this case, Medina discovers that both parties are articulate. There is a moderate level of conflict between the parties. Englebert has acquiesced to the hazing rituals that Elvis has inflicted on him. There may be a power imbalance in terms of their stature in C-Soft and their respective levels of assertiveness. Elvis feels secure in his job. As a new employee on a 1-year contract, Englebert fears that his contract may not be renewed. His complaint to his supervisor came with great reluctance, not wanting to look like a "stool pigeon" or complainer. Englebert comes from a cultural background where direct confrontation is unacceptable. Elvis comes from a culture where assertiveness is encouraged.

---

[10]The downside of allowing the parties to vent in individual sessions is that they do not hear one another's stories. The mediator may learn information about one party that the mediator believes should be shared with the other. Accordingly, the mediator needs to let both parties know from the outset that the mediator will encourage them to share information with one another. See Exercise 7 at the end of the chapter.

Medina determines that it would be useful to have a second premediation meeting with both parties to help them prepare for mediation. This will give her an opportunity to rebalance power between the parties, so they can negotiate fairly and fully. For example, she can help Englebert understand that his position in the company is not in jeopardy because he has brought a concern to mediation. She can also offer to teach him assertiveness skills that are consistent with his cultural values.

Elvis is incensed at Englebert for complaining about him. During the first pre-mediation session, Elvis made derogatory remarks about Englebert's nationality. During the second session, Medina allows Elvis to process his feelings. They discuss ways Elvis can communicate his concerns without using bigoted comments or putting Englebert down.

Although therapeutic mediators explain the nature of mediation during premediation, they generally provide a second explanation during the first joint meeting. This ensures that both parties hear the same messages, supporting the notion of mediator impartiality and encouraging their joint commitment to the process. The opening statement is similar to that of an interest-based mediator. However, therapeutic mediators may give greater emphasis to building a more positive relationship between the parties.

> My job is to help you talk about your concerns and negotiate a solution that works for both of you. We can also look at your relationship. What type of relationship do you have now? What type of relationship, if any, would you like to have in the future?

Transformative mediators use their opening statements to explain empowerment and recognition in terms that are easily understood by the parties. Medina, for example, might begin with this statement:

> My job is to help you talk about your concerns so that you have a better understanding of one another. Each of you has your own view of what has happened in the past and what you would like to do in the future. You do not have to agree with each other about what has happened, but at least you can get a better idea of where the other person is coming from.
>
> In order to decide what to do in the future, we can talk about various options. If both of you agree to some sort of solution, we can put that agreement into writing. If you do not come to an agreement, then you still come away with a better understanding of each another's positions and the options available to you.
>
> One of the main purposes of mediation is to ensure that both of you feel that you have greater control of the decisions affecting both of you. I am not going to make any decisions for you. You decide whether you want to mediate, what you want to mediate, and even how you want to mediate.
>
> My role is to help make mediation a safe place for the two of you to talk. I will help guide the discussion so that both of you can speak freely and be heard by one another. I will also help clarify any misunderstandings that may arise.
>
> If you have any questions about how to communicate or negotiate more effectively, I can provide suggestions, but you will be the ones making all the decisions.

Transformative mediators encourage the parties to set their own ground rules. Medina asks the parties whether there are any rules that they think would help them engage in a safe and beneficial dialogue. Elvis asks for an example because he does not know what Medina means. Medina says some clients agree to a rule of "No interrupting one another; when one person starts to speak, the other will give him time to finish what he is saying." Elvis and Englebert say this rule is too restrictive. Instead, they agree to give each other equal opportunity to talk, but there may be occasions when one person can interrupt the other. This empowers the parties by giving them greater say over the process. They also learn skills for dealing with conflict on their own. If their rule proves problematic, they can review it and try to negotiate a more effective one. They are not completely dependent on the mediator for guiding them through the process.

Most mediators have a standard *Agreement to Mediate* that they ask parties to sign during the first joint session. This gives them the opportunity to review the agreement with their lawyers after their individual sessions. The Agreement to Mediate describes the parties involved, the role of the mediator, the terms of confidentiality and privilege, the issues to be mediated, remuneration for the mediator, and important ground rules. Some mediators include a statement about legal advice, so that it is clear they have suggested that the parties obtain independent legal advice from the outset of the process. The signatures of the parties indicate their commitment to the process.

Transformative mediators may encourage parties to build their own Agreement to Mediate or tailor the mediator's standard form in order to meet their needs. Negotiating the Agreement to Mediate may be difficult because of the initial level of conflict between the parties, their lack of experience with mediation, and the possibility that they will insist on terms that are inconsistent with the mediator's model of practice.

Medina asks Elvis and Englebert to sign the Agreement to Mediate as per Figure 4.1.

This Agreement to Mediate is relatively simple, using plain language. Some mediators use more detailed and legalistic agreements. The Agreement to Mediate should reflect the mediator's approach to mediation and legal issues that may arise in the context of the conflict. Consider which approach to mediation this document seems to reflect. How would you alter it to suit each of the other approaches to mediation?

Parties who have never mediated before often require repeated explanations of the mediation process. They may be self-absorbed in their feelings about the conflict, making it difficult to focus on the mediator's explanation of mediation. People frequently confuse mediation with adjudication, thinking the mediator will make decisions for them in spite of the mediator's opening statement.

If the parties do not agree to participate in mediation, the mediator can help them explore other alternatives to resolving their dispute. Therapeutic mediators, in particular, view referrals to other resources as an integral part of their role. In any case, mediators can leave the door open for parties to return to mediation if they change their minds.

Figure 4.1 | Agreement to Mediate

1. PARTIES: Elvis John Cameron and Englebert Younas are employees of Conflictia Software Enterprises (C-Soft) who agree to mediate a conflict that arose between them at work. They agree to act in good faith and to share all relevant information so they can work out an agreement in an amicable manner.

2. MEDIATOR: Medina Sellers has been hired by C-Soft to help employees resolve workplace conflicts. Her role is to help the employees discuss their concerns and work toward an agreement that satisfies both of their interests. Medina will act as an impartial mediator, meaning that she will not side with either employee or make decisions for them.

3. VOLUNTARY: Mediation is a voluntary process. Although C-Soft encourages its employees to resolve disputes in an amicable manner, C-Soft will not impose any sanctions on the parties for refusing to mediate or for failure to come to an agreement. Either employee may terminate mediation at any time in the process.

4. CONFIDENTIAL AND PRIVILEGED: All information provided by the parties during mediation will be kept confidential and privileged, unless the parties provide express written consent or the mediator is required by law to disclose information (e.g., if a person is put at risk of physical harm). The mediator's records will not be shared with other employees of the organization. The parties agree that they will not subpoena the mediator or her records for any trial, hearing, or other legal proceeding.

5. AGREEMENT: If the parties reach agreement during mediation, the mediator will write down the terms of the agreement in a letter to the parties. The agreement will not become a legally binding agreement unless the parties agree to have their lawyers draft a formal contract based on the terms set out in the letter.

6. LEGAL ADVICE: The mediator has explained the benefits of independent legal advice to the parties. They have both chosen not to hire lawyers at this time. The mediator will not provide legal advice to the parties but will ensure that they have time to meet with a lawyer during mediation, on their request.

7. FEES: C-Soft will pay the mediator $200 per hour for up to 6 hours of mediation. If the parties choose to mediate beyond 6 hours, then they will each pay the mediator $100 per hour for any time beyond the initial 6 hours. All fees are due prior to the mediation session.

Signed on April 23, 2006, by:

_____   _____

Englebert Younas   Medina Sellers

_____

Elvis John Cameron

3. Issue Definition

The issue definition phase begins with storytelling by each party and concludes with the parties agreeing on the specific issues to be dealt with in mediation. Medina's earlier assessment suggested that Englebert tends to avoid conflict, only responding more assertively when the cause of the conflict has exacerbated. Accordingly, she decides to have him provide an opening statement first. She tells the parties that Englebert will go first since he is the one that originally raised the concerns about what was happening at C-Soft. She reassures Elvis that he will have an equal opportunity to speak. She provides both Elvis and Englebert with paper and pens to write down any thoughts that come to mind as they are listening to the other person. Elvis expresses concern that he is being put on trial. Medina notes the purpose of this phase of mediation is to allow each of them to hear what the other is concerned about; she is not going to make any judgments.

If Medina adopted a settlement-focused approach, she would ask the parties to focus on present concerns. "What concerns do you want to resolve here in mediation?" She would put relatively tight limits on their storytelling or expression of feelings. If Englebert started to discuss why he took a job at C-Soft or how angry he felt when Elvis shaved his head, Medina would acknowledge Englebert's views but quickly refocus Englebert on what needed to be resolved in mediation. A settlement-focused mediator wants to get to the crux of the negotiable issues as expeditiously as possible.

If Medina used one of the other models, she would allow for more storytelling, historical detail, and expression of feelings. She might begin by asking each party, "What concerns bring you to mediation?" Interest-based, therapeutic, and transformative mediators are interested in having the parties identify negotiable issues, but they realize the parties may still need to process feelings. People need to feel heard—by the mediator and by the other party—in order to be able to move forward and negotiate solutions. When people say, "I want my day in court," they typically mean that they want an objective third person to hear their story. Paradoxically, "getting one's day in court" is more likely to happen in mediation than court. In court, lawyers and judges control what the parties can say and when. A mediator will use active listening skills to demonstrate empathy, without taking sides. The mediator will also encourage each party to use active listening skills, particularly a transformative mediator who wants to foster recognition.

> Englebert, thank you for sharing your concerns with us. Elvis, what were some of the main points that you heard from Englebert? You don't have to agree with him—I am just asking what messages you understand from what he said.

Empathy refers to demonstrating emotional identification or communicating a sense of understanding (Broome, 1993). The active listening skills identified in Chapter 2 form the basis of providing empathy and recognition. Whereas most helping professionals use these skills to demonstrate empathy themselves, the mediator's role is somewhat different. Mediators teach these skills to the parties so they can demonstrate empathy to one another. Each party learns about the other's perspective. In the process, they may develop joint understandings.

An interest-based approach focuses on clarifying the parties' issues rather than facilitating recognition. Englebert tells of 10 different incidents in which

Elvis harassed him but does not specifically identify what he wants to deal with in mediation. Medina responds:

> From what you've been saying, I understand that you believe that Elvis has mistreated you ever since you began working for C-Soft. Now, given all that has happened, what specifically do you think we need to work on during mediation?

Note how the language directs Englebert to identify issues for work, not positions or possible solutions. Parties often want to move to solutions early in the process. Unfortunately, this may cause them to become entrenched in positions before trust has been built and before the underlying issues have been identified. For transformative mediators, the process of helping parties clarify interests contributes to their empowerment. If they do not have a clear sense of the issues and their underlying interests, they cannot help but operate out of ignorance.

Therapeutic mediators have already heard the parties' storytelling in premediation. This allows the parties to vent some of their emotions. This also enables the mediator to help them articulate their stories more clearly and rationally. Still, each party needs some time to tell their stories to the other party, rather than have the mediator simply summarize what each party has said. As with narrative therapy (Winslade & Monk, 2000), the process of storytelling in mediation allows each party to explore symbolic meanings of their experiences. For Englebert, the experience of hazing at work may bring back memories of being mistreated at elementary school. Elvis was not previously aware of this. Medina offers emotional support.

For transformative mediators, storytelling is particularly important for recognition. As each person reviews the history of events, the mediator encourages the other person to acknowledge new insights or information. Elvis says that he thought Englebert was consenting to the hazing process. Elvis tells how surprised and angry he was when his supervisor came up to him one day and said a harassment complaint had been laid against him. Englebert believes Elvis is minimizing his actions. He also has trouble believing that Elvis thought he had consented to the hazing. Medina responds:

> You think Elvis knew that you were opposed to being hazed. Is there anything Elvis has said today that you did not realize before?

This allows Englebert to acknowledge that he did not know Elvis was shocked and angry when he received the harassment complaint. Elvis has not agreed with Englebert's points, but he has demonstrated some understanding from Englebert's perspective. This helps build trust between the parties.

Maintaining mediator impartiality can be difficult where, as in the present case, one party is the obvious aggressor and instigator. However, mediation is not about blaming. If Elvis feels judged by the mediator, he is likely to withdraw from the process. The mediator might believe that an appropriate solution includes an apology, compensation, or even punishment. The mediator needs to be aware of these biases and allow the parties to come to their own solutions.

Throughout the storytelling, Medina takes notes to help her identify issues and to keep track of important information from one mediation session to the next. She limits her note taking so that she can give the parties generous eye contact. Further, she does not want to appear as though she is gathering evidence. She allows both parties to see her notes. Her notes are not particularly interesting to either of them, because they do not include any of the mediator's interpretations or suggestions.

In order to help the parties clarify the issues to carry forward in mediation, Medina lists both of their concerns on a flipchart. As she lists them, she tries to reframe the issues so that they are more positive, mutual, and future-focused (see Exercises 15 and 16 at the end of the chapter for further descriptions of reframing). The issues listed include the following:

- What to do about the hazing that has already occurred?
- Will Englebert press his concerns forward with the Harassment Committee?
- What type of work relationship do Englebert and Elvis want, if any?
- How will Elvis and Englebert handle any future conflicts at work?

Medina checks to see whether the list of issues is exhaustive, balanced, and clear. The parties say that they have no other concerns. For the first issue, Medina tries to reframe "hazing that has already occurred" to "past treatment between Englebert and Elvis." Englebert objects because he did not mistreat Elvis. Elvis admits to hazing, so he is comfortable with the initial phrasing. Both parties summarize the issues, indicating they have a common understanding about the issues that need to be resolved in mediation. They begin to prioritize which issue to deal with first. Englebert says that he is not currently planning to take the case to the Harassment Committee, so that issue is not urgent. They agree that the first issue needs to be dealt with first, before they can move on to the other issues. Medina believes it would be easier to talk about their relationship first, to help build trust and collaborative spirit. Dealing with easier issues first also fosters momentum of agreement. If she adopted a settlement-focused approach, she might be more directive. However, the other models suggest giving the parties greater control over the process, particularly if they can readily agree on process issues. Medina congratulates them on being able to come to a clear and comprehensive agreement about the issues for mediation.

4. Exploring Needs and Interests

Exploring needs and interests is the crux of the interest-based approach. It may also be used in the other approaches, though it may receive less emphasis. *During this phase, the mediator encourages both parties to identify their individual interests as well as interests which they have in common.* Settlement-focused mediators move through this phase quickly, giving more time to problem solving than analyzing the problem. In order to deal with the issue of past hazing, Medina asks each party to identify their own feelings about what has happened. Englebert says he feels embarrassed, degraded, and alienated. Medina explores why he feels embarrassed. Englebert admits that he was not able to confront Elvis directly and had to go to his supervisor for help. He thinks he should have been able to stand up for himself.

Elvis says he is "pissed off" at Englebert for putting his job in jeopardy when all he was doing was fooling around. Medina validates Elvis's feelings and explores what is underneath them:

> I can see you're very angry at Englebert. This tells me that these issues are very important to you. Besides feeling angry at Englebert, what else do you feel?

Elvis says he's not into this "touchy-feely stuff." Medina responds nondefensively:

> You don't need to talk about anything you don't want to. I'm just wondering, when you mentioned you were "pissed off," what exactly were you trying to say?

This gives Elvis the opportunity to say that he was scared he might lose his job over a couple of pranks. A therapeutic mediator may have helped Elvis talk about feelings during premediation sessions. If Elvis is still uncomfortable disclosing feelings, the mediator will not push the issue too far.

For a transformative mediator, the previous exchange produces several opportunities to encourage each party to recognize the other's situation. Each has also been empowered to disclose information that he previously found difficult to disclose.

Medina shifts discussion to their self-identities.

> How do you think your coworkers see you? How has this conflict affected their opinions about you?

Elvis says that his coworkers used to respect him. They thought he had a good sense of humor. Once rumors of a harassment case got out, they started to think he was a bully. Englebert, on the other hand, always felt his coworkers thought he was a wimp. Having to go to his supervisor for help probably just confirmed this opinion. Englebert starts repeating his life history of being hazed and bullied. Medina refocuses him on the present issues.

She explains the process of interest-based negotiations and asks them to identify their underlying interests.

> We've talked about many different issues. Now, let's focus on your key interests. When you think about what needs to be done to deal with the hazing that's already occurred, what is really important to you?

Elvis responds that he wants Englebert to drop the harassment charges and advise their supervisor that they had worked things out. This is a position or solution rather than an interest. Medina helps him explore what interests underlie his suggestion.

> When you say you want the harassment charges dropped, why is this important to you?

From this line of questioning, Elvis identifies "job security" as a primary interest. Medina continues the process of helping Elvis and Englebert identify underlying concerns. Eventually, they arrive at the following list:

- Job security (financial security)
- Respect from coworkers
- Respect from each other
- An end to the dispute, as soon as possible

They agree that these are mutual interests, although they may have different meanings or levels of importance to each party. Medina writes these on the flipchart and commends them once again for their hard work and good faith.

5. Negotiation and Problem Solving

Negotiation and problem solving are the central foci of the settlement-focused approach, as well as integral parts of interest-based and therapeutic mediation. Although negotiation and problem solving also occur in transformative mediation, recognition and empowerment receive greater emphasis. At this point, the mediator has established trust with the parties. They have committed themselves to dealing with particular issues and they have identified their underlying interests. This phase moves them from interests to solutions.

Strategies at this phase include option generation, identifying objective criteria, and drawing the parties' awareness to the cost of nonagreement. These strategies are similar to what was presented in Chapter 3 on interest-based negotiation, except the mediator facilitates the parties through these processes. For example, both parties have expressed an interest in job security. Medina asks them to brainstorm options for solution. She lists their suggestions: both parties continue to work for C-Soft; Elvis quits and finds another job; Englebert quits and finds another job; they start their own company; they work for different divisions of the same company; they return to their old jobs; or one of them wins the lottery and they split the winnings. They cannot think of any other options at this time.

Englebert thinks Elvis should quit because he was responsible for the conflict in the first place. Elvis thinks Englebert should quit because Elvis has seniority and Englebert is still on probation. Medina explains the need for objective criteria for decision making.

> Each of you has good arguments from your own point of view. What we need is an objective way to analyze this problem. What factors would a complete stranger suggest for how to resolve this issue? Someone who doesn't know either of you and has no stake in the outcome.

They agree that their decision should be based on two factors: fairness and practicality. They define *fairness* as equal treatment (Menkel-Meadow & Wheeler, 2004). If one person leaves the job, then both also have to. It would not be very practical for both to leave their jobs, so they agree to work out a solution where both continue to work for the company. They like their jobs and think that they can work things out where they can work together, side by side.

Englebert says that in order for him to gain respect from his colleagues, Elvis needs to get up in front of all of the employees and make a public apology. Elvis rejects this solution out of hand and threatens to terminate the mediation process. Both parties start to raise their voices. Medina acknowledges their frustration but notes how hard they have worked to get this far. She suggests a brief break to allow them to regain their composure. Transformative and therapeutic mediators might be less likely to call a break at this point in time. Their processes are geared toward helping people deal with strong emotions, rather than simply negotiate rationally and calmly.

After the break, Medina reviews the process, emphasizing their progress and acknowledging their feelings about the impasse. A settlement-focused mediator is most likely to be directive at this point, emphasizing the cost of disagreement (their BATNAs). In this case, if the parties do not come to an agreement, Englebert's BATNA is to pursue the case through the Harassment Committee. This process could be lengthy, adversarial, and embarrassing to both parties. Neither one knows how the Committee would decide this case. An interest-based or therapeutic mediator may also draw the parties' attention to their BATNAs, but in a less directive or manipulative manner. The parties themselves would identify the consequences of nonagreement rather than have the mediator suggest them.

Transformative mediators are the least likely to put pressure on the parties by emphasizing the cost of nonagreement. Rather, they focus parties on the benefits of agreement, particularly how it can alter the way they manage and experience conflict. If one or both parties want to terminate mediation, ultimately, that is a choice the mediator must respect.

In this case, Elvis and Englebert agree to move forward in mediation. Englebert is reluctant to back down from his request for a public apology, feeling that he will look like a wimp once more. Medina offers the following metaphor:[11]

> Have you ever heard the story about the ship that sees a light shining through the fog? As the ship approaches the light, the captain puts out a call on his radio: "This is the captain of the USS *America*. You are headed directly toward us. Please turn your vessel portside to avoid collision." The reply comes, "I am sorry we cannot oblige. Please divert your course." As the ship moves closer, the captain becomes more adamant: "We have the right of way. You must alter your course to avoid collision." The reply comes once more, "I am sorry we cannot oblige. Please divert your course." As collision is moments away, the captain says desperately, "You must divert your course. This is the USS *America*." The reply comes, "You must divert your course. This is a lighthouse."

The parties laugh at the joke and then discuss its lesson. Sometimes it is better to back down.[12] Medina reminds them that there is a difference between backing down from a position and backing down from an interest. She encourages both parties to pursue their interests, in this instance, the respect of their coworkers. A public apology is one option, but not the only one. Elvis says he respects Englebert for reconsidering this issue. He wants to come up with a solution that works for both of them.

They explore various options and come up with one that seems to satisfy both parties' interests. Although Elvis was not prepared to make a public apology, he offered Englebert a sincere apology in private. They agreed to send a memorandum to their coworkers, explaining that they had gone to mediation and come to an amicable agreement. They worked through exactly what would be written and what each of them could disclose orally to their coworkers. They did not want to disclose the full details of the conflict, because both still felt embarrassed about it.

Mediation continues until they come to tentative agreements about all of the issues in dispute. Some issues became immaterial when other solutions fell into

---

[11]Source unknown.

[12]This story can be used for other lessons, including the importance of clear communication. Innocent misunderstandings can lead to grave consequences.

place. By this point in the process, the parties are able to work together collaboratively, with less direction from the mediator.

6. Finalizing an Agreement

*Once an agreement in principle has been reached, the parties must decide how to
finalize it: as an informal understanding, as a legally enforceable agreement, or as an
order of a court on consent of the parties.* This is not a case that has been filed in
court, so initiating a case just to secure a court order is not practical. The parties
agree that there is no need for a legally binding agreement. They believe the issues are
more about their relationship than about their legal rights. The mediator offers them
an opportunity to obtain legal advice, but both decline. They opt for an informal
understanding that the mediator will summarize in a letter addressed to both parties.

Medina works through the letter with the parties. A settlement-focused mediator is likely to suggest the wording of the informal agreement since this is most
expedient. A mediator from one of the other approaches is less directive and therefore more apt to ask the parties to suggest its wording. Medina uses plain language,
avoiding legalese. Her letter includes the following paragraphs:

> The purpose of this letter is to summarize my understanding of the terms you have agreed
> to in mediation. This is an informal agreement that is not intended to be legally binding.
> The agreement will work as long as both of you remain committed to it. If there are any
> problems with the agreement, you may return to mediation to work these out.
>
> Both of you agree to treat each other with respect. In order to promote a positive
> working relationship, you have agreed that you will not participate in any hazing rituals
> at C-Soft. You have also agreed to circulate the attached memorandum to your cowork-
> ers. Neither of you will talk to coworkers about other details or issues discussed in
> mediation.
>
> If either of you has a concern about how the other has treated you, your first step will be
> to meet with the other in private to discuss your concerns. If the issue cannot be resolved
> through one-to-one discussions, then either of you can request the help of a supervisor or
> mediator.

Medina reviews this agreement with the parties to ensure that it reflects their
intentions accurately. She asks about potential problems in implementing the agreement. Elvis says that C-Soft needs to consent to distribution of the memorandum
before they distribute it to their coworkers. Elvis and Englebert agree to take the
agreement to their supervisor to ask for permission to circulate the memorandum. If
they cannot work out the arrangements with the supervisor, they will contact the
mediator to discuss other alternatives. Ideally, the mediation agreement is self-
enforcing; that is, the agreement can be enforced by the parties themselves, without
the need for a third party to monitor and enforce agreement. If external monitoring
or enforcement is needed, methods of enforcement should be specified.

Many mediators leave it up to the parties to decide whether to return for follow-
up. Transformative and therapeutic mediators typically include follow-up as part of
their process. Accordingly, they will schedule a specific time and place for follow-up
before dismissing the clients.

The mediator concludes this phase by reinforcing the progress that the parties
have made and by offering encouragement to move forward. Settlement-focused
mediators reinforce the fact that the parties have come to their own agreement.

Interest-based mediators congratulate the parties on being able to work coopera-tively and resolve their underlying interests. Therapeutic mediators emphasize the parties' improved relationship. Transformative mediators encourage their progress toward empowerment and recognition.

7. Follow-up

Follow-up with the parties serves a number of purposes: the mediator can reinforce the parties' progress; new issues can be mediated; the mediator can refer the parties to additional services, as needed; and the mediator can solicit feedback for research and program development purposes. Therapeutic mediators, in particular, recognize that conflict is not over just because an agreement has been reached. Implementation of the agreement can raise a whole new set of issues: resistance from other people or systems; problems with enforcement; frustration or despair when things do not work out as well as expected; and conflicts around issues that were not previously expected. Conflict is not necessarily resolved but managed. Ongoing issues are apt to arise, particularly if the parties expect to have an ongoing relationship. Ideally, the parties have gained CR skills through participation in mediation. This enables them to deal with conflict more effectively on their own. Sometimes, the mediator frames the parties' agreement as a "nonbinding interim[13] agreement" or "trial run," so that parties can test out whether the trial agreement is working and return to mediation to see if the agreement needs any tinkering or more substantial renegotiation. Parties who seem to be heading toward impasse might be more inclined to agree to a trial run than a permanent agreement. If both try to follow the tentative agreement in good faith, they will be better able to reach a more permanent agreement at follow-up.

Although follow-up is not emphasized in the other models, follow-up could be used for different purposes. For settlement-focused mediation, settlement is key. Accordingly, follow-up could be used to help the parties ensure that settlement en-dures. The mediator[14] uses follow-up to monitor compliance. If there are problems with compliance, the mediator could help the parties mediate a revised agreement or explore different means of enforcement.

For interest-based mediators, the focal points of follow-up are satisfaction and ongoing collaboration. If the parties are not satisfied with the agreement, the medi-ator can help them renegotiate. If the relationship between the parties has soured, the mediator can refocus them on the importance of cooperation.

Transformative mediators would use follow-up to continue the processes of empowerment and recognition. By this phase, the parties have learned to take responsibility for their decisions and have learned how to demonstrate empathy to

---

[13]*Interim* refers to an agreement or court order that is only expected to be followed until a more perma-nent agreement or order is made. Sometimes, interim orders or agreements are made "without prejudice," which means that the parties' rights and obligations are not prejudiced by the terms of the interim order or agreement. If there is a possibility that interim agreements will affect the parties' rights, ensure they have access to legal advice before agreeing to the interim arrangement. Consider a divorce situation in which the parents reach an interim agreement stating the children will have temporary residence with their mother. This could create a status quo that would be difficult for the father to contest in the future, because courts are reluctant to change a child's residence once it has been established.

[14]Follow-up could also be pursued by an administrative person from the agency rather than the mediator.

one another. Follow-up acts as a booster session, to provide support for their continued efforts.

In the present case, Elvis and Englebert return for follow-up six weeks after finalizing their agreement. They review implementation of the agreement, including successes and problems. Englebert reports that distribution of the memorandum and responses to it were positive. Elvis also affirms a more positive work environment at C-Soft. Medina cautions them that there may be rough spots in the future, pre-empting possible disappointment if things did not continue to go so well. She also congratulates them on making their agreement work.

Englebert does have one concern. C-Soft had just issued a policy against hazing new employees. He feels somewhat embarrassed because people were calling this the "Englebert policy." Elvis demonstrates recognition by acknowledging how these comments singled out Englebert. As Elvis and Englebert talk about the Englebert policy, they begin to realize that it was nothing to be embarrassed about. Elvis jokes that he is jealous that there was no "Elvis policy." Elvis and Englebert agree that when people at C-Soft referred to the Englebert policy, they would add, "You mean the Elvis and Englebert policy," taking pride in ownership of this policy and removing the sting that some coworkers may have intended.[15] Medina commends them on the progress they had made since their first mediation session.

This case demonstrates many of the decisions, skills, and activities that comprise mediation. Some aspects of the process have been abbreviated for demonstration purposes. It is not intended to be "the perfect case." Each of your own cases will present you with a different set of issues, level of conflict, and possible approaches.

COMPARING MEDIATION WITH INTERVENTIONS OF OTHER HELPING PROFESSIONS

One way to gain a deeper understanding of mediation is to learn how the role of a mediator is similar to and different from other helping professions. For example, how is therapeutic or transformative mediation different from therapy (Favaloro, 1998)? Is settlement-focused mediation simply a form of legal practice? To what extent do you have to change your skills, strategies, and ethical standards when you switch hats from your original professional identification to that of a mediator? Figure 4.2 provides a comparison of three professions: mediation, social work, and law. I use the interest-based model of mediation, the generalist model of social work,[16] and a traditional adversarial model of law for the purposes of demonstrating these comparisons.

---

[15]This fits with the children's motto "Sticks and stones may break my bones, but names will never hurt me." Name-calling hurts only if one lets it. Often, minority groups that have been labeled with derogatory terms will take these terms and adopt them as a badge of pride (e.g., gays who accept the moniker "queer").

[16]The Generalist Intervention Model is one of the more popular models of practice taught in schools of social work. This model provides the foundation of knowledge, strategies, and skills that frame many different interventions with individuals, families, groups, organizations, and communities. Generalist social workers work with various types of social systems, often focusing on the interactions between these different types of systems.

Figure 4.2 | Comparison of Mediation, Social Work, and Law

	Mediation[17] Interest-Based Model	Social Work[18] Generalist Intervention Model	Law[19] Traditional Adversarial Model
Definition	• A specialized problem-solving process in which an impartial third party helps disputing parties try to reach a mutually acceptable settlement, by facilitating communication and negotiation between them.	• A planned-change framework that guides practitioners to help clients deal with biopsychosocial problems issues using a broad range of knowledge, skills, roles, and strategies, rather than specializing in a narrow range of clinical interventions.	• An approach to resolving disputes over legal rights and responsibilities requiring each attorney to advocate zealously on behalf of the particular client he or she is serving.
Philosophy	• Assists clients in dealing with conflicts in a manner that satisfies their underlying interests. • Focuses on relationships rather than rules. • Encourages joint problem solving.	• Helps clients cope and adapt to their social environment, as well as change their social environment. • Promotes social and economic justice. • Incorporates generalist social work knowledge, skills, and values throughout the planned-change process.	• Provides each client with a specialized advocate who uses positional negotiation strategies in hopes of maximizing rights and gains for the client. • Focuses on rules rather than relationships. • Provides each client with a legal representative in court who will debate legal rights and present evidence in favor of the client. *(continued)*

[17]For a detailed analysis of interest-based mediation, see Mayer (2004b).

[18]This column is based on Kirst-Ashman and Hull's (2006) explanation of the Generalist Intervention Model.

[19]Note that this column focuses on a traditional approach to legal advocacy. Many lawyers now use collaborative approaches to practice (see http://www.mediate.com/collaborativelaw).

Figure 4.2 | *Continued*

	Mediation Interest-Based Model	**Social Work** Generalist Intervention Model	**Law** Traditional Adversarial Model
	• Focuses on the future. Avoids assigning blame (restoration; remediation).	• Focuses on the present and future. Emphasizes responsibility for change rather than judging or blaming.	• In litigation role, focuses on determining blame (or legal liability) and innocence (or superior rights) for past acts.
Objectives	• Promotes social justice, defined by empowering the weak by helping establish alliances among disadvantaged groups	• Influences interactions between organizations and institutions, particularly for the benefit of oppressed or vulnerable groups.	• Promotes justice, defined as individual rights, equality, freedom, democracy, and security of the person.
	• Promotes community of interest rather than individual rights.	• Assists clients with achieving goals as determined by the clients.	• Holds guilty people accountable for their actions.
	• Redistributes power to correct imbalances.	• Enhances client's coping skills and abilities.	• Provides compensation to people who have suffered due to the actions of others.
	• Promotes satisfaction and settlement by resolving conflict amicably, consensually, informally, and efficiently.	• Facilitates interaction between individuals and others in their environment.	• Ensures all parties have access to professional representation.
	• Fosters win-win outcomes. (Bush & Folger, 2005).	• Obtains access to resources and makes organizations responsive to people.	• Enforces the rule of law.

	Mediation Interest-Based Model	Social Work Generalist Intervention Model	Law Traditional Adversarial Model
Assumptions and Perspectives	• Conflict is a natural phenomenon, dealt with effectively through collaborative processes.	• Client problems relate to interactions and stresses in various systems, including family, community, work, and cultural systems.	• Truth and justice are most likely to emerge in an adversarial process in which each party has a professional advocate.
	• Clients should be responsible for making decisions over matters affecting themselves.	• Clients have a right to self-determination but may be prevented from fulfilling their potential due to lack of resources or discrimination.	• Judges may be required to make decisions and impose solutions on people involved in conflict.
	• Clients are more likely to follow through on arrangements that they have discussed and agreed on.	• Clients are expert in their own lives and are capable of handling a range of biopsychosocial issues on their own.	• Clients do not have sufficient legal knowledge and advocacy skills to represent themselves in a dispute.
	• Mediators can deal with power inequities by providing a process that focuses on interests rather than positions, effective communication, access to information, and access to advocates who can provide support during the mediation process.	• Clients are more likely to fulfill their potential if they are allowed to function in a more supportive environment, which can include the support of helping professionals.	• Disputes should be resolved on the basis of who has the best arguments, based on current laws, case precedents, and the most credible evidence to support a case. Lawyers are required to ensure that legal rights and responsibilities are enforced.

(continued)

Figure 4.2 | *Continued*

	Mediation Interest-Based Model	Social Work Generalist Intervention Model	Law Traditional Adversarial Model
Roles	• Impartial facilitator, intermediary, negotiation coach, coordinator, and educator (information, not advice).	• Enabler, mediator, coordinator, general manager, educator, evaluator, broker, facilitator, initiator, negotiator, mobilizer, and advocate. • As mediators, generalist social workers enhance interactions between individual clients and systems in their social environments.	• Advocate, mouthpiece, draftsperson; interviewer, assessor, advisor, and counselor. • (Alternative roles for attorneys: arbitrator, judge, mediator, and lawmaker).
Values and Ethics	• Respect for all people and their ability to make decisions for themselves. • Full disclosure (sharing information between parties). • Confidentiality. • Collaboration and win-win solutions. • Consensus. • Professional integrity. • Clients have a right to competent mediators.	• Acceptance of and belief in the dignity and worth of all human beings. • Access to information (education as power). • Confidentiality. • Social relationships and supportive social environments. • Diversity of belief and opinion. • Professional integrity. • Clients have a right to competent social workers.	• Respect for human rights and freedoms (e.g., equality, life, liberty, due process). • Limited disclosure (only what is legally required). • Confidentiality. • Competition and winning. • Ambivalence—Tolerating coexistence of different and opposing attitudes or beliefs. • Professional integrity. • Clients have a right to competent lawyers.

	Mediation Interest-Based Model	Social Work Generalist Intervention Model	Law Traditional Adversarial Model
Client- Professional Relationship	• Clients agree on the definition of the problem and on the solution; the mediator is impartial.	• Client and social worker must agree on the definition of the problem and on the solution (mutuality).	• Client defines the problem and decides on the solution, with advice of the lawyer.
	• Mediator neutrality is crucial to establishing trust and fairness of the process.	• Rejects worker neutrality and impartiality as part of "professionalism" (positive obligation to promote social justice).	• Lawyers advocate for one party; neutrality is rejected unless lawyer is acting as a mediator rather than as an advocate.
	• Mediator is a reflective practitioner.	• Worker self-awareness is necessary to minimize distorted or maladaptive communication.	• Ability to think like a lawyer requires objectivity, but self-awareness is not emphasized.
	• Uses neutrality and empathy to build trust.	• Uses empathy, genuineness, and unconditional positive regard to build trust.	• Trust depends on integrity and expertise of lawyer.
	• Debate ensues as to whether the mediator needs to ensure a balance of power between the parties (Taylor, 1997).	• Workers have specific obligation to challenge social and economic injustice, including oppression and discrimination.	• Lawyers have special obligations to serve and protect those who are disenfranchised or deprived of their rights.
Structure / Phases	• Preparation—The mediator receives the referral and assesses whether mediation is appropriate. In some jurisdictions, mediation is mandated by the court	• Referral—Some clients seek services voluntarily while others are mandated by court or encouraged by others to attend.	• Referral—The client determines whether to hire a lawyer.

(continued)

Figure 4.2 | *Continued*

	Mediation Interest-Based Model	Social Work Generalist Intervention Model	Law Traditional Adversarial Model
	• Orientation—The mediator describes mediation to the clients and determines whether they want to commit to the process.	• Engagement—The worker builds rapport with the client through outreach, demonstrating empathy and respect, and explaining confidentiality and terms of service.	• Engagement—The lawyer spends little time on engagement or orientation, perhaps explaining expertise if the client asks.
	• Issue definition—The clients tell their stories and the mediator helps them identify issues to resolve.	• Assessment—The worker and client gather information about the client's strengths and needs in order to jointly determine problem(s) for work, goals, and priorities.	• Problem identification—The lawyer helps identify the problem from the client's perspective.
	• Exploring interests and needs—The mediator helps the clients identify their underlying interests, including mutual concerns.	• Planning—The worker and client determine the best way to proceed.	• Option generation—The lawyer involves the client in the process of exploring potential solutions.
	• Negotiation and problem solving—The mediator uses various CR strategies to help move clients to agreement (brainstorming, metaphoric storytelling, reframing, etc.).	• Implementation—The worker and client carry out the plan (which could include counseling, advocacy, mediation, problem solving, referrals, etc.). The worker and client jointly evaluate progress on goals and determine next steps, if any.	• Advice and decisions—The lawyer provides advice based on the client's concerns and values. The lawyer encourages the client to make any decisions that are likely to have a substantial legal or nonlegal impact.

	Mediation Interest-Based Model	Social Work Generalist Intervention Model	Law Traditional Adversarial Model
	• Finalizing an agreement—The mediator helps clients ensure their agreement is sound and helps them determine how to formalize their agreement (e.g., formal contract, court order, or informal agreement).	• Termination—The worker and client work through any outstanding issues, including emotional issues and possible referrals.	• Implementation— The lawyer pursues rights of clients through negotiation or litigation, as agreed. Termination of process may include a court order or the signing of an agreement.
	• Follow-up—The mediator contacts clients to offer further services, to help problem-solve, and to evaluate effectiveness of prior services.	• Follow-up—The worker contacts client to evaluate ongoing results, offer additional services, and promote ongoing improvement.	• Follow-up— Typically, lawyers do not follow-up with clients, but leave open the possibility that clients will re-initiate contact if the need arises.

Both law and social work view mediation as one of the possible roles that these professions include. However, when you analyze the orientations, values, and methods of the three models as described in Figure 4.2, significant differences emerge. The traditional role of a lawyer is that of an advocate who pursues the rights and interests of one party involved in a conflict. Similarly, most social workers are used to advocating for particular clients or causes. In order to assume the role of a mediator, lawyers or social workers must suspend their orientation as advocates and become impartial facilitators. Mediators allow clients to advocate on their own behalf. Although mediators support each party's ability to negotiate, they do not support a particular position or solution. Impartiality is one of the most difficult transitions for helping professionals to make when they become mediators.

In terms of values, law, social work, and mediation each emphasize the right of clients to make self-determined choices. They respect individuality and the self-worth of all people. Some people view law as contrary to self-determination, because courts impose solutions on parties. However, court is an avenue of last resort, even for lawyers. Preferably, conflicts are resolved through party-to-party or lawyer-led negotiations (Ellis & Stuckless, 1998). Court is used only when the parties are unable to come to a solution on their own.

The similarities and differences between professions depend on the models of intervention being compared. For example, the therapeutic and transformative models of mediation adopt methods that are similar to those used by clinical social workers, psychologists, and other mental health professionals. The settlement-focused model of mediation focuses more on rights and resolving legal issues, similar to the traditional practice of law. As mediation continues to evolve, helping professionals must consider how it relates to their original professional identities and what changes they need to adopt in order to assume the role of a mediator.

CULTURAL ISSUES

Cultural issues affect mediation practice from a number of perspectives:

- If the conflict is between parties from different cultural backgrounds, the conflict may be based on cross-cultural miscommunication, conflicting cultural values or beliefs, or dividing resources between people from the different cultures.
- If the mediator is not from the same culture as either party, the mediator needs to determine which knowledge, values, and skills are necessary in order to mediate in a culturally appropriate manner.
- Each model of mediation has a number of assumptions that may or may not be valid when working with people from different cultures.

The following two sections deal with these concerns by exploring cross-cultural issues between clients, as well as between mediators and clients. Sections 3 to 5 re-examine the value, knowledge, and skill bases of mediation in light of cultural factors.

1. Clients from Differing Cultures

Mediators must be prepared to explore whether the nature of a conflict is rooted in cross-cultural issues. Some mediators are reluctant to explore issues such as prejudice and power because they are afraid about exacerbating the conflict. However, if cultural issues are left brewing below the surface, the parties cannot deal with the real basis of the conflict. On the other hand, mediators must be careful not to assume that a conflict is caused by cultural issues simply because the parties come from different cultures. The following strategies may be useful in dealing with cross-cultural issues:

- Use recognition strategies from the transformative paradigm to facilitate understanding, reconcile past miscommunications, and foster mutual respect (Dubinskas, 1992).
- Validate different cultural beliefs, values, and ways of doing things, because many conflicts do not have a right and a wrong; reinforce that conflict is a part of diversity (Rabie, 1994).

- Separate interests and values; help the parties understand the conflict between their values and focus the problem-solving component of mediation on satisfying interests that exist regardless of their difference in values.[20]
- Use cultural interpreters to help each party gain better understandings of one another. If clients have lived most of their lives in a homogenous culture, they may have difficulty explaining cultural norms to others in language that they can understand. Cultural interpreters have had experience with more than one culture, so they have learned how to translate cultural norms from one culture to another.
- If the conflict is based on intergroup conflict, consider group approaches rather than mediation between individuals (see Chapter 5).

2. Mediator's Culture

Some proponents of mediation suggest that one of its advantages is that the parties can select mediators who come from the same cultural background as themselves. Although this point may be true, it is not necessarily an advantage nor a given. Some individuals do prefer to deal with a mediator from their own cultural background: such mediators bring an understanding of cultural issues into the mediation process. Furthermore, some people do not like to air their conflicts in the general community. For example, if the parties come from a discriminated group in society, they may distrust mediators from outside their group. Conversely, some people prefer to take their conflicts to professionals outside their community. The cultural group may be small and closely knit. If the parties are concerned about confidentiality, they may believe their privacy is easier to protect with an outside mediator.

Mediators can and do come from a variety of backgrounds. In many regions, however, the vast majority of professional mediators are people from middle-class, Western cultures. To some extent, this reflects access to professional education and mediation training programs. In some jurisdictions, mediators require a law degree or a graduate degree in one of the helping professions in order to be eligible for certification. These requirements block access to those who are not interested in or who cannot afford such education.

All mediators can expect to work with people from different cultures; thus, cultural-specific education and experience are integral parts of professional development. Competence to work with people from one culture does not ensure competence to work with people from other cultures. Cultural competence requires specialized values, knowledge, and skills (Barsky, Este, & Collins, 1996).

3. Values

Two values that are particularly important for mediation with clients from different cultures are cultural relativism and respect for individuality. *Cultural relativism*

---

[20]Because values are so deep-rooted, they are difficult if not impossible to change in a brief intervention such as mediation. However, parties can learn to respect one another's values without having to agree with them.

suggests that no one culture is better or worse than another; they are simply differ-ent. Accordingly, mediators must demonstrate respect for cultures that are different from their own, rather than judge or impose values on them. Respect for individual-ity suggests that individual differences among people from the same culture must also be respected. Mediators need to caution against stereotypes or other generaliza-tions that ignore diversity within the cultural group.

Neutrality is not a universal value for mediation. Within some cultural traditions, mediators assume the role of an "insider partial," rather than "outsider neutral" (LeBaron, n.d.). Insider partials provide moral guidance or encourage the parties to resolve their conflicts in accordance with particular values or laws. Parties trust these mediators because of their local connection and moral authority, rather than their neutrality. Although professional mediators from outside the parties' culture must be wary of imposing values on the parties, a mediator from within the culture may have greater latitude to refer clients to moral principles accepted within their group. Such mediators should indicate their value biases to the clients up front (e.g., "Because this is an Ismaili mediation center, I may ask you to consider teachings from the Qu'ran to help you resolve your concerns"). If the parties consent to a mediator's biases, then neutrality may not be essential.

4. Knowledge and Process

Knowledge required for cultural competence depends on the context of the conflict. In general, the mediator needs to inquire into how the parties and their cultures view each of the following (LeBaron, 1997):

- What constitutes a conflict?
- How should conflict be approached?
- Which process is most appropriate for intervention?
- What constitutes resolution?

Consider the following case.

Conflictia High School recently suspended Raphael Florez for acting violently in the schoolyard. The Florez family believes that Raphael, subjected to racist taunting, was justified in defending himself.

In order to answer questions about conflict with this particular family, the mediator can draw on a number of sources: the family members themselves, cultural interpreters, other helping professionals from their community, readings, and research. Mediators tend to view conflict as something to be resolved. Members of the Florez family, however, have experienced ongoing racism. They believe that con-flict of this sort needs to be confronted and challenged. To them, resolution sounds as if they are being told to accept the status quo.

In terms of whom to involve in mediation, the mediator needs to identify how the family members would identify the parties. This family views the affront to Raphael as a family issue rather than an individual one. Accordingly, the mediator should consider involving family members, not just Raphael (Sue, 2006). In some cases, conflict is viewed as a group issue. The mediator may need to involve leaders or representatives of the group.

In terms of how to approach the conflict, the mediator needs to accommodate the school and the family. In this case, the school prefers to deal with conflict through a rational, structured dialogue. The family is accustomed to more open expression of emotion and informal discussions. The family wants to have a public forum, whereas the school wants to keep the process confidential.

With regard to developing an appropriate process, mediators have three primary options: (1) use their general model of practice, and try to be sensitive to the needs of people from different cultures within the general model; (2) adapt their model to meet the specific needs of the specific cultures; or (3) create a new model of conflict resolution by learning about the means of conflict resolution used traditionally within the culture. For the last alternative, the mediator works in partnership with the culture in order to develop the culturally specific approach to conflict resolution (LeBaron, 1997; Lederach, 1995). The process becomes more complicated when, as in the present example, the parties come from different cultures.

In this case, the mediator begins by having separate meetings with the family and with the school. This approach enables the mediator to explore their values and beliefs about conflict and the way it should be resolved. The mediator finds that the parties share some values: both want the conflict to be resolved, they are looking for a process that is fair, and they define fairness as having a mediator who does not take sides. Where the mediator identifies contradictory values and beliefs, the mediator will have to make tough choices. Believing that it will be more difficult to engage the family, the mediator decides to tailor some of the process to their needs. Also, the school is represented by teachers and the principal, professionals who should be willing to make accommodations for the family. The mediator develops and proposes a hybrid process to the family and the school. The mediation process is voluntary. Mediation only proceeds if both parties consent to the process.

5. Skills

Culturally competent mediators adapt their use of skills to the needs of different groups. This requires an understanding of the group's norms of communication and conflict resolution styles (Irving & Benjamin, 1995). The following mediator skills are particularly useful for situations where the parties' culture is different from that of the mediator:

- Checks out assumptions on meanings of terms and phrases
- Presents issues or ideas as they are perceived from the parties' perspectives
- Uses short, clear sentences
- Uses concrete examples and specific language
- Avoids idiomatic expressions, mixed messages, abstractions, or unfamiliar terms
- Indicates appreciation and respect for the dignity of the parties and the groups to which they belong

- Promotes an environment that allows for sharing of selected (appropriate) cultural information
- Tolerates ambiguity
- On making an interactive mistake, acknowledges it in a nondefensive manner (e.g., apologize, acknowledge your limitations, indicate your intent to learn how to avoid mistakes in the future)
- Acknowledges differences in beliefs, values, and norms
- Makes tentative suggestions ("I wonder if . . .")
- Acknowledges interest in and unfamiliarity with the parties' culture
- Recognizes that the parties know more than the mediator about their culture
- Thanks parties for helping the mediator understand the parties' culture
- Asks about the parties' natural or informal support systems (including who is involved in making different types of decisions)
- Uses appropriate self-disclosure to help build a positive working relationship (Barsky et al., 1996; Greey, 1994; Kavanaugh & Kennedy, 1992)

Mediators can expect to invest considerable time in order to learn how to work effectively with people from a different culture. Cultural competence develops over time through experience, feedback, reading, and reflection. Conflict occurs not only between the two parties but between each party and the mediator. Mediators can make positive use of conflict with the parties by modeling conflict resolution skills for them.

KEY POINTS

- The role of a mediator is to provide parties with support so they can negotiate more effectively.
- Mediation can be provided by both professionals and nonprofessionals, though each may operate on different assumptions about the nature of mediation and the appropriate roles of a mediator.
- A professional's choice of approaches to mediation depends on the professional's value base, as well as how the mediator views success.
- Settlement-focused mediators emphasize expedient resolution of manifest conflict.
- Interest-based mediators engage the parties in a joint problem-solving process in order to help them resolve the conflict and their underlying interests in a mutually satisfactory manner.
- Therapeutic mediators assist parties with emotional and relational issues in order to be able to resolve their conflict more effectively.
- Transformative mediators foster empowerment and recognition between the parties, helping them change the way they deal with conflict.
- When selecting or developing a model of mediation, mediators need to consider the following issues: voluntary or coerced participation, neutrality, impartiality, fairness, power imbalances, confidentiality, and definitions of successful mediation.

- Helping professionals can act as emergent or contractual mediators in a range of contexts, including family, mental health, cross-cultural, criminal justice, workplace, public policy, and community conflicts.

- Mediation can be broken down into seven phases: preparation, orientation, issue definition, exploring interests and needs, negotiating and problem solving, finalizing an agreement, and follow-up.

- In order to switch from one's conventional helping role to the role of mediator, a helping professional needs to identify key differences in skills, strategies, values, and manners of interaction with clients.

- When working with people from different cultural backgrounds, mediators need to decide whether to use a standard model of mediation, to adapt their standard model, or to develop a culturally specific model of mediation.

- Cultural competence in mediation requires that mediators develop knowledge, values, and skills to be able to work with people from specific cultural groups.

DISCUSSION QUESTIONS AND EXERCISES

1. MEDIATION SUCCESS: Identify a conflict situation in which you see yourself as a potential mediator. As a mediator, what would your goals for mediation be in these circumstances? Refer back to your answers to Exercise 2, "Negotiation Success," in Chapter 3. Are there any differences between how you view success as a mediator and success as a negotiator? Does it depend on the context of the conflict?

2. MEDIATOR VALUES: As a *mediator*, what are your primary values? List your top five in order of priority. Consider the following, but feel free to add your own: safety, fairness, respect for all individuals, empowerment, neutrality, autonomy, access to resources, harmony, change, privacy, competence, and mutual understanding.

3. IMPARTIALITY DILEMMA: You are facilitating a play therapy group for 6-year-olds who have experienced physical abuse from their parents. During the third session, two children start to fight over one of the puppets. You decide to use your mediative skills to help them resolve this conflict. You encourage them to come up with their own decision rather than impose one on them. You are able to help them work toward a mutually agreeable solution: rip the puppet into small pieces so neither of them can fight over it anymore. You personally find this solution troubling because it is violent and destructive. Still, you have encouraged the children to develop their own solution. Do you support their decision or direct them to a different type of solution? What factors do you consider in making your decision?

4. OTHER APPROACHES: This chapter focuses on four approaches to mediation. There are many other models of mediation and mediation-like interventions—for example, narrative mediation (Winslade & Monk, 2000), "mediating dangerously" (Cloke, 2001), Milanese family mediation (Fong, 2005), Native

North American healing circles (Green, 1998; Stuart, 1997), ho'opono pono in Hawaii (Wall & Callister, 1995), and sulha in Arab communities (Jabbour, 1996). Select one of these models. Conduct a literature review on this model to identify its key assumptions, components, and strategies. Compare this model to one of the models analyzed in this chapter.

5. CRITIQUING MEDIATION: Review the mediation case illustration between Englebert and Elvis. Select one phase of the process. Identify the strengths and limitations of how Medina handled this phase. What other issues and alternatives could have been considered?

6. CONFIDENTIAL OR NONCONFIDENTIAL: The examples of an *opening statement* and *Agreement to Mediate* in Elvis and Englebert's case describe **confidential mediation** (which some jurisdictions call **closed mediation**). In confidential mediation, information from the mediation cannot be used for court or other purposes. The parties are agreeing that the mediator and the mediator's files cannot be subpoenaed. If the parties agree to **nonconfidential mediation** (sometimes called **open mediation**), then either party can use information from the mediation in other processes, particularly if the parties do not come to a full agreement. In nonconfidential mediation, the mediator provides a report at the end of the process, summarizing the issues, underlying interests, and final offers or positions on the issues. The mediator does not provide recommendations. The parties can give the report to a judge, arbitrator, or other professional who may be hired to help them resolve their conflict. What are the advantages of confidential mediation? What are the advantages of nonconfidential mediation?

7. CAUCUSING DILEMMA: Some mediators never meet individually with the parties. Others meet with the parties individually to screen for safety issues, to help with power balancing, or to help parties resolve an impasse. What happens if a party shares important information with the mediator but refuses to allow the mediator to disclose it to the other party? Under what circumstances should the mediator disclose the information? When should the mediator keep the information confidential? How can the mediator pre-empt this sort of dilemma (Menkel-Meadow et al., 2005)?

8. POWER PLAYS: Bush and Folger (2005) suggest that it is appropriate for transformative mediators to empower parties but not to rebalance power between them. What is the difference, if any, between "empowering" and "power balancing?" How do mediators using different models view the appropriateness of each?

9. CONTRASTS: Earlier in the chapter, I provided a comparison between mediation, social work, and law. In order to conduct a similar analysis, select an approach to mediation (e.g., transformative, narrative, or therapeutic) and a model of intervention from your own profession (e.g., cognitive restructuring, solution-focused therapy, strategic family therapy, structured family therapy, psychoanalysis, radical social work, andragogy, restorative justice, Leininger's transcultural nursing model, or feminist counseling). Using a chart similar to that in Figure 4.2, compare these two models in terms of their definitions, philosophies, objectives, assumptions, roles, values and ethics, client-professional relationship, and structure. Which roles, ethics, methods, and so on, can you

transfer from your original profession to mediation? What are the key changes you need to make when you take on the role of a mediator?

10. COMEDIATION: *Comediation* refers to mediation conducted by two or more mediators. Identify the advantages and disadvantages of comediation. Under what circumstances is comediation advisable?

11. DEAL WITH THE DEVIL: Andrew is addicted to alcohol. One evening, he finds himself without cash or alcohol. Suffering from withdrawal symptoms, he screams out, "I'd sell my soul for a 12-pack of beer." Suddenly, the Devil appears. The Devil says, "I'll give you six beers for your soul." They haggle back and forth but are unable to come up with an agreement. They decide to hire you as their mediator. What ethical issues are raised by this case? How would you handle them? What techniques could you use if you wanted to balance power between the parties?

12. CULTURAL VALUES DILEMMA: As a mediator, you respect your clients' right to self-determination and their cultural diversity. You also believe in cultural relativism. Consider a case in which all the clients come from the same culture, but that culture is different from your own. The conflict is a noise-related dispute between two couples who live in adjacent apartments. During mediation, the husbands speak on behalf of their wives, even though the primary conflict occurred between the women. According to their culture, women are not permitted to speak directly with the mediator or with men other than their husbands. You find this belief offensive. How do you reconcile your values and deal with this situation?

13. CULTURAL HETEROGENEITY: In Exercise 12, you are asked to consider clients who "come from the same culture." Although there are similarities between people from the same culture, there are also differences (e.g., people from different subcultures, people with different personalities, people with different life experiences). Conversely, there are often more similarities between people from different cultures than differences. How can a mediator use information about culture without falling into the traps of stereotyping and overgeneralizing?

14. PEACEMAKING AND GENDER: Which gender attributes are more compatible with the role of a mediator, male or female? Which male attributes are associated with being a good mediator? Which female attributes might contribute to a woman's ability to act as mediators (Kolb & Williams, 2003)?

15. REFRAMING: *Reframing* refers to looking at a situation from a different context or perspective (Bandler & Grinder, 1982). Consider how a painting changes appearances when you change its frame or how different people look if you view them face-to-face as opposed to from an aerial view. To illustrate, consider the following figure:

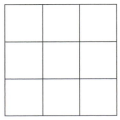

Count the number of squares in this figure and write down *the number of squares that you see*. Ask others in the class to do the same. Compare answers. If there are any differences, how do you account for these? Is there only one right answer?

16. REFRAMING, THE SEQUEL: Reframing is a key skill in mediation. One method for reframing is to restate what someone has said (a) to express it in positive terms, (b) to eliminate blame or accusation, (c) to identify underlying concerns, fears, interests, needs, values, or goals, or (d) to identify common ground. The following structure can be used to implement this method:

"You seem to feel . . ." (identifying an underlying concern or fear, in order to show you understand how the person feels)
"Both of you/All of us . . ." (identifying a mutual interest, need, value, or goal)
"Why don't we . . ." (identifying problem-solving approach)

To practice reframing, try using these suggestions to develop an appropriate response for each of the following scenarios.

Example: During mediation between Leo and Leona (two coworkers), Leona says, "You're a racist, male chauvinist pig." How could the mediator reframe this in a more positive tone, without ignoring or minimizing Leona's primary concerns?

Reframe: "Leona, I can hear that you're quite angry with Leo. . . . [pause for response] Both of you are planning on working for this company for a long time. Would both of you agree that it's important to develop a more respectful working relationship? [pause for response] Perhaps we could talk about how to ensure that this is a safe and comfortable place to work, regardless of one's sex or ethnocultural background. . . .

a. In a divorce mediation where child custody is in issue, one parent tells the other, "You're wrong. The children need to live with me." How could the mediator reframe this?

b. At a case conference, agency staff members are debating whether to admit a client for services even though he is an undocumented alien. Agency policy suggests that they only provide services to current citizens. One professional argues, "If we can't offer service to this client, then we might as well close up shop." How could the chair of the meeting reframe this?

c. A clinical supervisor is having a meeting with a client and a therapist. The client is upset about how she has been treated by the therapist. The client says, "Two thousand therapists in this city, and I ended up with you!" How could the supervisor reframe the client's statement?

d. A mediator in a child protection case has a client who seems resistant to any kind of help. The mediator wants to say, "If you're not going to cooperate, then I really can't help you." How could the mediator reframe this thought in a more positive fashion?

e. A client screams to an intake worker, "What do you mean there's a 6-month waiting list?" How could the intake worker reframe this concern?

f. Two residents in a nursing home, Juan and Talina, are arguing over which show to watch on the communal television. Juan says he has the remote control so he gets to decide. Talina responds, "Who made you dictator?" How could a staff member reframe this exchange and encourage the parties to focus on a mutual concern?

g. A student who is concerned about getting a B on a test tells her professor, "I get A's in all my other classes." How could the professor respond to this, using a reframe?

h. During a meeting of the Student Representative Council, one student says, "This council is useless. You never get anything done." How could the council president respond, using a reframe?

17. REPACKAGING PROPOSALS FROM LOSS TO GAIN: According to the concept of *loss aversion*, people will often accept risks to avoid a loss, but avoid risks when faced with a gain. Accordingly, people are more likely to risk going to court to avoid a loss but less likely to go to court if they perceive a gain that they might lose in court. This means that mediators can help parties accept an offer by repackaging offers that sound like losses into gains (Dubler & Liebman, 2004). Try repackaging the following proposals from losses into gains.

Example:

ETHEL'S INITIAL PROPOSAL: Fred must turn off his stereo by 10 P.M.

REPACKAGED: Fred may enjoy playing his stereo until 10 P.M.

Proposals to be repackaged:

a. Matilda will sell the house and give half the proceeds of sale to Gus.

b. Estaban will give up his claim to compensation for emotional pain if Noto-Corp gives him his job back.

c. As punishment for breaching confidentiality rules under the Conflictian Psychotherapy Association's Code of Ethics, Sabrina agrees not to practice psychotherapy for two years.

18. MEMORANDUM OF UNDERSTANDING: Consider the following memorandum of understanding, written by a mediator in a case between a mental health patient and a long-term care facility:

The parties of the first part and of the second part hereby agree that Mr. Paul Paterson will stop harassing the nursing staff by calling them in the middle of the night for trivial matters. If Mr. Paterson continues this immature behavior, he will be immediately discharged from the Shady Firs Residence. The residence accepts no responsibility for Mr. Paterson's welfare should the Residence need to discharge Mr. Paterson.

Critique this memorandum (identifying its strengths and limitations) according to the following criteria: clear, plain language; balanced and impartial; future focused; nonjudgmental; and sufficient detail so parties know what is expected of each. Rewrite the memorandum in a way that deals with the limitations you have identified. Feel free to use your creativity.

ROLE-PLAYS: GENERAL INSTRUCTIONS

The following role-play exercises are designed to help you practice each phase of the mediation process. Each of the first seven role-play descriptions includes an inventory of skills and activities that fit with the particular phase of mediation (Bush & Folger, 2005; English & Neilson, 2004; Irving & Benjamin, 2002; Leviton & Greenstone, 1997; Mayer, 2004b). You will use different skills or emphasize them in different ways, depending on the approach to mediation that you are using. For learning purposes, select an approach that you want to learn and then identify the skills and activities that you want to focus on. When you are mediating with real clients, your choice of approaches, skills, and activities will depend on your agency's mandate, the dynamics between the parties, the issues to be resolved, the wishes of the parties, and how you and the parties define success.

These inventories can also be used as a checklist for professional development and self-evaluation purposes.[21] Mark "C" for each area of competence and "W" for each area requiring more work. Use the exercises in this course to practice the Ws. If you are using these inventories to give others feedback on their mediation skills, identify positive examples of how they used different skills. For areas where they could use help, suggest alternatives that you might have tried.

The reason that each of the following mediation role-plays focus on a distinct phase is to facilitate learning. As you are learning new skills, it is easier to try to master the process one phase at a time. In practice, experienced mediators will not follow the phases in a linear fashion. There are many overlaps between phases and the skills required for various phases. Assessment of power and safety issues, for instance, occurs on an ongoing basis. In addition, mediators often circle back and forth between phases. If parties seem to be getting stuck at one phase, the mediator may loop back to an earlier phase or jump ahead to a later phase. As you become more familiar with the various components of mediation, you will learn to integrate them more flexibly.

ROLE-PLAY 4.1: "DIAS DIVORCE"—PREPARATION

Mrs. Dias and Mr. Dias have recently separated. Mr. Dias's lawyer, Ms. Lopez, filed an application in court asking for interim (temporary) custody of their two children, Lenny (5) and Skeeter (7). Mrs. Dias does not have a lawyer. A judge hearing the application ordered Mr. Dias and Mrs. Dias to go to mediation. Ms. Lopez is not a big fan of mediation, but she agreed to contact a mediator, Michael Moore, and arrange for the parties to go for mediation. This role-play involves a telephone call between Ms. Lopez and Michael.

Ms. Lopez will initiate the phone call and ask about mediation services for the Dias family. She will let the mediator know that she does not generally trust mediation because mediators tend to favor women, information in mediation could be used in court, and mediators do not know enough about the law to advise clients properly or help them win their rights. The only reason she is initiating the referral is because of the judge's order. Ms. Lopez suggests that Mrs. Dias is mentally ill, with

---

[21]For competencies specific to family mediation, see English and Neilson (2004).

paranoia or something, so mediation may be inappropriate. Both Mr. Dias and Skeeter have a speech impediment (stuttering).

Michael, a mental health professional by background, should select three or four items from the following inventory to focus on (Figure 4.3). Also, Michael should identify an approach to mediation that he plans to use (interest-based, therapeutic, etc.), so he can answer any questions about mediation that Ms. Lopez may ask.

Figure 4.3 | Inventory of Skills and Activities for the Preparation Phase

1. Receives referral
2. Makes contact with the parties
3. Screens for safety issues and appropriateness for mediation
4. If situation not appropriate for mediation, explores alternatives and develops safety plan, if needed
5. Decides whether to meet individually with parties first (for further screening, to allow parties to ventilate in privacy, to help prepare them for negotiation, etc.)
6. Arranges for interaction between the parties (together, shuttle mediation,[22] use of telephone, or other distance technologies)
7. Chooses and arranges the meeting space/environment conducive to mediation (quiet, impartial, comfortable, soothing, fun, creative, spiritual)
8. Ensures parties have access to legal advice, particularly where the decisions to be made have significant legal consequences
9. Speaks with lawyers or other parties who may have an influence over decision making, with permission of the parties (to explain mediation and obtain their support for the process)
10. Obtains agreement about who will participate in mediation
11. Provides parties with written information explaining mediation (e.g., brochure, Agreement to Mediate, website)

Debriefing: Which preparation phase skills and activities did Michael use most effectively? What challenges did Michael face when dealing with Ms. Lopez and how did he try to handle them? Given the information that Michael gathered in the role-play, is mediation appropriate for these clients? If yes, what does Michael need to do (if anything) to ensure mediation is safe and fair? If no, why is mediation inappropriate?

ROLE-PLAY 4.2: "PARKING PERILS"—ORIENTATION TO MEDIATION

Victor (Victoria) is a volunteer mediator for a community dispute resolution program in Conflictia. A police officer, Sgt. Pullitzer, has referred two neighbors—Nora and Nelly—to mediation in order to resolve their "parking feud." Over the past month,

---

[22]*Shuttle mediation* refers to meeting with the parties individually and shuttling between them. The two parties could be in separate rooms at the same time, with the mediator moving back and forth between them. Alternatively, the mediator could meet with the parties at separate times. Shuttle mediation may be used when there are safety issues, when the parties refuse to meet face to face, or where slowing down the process is needed to help the parties to cool off.

Nora has called the police on six occasions to complain that Nelly was parking in front of Nora's driveway. Nelly claims Nora lets the air out of her tires if she parks within 12 feet of her driveway. For this role-play, Victor will meet Nelly and Nora for the first mediation session. Assume Victor had no prior contact with the parties.

To prepare, Victor should plan an opening statement using some of the topics identified in the inventory below (Figure 4.4). He could create crib notes to ensure he covers the key points, but he should not read a script. The opening statement should reflect one particular approach to mediation (e.g., transformative, settlement focused, or whichever approach that the person playing Victor wants to learn). Victor should ensure eye contact with both parties and remain flexible, answering questions of the parties that may arise. Nora and Nelly should be relatively cooperative with Victor. Periodically, one or the other could interrupt by asking naïve or pointed questions (e.g., "What type of meditation do you practice?" "What happens if I need to go to the restroom?" "When are you going to decide who is right and who is wrong?" "How do I know you're not going to side with her?"). The main learning goal for this role-play, however, is for the mediator to become comfortable with the orientation phase of mediation.

Figure 4.4 | Inventory of Skills and Activities for the Orientation Phase

1. Puts clients at ease during introductions to parties
2. Opening statement: Explains the mediation process—structure of the communication; purposes; how mediation differs from court or therapy; role of mediator; credentials; role of the parties; what happens if a tentative agreement is reached or not reached
3. Asserts control over process
4. Emphasizes parties' responsibility for decision making
5. Identifies the timing (beginning; duration; finishing; possibility of future meetings)
6. Screens candidates for suitability—readiness; balance of power; safety; ability to negotiate fairly (considering impact of any mental illness, substance abuse, etc.)
7. Assesses cultural factors that may affect the process: values, preferred ways of dealing with conflict, traditions related to the subject of the conflict
8. Determines need for further premediation interventions
9. Obtains parties' agreement about ground rules for communication and process (e.g., one person speaking at a time, use of notes, use of respectful language, smoking, protocol for calling breaks, and other terms that the parties agree on)
10. Describes standards of practice in terms understandable to parties:
    - Neutrality or impartiality
    - Confidentiality (giving permission to speak freely, within limits)
    - Communication with parties, their lawyers, or other parties
    - Use of caucusing (meeting individually with parties during mediation)
    - Safety issues
    - Voluntary involvement/Ability to withdraw or terminate
11. Fosters rapport and trust with clients (by demonstrating genuineness, unconditional positive regard, empathic understanding, patience, impartiality, concern, optimism, and active listening skills)

(continued)

12. Clarifies the terms of the Agreement to Mediate (the retainer or contract for the mediator's services, including fees or how mediator will be paid)
13. Encourages informed commitment to the process (including commitment of time, effort, and good faith)
14. Reaches Agreement to Mediate (written or oral agreement)
15. Obtains preliminary information about presenting problem (may do this at beginning or toward end of this phase)
16. Identifies motivations of parties for mediating
17. Assesses the nature of the conflict: e.g., difference of understandings, ideologies, or interests (see the Negotiation Preparation Tool in Chapter 3 for more detailed analysis of conflict)
18. Congratulates or thanks the parties on their decision to commit to the process
19. Encourages positive expectations of the mediation process
20. Invites feedback and criticism from the parties
21. If a party expresses reluctance to mediate, explores why (in joint session or in caucus)
22. If parties do not agree to mediate, explores alternatives with parties and reinforces that the parties are in the best position to decide on how to proceed
23. Empowers clients (e.g., supporting their negotiating skills, giving each a fair opportunity to speak, reinforcing their strengths)
24. Clarifies the agenda, and invites parties to commit to it

Debriefing: Which orientation skills and topics did Victor(ia) demonstrate well? Give examples of what he or she said. What challenges arose in the orientation stage? How did the mediator handle these?

ROLE-PLAY 4.3: "MUTUALLY NOISY NEIGHBORS"—ISSUE DEFINITION

This role-play involves a community mediator, Coco, and two neighbors, Ms. Thibault and Mr. Omar. In the two months since Ms. Thibault moved into the apartment unit directly above Mr. Omar's, they have been embroiled in a bitter dispute. Mr. Omar is a 71-year-old widower who has lived in his apartment for more than 20 years. Ms. Thibault is a 22-year-old university student. She has made several complaints to Mr. Omar about the noise coming from his apartment. Mr. Omar has a hearing impairment. He turns up the volume on his TV or radio in order to be able to hear them. Mr. Omar likes to go to bed early and wake up early. Mr. Omar keeps the TV or radio on all the time because he likes the company; also, it is his only way of keeping up with what's going on in the community.

Ms. Thibault is away at school during the afternoon, but she likes to work at home in the morning and in the evening. She finds it difficult to study with Mr. Omar's noise, but she needs to work at home because that is where her computer and her books are. She is also awakened early (about 5:30 A.M.) when Mr. Omar gets up and turns on the radio. Ms. Thibault has told Mr. Omar about the problem several times, but he continues to leave the volumes at the same levels. In frustration, Ms. Thibault has begun to respond by playing her stereo at blaring levels or by stamping on her parquet floors. When this happens, Mr. Omar just raises the volume of his TV or radio. With the escalating noise war, other neighbors have complained to the building manager. The manager has told Mr. Omar and Ms. Thibault to get together to work it out themselves. Management does not want to hear anymore problems from either of them. Ms. Thibault and Mr. Omar agree to go to the Conflictia Mediation Center, on neutral ground, to try to work out a solution.

This case can be role-played using a variety of negotiation styles: hard, soft, positional, chicken, compromising, tit-for-tat, interest based. Mr. Omar and Ms. Thibault should each select a style and not disclose it to the others. In preparing for the role-play, they should write down examples of tactics and strategies they will use in playing their designated negotiation style (refer back to Chapter 3 for different styles and approaches to negotiation).

The main purpose of this role-play is to give the person playing the mediator practice at the issue definition phase of the mediation process. Coco should select an approach to mediation and use the inventory in Figure 4.5 to prepare for this role-play. Assume that Coco has introduced the parties to mediation. She will move onto the issue definition phase with a statement such as "Now that everyone has agreed to mediate, let's begin by hearing what brings you to mediation and what you want to accomplish here."

Figure 4.5 | Inventory of Skills and Activities for the Issue Definition Phase

1. Provides rationale for "who goes first"
2. Allows each party the opportunity to identify their concerns
3. Allows parties to ventilate feelings
4. Puts appropriate limits on storytelling and expression of feelings
5. Assures each party hears and understands the others (e.g., encourages each party to use active listening skills to reflect back or summarize what the other has said; helps parties with language to validate each other's needs and views as legitimate, even if they do not agree; makes constructive use of silence and pacing)
6. If a party seems surprised about information provided by another party, explores how this new information changes the first party's understanding of past events
7. Identifies, clarifies, and summarizes interests of each party, including relationship issues
8. Identifies areas of agreement and mutual interest (reinforces ability to agree)
9. Develops a list of concerns that is balanced, exhaustive, and clear
10. Obtains consensus about how to proceed (priorities of parties; order of issues to be addressed—e.g., by most important, least important, most urgent, easiest, or most difficult first)
11. Responds appropriately to different conflict styles
12. Validates identity and role of each party
13. Avoids taking sides (e.g., uses neutral statements to demonstrate active listening)
14. Conducts own analysis of underlying concerns

Debriefing: What issues did the mediator discern from this session? What were each party's original positions on each issue? Identify three strengths of the mediator's performance, using the inventory for the issue definition phase. Identify one additional skill or activity that the mediator could have demonstrated.

ROLE-PLAY 4.4: "ANTIDISCIPLINARY TEAM"—EXPLORING INTERESTS AND NEEDS

This is a role-play between Norman (a nurse), Sonia (a social worker), and Penelope (a psychologist who will assume the role of an emergent mediator). These three professionals work on a specialized, interdisciplinary team at Conflictia Hope Hospital. The team provides assessments and supportive interventions for children who are suspected of having been sexually abused. Norman and Sonia personally cannot stand one another. Norman sees Sonia as arrogant, uncooperative, and indecisive. Sonia sees Norman as petty and backstabbing. Recently, they returned a child (Chelsey) home with her parents. Chelsey was abused further. Norman told administration that he had nothing to do with the case, laying blame at Sonia's feet. During a case conference regarding another family (the Farqhuars), Norman and Sonia start arguing about Chelsey's case. Penelope gets caught in the crossfire and tries to use her mediative skills.

Since Penelope is not a contractual mediator, there is no formal introduction or Agreement to Mediate. The parties should begin the role-play with Norman and Sonia arguing about who is at fault. The focus of this role-play is to explore the parties' interests and needs, *not* to do any problem solving or to bring the parties to agreement. The person playing Penelope should use the inventory in Figure 4.6 to prepare for this role-play. Focus on practicing just three or four skills at a time.

Figure 4.6 | Inventory of Skills and Activities for the Exploring Interests and Needs Phase

1. Asks parties to identify their feelings around their own issues
2. Asks parties to identify their perceptions of the other's feelings around the issues in conflict (facilitates recognition)
3. Helps parties explore underlying interests and needs
4. Helps parties explore their self-images and how these contribute to the conflict and its possible resolution
5. Asks clear, open-ended, and relevant questions
6. Encourages parties to share information
7. Maintains safe environment for clients
8. Maintains appropriate level of control over emotional climate (e.g., exhibiting relaxation through body language, calling for a breather, exploring immediacy, using humor)
9. Keeps parties focused on one issue at a time
10. Maintains control over disruptive behavior
11. Partializes issues
12. Establishes priorities with parties
13. Achieves understanding or closure on relevant feelings
14. Uses interventions appropriate for

    - Balancing power,
    - Maintaining problem-solving focus, and
    - Responding to emotional needs.

Debriefing: What challenges did the mediator face in this role-play? Which skills did the mediator use to deal with these? What were the parties' original positions, and what underlying interests and needs did the mediator help the parties identify?

ROLE-PLAY 4.5: "SEQUELS"—NEGOTIATION AND PROBLEM SOLVING

For this role-play, use the fact situation from one of the previous three role-plays. The mediator should conduct a brief introduction and allow the parties to tell their stories. The parties should be cooperative up to this phase, so this role-play can focus on negotiation and problem solving. As you work on developing your skills, focus on three or four skills from the inventory in Figure 4.7. Master these skills, and then move onto additional ones.

Figure 4.7	Inventory of Skills and Activities for the Negotiation and Problem-Solving Phase

 1. Clarifies the goal or purpose of coming to an agreement (including how this empowers clients to take control over their own decisions and lives)
 2. Moves from broad principles (where parties can more easily agree) to more specific topics
 3. Encourages cooperative problem solving
 4. Encourages generation of options for each issue
 5. Offers substantive suggestions and proposals (without losing neutrality)
 6. Avoids imposing mediator solutions
 7. Avoids moving to solutions prematurely
 8. Provides a structure for problem solving
 9. Helps parties develop objective criteria for deciding between options
10. Narrows issues in dispute (if full agreement not reached)
11. Uses pre-emptive strategies
12. Helps parties reframe statements that are *negative, self-centered, past focused, judgmental, or positional* into perspectives that are more *positive, mutually acceptable, future focused, nonjudgmental and interest-based* (offering alternative ways of looking at issues rather than trying to impose these perspectives on the parties)
13. Maintains appropriate control over process—may turn over more control to the parties as they begin to work more collaboratively
14. Uses decision trees, charts, notes, or other visual aids
15. Encourages parties to use lateral thinking (viewing problems from different angles to try to come up with innovative solutions)
16. Proposes possible concessions (as options rather than as advice)
17. Rewards party concessions
18. Takes responsibility for concessions
19. Links the parties with outside experts or resources to help enlarge their perceived option set
20. Helps parties identify information that needs to be produced

(continued)

21. Supplies and filters missing information, or seeks agreement on how parties will obtain it for themselves
22. Pre-empts or corrects counterproductive negotiation behavior
23. Praises constructive negotiation behavior
24. Identifies the function or effect of parties' behaviors or attitudes on negotiation
25. Allows all interests of the parties to be discussed
26. Recognizes or legitimizes the rights of others to be involved in the process, where appropriate
27. Explores cultural differences and misunderstandings
28. Adapts language and behaviors to fit with culture(s) of parties
29. Explores power dynamics and concerns for fairness
30. Helps one party package a proposal in terms that the other is more likely to accept
31. Brings others into the mediation process to contribute to agreement
32. Educates the parties about constructive negotiation skills and principled negotiation strategies
33. Helps parties re-evaluate their expectations (e.g., through reality testing questions, role reversals, looking at hypothetical situations, evaluating the pros and cons of different options, metaphoric storytelling; see Appendix 3)
34. Focuses the parties on the future, rather than on the past
35. Focuses on one issue at a time (or a manageable number of related issues)
36. Explores relationship issues
37. If parties express judgmental statements, helps them see one another in a more positive frame of reference
38. Asks parties to consider possible changes in future circumstances
39. Helps parties separate personality issues from the substance of the negotiations
40. Prescribes homework tasks for parties to carry out between sessions
41. Asks parties to consider the interests of parties affected who may not be at the mediation table
42. Uses constructive confrontation (e.g., helps a party to identify incongruencies between two pieces of information the party has given, or between a statement and the party's behavior)
43. If parties have forgotten issues raised earlier, gives parties an opportunity to put them back on the table
44. Helps parties resolve impasse by
    - Caucusing (meeting individually with both parties to explore possible blockages to moving forward and ways to resolve them, to allow ventilation of feelings, to encourage candor, to correct unproductive behaviors, to reality test, or to deal with power imbalances without losing parties' faith in mediator's neutrality);
    - Encouraging parties to remain at the table;
    - Helping parties save face or undo a commitment (see Chapter 7);
    - Helping parties do a cost-benefit analysis of nonagreement (e.g., "What is the best alternative to a mediated agreement, and what can you expect in terms of costs in time, money, and aggravation, to yourselves and others affected by this conflict?" "What are the risks and benefits of terminating mediation without agreement?");
    - Listening carefully to what is happening in the moment and improvising in a manner that motivates the parties to move forward, or even laterally (e.g., saying something for shock value, surfacing unspoken feelings, reaching into a negative and extracting a positive, or reversing ground rules such as "one person speaks at a time" or "everyone speaks respectfully")

In order to compare and contrast different approaches to mediation, you could assign different approaches to different people who will play mediator in each successive role-play.

In addition to the skills that can be used to advance the mediation process, mediators must also consider what types of behaviors to avoid. *Dysfunctional mediator behaviors* are mediator responses that impede effective mediation. Many of these are the inverse or opposite of the positive skills and activities described in Figure 4.7. For example, if "allowing all parties to discuss their interests" contributes to the process, then "failing to provide all parties with an opportunity to discuss their interests" impedes the process. The list in Figure 4.8 identifies dysfunctional behaviors to avoid. During the role-plays, observers should watch for the use of any of these dysfunctional skills. When debriefing, remember to provide constructive feedback in a respectful, behavior-based manner.

Debriefing: What skills and strategies did the mediator use effectively? What were the key differences in the process when different people used different approaches to mediation? Which approach seems most appropriate for this case situation, and why? Which dysfunctional behaviors, if any, did the mediator demonstrate?

Figure 4.8 | Dysfunctional Mediation Skills

1. Demonstrates bias to one party
2. Follows agenda too rigidly, ignoring what is going on for the parties
3. Allows assumptions and misunderstandings to go unchecked
4. Allows threats or blaming
5. Uses inflammatory language
6. Lacks genuineness (sounds artificial or disinterested)
7. Exhibits lack of confidence (in self as mediator or in mediation process)
8. Focuses on the parties' positions
9. Judges or blames parties for their role in the conflict
10. Glosses over serious problems to try to reach settlement
11. Denies opportunity for parties to discuss feelings
12. Mismanages information provided by the parties
13. Leads parties into a settlement that pleases the mediator
14. Pressures parties into agreement
15. Tries to solve problems for the clients
16. Ignores cultural and other diversity factors that may affect client interactions
17. Moves parties through phases too quickly
18. Allows one party to take control of the process
19. Becomes defensive when challenged by a client
20. Assumes a nonmediator role (e.g., crosses boundary into therapy, law, etc.)
21. Asserts own reality rather than allowing parties to express their own realities
22. Offers advice rather than information or options

ROLE-PLAY 4.6: FINALIZING AN AGREEMENT

Building on the scenario that you used in Role-Play 4.5, use this role-play to practice finalizing an agreement. The mediator should prepare by identifying three or four skills to focus on from Figure 4.9. If the parties did not reach agreement in your prior

---

Figure 4.9 | Inventory of Skills and Activities for the "Finalizing an Agreement" Phase

1. Uses appropriate language in the agreement or memorandum of understanding:
   - Oral or written (as appropriate for the case)
   - Plain language (rather than legalese or professional jargon)
   - Impartial, balanced, and mutual
   - Comprehensive, clear, and concise
   - Future focused (rather than reviewing past or assigning blame)
2. Tests agreement with parties to ensure it is realistic (e.g., do they see it as practical, fair, enforceable, and something they can live with over the long term?)
3. Deals with contingencies (including possibility of future disagreements)
4. Clarifies the roles and obligations of each party (the agreement explains who is responsible for doing what, when, and how, and what happens if one or both do not fulfill their obligations under the agreement)
5. Ensures commitment (e.g., do they fully understand the agreement and its implications, do they accept responsibility for making the agreement work?)
6. Explores doubts expressed by either party
7. Ensures access to independent legal advice
8. Deals with how the tentative agreement will be finalized (e.g., legally binding agreement drafted by lawyers and signed by parties,[23] court order on consent of parties, informal letter rather than legally binding agreement, or confirmed as an oral agreement based on the parties' good faith)
9. Helps devise ways to monitor performance and enforce the agreements (defining terms of implementation, evaluation, follow-up, and review, including sanctions or other provisions that take effect if certain terms are broken)
10. Summarizes the process that has taken place
11. Reinforces the parties' efforts and decisions (end on a positive note; shake hands, have a meal together, have a drink, or some other ritual)
12. Arranges for follow-up (date, time, place, who is responsible for doing what)
13. If no agreement is reached:
    - Summarizes areas of agreement and disagreement
    - Explores possible alternatives for resolution of outstanding issues
    - Explores parties' feelings and frustrations
    - Links parties to desired resources
    - Reinforces parties' efforts and successes (including empowerment and recognition)
    - Offers opportunity to return to mediation at future date

---

[23]See http://www.abanet.org/dispute/resolution2002.pdf for the American Bar Association's policy on whether drafting an agreement constitutes "unauthorized practice of law."

role-play, you could focus on the skills in Point 13 for how to end mediation when the parties do not reach agreement. Alternatively, you could work out a tentative agreement before you begin this role-play, so you can focus this exercise on finalizing the agreement.

Debriefing: What decisions did the parties make relating to whether the agreement was oral or written, and submitted to court, lawyers, or neither? What are the pros and cons of how they finalized the agreement? Which skills did the mediator use most effectively for this phase?

ROLE-PLAY 4.7: FOLLOW-UP

Using the scenario that you used in Role-Play 4.6, prepare for a follow-up contact, as per the skills and activities in Figure 4.10. Select one type of method for soliciting feedback (e.g., a structured telephone interview with just one party or an open-ended, face-to-face meeting with both parties together). Make sure your methods of soliciting feedback and your use of skills fit with the approach to mediation that you used in the prior role-plays (e.g., a transformative mediator would ask for feedback on how the parties are interacting with each other since mediation, rather than whether they are satisfied with the particular agreement they reached).

Figure 4.10 | Inventory of Skills and Activities for the Follow-up Phase

1. Contacts the parties (by mediator or other person; sets up face-to-face meeting, conducts the interview by telephone, or asks for written feedback by mail)
2. Solicits feedback (structured interview for quantitative or qualitative research, written feedback on evaluation forms, or informal request for feedback)
3. Provides mediation reviews at specific time intervals (e.g., to look at short-term or trial agreements, to consider longer-term arrangements, to consider progress and problems since finalizing the agreement)
4. Reinforces positive outcomes
5. Offers additional services

Debriefing: What were the main issues that arose during follow-up? Which skills did the mediator use to handle these? Critique the overall effectiveness of this role-play, focusing on the mediator's strengths and the degree to which the parties achieved the primary goals of the particular approach to mediation (e.g., for transformative, to what extent were the parties empowered and how well did they demonstrate recognition?) Give specific examples.

ROLE-PLAY 4.8: "TOUCHY ISSUE"—EMPOWERMENT AND POWER BALANCING

Diversity Plus has a special unit, Cultivate Your Aptitudes, that provides support services to people with cognitive disabilities. Vince is a vocational counselor. Clara is one of Vince's clients. Clara has moderate cognitive impairment related to brain damage that occurred during birth. During a meeting with Vince, she believes he has touched her in an inappropriate manner: He touched her shoulder, without her permission. Although he did not mean to do this in a sexual manner, Clara took offense. As Clara came out of Vince's office, Don (the director of CYA) saw she was distressed and asked her what was wrong. Don tries to mediate the conflict.

Ordinarily, the person playing a mediative role in this situation would not have time to prepare. For learning purposes, Don should strategize in advance. What types of power issues are raised by this scenario? The first person playing Don should identify and focus on two or three strategies to "empower" the parties. The second person playing Don should identify and focus on two or three strategies to "balance power" between the parties.

Debriefing: Which empowerment or power-balancing strategies did Don use effectively? What is the difference between empowerment and power balancing, from Clara and Vince's perspectives? Was mediation appropriate for this scenario? Why or why not?

ROLE-PLAY 4.9: "FAMILY PLANNING"— CULTURAL INTERPRETER

For this role-play, team up with a person from a different cultural background (if possible, someone who is also from a different professional background). One of you will role-play a mediator. The other will play a cultural interpreter. The mediator is helping a couple negotiate a prenuptial agreement. The couple wants to mediate the following issues: the number of children and approximate timing for having children; whether one or both spouses will work outside of the family home; and how they will make decisions about parenting issues such as discipline and education. The couple is from a different background than the mediator, so the mediator arranges to meet with a cultural interpreter in order to gain a better understanding of cultural issues that may be raised in this case.

The mediator should plan what types of questions to ask the cultural interpreter in order to prepare for this meeting (e.g., "What are the norms within this culture about parenting?" "What happens within the community if people do not follow the norms?"). During the meeting, the cultural interpreter should draw from his or her culture in order to answer the mediator's questions. The role of the cultural interpreter is to educate the mediator. The interpreter may not feel comfortable making generalizations about his or her culture. If so, the mediator can validate these concerns and negotiate what types of information the interpreter would be willing to share. If you want further information on the process of ethnographic interviewing, consult a diversity textbook such as Anderson and Carter (2003).

Debriefing: What did the mediator learn about the family's culture? How would this information affect the way that you mediate with the couple? What ethical issues does this scenario raise for the mediator?

ROLE-PLAY 4.10: FOUR CASES OF EMERGENT MEDIATION

The following cases involve emergent mediation. For each case, identify the issues in dispute and the nature of the conflict. What challenges do they pose for the third party? What strategies would you use to deal with them? Would it be appropriate for you to act as an emergent mediator? If so, what would you need to do to improve the chances that the parties accept you as a mediator? Try role-playing these situations from beginning to end (about 3 to 6 minutes per role-play, plus preparation and debriefing).

a. Family Feud

Richard and Jane are adult siblings who come from a family that deals with conflict by slamming doors, screaming, or throwing things. Francis is their longtime friend. During dinner at a restaurant, Richard and Jane start to argue about who is going to pick up the tab. Francis feels caught in the middle. Francis feels embarrassed about making a scene and offers to pay the bill. Jane says, "No way! It's Richard's turn. Don't let him walk all over you." Richard replies to Jane, "You're full of it! You're the one who's always bragging about how much money you make!" As a friend, what strategies should Francis use to help mediate the dispute? Try role-playing this situation.

Debriefing: What strategies did Francis use? How effective were each of these? Were the parties ready for Francis's help? How could Francis assess whether she should intervene? If Francis were Jane and Richard's counselor rather than their friend, how would she help them with this conflict? How would a counseling role be similar to that of the friend? How would it be different?

b. Crabby Coworkers

Bea and Jay work as receptionists in Diversity Plus. Jay always complains that Bea is late, takes long lunches, and leaves early. Jay thinks Bea is lazy and is taking advantage of Jay's good nature. Bea has a number of excuses—having to drop off and pick up the kids at daycare, needing time to do the shopping, and being tired from working too hard. Besides, Bea says that she's more efficient than Jay and makes up for the time off. Jay finally can't put up with Bea and goes to Orville (the office manager) to "fire Bea and get someone competent." Because of Bea's seniority and position, Orville is reluctant to fire Bea and would prefer to work it out amicably. Also, Jay is not responsible for deciding who to hire or who to fire. Orville has arranged for a meeting with both of them.

Debriefing: What challenges did Orville face in this situation? How did he handle them? What issues can Orville be neutral about and what are the limits of his ability to be neutral? Is emergent mediation an appropriate role for Orville? Why or why not?

c. Gossipy Group

Ashley and Gerry are members of a recreational softball team. Cayla is team captain. In recent weeks, Ashley has been saying that Gerry is having an affair with someone 15 years older. The team is out on the playing field. Gerry has just caught wind of this story from the shortstop and decides to throw the next ball that comes his way at Ashley's head. Gerry has a bad arm, so the ball misses Ashley. The two start cursing and threatening each other. As captain, Cayla intervenes and leads them into the locker room to "talk it out."

Debriefing: Which mediation strategies did Cayla use, and how did the parties respond to these? What are the advantages or disadvantages of Cayla using a combination of authority and mediation in helping Gerry and Ashley? Contrast this baseball team scenario with a group of social workers, nurses, psychologists, and doctors who worked together in a hospital. How are the roles of baseball team captain and interdisciplinary team leader similar regarding conflict management roles? How are they different?

d. Catch-22 Couple

Fanya is a family therapist who has been seeing Andy and Michelle over the past 3 months for couples counseling. Andy and Michelle are trying to decide what to do for their fifth anniversary. Andy wants them to go on a nostalgic trip back to their birthplace, Bohemia, where they also met and married. Michelle wants to throw a big party here in Conflictia. They do not have the time or money to do both. They come to Fanya, their trusted therapist and friend, to tell them what to do or where to go. If Fanya sides with one, she will offend the other. If Fanya gives them a third option, they will both get angry with her. If Fanya refuses to help, then they'll think Fanya is "a wuss."[24] Role-play this with Fanya choosing to help as an emergent mediator.

Debriefing: How did Fanya handle Andy and Michelle's request to tell them where to go? What were the risks for Fanya, as a therapist, in using a mediation approach with this couple? How would her use of skills differ depending on whether she used an emergent mediation approach or a traditional therapist approach?

---

[24]A derogatory term, suggesting you are a coward.

MAJOR ASSIGNMENTS

The following role-plays can be used for major assignments. See the section on Major Assignments in Chapter 3 for instructions on how to prepare a written analysis. These role-plays give you broad latitude about how to prepare and how to intervene. You can use theory from this chapter or from other mediation books and articles.

ASSIGNMENT 4A: GUN PROHIBITION CASE

The three roles to choose from in this case are Adelle (who will take on a mediator role), Faith, and Connie. If any of the role-players are male, they could be Arnie, Foster, or Constantine.

Adelle is the administrator for Conflictia's Seniors' Center (CSC). At CSC's last annual meeting, many members said they were concerned about their safety on the streets of Conflictia. They believed that the elderly were especially vulnerable to violent crime because of concerns such as physical frailties, dementia, and lack of awareness about potentially dangerous situations. A motion was passed at the meeting that the Center should send a position paper to each of the three major political parties in Conflictia: ROC, LOC, and SIM. The LOC Party has recently proposed that Conflictia pass a constitutional amendment to ban possession and sale of all guns and rifles.

Among members of CSC, there is rift between (1) those who believe prohibiting guns would go a long way to promoting safety and (2) those who believe that prohibiting guns not only would be ineffective but also would impose a gross infringement on the rights and freedoms of law-abiding citizens. In order to resolve their differences, Adelle suggested that they try a two-party mediation process, in which she would act as mediator.

Each side of the debate has met as a group and appointed a leader to represent its viewpoint. Faith will represent those who favor the proposed constitutional amendment to ban guns. Connie will represent those that oppose the proposed gun prohibition. They will meet with Adelle to try to work out a joint position paper that they will present to the three political parties. They believe the Center will have a stronger voice if it submits a single, consensus report, rather than have members with different viewpoints submitting their own suggestions. They also believe this process can bring members of the community closer together if the process is successful; on the other hand, an unsuccessful process could be alienating and divisive.

Connie's Confidential Facts

Connie is a member of a rifle association and has a collection of guns, some of them antiques. She doesn't hunt, and they stay in a special locked case. If the gun prohibition laws are passed, Connie would not turn in her guns as a matter of principle. Prohibition is just another attempt by government bureaucrats to enter the bedrooms and basements of law-abiding citizens. Money could be better spent on food for the hungry or housing for the homeless. Although Connie does not agree, most people at CSC who oppose gun prohibition believe that the government should be spending more money on law enforcement and prisons in order to make the streets safe for all citizens.

Connie does not like conflict—particularly conflict involving arguments and raised voices. She is concerned that Faith might get carried away and start yelling. If this happens, Connie will withdraw into silence. Better to avoid this type of trouble. In addition, Connie isn't sure the mediator (Adelle) can handle Faith.

Faith's Confidential Facts

Faith tends to express feelings openly, verbally, and with broad hand gestures—perhaps it is a cultural thing. The issue of gun control is an emotional issue for Faith, having been mugged at gunpoint only 18 months ago. Faith realizes that she represents a group from her agency, and will try to keep her personal experiences in check—most of the time. She also wants to ensure their position paper will have a significant impact on the political debate. There is no use in coming up with suggestions that government will just ignore. The LOC already favors the constitutional amendment, but it needs to convince members of the SIM Party, and even a few of the softer heads of the ROC, in order for the amendment to have any chance of passing.

Faith and her constituency believe that the purpose of government is to keep peace and order. They see gun prohibition as a legitimate way to reduce the incidence of violent crime and injury. Faith is also aware of suicide statistics showing that the availability of guns is associated with a higher incidence of completed suicides. If people having suicidal thoughts have direct access to an effective means of killing themselves, then they are more likely to kill themselves. Also, unplanned murders (committed in the heat of passion) are more likely when guns are accessible. Spousal violence, in particular, can result in death rather than lesser injury when guns are readily available.

Faith is subject to occasional, short-term memory lapse. At one point in the meeting, Faith might lose her train of thought and start asking about why the food in the Senior's Center is so bad. She is embarrassed about her memory lapses and will try to cover them up—perhaps pretending she has a hearing problem. Consensus is very important to Faith. She likes to get along with everyone and doesn't want this debate to leave any scars on CSC. On the other hand, Faith is a tough bargainer, particularly when the stakes are so high.

Adelle's Confidential Facts (Mediator)

Although Adelle has a degree in public administration, she is also a former navy admiral. In the military, she learned to deal with people straight on—no nonsense. Adelle personally favors gun prohibition, not just for the public but for the police.

Only the national armed forces should have access to guns. Adelle has seen the damage people can do when they do not know how to use a gun properly. Adelle is also a registered member of the LOC Party, which favors gun control.

In order to prepare for this meeting and plan out a process, you may want to meet with another person from your class who is also playing the mediator. Brainstorm issues that you might expect and identify strategies to help you deal with them. For instance, is the main issue whether to pass a constitutional amendment to prohibit guns? How can Adelle help to heal the divisiveness within the senior's center and encourage both sides to work together? Consider bringing snacks or drinks to the meeting in order to make the meeting feel more relaxed and friendly. Consider whether there are any special considerations as to how you conduct the meeting, given that the participants are seniors. Also, take care to avoid making ageist stereotypes.

ASSIGNMENT 4B: MESSY ESTATE DISPUTE (THE MED CASE)

The three roles to choose from are Suzie, Selma, and Mona. Mona will play the mediator. If any of the role-play participants is male, he could be Sheldon, Simon, or Malcolm.

Suzie (38) and Selma (41) are siblings. Their parents died 5 months ago, leaving them shocked, angry, and saddened. The sisters have not gotten along very well for years, dating back to their envy and competitiveness in high school days. However, they somehow managed to act "good" in front of their parents. Relations have soured further given their reaction to the loss of their parents and the present task of how to divide their parents' estate. Neither parent had a valid will. Selma and Suzie are the only children, and (now that Selma has paid the parents' bills) no other parties are making claims in the estate.

The main assets include a joint bank account with $15,000, life insurance and pension benefits worth $40,000, a condominium (purchased 5 years ago for $240,000 with an outstanding mortgage of $130,000; present market value unknown); Mom's diamond engagement ring; two wedding rings; a gold bracelet; Grandma's brooch (low monetary value, but sentimental to both); six photograph albums; a china set (serves 12); furniture (bedroom/living room/dining room); and a 2004 Mazda (which neither daughter wants due to car repair needs). Selma is the more financially secure of the two women and has threatened to take Suzie to court (mostly out of spite). Suzie works part-time and rents an apartment; she would like to move into the condo to save money. Besides, the market value is currently depressed due to the recession in Conflictia. Suzie believes it would be best to wait before selling. Selma thinks that Suzie is already living in the condo and that she has started to sell off pieces of furniture.

Both Selma and Suzie have independent legal advice; the lawyers referred them to mediation to try to work out a memorandum of understanding. If and when the issues are resolved, the lawyers will draft the final agreement. Selma and Suzie have agreed to try to work things out with Mona, a family mediator recommended by one of Selma's friends.

Suzie's Confidential Facts

Suzie is not sure she can trust Mona, the mediator. Mona seemed to know Selma from before. Suzie is worried that Mona and Selma are good friends. Suzie does not want to make any accusations, because her lawyer said she should try to make a good impression with the mediator.

Suzie is not very knowledgeable about real estate values or investments. Her parents used to help her budget and told her what to do with her money. Suzie was quite dependent on them, emotionally as well as for concrete support and advice. When she found out her parents were killed in a car crash, she was devastated. Suzie is not living in her parents' condo. She has mixed emotions about doing so. On the one hand, she could save rent money. On the other hand, she would be living with a constant reminder of her parents and their recent tragedy.

Suzie can be accommodating, but she will become competitive if backed into a corner. She might even start to decompensate or regress into childish name-calling if she feels threatened. Suzie may be willing to compromise on certain monetary items in her parents' estate, but if there's one thing that she wants—whether through litigation or through mediation or whatever—it's Grandma's brooch. Grandma promised it to her when she was 12.

Selma's Confidential Facts

Selma is the older, wiser, and stronger sibling. She has mixed emotions about dividing her parents' estate. On the one hand, her parents always told her to take care of Suzie; on the other hand, she hated that. Moreover, Selma is still in shock about her parents' sudden death in a car accident. She was supposed to meet them earlier that day. She still feels guilty for backing out at the last minute.

Selma may approach the mediation in a "tit-for-tat" manner, willing to trade off one item for another. However, if Suzie rubs her the wrong way, Selma will shoot back. There are some items that Selma must have: the entire china set, the diamond engagement ring, and Grandma's brooch (which she promised Selma when she was 14). She does not think that Suzie should get anything of value, since she is not good with money. Selma believes Suzie is likely to lose any investments and sell family heirlooms to pay for her day-to-day needs. She spoke to the superintendent at her parents' condo. He thought that Suzie had already emptied out most of the furniture.

Selma wants to get things settled in one session. She is quite willing to go to court. She is only mediating because her lawyer strongly suggested it. She has difficulty maintaining attention for long periods. She may get up once in a while to wander around. Selma has never participatd in mediation before. She finds that Mona can sometimes be "too nice."

Mona's Confidential Facts (Mediator)

The only case facts that you have are the common facts identified at the beginning of this section. You may want to meet with another person in your class who is role-playing the mediator, to help you prepare and plan your approach to mediation. Brainstorm issues that you might expect the parties to raise. Identify theories and strategies that will help you deal with them.

*Good communication is as stimulating as
black coffee and just as hard to sleep after.*

—Anne Morrow Lindbergh

Group Facilitation CHAPTER 5

Group facilitation refers to helping a collection of people communicate more effectively. Essentially, a facilitator uses listening, questioning, and focusing skills (described in Chapter 2) to promote positive interaction and pre-empt barriers to effective communication. A facilitator plays an impartial role regarding the content of group communication but guides the process in a manner that balances participation and results (International Association of Facilitators, 2004). Facilitators also use a range of techniques to help groups think together, discuss difficult issues, make critical decisions, and ensure that decisions are properly implemented and evaluated. Mediators often refer to themselves as facilitators, though mediators comprise just one type of facilitator. Helping professionals use facilitation skills in various roles, for instance, as administrators, committee chairs, group counselors, community organizers, and educators. Some professionals view facilitation as "a way of life" as opposed to a specific role, because facilitation can be used in so many different roles (Eller, 2004).

This chapter begins with an overview of the types of groups and typical stages of group process. The manner in which a facilitator responds to conflict depends on the nature of the group as well as its stage of development. The following section identifies common challenges to group communication and provides suggestions for dealing with each. The middle sections of this chapter identify various approaches to facilitation, showing how each approach deals with conflict in a different manner. The latter sections provide an inventory of facilitation skills and a series of exercises you can use to practice these skills. As you work through this chapter, reflect on a group in which you participated: what type of group was it, what were its goals, what group process issues arose, and what approaches and skills did the facilitator use to pre-empt or deal with group conflict?

TYPES OF GROUPS

Groups can be categorized as task, psychoeducational, counseling, or therapeutic groups. *Task groups* are designed to plan and implement specific jobs or undertakings; for instance, a committee is struck to assess an organizations needs, a community

185

group decides to build a recreational facility for elders, or a coalition of child welfare agencies develops in order to coordinate their services. *Psychoeducational groups* are designed to foster cognitive, affective, or behavioral skills through the use of structured activities; for instance, a substance abuse group might include education about the causes of substance abuse and offer role-plays to help clients develop healthier methods of coping. *Counseling groups* help people deal with common living problems through the use of support, problem solving, and skill building; for instance, a self-esteem group might help participants compare the perceptions they have of themselves with the perceptions others have of them, and use mutual support to help each other build stronger senses of themselves. *Psychotherapy groups* help clients remediate psychosocial problems through the use of therapeutic techniques such as exploring unconscious psychological processes, dysfunctional relationships, and deep-rooted fears; for instance, a group for people with anxiety disorders might include dream analysis, behavior modification, hypnosis, or relaxation training (Corey & Corey, 2006).

Although conflict can emerge in each type of group, a facilitator's response must take the type of group into account. It would be inappropriate, for instance, for the facilitator of a task group to respond to conflict by using therapy with group members. In order to help the group accomplish its tasks, however, the facilitator does need to attend to emotional and relational issues. The facilitator could use team-building activities to restore collaboration or allow group members to vent feelings, before refocusing on the tasks to be accomplished. Exploring childhood memories to see how they might affect current behaviors, however, crosses the boundary into therapy.

Although conflict can transpire in any group, some groups are specifically designed to deal with conflict. An agency with high levels of staff conflict, for instance, might create a task group to explore ways of fostering more effective conflict resolution. A psychoeducational group could be designed for perpetrators of violence, teaching them about the impact of their behavior and providing alternate ways of dealing with anger or stress. A counseling group could be developed for children with poor impulse control, offering them support and fostering problem-solving skills. A therapeutic group for survivors of intimate partner abuse could help them resolve feelings of embarrassment, self-loathing, or fear and avoid abusive relationships in the future.

GROUP STAGES

Groups typically go through a series of stages, each marked by certain types of group dynamics and issues (Corey & Corey, 2006). By understanding these stages, facilitators can pre-empt destructive patterns of conflict and promote more positive approaches to dealing with it. The basic stages of group development include forming, norming, storming, performing, and adjourning.

When groups are *forming*, facilitators must decide who to bring into the group and how to structure it. Inviting members with similar backgrounds and views may decrease conflict, but diversity of backgrounds and perspectives may bring greater richness, expertise, and legitimacy to the group (Ting-Toomey & Oetzel, 2001). Leaving certain people out of the group can create resentment, rumors, and further conflict (Wilmot & Hocker, 2007). Seating people theater style tends to formalize discussion and make the audience passive, whereas a circle opens up dialogue and invites participation from everyone. Even decisions as simple as naming the group can have an impact on how conflict is handled. Some facilitators avoid names such as "Task Force" because "*force*" implies violence. A "Complaints Committee" invites people to complain, whereas a "Think Tank" or "Creative Response Team" promotes imaginative problem solving.

In the *norming* stage, members may have unclear expectations about the goals of the group and expectations of them as group members. Facilitators can pre-empt conflict by clarifying the group's goals and rules. This does not mean imposing goals or rules but rather inviting the group to develop them. For large groups, it may be useful to have a subcommittee meet in advance to help establish goals, rules, and an agenda for the first meeting. At the first meeting, the facilitator could present this information and ask the larger group whether they can agree to these goals, rules, and agenda items.

The beginning stages of a group are often marked by a honeymoon stage, where everyone is a bit nervous and self-conscious, avoiding conflict in order to give the facilitator and group a good impression. Facilitators can encourage surfacing of conflict through ground rules and modeling. It may be tempting for a facilitator to establish a norm such as "people will keep their emotions in check" or "members must not argue with one another." Such rules quell not only destructive conflict but also constructive conflict. Facilitators need to foster an environment where members are free to raise differences and express emotions (Cloke, 2001). If a group member criticizes the facilitator, for instance, the facilitator could thank the member for raising this issue and validate the concern. Validation could include paraphrasing and showing understanding. The facilitator can disagree, but still show respect.

During the *storming* phase, members have moved past the honeymoon stage and are more willing to express conflict directly. Some may question the goal of the group, the lack of resources required to achieve the goal, the motivations or abilities of other group members, or even whether they want to be a part of this group. People with different views may express anger or frustration toward those with whom they disagree. Facilitators must allow for venting of emotions and working through these issues. Although the facilitator may need to put some parameters on venting (e.g., no physical violence), the facilitator needs to help the group work through the problems rather than stifle discussion.

Working through conflict strengthens the group and prepares it for the *performing* stage, a phase where the group is able to focus on its goals or tasks. Facilitators must be careful not to do the work of the group. If a facilitator is working too hard, this is a sign that group members are not working hard enough. The facilitator must surface this issue with the group. Ideally, the facilitator has provided the group with time, space, skills, and structure to allow them to take the lead in doing their work. When conflict emerges, the group is better prepared to deal with it. The facilitator helps the group build on its successes and helps it work through problem areas.

In the *adjourning* stage, members prepare for the end of the group as it was originally constructed. Some groups terminate because they have completed their task; other groups terminate because they are time limited, they have run out of money or other resources, or the group is not able to achieve its goals (Corey & Corey, 2006). Conflict at this stage could include disagreement about whether to continue the group, frustrations about unfinished work, or emotional reactions to the termination of a group that has provided positive experiences (e.g., anger, sadness, or anxiety about the future). Again, the facilitator must balance task and process, helping the group decide how to proceed with unfinished goals and helping them work through their feelings about the disbanding of the group. Some groups do not merely disband; they morph into another form. For instance, a formal group with a leader may end, but group members may continue to meet informally on their own. Alternatively, the facilitator could help the group terminate "Phase 1" of the group, and then invite those who are interested to participate in "Phase 2."

The skills needed to **facilitate** a group change over its course. In some groups, a facilitator may be more directive at the initial stages, giving the group greater control of the process as it works through conflicts and establishes positive norms. In the beginning stages, facilitators often use trust-building skills (e.g., demonstrating empathy). In later stages, when trust has been built, facilitators may be more likely to use constructive confrontation skills to help the group work through conflicts. Throughout the group process, the facilitator should respond openly to conflict rather than deny it or respond defensively.

CHALLENGES TO GROUP PROCESS

Facilitators may face a range of challenges to effective group process: individuals have different agendas; the discussion has no focus; the discussion is dominated by certain individuals; some individuals keep interrupting; some individuals remain silent; individuals lose their attention; individuals have difficulty listening to other's ideas; statements or questions put some people on the defensive; individuals are not saying what they really think; individuals are confused about what decisions they have made (Eller, 2004; Kaner, 1996; Kosmoski & Pollack, 2000). To illustrate facilitation strategies for each of these obstacles, I will use a conflict situation between various helping professionals with conflicting ideas about how to regulate their professions.

1. Different Agendas

In a room full of 50 people, you might have 51 different opinions about the purpose of the meeting. If people come into a meeting with different agendas, at least some of them will come away feeling disappointed. Conflict resolution begins before people meet, particularly with large groups. Everyone must be prepared ahead of time with the following types of information: the goals for the meeting, who will be attending, who will be facilitating the process, the roles of various participants, and what materials or information people need to bring to the meeting. Proper preparation means pre-empting surprises. Some surprises are entertaining. I remember one evening meeting in which I told everyone the coffee was decaffeinated but later found out my colleague accidentally had used full-strength. We were hoping that decaf would help calm participants, but we kept noticing people becoming more stimulated as the night wore on. Note how this section is titled Agenda Setting, but I have gone off on a tangent with my own agenda, telling a cute anecdote. Let's refocus.

In order to prepare for a meeting, the facilitator must decide whether to meet with individuals or subgroups that will be participating at the larger meeting. Meeting with individuals or small subgroups is particularly desirable when the level of conflict is high and many different points of view emerge. In some cases, the facilitator can meet with representatives of each group in order to develop an agenda. The representatives for each group are responsible for ensuring that their members are prepared and agree with the agenda prior to the larger meeting.

Where the relevant parties do not agree on the agenda, the facilitator could use mediation skills to help them develop a mutually acceptable agenda. The facilitator may need to shuttle back and forth between the parties until an agreement is reached. Often, the toughest negotiations go on before the parties ever agree to an agenda and sit down together. Each party may be positioning for certain advantages—for example, a time and place that is favorable to their own group, a wording of the issues for discussion that limits the possible solutions in their favor, or a conflict resolution process that is biased in their favor. The facilitator must recognize these tactics and promote more constructive negotiation strategies (see Chapter 3 for examples).

2. No Focus

Once an agenda is set, the facilitator needs to keep parties focused on the agenda. If necessary, the parties can renegotiate parts of the agenda. However, this should be a deliberate process. Too often, the facilitator and the parties wander from one issue to another without any clear focus.

Punctuation refers to the skill of clearly separating each issue from other issues. The facilitator lets participants know which issue is up for discussion, guiding participants through different phases of the discussion (Kraybill, 2005a).

> We are now moving on to the issue of standards for accreditation. We have 45 minutes to discuss the proposal put forward by the Accreditation Committee. We will then take a 5-minute break. After the break, we will move on to the issue of professional discipline.

Punctuation emphasizes the transitions from one topic to another. Topic separation can be enhanced by making conscious changes in time and environment: taking a break between topics, moving to a different room, moving people from large groups to small groups, changing the lighting in the room, and so on.

When people stray from the topics on the table, the facilitator uses refocusing skills. The facilitator can remind the parties that they have agreed to a specific agenda, that they have limited time, and that they have made time for all issues to be discussed.

I understand you're concerned about professional discipline. We'll get to that after the break. I'll make a note that you want to speak to this issue. Did you want to add anything to our discussion on accreditation?

If people sense they have ownership of the agenda, they are more likely to keep focused. If the facilitator notes a certain pattern to the interruptions, the facilitator should assess the reasons for the interruptions—for example, individual difficulties maintaining focus or attention, a tactic to prevent constructive problem solving, or underlying emotional needs that require attention.

In the current example, one participant, Paul, keeps talking about how he was brought up on charges of professional misconduct. Other participants are getting frustrated because the issue is not about Paul but professional issues more generally. The facilitator assesses that for Paul, the issue *is* about Paul. He has unresolved anger about how he was treated. For Paul to participate more constructively as a group member, he needs help with this issue. The facilitator needs to decide whether to allow Paul time within the structure of the group or to meet with him outside the group in order to help him work through the anger. In this case, the facilitator finds a way to mesh Paul's needs with the needs of the group. With the group's approval, the facilitator sets aside a specific time for professionals to share horror stories; the group will use the stories to identify common themes about problems in the current regulatory system.

3. Domination

In any group interaction, certain people might dominate discussion. This may be due to individual or cultural differences: some people speak more loudly than others, some require less time to think before they speak, some demonstrate more passion, and some are more articulate. To ensure that everyone is able to participate fairly in the process, the facilitator can use empowerment and power-balancing strategies described in Chapter 4: giving everyone in the room a turn to speak, giving less empowered people the opportunity to speak first, teaching people effective communication skills during preparation for the meeting, slowing down the pace of the discussion, reminding participants of ground rules such as "demonstrating respect for others," or using a combination of written and oral presentations so that everyone can communicate in his or her preferred mode.

In the regulation illustration, a group of vocational counselors has not prepared for the meeting. A group of family therapists has prepared thoroughly and tends to dominate the discussion. The facilitator recognizes the imbalance and asks the parties to consider adjourning the meeting so everyone can contribute. The family therapists may perceive a bias against them: everyone had the same chance to prepare, so why should they have to come back for another meeting just because another group was negligent? The facilitator acknowledges their frustration and gives the other groups an opportunity to do the same. The facilitator then encourages the parties to consider the purpose of the meeting: to come up with the best decisions possible. In order to do this, each group must be prepared.

Competitive groups or individuals use domination as a strategy—to win. Facilitators can recognize this tactic when people are arguing positions rather than needs or interests. As with mediation, the facilitator must encourage the parties to look at interests and needs rather than positions. In addition, the facilitator can move the parties toward cooperation by helping them understand the costs of adversarial relations and nonagreement.

When a facilitator tries to prevent or remedy domination by a few individuals, the facilitator must be careful not to shut people down. An essential aspect of group interaction is to promote a full discussion of the issues, with everyone's input.

4. Interruptions

Group participants may interrupt discussion by switching topics, speaking over another person, making noises, or behaving in a distracting manner. With occasional interruptions, the facilitator can simply use focusing skills.

> Excuse me, Sharon. If we can finish hearing what Paul has to say, I'll put your name down to speak next.

The challenge is how to deal effectively with an interruption without putting the person who interrupted on the defensive. Some facilitators use a process called *stacking*, listing people who want to speak and then recognizing them in the order that they asked to speak (Kaner, 1996). If one person is talking and another wants to respond, the second person raises a hand, and the facilitator adds that person to the list. This prevents interruptions. Unfortunately, it formalizes the process and stunts the natural flow of discussion. By the time a person gets a chance to speak, the topics may have changed. *Linear problem solving*, in which one person speaks at a time and the focus is on one issue at a time, works better for some cultures than for others. The facilitator needs to determine how flexible to be about interruptions and the flow of communication. Some groups can tolerate interruptions and still work constructively. In fact, sidetracking can lead to creative solutions.

When certain people constantly interrupt the process, this behavior may indicate that they have a different agenda or they are using interruptions as a competitive tactic. They may also have emotional needs that require addressing (as discussed earlier). Some facilitators use a talking piece to discourage interruptions and to promote more equal participation. A *talking piece*, originally used in Native American healing circles, is a feather, stone, stick, or other object that participants pass between them. Whoever has the talking piece is allowed to speak without interruptions. When finished, the speaker passes the talking piece to the next person.

5. Silence

Silence among certain participants is difficult to assess. Often, people assume that if someone is silent, the person is agreeing with what is being said. However, silence could also mean the person is not comfortable speaking in front of a group, the person disagrees but does not know how to respond, the person does not feel safe presenting a contrary point of view, the person is not paying attention, or the person does not understand what is being said. Because sharing information is vital to group decision making (Schittekatte, 1996), facilitators need to address any issues related to silence.

Facilitators can establish several ground rules at the beginning of the process to pre-empt some problems related to silence:

- All participants will be given an opportunity to speak.
- Everyone's needs and interests are important to the group and its decisions.
- Diverse opinions will be valued and respected.
- If anyone has difficulty speaking in front of the group, he or she can discuss alternatives with the facilitator (e.g., practicing communication skills in order to prepare, using an advocate, or submitting a written brief).
- Although participation in discussion may be encouraged, nobody will be forced to speak.
- The group will not assume that silence means agreement.

Some people do not bother to speak up at meetings because they do not believe their input will have any bearing on decisions to be made. In order to pre-empt this problem, the group needs to know how decisions will be made from the outset. In some cases, the group will operate on a consensus model. That is, decisions will require general agreement of the group.[1] For some decisions, the group may require unanimity. For others, it may require majority or supermajority votes (e.g., over two-thirds of the people present). Voting procedures ensure that everyone has a say in the outcome; consensus approaches are more likely to encourage win-win solutions and collaborative problem solving. Voting procedures could include either open voting or secret ballot. Secret ballot allows people to vote their conscience without fear of recriminations from others. The downside of secret ballot is that no one knows why people voted a particular way. This allows individuals to vote a particular way without ever letting others know of their true concerns.

In some instances, people are asked to participate in a discussion in which they have no decision-making power. For example, at the end of the discussion, a small group will be responsible for actually making the decisions. In such a case, the facilitator needs to ensure that the decision makers will actually take everyone's input into account. The facilitator could ask the decision makers directly, "Why are we having this discussion with 50 people when only 5 of you will actually decide what happens?" The decision makers can explain that they value the knowledge and opinions of all group members. They can also note that the decisions will need to be implemented by the membership; therefore, a decision that does not reflect their needs and interests cannot be implemented effectively.

One of the best ways to find out why a person is remaining silent is to ask, either in the group or in a private caucus. The facilitator should allow the person to speak, without feeling pressure or embarrassment.

Veronica, we haven't heard from you for a while. I'm not sure whether this is because you're agreeing, disagreeing, or just need more time to think this through.

---

[1]Susskind (2005) suggests that if there is overwhelming agreement but not unanimity, each person must be asked, in person and out loud, about whether he or she can live with the agreement. If each person can live with the agreement, then consensus may be declared. Otherwise, the group needs to hear and try to accommodate the concerns of those who say they cannot live with the agreement. If the group cannot satisfy these concerns, then there is consensus that no agreement is possible.

Asking people a direct question and looking at them as though you expect an answer generally provokes a response. However, you may also want to respect a person's right not to speak. For some individuals, observing and listening is a sufficient form of group participation. Their body language may indicate whether they are agreeing or disagreeing with the direction of the meeting.

People who are silent may have difficulty expressing themselves. In order to draw them out, the facilitator can use reflective listening skills and exploration skills.

You seem to agree that higher standards are needed. Can you please say more about that?

In spending time to draw out particular individuals, the facilitator must be careful about losing impartiality. Often, facilitators are tempted to draw out people whose opinions fit with their own or whose ideas might lead to a speedy solution. The facilitator must ensure that all people have an opportunity to speak, regardless of whether the person's ideas are interesting or realistic (Kaner, 1996).

6. Lost Attention

Group participants may lose their attention for a number of reasons: the content is not interesting to them, the process is long or dull, there are outside distractions, or they have a relatively short attention span.

If the parties have agreed to the agenda and the facilitator keeps discussion focused on the agenda, then the content should be of interest to the participants. If some participants seem disinterested in the topics being discussed, the facilitator could ask directly whether this is so. The agenda may require renegotiating in order to focus on what really matters.

In order to ensure participants do not feel the process is dragging, keep meetings to less than 90 minutes, or have breaks at specified intervals. Use a variety of formats for communication: small-group discussion, panel discussion, brainstorming session, keynote presentation, written submissions, experiential exercises, and so on. Make use of audiovisual equipment, such as flipcharts, LCD projectors, CD players, and DVD players. Allow for humor to lighten up the discussion.

External distractions could be physical or emotional. Physical distractions include noise, hunger, fatigue, or discomfort (e.g., too hot or too cold). Simply assuring that participants are well fed and comfortable goes a long way to ensuring that they can participate constructively. Dealing with emotional distractions may not be so easy. People may have a number of things on their mind that distract them from the process, many of which have nothing to do with the group's objectives. Ideally, try to set a time for meetings when people are less likely to have emotional distractions (e.g., not when a key participant is dealing with a family emergency or not just before a major holiday). If a person seems distracted, this may be occasion for the facilitator to approach the person privately, during a break, to see whether there is a problem.

Another method to ensure people remain attentive is to provide everyone with a specific role: meeting chair, timekeeper, recorder, and so on. Some people could be designated in advance to present on particular topics within their realm of expertise (e.g., suicide, crime prevention, or alternative cancer treatments). This gives people something to do and shows that their participation will be valued.

Avoid assigning people to represent particular positions or interests. This tends to push people into polarized positions. For example, a person trying to represent the interests of vocational counselors might push their agenda to the exclusion of the interests of human service workers. Instead, encourage people to draw from their own area of expertise, while also exploring issues from a global perspective.

> Each one of us comes from a different professional background, with different views and areas of interest. The issue of professional regulation, however, cuts across all professions. Perhaps we can focus on our common concerns.

The facilitator tries to foster joint problem solving. This approach encourages participants to listen to one another because the discussion affects all of them, regardless of whether the speaker is a psychologist, family therapist, probation officer, or pastoral counselor.

7. Difficulty Listening to Others

One of the most common causes of conflict is miscommunication. Often, this means that group members have had difficulty listening to one another. People involved in destructive conflict tend to focus on their own needs and agenda. As with mediation, a facilitator can foster mutual recognition by helping group members listen to one another. This can be done through modeling or teaching people active listening skills.

> Frank, you're scheduled to speak next. Before you share your ideas, would you mind providing a brief summary of what you understood Sharon to say?

The facilitator encourages participants to hear what others have to say, from their point of view. This does not mean that they have to agree with one another. However, mutual understanding can go a long way to fostering effective team work and managing conflicts.

Facilitators must accept that misunderstandings—and even chaos—are virtually inevitable. They can acknowledge that misunderstandings are stressful for everyone, but each group member has potential to gain a better understanding of one another. Rather than rescue a group from chaos, facilitators help groups work through it, thereby developing a stronger sense of team or community (Eller, 2004).

8. Others Put on Defensive

Insults, insinuations, and direct attacks can put participants on the defensive. Often such remarks are unintended. Where a high level of conflict exists, people often impute negative connotations to remarks that the speaker did not intend. In order to prevent problems of this kind, the facilitator can establish ground rules like the following:

- Everyone will speak to one another with respect.
- If individuals feel slighted or harassed by another person, they can state how they feel and ask what the other person intended.
- Participants will act in good faith and take responsibility for what they say.

If participants breach their ground rules, the facilitator can remind them of their previous agreement and explore whether the ground rules need to be renegotiated. This encourages positive interaction without embarrassing specific individuals. Another strategy is to involve the group in a discussion of the costs of noncooperative relations. Encouraging people to show respect, however, does not mean that people have to stifle their different views or suggestions, as the following section explains.

9. Not Saying What They Think

One of the most difficult issues for a facilitator to assess is whether participants are saying what they think (Stone, Patton, & Heen, 2000). People may self-censor themselves in order to avert conflict, fit in, or look good. This may be because they are conflict avoiders, conflict accommodators, or naturally shy. The facilitator's role is to ensure the environment for discussion is safe for all members. Facilitators can foster such an environment by developing explicit ground rules with the parties.

- The group encourages all individuals to express their opinions, even if they may sound contrary or unpopular to others.
- All participants will try to understand diverse opinions expressed by others, before making any comments about them.
- People can disagree on various issues, while still maintaining respect for those they disagree with.

The facilitator can also encourage participants to use active listening skills with one another in order to build a sense of trust.

> Veronica, Sharon . . . the two of you seem to have different opinions about disciplinary procedures, but I'm not sure I understand what the difference really is . . . Veronica, could you try to restate what Sharon is saying? After, I'll ask Sharon about Veronica's statement.

Because each person knows that the other will be paraphrasing his or her statements, each will try to restate what the other has said in a respectful and accurate manner.

10. Confusion about Decisions

Groups can make decisions by general consensus, vote, or determination of the group's leader(s). When the group makes decisions, it needs to know exactly what decisions have been reached. When many individuals are involved in decision making, there is enormous opportunity for confusion. Record keeping or note taking is vital. The facilitator, or someone else who has been designated, should take notes throughout the process and periodically ask for feedback to ensure that the notes accurately reflect what the group has decided.

Records or notes can take various forms. A video or audio recording of a meeting can be used to prepare a verbatim (or word-for-word) *transcript* of the meeting. *Minutes* include the topics discussed, key issues, votes taken, decisions made, and who is responsible for which tasks in order to implement decisions. A *summary of decisions* only lists the decisions reached by the group. Transcripts are the most detailed and accurate, because the recorder does not have to make any interpretations of what has been said. Unfortunately, they are lengthy and costly to produce. In addition, few people have time to spend reviewing transcripts. Minutes require the recorder to make interpretations. Tentative minutes can be passed around the group for feedback to ensure their accuracy. A summary of decisions is less detailed than minutes. The group can work through the wording of the decisions or agreements as they are being reached. The recorder can use a flipchart or overhead transparency to record decisions in a manner that the group can respond to immediately. Decisions are the most important parts of the meeting to record. Transcripts or minutes of the process often generate further conflict between the parties (e.g., "I didn't say that," "That's not what I meant," or "Why didn't you include my suggestions?"). In order to avoid future misunderstandings, the facilitator should suggest that notes from a meeting include at minimum what the group decided, who is responsible for doing what, what is the expected time frame for getting tasks accomplished, and how the group will monitor and follow up on its decisions.

GROUP FACILITATION SKILLS AND ACTIVITIES

The inventory in Figure 5.1 identifies key skills activities for group facilitation. As with previous inventories, this one can be used as a checklist to help you prepare for a specific intervention or to help you identify skills that you want to work on.

Figure 5.1 | Inventory of Group Facilitation Skills and Activities

1. Assesses presenting problem(s) or conflict situation with people affected in order to determine the best time, place, and process for bringing people together
2. Invites and encourages essential people to attend the meeting
3. Obtains agreement on the agenda and goals for the meeting (either prior to or during the meeting)
4. Establishes ground rules to promote effective communication
5. Clarifies the roles of the people participating
6. Keeps participants focused on the agenda
7. Punctuates topics and transitions between topics
8. Allows for flexibility in the agenda to meet specific needs of the group
9. Provides all participants with an opportunity to contribute to the process
10. Assists individuals needing support to communicate without losing impartiality
11. Constructively confronts people who dominate, disrupt, or interrupt, without putting them on the defensive
12. Promotes safe environment for expressing divergent or unpopular opinions
13. Establishes clear understanding about how decisions will be made (e.g., by group, by certain individuals, by consensus, or by majority vote)
14. Shares facilitation tasks, where appropriate (e.g., clarifies who is responsible for note taking, time keeping, sharing expertise, enforcing ground rules)
15. Uses reflective listening skills or exploratory questions to draw out nonverbal participants

16. Makes use of audiovisual aids and various formats for discussion to ensure the process is interesting and productive
17. Paces the meeting, balancing time constraints with the needs of various participants to express themselves
18. Pre-empts or attends to external distractions (e.g., noise, uncomfortable environment, hunger, emotional distractions)
19. Encourages participants to use active listening with one another to foster mutual understanding and recognition
20. Clarifies misunderstandings between participants
21. Encourages participants to demonstrate respect to one another, regardless of expressed differences of opinion
22. Fosters collaboration (e.g., a team approach)
23. Provides participants with constructive responses for dealing with potential insults, insinuations, or attacks
24. Boomerangs (or reflects) questions posed to the facilitator back to the group (if members ask the facilitator questions that the group is responsible to answer)
25. Ensures decisions or agreements are accurately recorded (flipcharts, typed notes)
26. Helps the group plan for implementation, monitoring, evaluation, and follow-up

APPROACHES TO FACILITATION

Different facilitators use the skills listed in Figure 5.1 in different ways, depending on their approach to facilitation. The following discussion focuses on four of the many approaches to group facilitation: debate, dialogue, problem solving, and identity-based facilitation. I selected these approaches because they represent very distinctive frameworks for interaction.

To illustrate each approach, consider the following conflict scenario:

Amanda is a woman of African descent living in an area of Conflictia where the majority of the residents are of European descent. On her way to and from work, she passes the high school. Often, she is confronted by a group of teenagers who taunt her with racial slurs. One day, she hears about a new Center for Community Facilitation. She decides to call the Center to see what it can offer. The Center says it could offer to facilitate discussion between Amanda and the specific group of teenagers. However, it has received similar complaints from others and believes that the issue should be dealt with on a community basis.

1. Debate

A *debate is a forum for discussion where conflicting parties advocate for particular positions.* In a formal debate, the facilitator (often called a **moderator**) guides the participants through a particular sequence of presentations (International Debate Education Association, n.d.):

1. The moderator introduces the question for debate, often in the form of a statement that requires the participants to take a stand, pro or con. In the present example, the statement to be debated could be "Students who commit racial slurs should be suspended from school."

2. People who agree with the statement (the pro side) present a brief introduction to their argument (i.e., give reasons to back their point of view).
3. People who oppose the statement (the con side) present an introduction to their argument.
4. The pro side presents its full argument.
5. The con side provides a response to the pro side's argument.
6. The con side presents its full argument.
7. The pro side provides a response to the con side's argument.
8. The moderator facilitates taking questions from the audience or a panel of people designated to ask questions.
9. The con side summarizes its case.
10. The pro side summarizes its case.
11. A decision is made by a panel of judges or a vote by the stakeholders.

In some ways, the role of a moderator is similar to that of a mediator. A moderator helps parties communicate with one another and guides them through a conflict resolution process. The moderator establishes ground rules and keeps parties to them. The facilitator has no decision-making power. The decision is generally left to a panel of judges or a vote of the stakeholders. The structure of the debate is designed to inform participants about a range of issues and arguments, with each side trying to convince the decision makers of a particular view. In contrast to the role of a mediator, a moderator does not help the parties work toward a mutually satisfactory agreement, does not try to foster amicable relations, and does not promote transformation. The debate format tends to be adversarial, similar to court proceedings or positional negotiation.

Public discussions often take on the qualities of a debate, even if the forum is not set up as a formal debate. For example, the Center for Community Facilitation decides to organize a town hall meeting to discuss the issue of racial taunting among students. Various stakeholders are invited: Amanda and other targets of harassment, students, parents, directors from the school board, teachers, guidance counselors, community workers, police, and equal rights advocates. During the meeting, the town hall facilitator invites everyone to respond to this issue. Some suggest that the students should be suspended. Others reject this idea. The two groups become polarized, each arguing its own point of view without considering the other's perspective or their mutual interests. The facilitator acts as a referee or peacekeeper, encouraging the parties to demonstrate respect, speak in turn, and focus on the key issues. However, the facilitator does not help them negotiate a mutually acceptable agreement.

One of the primary advantages of a debate is that a decision is guaranteed at the end of the process. The judges or other participants make a decision by majority vote. Consensus is not needed. Debates also tend to simplify the issues. The options for solution are narrowed into a clear choice: in this case, for example, to suspend or not to suspend. Debates highlight the issues and the areas of disagreement. They also allow for a broad range of participation. All stakeholders can have an opportunity to express their point of view—having one's day in court, so to speak. At their best, debates include thoughtful critique of an issue, providing decision makers with the information and analysis they need in order to make highly informed decisions.

The downside of debating is that debaters tend to become entrenched in positions. Debates encourage participants to use rhetoric to support their positions rather than look at underlying interests and ways of working toward creative, win-win solutions (Chasin, Herzig, Roth, Chasin, Becker, & Stains, 1996). Often, debates become provocative rather than thought provoking (Tannen, 1998). The question for debate is posed as *pro* or *con*, meaning the debaters typically ignore other options for solution. Although participants are encouraged to look at issues from the other group's perspective, this is only for the purpose of being able to counter their arguments. Debates lead to final decisions, but these are not necessarily decisions that both parties can live with. If follow-through on the decision requires cooperation of the participants, this may not be forthcoming from a group that is not happy with the decision.

Debates certainly have a place in determining intergroup and community conflicts. A helping professional's choice of approaches will depend on the type of issue in dispute, the nature of the conflict, the willingness of the parties to engage in a particular type of process, and the type of outcomes that are desired. Sometimes a combination of approaches can be used.

Consider: In the racial taunting case, is a debate really appropriate? If so, what is the most germane question for the debate? If not, what are the problems with this process for Amanda and the other interested parties?

2. Dialogue[2]

Whereas debates tend to place people on opposite sides of issues and foster adversarial relations, *dialogues are designed to build understanding, cooperation, and positive relationships*. The dialogue approach draws a number of elements from family therapy:

- The facilitator works in a nonhierarchical manner with the participants, establishing a collaborative relationship with each of them as they endeavor to realize their conflicting desires.
- The facilitator conducts much of the work prior to bringing the participants together: assessing their skills, hopes, and fears; preparing them with constructive communication skills; obtaining commitment to the dialogue process; and identifying old, destructive patterns of relating that they need to discontinue for the dialogue to be effective.
- During the dialogue, the facilitator promotes an atmosphere of safety, where people can express divergent points of view and still demonstrate respect for one another (Chasin et al., 1996; Schirch, 2004).

Whereas participants in a debate represent a position, side, or stereotype, participants in a dialogue are encouraged to speak as individuals, from their own personal experience. In debates, advocates or representatives are often selected as spokespeople for each group. The dialogue approach encourages broad participation, as individuals speak on their own behalves rather than through designated

---

[2]Some people use the word *multilogue* rather than *dialogue* to connote that many different parties and perspectives are involved rather than just a communication between two.

leaders. The dialogue approach encourages participants to listen to one another in a way that builds insight and mutual understanding. In this sense, dialogue is similar to transformative mediation (Bush & Folger, 2005). Facilitators may remind participants to be kind or compassionate with each other, noting that everyone has strong feelings and legitimate concerns (Wilmot & Hocker, 2007). Sometimes, facilitators bring a playful attitude toward the dialogue, encouraging participants to have fun, use their imaginations, and be creative.

If the Center for Community Facilitation decides to orchestrate its town hall meeting as a dialogue, the first step is to meet with the various stakeholders. The facilitator encourages victims of harassment to speak on their own behalves rather than through lawyers or human rights advocates. The facilitator helps Amanda and others like her so they can articulate their personal experiences of how the harassment affected them. Likewise, the facilitator works with students to speak on their own behalves rather than through their parents or teachers. Initially, the students are reluctant to engage in the dialogue, believing they are being set up in a process bent against them. The facilitator needs to ensure the process is fair and students feel safe participating. The participants agree to the following ground rules: participants will speak to one another in respectful terms; participants will listen to each other as allies; the focus of the discussion is not to establish fault or blame but to promote understanding; the dialogue will not result in any decisions about the students' status at the school.

The issue for the dialogue is not "Should the school suspend the students accused of harassing?" but "How have each of the participants experienced this conflict?" This question opens the discourse and allows participants to explore the conflict from a broader perspective. Those who have experienced harassment will learn about the views and motives of the students. The students, in turn, will learn how their actions have affected the people they have taunted. As a result of this exchange, the students may apologize for their actions, or the group may come to an agreement about what to do from now on. However, success of the dialogue does not depend on coming to an agreement. Success may occur through fostering better communication, understanding, and healing of relationships.

The primary goals of dialogue are to provide everyone with an opportunity to speak and to gain a better understanding of one another. Although a dialogue might help parties work toward resolution of conflicts, it might also make differences between parties more pronounced. Given that reaching agreement is not a primary goal, is a facilitated dialogue a form of mediation?

The dialogue approach may be particularly appropriate when reaching agreement is not a realistic goal. When people have conflicting values, for instance, these are difficult to reconcile. Consider the controversy over euthanasia. Those who support the use of euthanasia value individual autonomy over the sanctity of life. Those who oppose euthanasia value sanctity of life over individual autonomy. Because these values are deeply held, a short-term conflict resolution process designed to reconcile these values is likely to fail. Dialogue, however, allows the parties to learn more about one another's perspectives, without expecting them to compromise their values. By establishing mutual understanding, the participants learn to respect one another, including their differences. Over the long term, dialogue can affect the values of each group as well as the common values that they develop.

In some instances, dialogue can be used as a prelude to an agreement-oriented CR process. Where the level of conflict between participants is high and level of understanding is low, dialogue provides the participants with an opportunity to engage with one another in a nonthreatening process. They know coming into the dialogue that they are not being asked to "compromise with the enemy." Dialogues ask people to sit down and talk, without requiring any further commitment. Mistrust builds over time; thus, rebuilding trust also takes time. Dialogue can be structured as a process that occurs over time rather than as a one-time event. The helping professional develops a sequence of opportunities for conflicting groups to engage in dialogue. During initial stages, the structures for dialogue tend to be more formal. As trust builds, the structures become less formal. Decision making may emerge from the process, but the facilitator does not try to force it on the parties.

3. Problem Solving

According to the problem-solving approach, a facilitator guides group members through a series of phases designed to help members analyze and resolve the issues confronting them. This approach could use the same steps as the interest-based approach to mediation described in Chapter 4: preparation, orientation, issue definition, exploring interests and needs, negotiation and problem solving, finalizing an agreement, and follow-up.

Whereas the interest-based approach in Chapter 4 focused on problem solving between individuals, this section focuses on a problem-solving process between groups. Consider the harassment scenario again. At the beginning of the preparation phase, the Center for Community Facilitation needs to consider who are the parties and how will they participate. If this were mediation between individuals, the primary parties would be Amanda and the students that she claims harassed her. However, the Center has decided to approach this as an intergroup conflict. The primary groups are the students and the various complainants against the students. Teachers, parents, and counselors could also be brought into the process. Some facilitators prefer to limit the number of participants in order to streamline the process. Others prefer larger groups because of the advantages of pooling information and expertise from a broad range of participants (Stewart & Strasser, 1998). In this case, the Center decides that the conflict pervades the community and requires broad participation. Participants will act as individuals rather than as representatives of particular groups. Any decisions will be made by consensus of the participants.

Given the large number of participants, the Center opts for two people to cofacilitate. They select one facilitator of African descent and one facilitator of European descent, hoping to pre-empt fears that the process is biased against either group. The facilitators meet with each group separately, in order to hear their concerns, explain the group process, obtain their commitment, and help them prepare. Preparation is particularly important for intergroup conflict given the large number of people and potential for the process to get out of control. Smaller meetings also provide the parties with a chance to vent feelings, so that they may be able to focus more on problem solving during the joint meetings.

Of all the groups involved in the process, the students are the most reluctant participants. On meeting with them, the facilitators offer suggestions about how to articulate their needs and interests. This empowers the students and helps the facilitators establish trust with them.

The group complaining of harassment expresses concern about how to deal with racist comments that may arise during the joint meetings. The facilitators offer ground rules to try to pre-empt this type of conflict from escalating. They also describe techniques such as *I statements* and *constructive confrontation* that can be used to respond to hurtful remarks.

During meetings with the teachers, the facilitators discuss how the teachers can contribute to the process without taking a dominant role. The teachers are used to resolving conflict on their own, so the facilitators acknowledge the teachers' expertise in conflict resolution. Following some negotiations, the teachers agree to act as constructive participants—looking for mutual interests, focusing on the future, brainstorming options for solution, and so on. However, they will leave control of the process to the facilitators.

The preparatory meeting with the parents is marked by a high level of conflict. Various parents accuse one another's children of being racist, rude, or degenerate. Conflict resolution between individuals *within* a group is often more important than conflict resolution *between* groups. The facilitators do not try to get the parents to agree on who was or was not responsible for the problem. Instead, the facilitators focus the parents on their mutual interests. All parents agree that they do not want past incidents to interfere with their children's ability to complete their education. They also agree that they do not want their children or community to be known as racist.

By the time the first joint meeting takes place, the parties are oriented and committed to the process. The facilitators review the problem-solving process and comment on the positive level of participation from all groups during the preparatory meetings. The facilitators review an agenda that has previously been distributed to the participants. Today's meeting will last 3 hours. The first 90 minutes is designated for an open dialogue about the concerns that brought people to this meeting. The facilitators have prepared the parties with ways of expressing concerns from personal perspectives, without inflaming conflict. After a break, the discussion will turn to identifying issues and exploring underlying interests. A follow-up meeting is scheduled a week later to work through the latter stages of the problem-solving process. The facilitators keep the parties to a relatively fixed time schedule. They also tend to be more directive about the agenda than for mediation between individuals, in order to maintain control over the process. Still, they need to ensure that they have consensus on the agenda before moving forward.

The storytelling portion of the process goes ahead as planned. Various individuals describe what has been happening. Others start to focus on the future. The group is too large for everyone to have as much say as they would like, so the facilitators decide to place limits and keep the parties focused. They consider dividing participants so they can engage in small-group discussions but decide that today's meeting should focus on discussion between all members. Some students seem intimidated, so the facilitators try to draw them out with exploration questions.

After the break, the parties begin to identify issues. Some participants offer solutions, such as suspending the students, having the students do community service, or having the complainants avoid passing by the school. The facilitators explain that it is too early to focus on solutions, because the issues have not even been clearly identified. Some teachers take the lead, helping others understand the difference between issues and solutions: how to hold students accountable for their behavior, how to make amends to those who have suffered from harassment, and what the school can do if similar incidents arise in the future. The big issue that emerges is what to do about racism in the school and in the general community. To the facilitators' surprise, everyone seems to coalesce around this one issue. The students are not singled out as the problem. Rather, the community seems prepared to look at racism as a broad community issue. The people who originally complained of harassment are encouraged that people are accepting responsibility for what has happened.

The facilitators move the participants into a discussion of their interests. Initially, individuals focus on their own interests. The facilitators remind them of their primary issue: racism in the school and the community. This helps them focus on mutual interests. Once the participants get going, they start to flood the facilitators. The facilitators list the ideas on a flipchart. Once an exhaustive list is completed, the facilitators help them draw out themes and common interests. The participants achieve consensus on three key interests: respect for all individuals and groups, regardless of race or ethnic background; racist-free education; and the ability to walk down the streets without being harassed. The facilitators congratulate the participants on their progress in this first meeting. In order to prepare for the next meeting, the facilitators ask them to brainstorm ideas for how to satisfy these interests. The facilitators advise participants to keep their ideas tentative: during the next meeting they will explore a broad range of options before deciding how to proceed.

During the second meeting, the facilitators review the process to date, remind everyone about the ground rules, and confirm everyone's commitment to the agenda. Notes on flipcharts list the issues and interests identified at the last meeting. The facilitators engage the parties in brainstorming by going around the room and asking each person to identify one possible solution, not necessarily their favorite one. The facilitators write each idea on the flipchart, as it is suggested.

At one point in the brainstorming, a parent uses the term *colored people*. Some participants jump all over him for using such an offensive term. Others come to his defense, saying they do not believe in political correctness. The facilitators suggest that they suspend brainstorming for 15 minutes in order to discuss this issue. One facilitator takes the parent through a series of questions: What did you mean when you said "colored people"? Where did you learn this term? Did you mean it to be offensive? Do you understand how others might find it offensive? The facilitator asks for a volunteer who is offended by the term. The facilitator asks the volunteer the following questions: When you heard someone say "colored people," how did it make you feel? Why do you think you felt this way? Do you think that it was intended to be a racist remark? What words could you suggest other than "colored people"? The facilitator uses this exchange to promote mutual understanding. The facilitator also models how to confront racist comments in a constructive manner. Not everyone is satisfied that the issue has been resolved. The facilitators validate their concerns and suggest that this may be one of the issues for the group to deal with over the longer term. The facilitators do not try to put closure to this issue.

The facilitators make a transition back to brainstorming. Once an exhaustive list has been ascertained, the facilitators divide the participants into three groups. Students, teachers, complainants, and others are randomly dispersed through the groups. Each group is assigned responsibility for one of the key underlying interests. They are allotted 30 minutes to review the list of options and to develop a general plan to deal with this issue. Each facilitator works with one group. They have also prepared one teacher to facilitate the third group. One advantage of smaller groups is that individuals have greater opportunity to participate. Another advantage is that they can tackle more than one issue at a time.

Each group reports back to the full forum. Following each presentation, individuals are invited to provide comments. The facilitators encourage them to build on the ideas of subgroups rather than offer completely different options. Eventually, the group comes to consensus on the following plans:

- A joint teacher-parent-student committee will be established to review the curriculum at the school to ensure that racism, discrimination, and other forms of bigotry are dealt with effectively in all grades.
- The school will develop a Harassment Committee to deal with any complaints about student harassment or racism.
- The community will develop a public campaign to raise awareness about the effects of racism and to promote greater respect for people from different backgrounds.

The facilitators ask questions to ensure that these plans are feasible. They explore who will be responsible for what, how they will secure sufficient resources to do what they want, and how they will ensure that people follow through on the tasks they accept. They also encourage broad participation in these tasks so the whole community takes ownership of the solutions. Certain people accept leadership roles. The facilitators offer to provide these leaders with further information and support about how to facilitate the implementation of their decisions. The work has just begun.

4. Identity

Identity-based approaches to facilitating intergroup discussion are designed for identity-based conflict. In contrast to conflict based on miscommunication or division of limited resources, identity-based conflict is rooted in the ways that conflicting groups view themselves and the other group. Archetypal examples of identity-based conflicts include the conflicts between Roman Catholics and Protestants in Ireland, Sunni and Shia Muslims in the Middle East, and Blacks and Whites in South Africa and the United States. Identity-based conflicts may originate as disputes over land, money, values, or power, but they develop into identity issues as the conflict becomes protracted. Each group tends to view itself as innocent victims. In addition, each group imputes blame to the other group as the oppressors, transgressors, or evil adversaries. Stereotypes and discrimination can also develop through lack of contact and intergroup ignorance. In some cases, groups promote certain identities in order to further their political causes. Osama bin Laden and Al Qaeda promote certain identities for Americans (aggressors and infidels) and Muslims (righteous victims, martyrs, and holders of truth) in order to mobilize Muslims to fight against Americans.

Identity-based CR (Desivilya, 2004; Halabi, 1998; Rothman, 1997) is based on Kurt Lewin's (1948) identity theory. Lewin studied the issues of majority-minority relations in democratic, pluralistic societies. He posited that intergroup hostilities are often grounded in identity issues. A significant portion of individual behavior is determined by group membership. Therefore, the manner in which people from a majority group perceive and respond to a minority group depends on how the majority group views itself and the minority. The same applies to the way that a minority group perceives and responds to the majority group. If a conflict is rooted in identity issues, then it is difficult to redress unless the CR process helps individuals change within the context of their social groups (Bargal & Bar, 1997).

According to role theory, each individual in a social group has a particular position, similar to an office or job. People come to expect certain behaviors of the individual associated with that job. If the individual does not behave as expected, then stress occurs in the system: others in the system punish or alienate the person; alternatively, they reward the person for taking steps back toward the expected behaviors for the role. In order for the intergroup process to be effective, the facilitator must help each group alter its role expectations.

Changes in self-perception and role expectations require experiential workshops rather than just educational lectures or abstract discussions. Accordingly, the facilitator needs to design interactions that enable participants to see themselves in new roles. The facilitator helps them re-evaluate perceptions of themselves as powerless victims or innocent bystanders. Each group challenges the other's stereotypes, generalizations, and self-perceptions. In a sense, each group acts as a mirror for the other group, allowing group members to see themselves in a different light (Halabi, 1998).

Groups tend to define themselves by similarity of background, experiences, or values. Accordingly, groups with different backgrounds, experiences, or values often find themselves at odds with one another. One method of altering identity-based conflict is to encourage different groups to see themselves as one group, bound together by an interdependence of fate (Lewin, 1948). Conflicting groups must come to the realization "Whether we like it or not, we are in this together." Rather than focus on past differences or present crises, focus on the opportunity to build better relations in the future.

Common obstacles to improving intergroup relations are low self-esteem and lack of confidence among people from a minority group. The facilitator can help the minority group by teaching CR skills and by fostering ethnic pride. Raising collective consciousness is another method of boosting confidence (Freshman, 2005). A single woman may feel that she is not worthy enough to confront a male boss and ask for higher salary; by raising the woman's awareness of other women in her situation, a facilitator empowers her to be more assertive. Some facilitators use confidence-building and mindfulness-raising measures by meeting separately with the minority group. Other facilitators refer the minority group to community developers or advocates for this type of support.

When intergroup conflict is deeply entrenched, the goal for facilitation may not be to resolve conflict, but to alter its course. At the end of the facilitated meetings, for example, the two groups will likely retain their core values. However, they will have a greater appreciation of their respective roles in maintaining or alleviating their conflicts. They can focus their energies on resolving pragmatic problems rather than philosophical ones. They can also establish ongoing interactions to help them build the sort of trust needed to handle larger issues over the long run.

The focus of identity-based facilitation is an encounter between groups rather than between individuals. In sharp contrast to the dialogue and problem-solving frameworks, participants are encouraged to see themselves as group members (Halabi, 1998). They must take responsibility for themselves, as well as others in the group. For example, European participants might agree that Africans have been mistreated but claim that they are not personally responsible for this. By focusing participants on group issues rather than personal ones, the European members are compelled to look at their role in discrimination against Africans.

Identity-based approaches use either a "cultural island" or a "community-based" process. *In the cultural island process (sometimes called an encounter group), the facilitator selects certain members from the conflicting groups to participate in a series of interactions.* These may be structured as weekly meetings or as a concentrated retreat. The advantage of a concentrated retreat is that the parties live together in a controlled environment for a period of a few days. This helps them learn about one another's cultures, including food, music, and religious rituals. The two groups are treated as a microcosm of the dynamics that occur in broader society, including oppression, anger, and other manifestations of the intergroup conflict. The facilitator helps participants relate their issues to external influences, but the primary focus of the intervention is on the participants in the cultural island (Halabi, 1998).

In a community-based process, the interventions take place in the community rather than in a controlled environment. The facilitator extends invitations to the whole community rather than to selected individuals. The participants may focus on current community conflicts and each group's roles in these conflicts (Fisher, 1997). The facilitator uses structured dialogues and noncompetitive activities to promote understanding and trust between groups. In an approach akin to community development, the facilitator helps the groups work through community conflicts in a collaborative manner. Research shows that competition over resources tends to inflame stereotypical attitudes and discriminatory behavior; in contrast, when rival groups are assigned to work together on superordinate goals, they tend to move beyond prejudice and work collaboratively (Platow & Hunter, 2001).

Consider relations between the rich and poor. Whenever a theft or other crime occurs, rich people blame poor people. Because of this, the rich people may support socioeconominc profiling by police (if certain people look like they do not belong in the rich neighborhood, police will stop and question them). People from the poor community perceive this treatment as prejudiced and unjust. A facilitator might bring these two communities together, not to work on the crime issue but to work on a mutual, uncontentious goal. Perhaps the goal is to clean up the community park and install a playground for all children from the area. By working collaboratively on an issue that is not a hot-button topic, the two groups experience each other and themselves in a different light. Essentially, the facilitator uses work on a common goal as an opportunity to build a bridge between the two groups. At some point, the facilitator may also encourage the groups to surface and work through the identity-based roots of past conflicts (Rothman, 1997). However, they may benefit from simply working together without expressly discussing identity issues.

Identity-based approaches tend to be less structured than problem-based approaches. Although the facilitator leads participants through a series of stages, the facilitator does not provide participants with an explicit agenda or structure. Instead, the facilitator lets the participants know the purpose of the interaction in general terms. The facilitator guides the participants through a series of stages, without making the transitions between stages explicit.

In Halabi's (1998) cultural island model, the facilitator guides the participants through group formation, storytelling, confrontation, and resolution.

- *Group formation*: When the groups are brought together, the facilitator and participants introduce themselves. Initially, no direct reference is made to the conflict. The participants tend to be courteous and pleasant toward one another. The group is permitted to set the agenda, at which point the dominant group tends to take control of the process and dynamics.
- *Storytelling*: The oppressed group begins to tell stories of the oppression and discrimination they have experienced in society. The polite relations between groups begin to become more tense. The oppressed group starts to feel a moral advantage in the discussion. The dominant group starts to lose its tolerance and respond more defensively, offering rationalizations for the suffering endured by the oppressed group. The two groups begin to challenge one another's versions of events.
- *Confrontation*: The dominant group raises concerns about the oppressed group's role in the conflict, trying to assert its control. Anger and frustration among both groups start to emerge. The oppressed group maintains greater strength and does not back down. When the smoke begins to clear, there is a possibility for a more equal relationship between the groups.
- *Resolution*: The dialogue becomes more equal. Rather than rationalize oppression, the dominant group becomes more willing to recognize the legitimate rights of the oppressed group. Better understandings emerge and each group has developed a different sense of its role in the broader conflict. (pp. 4–5)

According to this approach, success is measured by a change in each party's self-perceptions. Participants need not make decisions or take specific actions, though these may occur as incidental results. Other variations of identity-based approaches, however, add components of the problem-solving approach to the end of the process (Rothman, 1997). Following the resolution stage, the parties go on to action planning: given their new understandings of themselves and the others, what actions can they take in order to deal with community issues or other problems?

Consider the conflict between Amanda and the students. Assume the Center for Community Facilitation views this as an identity-based conflict. The roots of the conflict extend beyond the parties directly involved in the harassment. The Center decides to use the cultural island model, bringing a selected group of African and European students together for a two-day retreat. It opts to invite students who teachers have identified as troublemakers and antagonists. Even though these may be

the most difficult people to work with, they represent the greatest need.[3] Cofacilitators are used, one African and one European, in order to demonstrate balance and
to model positive relations between people from the two groups.

The facilitators explain the purpose of this retreat is to explore issues between
the African and European communities in Conflictia. Neither group really knows
what to expect. Participants are nervous and look to the facilitators for guidance.
The facilitators encourage the participants to set the agenda, giving them ownership
over the process. At first, everyone is reluctant to suggest agenda items. Eventually,
informal leaders emerge. Europeans tend to take control with well-intentioned suggestions: to improve African-European relations, to deal with complaints of racial
harassment, and to deal with discrimination in the community.

Some European participants rebel. They think this is turning into an exercise in
European bashing. They make claims about drug use, race riots, and unemployment in the African community. They lay blame squarely with the Africans. The
facilitators do not take sides on the issues but try to balance the dialogue by encouraging African participants to respond. The facilitators ask the African group to
share their experiences of African-European relations. Various participants begin to
tell personal stories of discrimination: being pestered by police, being thrown out
of stores, and being scolded by teachers, for no reason other than being African.
Initially, the Europeans are hesitant to contradict these stories. They become uncomfortable and eventually start to challenge the credibility of the stories they are
hearing.

The facilitators allow the conflict to escalate. Members from each group become defensive and make verbal attacks on the other side. The facilitators maintain
certain ground rules to ensure the conflict does not escalate into violence, but they
provide participants with significant leeway for arguing. During breaks, the facilitators notice that each group sticks together. The facilitators encourage participants to
continue their dialogue and interactions with each other during breaks in the formal
discussions.

The facilitators provide a summary of the concerns raised by both groups. They
surface and label the anger and frustration that each side has expressed indirectly.
This encourages both sides to discuss their feelings. The level of conflict begins to de-
escalate as both groups come to realize they have much in common. By allowing
both sides to vent their prejudices, anger, and frustration, catharsis occurs. They are
ready to start dealing with issues in a more constructive fashion.

The facilitators place more structure on the dialogue, guiding the participants
through various issues they have raised. One of the stereotypes, for example, is that
Africans are lazy. The facilitators explore where the Europeans learned this stereotype. The facilitators ask the Africans questions that allow them to speak to the

---

[3]Other writers suggest inviting the people most amenable to the conflict resolution process, because they
are easier to engage and the process is more likely to be successful. This may sound like "preaching to the
converted," but the hope is that participants will go back to their communities with greater skills and abilities to influence others. Some models are specifically designed for educators and helping professionals
from the two conflicting groups (Desivilya, 2004).

stereotype, from their perspectives. Other intergroup stereotypes are discussed in a similar fashion. The facilitators encourage each group to reassess its own role in perpetuating myths and prejudices.

Throughout the process, the facilitators strive to maintain objectivity and impartiality. They check with one another to ensure that neither is demonstrating sympathy, anger, or other biases toward either group. The facilitators also ensure that each facilitator contributes equally, rather than one facilitator dominating control over the process.

The dialogue tends to become more constructive and balanced between the parties. They begin to appreciate one another's perspectives and question their own biases. The facilitators ask how the confrontations during this process relate to dynamics in the broader community. Although the groups have gained a new sense of their roles in the intergroup conflict, they realize that the old conflicts will still exist when they return to the community.

The facilitators in this situation did not intend to take the groups to the next level—action planning. Their primary goal was to have members of each group redefine their identities in relation to the other group. Some participants decide on their own to carry the process forward. They plan an ongoing committee at the school to work on intergroup relations. The committee will develop educational materials to promote better understandings. In addition, it will develop forums for further dialogue between the groups. The facilitators offer consultation and support, but they allow the participants to take the lead.

Identity-based interventions have had varying success. They tend to be most successful in dealing with specific disputes and developing better relationships between people from antagonistic groups (Rabie, 1994). Eradicating racism and prejudice on a larger scale is difficult (Platow & Hunter, 2001). There is no quick fix. Identity-based CR may be part of a solution, but expectations for any brief intervention must be realistic. Social change at a grassroots level is more likely to be successful when accompanied by support from political powers and other structures in society. Accordingly, facilitators must work with community leaders in order to secure ongoing political, financial, and moral support.

KEY POINTS

- The role of group facilitators is to improve the flow of communication between participants, pre-empting or responding to barriers to effective interaction as they may arise.

- Facilitators help participants decide who speaks when, what issues to focus on, and how to structure their interaction.

- Facilitators must attend to conflict at three levels: between groups, within groups, and between group members and the facilitators.

- Facilitators can anticipate different types of conflict at different stages of group development: forming, norming, storming, performing, and adjourning.

- Intergroup conflicts may be caused by differences in values, beliefs, or interests; such conflicts are often complicated by stereotyping, prejudice, miscommunication, and other forms of misunderstanding.

- In the debate approach, each party takes a stance and presents arguments to support its position. The moderator facilitates discussion but does not guide the parties toward consensus. A panel of judges or the parties themselves make decisions based on majority votes.

- The dialogue approach to facilitation encourages people from conflicting groups to communicate with one another as individuals. The facilitator coaches participants on how to speak and listen to one another. The primary goal of dialogue is to promote understanding rather than to come to agreement on the issues.

- The problem-solving approach is specifically designed to help conflicting parties come to agreement on the identified problems. The facilitator guides the parties through a problem-solving process (similar to interest-based mediation) and encourages the groups to work toward mutually satisfactory solutions.

- Identity-based approaches to facilitation are designed to change the way that members of each group view their roles in relationship to members of the other group. The facilitator helps participants confront stereotypes, myths, and prejudices that exist between the groups.

- In order to determine which facilitation approach to employ, the facilitator should consider the type of conflict, the goal for facilitation, and the readiness of each party to participate in a particular type of process. In some situations, different approaches can be used in combination.

DISCUSSION QUESTIONS AND EXERCISES

1. ASSESSING CONFLICT: Identify an intergroup conflict that has persisted in your community for several years. Who are the key players in the conflict? What is the nature of the conflict? How could each group be persuaded to participate in an intergroup facilitation process? How could the parties select a facilitator? Would it be better to have a facilitator or cofacilitators who come from within the community or from outside? Provide reasons for each of your suggested answers.

    As an alternative to assessing an actual conflict in your community, you could assess a conflict portrayed in a movie. For this alternative, select and watch a movie that depicts a conflict between two groups in society (e.g., one of the racial or ethnic conflicts depicted in *Crash* [Haggis, 2005] or the conflict between gays and heterosexuals as depicted in *Brokeback Mountain* [McMurtry & Ossana, 2005]).

2. STAGED CONFLICT: Consider the following scenario:

    A group of students is working on a term project, a class presentation on diversity issues. They agree that Fran will act as their group facilitator, helping them arrange meetings and keeping everyone task focused. Initially, everyone seems to be getting along, agreeing on how to divide the work and the timelines for completing various parts of the assignment.

In the second meeting, Ronald suggests they focus on race, because race is the most important aspect of diversity. Fran notices the other group members, Hailey and Henry, look uncomfortable with this proposal, but they remain hushed, seemingly going along with Ronald's suggestion. Fran notes that Ronald is the only one of them from a racial minority group.

Identify the group's current stage of development, and suggest which skills or approaches the facilitator (Fran) should use in order to help group members work through their conflict.

3. ALTERNATIVE INTERVENTIONS: Select one of the following terms: *community development, participatory decision making, consensus building, Samoan circle,* or *fishbowl* (Kirst-Ashman & Hull, 2005; Kraybill, 2005b; Susskind, 2005). Conduct a literature search of your chosen term using library databases such as PsychINFO, Sociofile, Social Work Abstracts, and ERIC. How does the literature define your chosen term? Compare and contrast your chosen term to one of the approaches to group facilitation described in this chapter. Try to isolate differences in assumptions, values, goals, and methods.

4. OPPRESSED WITCHES: Witches comprise one of the most oppressed groups in Conflictia. Their religion is not even recognized by the state. They have no elected representation. Most Conflictians are ignorant about Wicca—some fear that Witches cast evil spells, use children for witchcraft experiments, and bring Satan into the community. Develop a proposal for an intergroup conflict resolution process to deal with the conflict between Witches and the rest of the community. Your proposal should include answers to the following questions: What is the nature of the conflict? What is the purpose of the intervention? Which approach best suits this purpose? What are the main barriers to communication between these groups? How can a facilitator deal with these?

5. LOBBY GROUP CONFLICT: A group of mental health counselors is lobbying Conflictia's government for more funding for mental health services. A group of probation officers is asking the same government to invest more money in the criminal justice system. Each group believes that more money to one cause means less money for the other cause. What is the nature of the conflict between the groups? Which approach to group facilitation would be most appropriate for dealing with this conflict? Why?

6. CRITIQUING FACILITATION: Review the problem-solving example described earlier in this chapter. Identify each facilitation skill used by the facilitators. Which other skills would have been useful and for what purposes?

7. CONFIDENTIALITY: Chapter 4 discusses the issue of confidentiality in mediation between individuals. Does confidentiality apply in a facilitated process that involves large community groups? If it does apply, how would you explain confidentiality and obtain agreement from all participants? How would you enforce confidentiality? What laws, if any, does your jurisdiction have concerning whether government-related dialogues need to be open to the public? How would a law requiring principle openness affect the way you would facilitate public policy discussions (Susskind, 2005)?

ROLE-PLAY 5.1: "PROFESSIONALS AND PARAPROFESSIONALS"—SKILL DEVELOPMENT

This role-play involves the entire class. Two people will play the conflict resolution professionals (CRPs).[4] The rest of the class will be divided into two groups of equal size. One group comprises the professionals who work for Diversity Plus. The other group comprises paraprofessionals who work for the same agency. Identify the type of helping professionals and paraprofessionals based on who is in your class (e.g., educators, mental health counselors, social workers, human service workers). The purpose of this exercise is to practice facilitation skills in an inter-group conflict situation.

A severe rift has developed between the employees at Diversity Plus. The para-professionals believe they are being mistreated: their wages are lower, they carry higher caseloads, and they have no room for advancement in the agency. The pro-fessionals believe that the status quo is necessary and desirable. The agency cannot afford to pay everyone the same rate of pay, so salaries are based on educational background and level of experience. The professionals have at least a graduate de-gree, whereas the paraprofessionals have college diplomas or baccalaureate degrees. The professionals justify their smaller caseloads because they deal with more diffi-cult cases. They suggest that the paraprofessionals can go back to school if they want to advance their careers. Doing graduate work is not feasible for most of the paraprofessionals; some cannot afford to go back to school, and others do not have sufficient grades.

The two CRPs for this role-play are actually two of the senior supervisors of the agency. Prior to the role-play, the CRPs will ask certain members of the class to introduce one of the following obstacles into the dynamics: individuals have differ-ent agendas, the discussion has no focus, the discussion is dominated by certain individuals, some individuals keep interrupting, some individuals remain silent, in-dividuals lose their attention, individuals have difficulty listening to others' ideas, statements or questions put some people on the defensive, individuals are not saying what they really think, or people are confused about the agreements. This will en-able the CRPs to identify and practice facilitation skills that can be used to deal with each type of challenge.

Conduct this role-play in 15-minute segments. Switch CRPs for each segment and try to deal with a different obstacle.

Debriefing: How did the CRPs attempt to deal with each prescribed obstacle? What worked? What other skills or strategies could be used to deal with each of these problems? What were the underlying causes of the problem behaviors? What strategies could be used to deal with these underlying causes?

---

[4]Pronounced "carps," as in the fish, not "craps."

ROLE-PLAY 5.2: "WEIGHTY PROBLEM"— DEBATE AND DIALOGUE

Conflictia Police Services have a policy that all employees must be within 15 pounds of their ideal weight for their height, according to guidelines established by the Health Department of Conflictia. This applies to all employees, regardless of their age, sex, or position in the Police Services. Proponents of this policy claim it is necessary to protect the image of the Police Services in the community. The guidelines also promote good health, reducing costs for sick leave, early retirement, and accidents related to obesity.

A group within the police force opposes this policy. They find it discriminatory and unduly restrictive. Many positions within the organization do not require peak physical condition. Different people have different metabolisms, making it impossible for some people to fit within the policies. Also, as police officers age, they should not be fired simply because they are gaining weight.

For this role-play, divide the class into two groups. One group will role-play this exercise as a debate. The other will role-play it as a dialogue. Within each group, assign one facilitator, and divide the group into proponents and opponents of the policy.

Each group can prepare for this exercise by reviewing suggestions from the negotiation chapter. Start off as positional negotiators. The facilitator may or may not move you from this style, depending on the approach that the facilitator is using.

The facilitators can prepare for this exercise by reviewing the description of their respective approaches, debate or dialogue. Also, identify two or three skills from the Inventory of Group Facilitation Skills that you want to remember to incorporate. Each of the two role-plays require approximately 30 minutes. Ideally, the two groups will have separate rooms and video the role-play to show to the other group.

Debriefing: How were the two role-plays similar? How were they different? What impressed you the most about how each facilitator carried out the facilitation role? In this type of conflict, which approach to facilitation seems most appropriate? Why?

ROLE-PLAY 5.3: "CLIENTS AND STAFF"—PROBLEM SOLVING AND IDENTITY

This role-play takes place in the Conflictia Group Home, a residential treatment facility for teenagers with emotional and behavioral problems. Select two people from the class to act as group-home supervisors (in the role of facilitators). Divide the rest of the class into two equal groups: one group will play teenaged clients; the other group will play residential staff.

In recent weeks, turmoil has erupted at the Group Home. The residential staff is unionized. The union is currently negotiating a new collective agreement with the Group Home. Staff is unhappy with the way negotiations are proceeding, so they have begun a work-to-rule campaign: they are performing all of their required duties, but they are not taking on the additional jobs that they normally would assume. For the clients, this has meant fewer recreational activities, more house chores, skimpy meals, and earlier curfews (because staff will not perform any overtime activities, such as escorting clients to movies, concerts, or even school dances). The clients have responded by acting out in various ways: refusing to do chores, sleeping late, messing up the house, and making verbal threats toward staff.

Staff feels like double victims. First, the Group Home pays little, expects lots, and provides little support for them to do a tough job. Now, they are being attacked by the clients when they are just doing their jobs. The clients also feel like victims. They do not want to be in the Group Home to begin with. With the work-to-rule campaign, they feel like they are caught in the middle of someone else's fight.

In order to respond to this conflict, the supervisors call a house meeting. One supervisor will begin the process using the problem-solving approach. At 20 minutes into the role-play, the other supervisor will take over using strategies from the identity-based approach. This segment will also take 20 minutes. During the role-play, both clients and staff will begin with positional styles.

Both supervisors can prepare by reviewing the materials on their respective approaches to facilitation. Two or three clients and staff can be designated to introduce special challenges into the process (e.g., silence, disturbances, demonstrating anger).

Debriefing: Which skills did the problem-solving supervisor successfully employ? Which skills did the identity-based supervisor successfully employ? What changes did the staff and clients notice when the facilitators switched from one approach to the other? Which approach was more appropriate for this situation? Why?

MAJOR ASSIGNMENTS

The following assignment is based on *observation of an actual group process.* For *role-play assignments involving facilitation skills,* see the major assignments at the end of Chapter 6. In each of these assignments, there is a facilitator designated to guide a conflict resolution process among a group of advocates. The advocates will prepare by using the material in Chapter 6. The facilitators will prepare by using material from this chapter.

ASSIGNMENT 5A: PROCESS ANALYSIS OF A REAL CONFLICT

For this assignment, you will need to video-record a television program involving a facilitator and two or more parties who are discussing a controversial issue.[5] This could include a debate or roundtable discussion of current events, or coverage of a decision-making body's actual meeting. Check program listings of news channels, local cable stations, or C-SPAN to help you identify an interesting process to analyze

---

[5]Alternatively, you could attend an actual group process and take detailed notes. You may need to ask permission to attend and take notes, though most public meetings are open to anyone who wants to attend.

(e.g., congressional debates or hearings, local school board meetings, or discussions among professionals who are expressing conflicting opinions). As you review the video of this process, take notes on the process issues that arise, as well as the ways in which the facilitator uses certain skills and strategies in order to deal with these issues.

Your written process analysis should include the following information:

1. INTRODUCTION: What was the stated purpose of the process? Who was present at the meeting (describe their roles or positions, rather than just their individual names)? What term was used to describe the facilitator's role (e.g., moderator, chair, speaker, mayor)? What type of group was this? What was the group's current stage of development? Which approach to group facilitation did the facilitator use? Provide brief explanations for each of your answers (e.g., how did you decide that the group was using an interest-based, problem-solving, or other approach?). [1 to 2 pages]

2. CONFLICTS: Describe the types of conflicts that were raised in this process (e.g., differences over beliefs, values, limited resources, identities). Which skills and strategies did the facilitator attempt to use in order to deal with these? [2 to 3 pages]

3. CHALLENGES: What specific challenges did the facilitator have to pre-empt or deal with? Which skills and strategies did the facilitator use in order to deal with each of these? [2 to 3 pages]

4. ALTERNATIVE: Identify another approach the facilitator could have used to help the participants manage their conflict more effectively. Explain why you think this approach would be more appropriate or effective. Provide examples of how the facilitator could use specific skills and strategies to implement this approach, given the same conflicts and challenges that you describe in Points 2 and 3. What are the risks or potential downsides of using this type of approach? [2 to 3 pages]

5. REFERENCES: List the books, articles, and other scholarly CR resources cited in your analysis. [5 to 8 references]

You must be the change you want to see in the world.
—**Mahatma Gandhi**

6 | CHAPTER | **Advocacy**

Advocacy refers to influencing decisions affecting the welfare or interests of another individual or group. Whereas a mediator is an impartial third party who assists both parties negotiate, an advocate is partial to one party or cause (Mayer, 2004a). The word *advocate* derives from the Latin *avocare*, meaning "to summon one's help" (Hopkins, 1994). An advocate can work with clients in order to help them negotiate more effectively, on their own behalves. Alternatively, an advocate can act on behalf of clients representing or defending them in a conflict resolution process. Working with clients tends to be more empowering. Acting on their behalves may be necessary or more efficient, depending on the circumstances. In many cases, an advocate combines both methods.

All helping professionals have an obligation to advance the interests of their clients. Most codes of professional conduct also impose an obligation to advance the broader causes of justice, health, or social well-being. Many professionals engage in advocacy because of their personal values, wanting to advance causes that they support. The greatest needs for advocacy generally come from disadvantaged groups in society, such as children, the elderly, people with mental illnesses or disabilities, people with low incomes, victims of abuse, people charged with crimes, and minority groups who are subjected to discrimination (Ezell, 2000; Hoeffer, 2006).

This chapter encompasses the following topics: approaches to advocacy, the relationship between advocates and decision makers, advocacy activities, using power, advocacy skills, and ethical issues. As you read through the chapter, note the similarities and differences between advocacy and the other methods of CR explored earlier in this book.

APPROACHES TO ADVOCACY

The manner in which helping professionals advocate partially depends on their theoretical orientations, including their views on what influences people and how social institutions change. For helping professionals with a systems orientation, change occurs by altering the transactions between people. Accordingly, someone coming from a normative education perspective might advocate by teaching clients communication and assertiveness skills (Southwest Educational Development Laboratory, n.d.). In contrast, Marxist or radical feminist helping professionals believe that change occurs when the disenfranchised and divided proletariat band together. In this instance, one of the key means of advocacy is coalition building, mobilizing people to work together for a common cause (Kirst-Ashman & Hull, 2005). Social exchange theory suggests that negotiation is a process of trading resources (Wilmot & Hocker, 2007). Applying this theory, an advocate would try to bolster a client's resources prior to entering into a negotiation process with competing parties, improving the prospects for a more positive exchange for the client. Similarly, advocates could adopt many of the other theories underlying conflict resolution described earlier in this book.

Advocacy can target three different levels: individual, administrative, or policy. *Individual advocacy*[1] *helps a specific client deal with a single, concrete conflict*—for example, advocating for an HIV-positive client to receive service from an agency that traditionally restricts service to people with full-blown AIDS. *Administrative advocacy is directed at changes in an agency's policies*. Rather than advocating for an exception for a particular client, one advocates for a change in the general procedures of the agency. *Policy advocacy is directed at changes in rules or laws that go beyond a single agency* (Fowler, 1989; Kumari & Brooks, 2004). In the HIV example, a policy advocate might seek to change the way that government funds social agencies so that clients with HIV have greater access. Helping professionals often focus on one level of advocacy in their work; however, advocacy coordinated at all three levels may be advantageous (e.g., using individual advocacy in the short term to help a client with an immediate need, but using administrative and policy advocacy to help a class of clients over the long term).

RELATIONSHIPS BETWEEN ADVOCATES AND DECISION MAKERS

The strategies of an advocate depend on the type of relationship between the advocate and the decision makers: alliance, neutrality, or adversarial. *In an alliance situation, the decision makers view the advocate as someone who is on the same side.* They tend to have common beliefs, goals, or mandates. *In a neutral situation, the decision maker views the advocate as an objective source of information or opinion.* The decision maker does not see the advocate as an ally or an adversary. *In an adversarial situation, the decision maker views the advocate as an enemy.* Typically, the level of disagreement is so large or so fundamental that the decision makers view the advocate with little legitimacy (Sosin & Caulum, 1983). The easiest situation for an advocate to have influence is as an ally.

---

[1] Individual advocacy is sometimes called *case advocacy*, as opposed to *cause advocacy*, which includes both administrative and policy advocacy.

Often, decision makers have certain preconceptions about advocates—for example, "This professional can be trusted" or "This person is biased." The advocate can either try to foster a different type of relationship or employ strategies that are most likely to be effective given the confines of the existing relations. Consider the following scenario:

> Mr. and Mrs. Pinder are proud new parents of a baby girl. Both parents use cocaine and other drugs. The hospital called child protective services when the baby was born. The child protection worker, Warren, needs to determine whether to allow the baby to go home with her parents. He speaks with three helping professionals at the hospital: an addictions counselor, a nurse, and a parent support worker.

1. Ally

The addictions counselor happens to have a previous relationship with Warren, who sees the addictions counselor as an ally. They share similar views about the needs of children and their right to proper parenting. The addictions counselor believes the baby would be put at risk of abuse and neglect if the Pinders took her home. In order to advocate for the baby's welfare, the addictions counselor builds on the values she has in common with Warren. Because Warren already trusts the addictions worker, the worker does not have to put much effort into building the relationship. He can focus on providing cogent arguments that substantiate the need for intervention required to safeguard the welfare of the baby. Allies can generally be persuaded to provide support if the advocate uses a bit of friendly reasoning or a moral or emotional appeal (Conflict Research Consortium, 1998).

2. Neutral

The nurse happens to have no prior relationship with Warren. Accordingly, he has no initial bias toward or against her. In order to build credibility as an advocate, the nurse tries to demonstrate her professionalism. She is knowledgeable, articulate, conscientious, and objective. She believes the baby can be returned home with the Pinders, provided they agree to cooperate with in-home support to monitor the situation and ensure the baby's needs are met. She bolsters her credibility by showing that she has considered all possible options. She reviews the advantages and risks of both options before showing how she arrived at her conclusion. Although Warren initially views the nurse a neutral, he begins to see her as more of an ally (someone with shared interests who wants to help him carry out his mandate effectively). In order to gain the support of a neutral, advocates may need to provide more comprehensive arguments or lines of reasoning, knowing the neutral will provide you with a fair hearing (Conflict Research Consortium, 1998).

3. Adversary

The parent support worker has a reputation for supporting the rights of parents over the rights of the child. Warren views the support worker as an adversary who will try to push him into releasing the baby to the Pinders, even if there are substantial protection risks. The support worker can choose between two different courses of action. The first is to try to move toward a relationship of neutrality or alliance: How can we work together? What are our common interests? How can I demonstrate that my opinions are valid and reliable? With this approach, the support worker focuses on establishing a more positive relationship before advocating a particular position. The second approach is to remain in an adversarial relationship and make use of competitive strategies (Hoeffer, 2006). For example, the support worker could engage Warren in a debate and try to provide stronger arguments (e.g., moral or factual arguments). The worker could also try to coerce Warren by threatening to go to his supervisor or to take the case to court.

Some adversaries may not agree with you in principle, but they may be willing to engage in an exchange of resources or commitments (e.g., "You scratch my back, if I scratch yours"). Other adversaries may refuse to listen or deal with you, regardless of what you have to offer. They may be holding onto extremist or prejudicial views that cannot easily be changed (Conflict Research Consortium, 1998).

In deciding which course of action to take, an advocate should first consider more collaborative and peaceful approaches (discussion, persuasion, joint problem solving, and mediation). Only when these have been exhausted or ruled out as infeasible, should the advocate consider more competitive or coercive approaches. Collaborative approaches reflect professional values such as peace, nonviolence, respect, and partnership. Before adopting competitive or coercive methods, an advocate must consider the potential costs. Even if a coercive strategy works in the short run, there may be a price to pay at a later date; for example, harmed relationships, retaliation, and backlash. An advocate's selection of approaches is essentially the same as a negotiator's BATNA analysis, as described in Chapter 3: what is the best alternative to a negotiated (or collaborative) agreement? Too often, advocates fall back on adversarial approaches when more constructive and creative approaches have not been fully explored.

ADVOCACY ACTIVITIES

The range of advocacy activities is virtually limitless. The following lists encompass the more common means of helping clients advocate and advocating on their behalves (Ezell, 2000; Kumari & Brooks, 2004; Nicol, 1997). Consider which activities are more collaborative and which activities are more competitive.

1. Helping Clients Advocate on Their Own Behalves

- Helping clients set reasonable goals
- Educating clients about their rights
- Teaching client how the system works
- Facilitating access to information for your clients
- Helping people listen to your clients (raising clients' visibility, giving clients a forum to express themselves)

- Coaching clients on how to negotiate for themselves
- Helping clients identify triggers that spur anger, hurt, and counterproductive responses to conflict, and develop strategies for dealing with such triggers
- Asking clients questions to facilitate insights about the best ways to proceed
- Teaching problem-solving skills to clients
- Organizing coalitions among clients
- Helping clients write an advocacy brief
- Role-modeling advocacy skills and techniques
- Facilitating opportunities for your clients to influence (e.g., setting up meetings between clients and professionals in the system; promoting mediation or other CR processes that involve clients in decision making)
- Supporting client self-confidence
- Supporting risk taking by clients if this is required to pursue a worthwhile cause
- Providing practical support (e.g., use of space and computers)
- Accompanying clients during negotiations or hearings
- Being available for clients and maintaining patience even when they seem to reject your help
- Providing constructive feedback
- Helping clients implement, monitor, and evaluate agreements or decisions

2. Advocating on Behalf of Clients

- Listening carefully to clients to ensure that you understand their needs, concerns, and wishes
- Educating the public on an issue
- Negotiating with agencies or other social systems (for access to services, better services, honoring client rights, etc.)
- Monitoring other agencies' performance (including follow-up on their promises)
- Appealing to an external ombudsperson or other statutory authority mandated to investigate or enforce client rights
- Preparing an advocacy brief (Kaminski & Walmsley, 1995)
- Giving testimony to decision makers (Barsky & Gould, 2002)
- Encouraging decision makers to pay attention to the client's demands (e.g., lend credibility to client group by demonstrating your support)
- Creating or sustaining a crisis environment in order to stimulate conditions for change (e.g., organizing boycotts, demonstrations, street dramas, vigils, or nonviolent civil disobedience[2])
- Lobbying individual policymakers (conveying demands, placing pressure on decision makers)
- Mobilizing constituent support (facilitating petitions, organizing community groups, creating nongovernmental organizations [NGOs])

---

[2] Nonviolence is a means of raising public awareness and sympathy through assertive means. Ideally, nonviolence demonstrates the interdependence among people and the need to address the concerns of a disempowered group (Schirch, 2004). When used effectively, nonviolence builds the moral power of the vulnerable group.

- Directing complaints to the agency's funding body
- Litigating or seeking legal remedies
- Conducting research or publishing articles in order to produce and disseminate information required for decision making (Barsky, in press-b)
- Instituting demonstration projects to show the effectiveness of certain interventions
- Representing a client in a case conference or at an administrative hearing
- Influencing administrative rule making in other agencies
- Political campaigning
- Influencing media coverage of an issue (raising awareness of issues or manipulating public opinion)
- Conveying positive attitudes to the community about your clients (countering negative stereotypes)

Deliberate and controlled advocacy processes are generally more effective than unplanned ones. A problem-solving process can be used to help strategize:

1. What is the nature of the problem?
2. What are the objectives for the advocacy?
3. What levels should be targeted for advocacy—individual, agency, policy?
4. What resources can the helping professional and client draw on for advocacy?
5. Given the range of advocacy activities, which are most likely to lead to a satisfactory resolution of the conflict?
6. Who will take which responsibilities for implementing the advocacy plan?
7. How will the results be evaluated and fed back into the problem-solving process?

Empirical studies have identified many factors associated with the effectiveness of advocacy interventions. One of the keys to successful advocacy is leadership. Leaders initiate advocacy organizations, establish organizational track records, and revitalize stagnant organizations. Advocates often operate with limited financial resources. Accordingly, they must find ways to use resources in a cost-effective manner. Many advocates depend on volunteers, donations, and creative use of nonfinancial resources to advance their causes (e.g., by linking advocacy and service delivery activities). Working in coalitions with like-minded organizations also contributes to effectiveness. In addition, advocates must balance organizational flexibility with consistency and continuity (Reisch, 1990). Finally, early intervention is generally more effective than later intervention (e.g., presenting the draft of a bill to help government develop legislation, rather than waiting to comment on legislation that the government has already drafted and presented to the public for comment; Hoeffer, 2006).

POWER

Power, the relative capacity of different parties to influence one another, plays a significant role in advocacy. As mentioned earlier, helping professionals often work on behalf of disadvantaged groups in society. In order to advance their concerns, helping professionals need to know how to affect the balance of power between individuals or groups involved in a conflict situation. Professionals familiar with systems and structural theories can use these theories to assist their analysis of power and the reciprocal influences that individuals or systems have on one another (Goldberg-Wood & Middleman, 1991). This section provides a means of analyzing power and intervening based on the ten sources of power: expertise, associations, possession of resources, control of procedures, legitimacy, sanctions, nuisance, habit, morality, and personal attributes (Lang, 2004).

To illustrate how the various sources of power can be used, consider the following scenario:

> Stella is a 12-year-old student with a learning disability. She has been going to a mainstream school. Although she takes regular classes, she also has a special education teacher who provides extra support. Because of budget cuts, the Conflictia School Board now says she must go to a school specifically designed for students with disabilities. The Board says it can no longer afford to have special education instructors in all of its schools. Stella and her parents believe that Stella is better off in her mainstream school.

1. Expert Power

Expert power derives from having expertise or special knowledge. Expert power is sometimes called information power because expertise is based on possessing certain wisdom, knowledge, or data. Helping professionals can lend their support to clients by providing information on their behalves or providing clients with access to information (Freire, 1994).

Some helping professionals see themselves as experts; others reject this title. For example, feminist counselors try to reduce the distance between counselor and client by presenting themselves as facilitators rather than experts. They prefer to help clients gain access to information rather than directly provide expertise to clients (Kumari & Brooks, 2004). Still, all helping professionals have knowledge that they can make available to clients.

One of the key areas of knowledge required for advocacy is knowledge about agency policies, procedures, and structures. In the case example, an advocate could provide Stella's family with information about the structure of the Conflictia School Board, how it makes decisions, and whether there are any avenues for appeal (e.g., administrative or court challenges). Many bureaucracies are complicated systems, with their peculiar jargon and norms. Advocates who are familiar with these norms and jargon can act as interpreters for clients.

An advocate may also have knowledge about the formal and informal power structures: Who are the people who make the decisions, and what tends to influence their decisions? If the Conflictia School Board is accountable to the municipal council, an advocate may suggest that Stella's family try to find an ally from this council. If there are upcoming elections for the School Board, Stella's family might be able to use the campaign to raise their concerns.

Clients also need to know about the probable consequences of escalating issues. If Stella's family decides to appeal the Board's decision, what are the potential benefits and risks? Will Stella have to face the media? What are the chances they will succeed? What are the chances of retribution (e.g., teachers becoming harder on Stella as revenge for her family taking the case to an appeal)? Decision Tree Analysis can help the family view its alternatives and make informed choices. *Advocates can provide access to government documents and other data sources* (Kirst-Ashman & Hull, 2005). Unless family members have been educated about social research, it is unlikely that they will know how to conduct a literature review on special education. An advocate can help locate empirical research (Lens, 2005) comparing students who are mainstreamed versus those who go to specialized schools.

Advocates can teach clients advocacy strategies, tips, and tricks. For example, get everything in writing, and date your notes in order to improve their credibility. If Stella's family documents all of its interactions with the school and the School Board, it can use these documents to support its case in any future hearings. Advocates can also help clients recognize problems and suggest CR strategies for dealing with them. For example, Board representatives may be using stalling tactics, not returning telephone calls, or saying they do not have the authority to make decisions. An advocate informs the family that they can move up one level and speak to a supervisor rather than wait for a response (Nicol, 1997). Similarly, if Board members are using bluffs or other forms of deceit to secure a competitive advantage, the advocate can teach the family how to use questions to invite information sharing and counter these tactics (e.g., "When you say that Stella can be denied any educational support if she does not comply with your wishes, which laws are you basing this on?").

2. Associational Power

Associational power comes from having a positive relationship with other people who have power. Also called *referent power* or *integrative power*, associational power allows clients to combine resources, build alliances, and gain moral influence.

One way to bring clients together is through consciousness-raising. Individual clients often feel alone in their problems and believe that their plight is caused by personal deficits. Advocates can help clients understand how various sociopolitical systems limit and devalue them. By working in concert, clients are in a better position to challenge existing power structures (Kirst-Ashman & Hull, 2005).

In Stella's situation, an advocate could develop associational power by bringing families together who share similar concerns. They can speak with a collective voice and share the cost burden of pursuing their cause. One of the downsides of a narrowly based interest group is that the group is seen as self-interested and biased. If the advocate can attract individuals and families who do not have children with disabilities, then the group no longer looks self-interested. Drawing a larger coalition ensures that more people are included in its joint efforts or initiatives. When certain individuals or groups are excluded from a coalition, they may form other coalitions that compete for resources, positions, or favors.

Advocates can foster associational power by bringing specific individuals into the cause. Cultivating support from people with high profiles, special expertise, moral reputations, or other desirable characteristics helps raise awareness and lends credibility to an advocacy plan. Stella's family would benefit, for instance, from associations with leading experts on special education who espouse mainstreaming.

Some advocacy groups connect with sports or entertainment celebrities to advance their cases. A celebrity spokesperson can be very influential, particularly among groups that identify with the celebrity. Unfortunately, associational power works in two directions. If a celebrity's reputation falters, an association with the fallen star will also have a negative impact on the advocacy group and its cause (consider the fluctuating reputations of Michael Jackson, O. J. Simpson, and Martha Stewart).

Advocacy within a group is generally safer than "going it alone." Suppose one teacher speaks up in defense of Stella's wish to remain in the school. In effect, he is going against the position of his employer. The School Board might impose sanctions to keep teachers from opposing the Board's decisions. If several teachers banded together in support of Stella, it would be more difficult for the Board to impose sanctions.

Another aspect of associational power is emotional support. If Stella's parents had to testify at an administrative hearing, for instance, the experience could be daunting. An advocate can offer emotional support by being there for the clients, escorting them to the hearing, sitting through the hearing with them, and helping them debrief afterward (Barsky & Gould, 2002). This type of support provides clients with confidence and a sense of hope.

Associational power can be used for "power with" another party, rather than "power over" another party. The power of two or more parties is integrated rather than used in a combative fashion (Mayer, 2000). In the previous examples of associational power, the advocate is making use of associational power to gain influence over another party. In order to move toward a more collaborative approach, the advocate could try to facilitate a joining of power between conflicting parties. Instead of using their power to try to gain favor over the other, they can form an association to gain power to pursue goals that meet both their interests.

Love is a very strong form of associational power (Conflict Research Consortium, 1998). When people develop loving relationships, love enhances many of their capacities, helping them feel better about themselves, supportive of one another, and motivated to do whatever is necessary to ensure their loved ones are safe, healthy, and happy. Just think of the power shift that occurs when an adversary is transformed into to a loved one, such as a close family or community member. If School Board members get to know Stella as a person, an adorable young woman, they may develop a special bond with her and become more motivated to help her. Metaphorically, associational power is sometimes referred to as a "hug," in contrast to sanction power (a "stick" used for force) and resource power (a "carrot" used for enticement) (Dugan, 2003).

3. Resource Power

Resource power stems from control over valuable assets; for example, money, materials, labor, or other goods and services. The inverse version of resource power is the ability to deny needed resources or to force others to expend them. In other words, resource power allows people to resolve conflict through an exchange of resources or through refusal to exchange resources. In many situations, resource power is a key area where clients are at a disadvantage. If the conflict is with a social agency, for instance, the agency is likely to have access to greater resources, both professional and monetary.

Advocates can help clients gain resource power by helping them secure assets from external sources. Clients may not know of social assistance benefits, legal aid funds, or other entitlements they can claim. In Stella's situation, there may be a charitable foundation that could provide financial support for her cause. Lawyers, educators, or other helping professionals may be willing to donate their time. When resources are scarce, advocates also need to explore creative ways to make better use of what they have.

A growing area of power imbalance concerns technology. People with more money and better education are more likely to have access to technology. In public policy, for example, interest groups are using fax and email to convey opinions to governmental decision makers. Other groups use websites to solicit memberships and fund-raise for their causes. Advocates can relieve these types of inequities by promoting broader access to education and equipment in schools, libraries, and other public institutions. Advocates may also need to promote literacy programs, because many of the new technologies require higher rates of literacy for people to participate.

Another method of enhancing resource power is to assist with an exchange of resources. Clients may be lacking in some resources but flush with other resources. For instance, Stella's family may not be able to afford private school for her, but they may have time to volunteer to help out at her school. Advocates can assist clients by helping them exchange certain resources for ones they need. This may include helping clients find the best price and quality, teaching them negotiation skills, or working with the other party to ensure the clients are treated fairly.

4. Procedural Power

Procedural power refers to control over the processes by which decisions are made. Procedural power is not the same as control over the decisions themselves. Consider various CR alternatives: negotiation, mediation, administrative hearings, and court trials. In negotiation, the parties have control over the process as well as over the decisions to be made. They can decide to have informal meetings, formal meetings, long meetings, short meetings, and so on. If one party is more powerful than the other, it may be able to dictate some of the terms of the process. For example, the School Board might insist that any discussions about Stella's case take place at its offices. This gives the Board "home field advantage." By having the meeting in their offices, they have access to secretarial support, computers, and so on. Stella's parents may also feel intimidated because they are not familiar with the surroundings. The Board might also say that Stella's parents cannot bring a lawyer. An advocate could assist Stella's parents by helping them negotiate a more equitable process: if the Board can bring its professionals to the meeting, then Stella's family should be able to bring its own.

In mediation, the mediator controls the process and the clients control the decisions. As noted in Chapter 4, a mediator has an ethical obligation regarding impartiality. Accordingly, the process should not be biased toward one side or another. If there is an imbalance of power between the parties, the mediator could make use of power-balancing strategies.[3] Essentially, the mediator could manipulate any of the 10 sources of power described in this section in order to redistribute power. For instance, if the problem were caused by an informational imbalance, the mediator could refer the less powerful party to an advocate who could ensure equal access to relevant information.

In an administrative hearing, the administrative board typically has control over both the process and the decision. In order to maintain its moral authority, the board must try to ensure that its process is fair and seen to be fair. The School Board, for example, might have an appeals process that allows parents to make written submissions. Stella's parents want an opportunity to present their case at an oral hearing. An advocate may be able to push for changes in the procedure by negotiating with the Board or by advocating that the government establish mandatory regulations. If an administrative process is unfair, legal advocates could also explore the possibility of going to court to have the case reviewed.

In a court hearing, the judge has control over the process and the decisions.[4] Court procedures are established by government, and the court has an obligation to ensure that the process is fair. Judges are less likely than administrative boards to have a stake in the outcome. If, however, a judge demonstrates bias or conducts the process contrary to the law, the decision can be appealed to a higher court. Only lawyers can represent clients in court. Nonlawyer advocates can provide support for clients; however, providing legal advice or representing them in court generally constitute unauthorized practice of law.[5] Clients and nonlawyer advocates have little control over the court process.

Advocates can help clients make informed choices about CR alternatives, as well as helping them negotiate processes that treat them more fairly (e.g., before participating in a facilitated community dialogue, advocate for certain ground rules such as everyone gets an equal opportunity to speak). Sometimes, just the presence of a third party (such as a mediator or ombudsperson) will help balance power and ensure a client is not coerced or mistreated (Nelson, Netting, Huber, & Borders, 2001). If legal issues are involved, then the advocate should also refer them for legal advice.

5. Legitimate Power

Legitimate power derives from having an official position or authority, as from legislation or policies of an organization. The School Board, for example, is mandated by state regulations to make decisions about how to use funds targeted for education.

---

[3] This raises the ethical issue concerning the appropriate role of a mediator when there is a power imbalance: Should the mediator balance power to ensure fairness or reject power balancing in order to remain impartial? Refer back to Chapter 4 for further discussion of this dilemma.

[4] There is an exception for jury cases, in which the jury makes findings of fact (Barsky & Gould, 2002).

[5] The helping professional could be fined, sued by an unsatisfied client, and risk his or her professional accreditation.

Teachers are authorized to discipline students who do not act in accordance with school policies. A broad range of helping professionals and government officials have these types of power over clients. For the most part, helping professionals try to limit their use of legitimate power. Even if a helping professional has the ability to impose decisions, codes of ethics dictate that clients have a right to self-determination. Exploiting a client is not in the professional's best interests. It is generally easier to work with clients on a voluntary basis than try to impose authority (see nuisance power, later).

Advocates may be able to intervene at a peer level with other helping professionals or officials who are making inappropriate uses of their authority. Ideally, the issues can be resolved informally and collaboratively. If necessary, an advocate can bring in a supervisor, administrator, mediator, or other professional to help resolve the conflict in a constructive manner. If the law or policy authorizing legitimate power is problematic, then the preferred target of advocacy may be at the policy level.

Within some organizations, only certain types of professionals are viewed as legitimate participants in decision-making processes. For those professionals who are recognized, each profession's position on the organizational hierarchy may help or hurt its legitimate power as advocates. For medical decisions, for instance, nurses may not be recognized in the same manner as doctors. For legal decisions, social workers may not be recognized in the same manner as lawyers. And for mental health decisions, psychologists or other mental health professionals may not be recognized in the same manner as psychiatrists. To overcome such obstacles, helping professionals may need to advocate first to be recognized as advocates and have a place at the decision-making table; only then can they have an effective voice for the clients they serve (Dodd & Jansson, 2004). If they are recognized but hold a low place in the organizational hierarchy, they may need to rely on personal power or other sources to gain influence.

Using legitimate power is a rights-based approach to advocacy. When a conflict exists within an agency, an advocate can make sure that the organization is living up to its own rules, including fair treatment of clients or others. When working with minority groups or vulnerable populations that have been subjected to discrimination, advocates may need to rely on civil rights legislation, including state and federal constitutions and international human rights laws (Schirch, 2004). Enforcing human rights can be time-consuming and expensive. Advocates may be able to secure the support of large advocacy organizations (e.g., Amnesty International, American Civil Liberties Union, or Human Rights Campaign) to assert a client's rights, including life, liberty, privacy, and equality.

6. Sanction Power

Sanction power emanates from the ability (or perceived ability) to inflict harm or to interfere with a party's ability to realize its interests. A typical sanctioning problem for clients occurs when an agency threatens to refuse services or impose other sanctions if the clients do not acquiesce to the agency's demands. For example, Stella's parents might fear that teachers would sanction Stella if the conflict is escalated.

When sanctions are legitimate, they are difficult to counteract. For example, if Stella becomes violent, then the school would have legal authority to suspend her. If the sanctions are not legitimate, then an advocate could counteract them by surfacing the issue. Consider, for instance, school officials who sanction Stella's family by belittling them. Initially, the advocate could discuss the issue of inappropriate sanctions with the people trying to impose them. If informal negotiations are unsuccessful, then the advocate could raise the issue in a more public forum (e.g., with elected politicians or the media). Perhaps the ultimate method of confronting legitimate power is to target the laws or policies granting the power—in other words, working for law reform or policy reform to alter the allocation of power in a manner that promotes fair treatment or social justice.

7. Nuisance Power

Nuisance power is based on the ability to cause discomfort to a party, falling short of the ability to apply direct sanctions. Nuisance power is often used by people who are at a disadvantage in terms of sanction and legitimate power. Clients who feel oppressed by agencies or other systems may rebel, using nuisance power without being conscious about it. Bureaucratic systems often respond more quickly to individuals who are causing them distress. Unfortunately, this teaches clients to use confrontational approaches to CR rather than collaborative ones.

Advocates can help clients use nuisance power in a deliberate manner. Nuisance power is risky, because it escalates the conflict. The other party may respond by trying to re-impose its power or by escalating conflict even further (Conflict Research Consortium, 1998). If the Board required Stella to go to a special school, she could rebel by misbehaving at the new school. The Board might decide that it is easier or better for Stella to be returned to her old school, where she did not pose problems. However, it also might decide to expel her.

Advocates should help clients assess the risks and benefits of using nuisance strategies. Generally, nuisance strategies should be used only after other strategies have been exhausted. Protests, strikes, sit-ins, and nonviolent civil disobedience are examples of nuisance strategies. Different types of nuisance strategies pose different levels of risk, for instance, noncooperation may be less risky than acting up, because noncooperation is more subtle. Stella's family could invoke noncooperation by boycotting meetings or slowing down their process (Schirch, 2004). In contrast, Stella could act up by singing the national anthem at the start of each meeting. If Board members try to stop her from singing, her family could raise the inference that they are unpatriotic or oppose American ideals such as freedom and justice for all. Alternatively, members of Stella's family could initiate a fast in order to bring attention to their daughter's plight. In addition to helping families consider the risk of negative consequences, advocates must also help them consider ethical issues in relation to the use of nuisance strategies (discussed later).

Sometimes, nuisance strategies such as strikes and protests are required to kindle or inspire widespread social change. Consider, for instance, Rosa Parks' refusal to surrender her bus seat in 1956. If Rosa and the Montgomery, Alabama, bus company were referred to mediation, they might have resolved their immediate dispute privately and amicably. Unfortunately, the agreement would do little for other

African Americans who were being subjected to the racist Jim Crow laws and other forms of discrimination. The protests and nonviolence that followed Parks' arrest awoke the nation to the issue of racism and the needs for legal and social change.

8. Habitual Power

Habitual power rests on the premise that it is generally easier to maintain a particular arrangement or course of action than to change it. Decision makers may also be persuaded by arguments in favor of maintaining traditions.

In Stella's case, the status quo suggests that she should remain in her old school. An advocate could argue that it is unfair to disrupt her education and have her move to a new school. Alternatively, another advocate might persuade the School Board to phase out special education in general schools but allow students currently enrolled to complete their education.

Prolonging the status quo is a common tactic in positional negotiations. If Stella is in her old school while the decision about special schools is being considered, Stella's family might want to prolong the decision-making process. The longer the process takes, the longer the status quo is maintained and the more difficult it is to make changes. She might even graduate before the School Board makes its final decision.

9. Moral Power

Moral power extends from appeals to widely held values, such as family, charity, freedom, privacy, fairness, and democracy. In order to finesse moral power, advocates use language that frames their cause in a positive light. For instance, groups that support women's rights to abortion call themselves "Pro-Choice" rather than "Pro-Abortion." Stella's parents could lay claim to values such as equality and respect. All they want is for their daughter to have the same friends and opportunities as everyone else's child.

At its best, using moral power helps people make decisions based on values and interests rather than positions. Unfortunately, appeals to morality often turn into positional bargaining. Each party claims moral superiority: "We stand for everything good; the others stand for evil." Once people establish values, it becomes difficult for them to compromise. Advocates may be able to intervene by helping the parties focus on common values. Demonizing another party also runs contrary to professional ethics, such as respect for individuals and diverse groups.

Some groups claim moral power by presenting themselves as victims. This may be effective in gaining public sympathy and support. In fact, they may actually be victims (of oppression, abuse, crime, etc.). Over time, however, victim mentality can be damaging. When people see themselves just as victims, they may not take responsibility for helping themselves. They operate on fear and mistrust. They become unable to consider constructive CR processes, even when safety and fairness can be ensured (Chetkow-Yanoov, 1997). Advocates can support such clients by validating their concerns but also by helping them build confidence and self-efficacy in their identities. When an advocate helps victims of violent crime view themselves as survivors, for instance, the advocate is also helping them take responsibility for moving on.

Advocates can help disempowered groups gain moral power by encouraging them to act morally—for example, using nonviolence rather than violence to assert their concerns. If Stella's parents slashed the tires of Board members who opposed them, they would lose moral power. A nonviolent approach could include "monitoring issues," such as keeping track of how the Board members respond to their requests for fair treatment. By creating a record of any abusive behaviors and sharing this information with the public, Stella's parents can demonstrate unfair treatment by the Board and win public support for their concerns. In order to use this method effectively, they must be careful to shame the *behaviors* of the Board, rather than shame the Board members personally (Schirch, 2004).

10. Personal Power

Personal power is based on a variety of individual attributes. Characteristics that contribute to a client's personal power include self-assurance, the ability to articulate one's thoughts and understand one's situation, determination, and endurance (Mayer, 1987). Some aspects of personal power come naturally. Others can be learned. Advocates can help clients raise their level of personal power by teaching them advocacy skills (e.g., listening skills, assertiveness, and other skills listed in the Inventory of Advocacy Skills and Activities in Figure 6.1). In the case example, an advocate might help Stella's family gain comfort using political processes and speaking in public forums. If they have a low tolerance for conflict, an advocate can teach them strategies for dealing with it more effectively (Kirst-Ashman & Hull, 2005). If their speaking styles are dull or unconvincing, the advocate can teach them how to use speaking devices such as alliteration, rhetorical questions, metaphors, visual imagery, recurrent themes, and dilemmas (Lens, 2005).

* * *

Power issues are pervasive in conflict resolution. As the forgoing discussion indicates, there are a number of ways in which advocates can use power bases to advance the interests of clients. This does not mean, however, that advocates must rely on positional and competitive strategies for conflict resolution. Wherever possible, advocates should promote collaborative strategies. By doing so, they can foster win-win solutions, improved relationships, mutual understanding, and client empowerment. Using the least force necessary to achieve advocacy objectives also minimizes unwanted counterforces (Kumari & Brooks, 2004).

INVENTORY OF ADVOCACY SKILLS AND ACTIVITIES

Skills for advocates include many of the same skills that are used by mediators and negotiators. The inventory in Figure 6.1 identifies key advocacy skills and activities. The inventory is broken down into three parts: preparation, oral advocacy, and written advocacy.

Figure 6.1 | Inventory of Advocacy Skills and Activities

Name of Advocate: _____
Person Giving Feedback: _____

Preparation for Advocacy

_____ Assesses the nature of the conflict

_____ Assesses the individuals and social systems affected by the conflict

_____ Becomes informed with all sides of the issues

_____ Reflects on personal and professional motivation and mandate for becoming involved as an advocate

_____ Understands who must be persuaded

_____ Considers a range of advocacy techniques and determines which are most likely to be effective and ethically appropriate

_____ Takes steps to improve power dynamics before primary intervention

_____ Plans agenda and structure, or receives the information from the facilitator

Oral Advocacy

_____ Identifies own and mutual purposes of the meeting

_____ Isolates key issues to be decided

_____ Seeks consensus on process and issues to be determined

_____ Provides relevant and persuasive information

_____ Identifies information that needs to be produced

_____ Asks questions to raise consciousness or insights

_____ Encourages positive expectations for the process

_____ Facilitates linkages between people and resources

_____ Joins with others (using associational power)

_____ Identifies common values and entitlements (using moral power)

_____ Articulates specific needs and interests (firm on interests, flexible on positions and means of addressing interests)

_____ Separates people from the problem (including use of nonjudgmental language)

_____ Generates options

_____ Identifies legitimate or objective criteria for evaluation

_____ Uses clear and concise language

_____ Checks out assumptions

_____ Uses visual aids or other presentation devices

_____ Uses active listening to demonstrate empathic understanding and build trust: paraphrase, summary, reflection of emotions, appropriate body language to show attending

(continued)

Figure 6.1 | *Continued*

_____ Identifies specific commitments for self and others

_____ Uses emotional appeals appropriately

_____ Demonstrates respect for diversity and difference of opinion

_____ Presents with confidence

_____ Presents in an assertive manner (rather than passive or aggressive)

_____ Uses creative strategies (indicate example: _____)

_____ Keeps focus on agenda and most important issues

_____ Responds pre-emptively to another party's argument (deals with an issue before the other person even raises it)

_____ Narrows issues in dispute (if full agreement has not been reached yet)

_____ Helps other parties save face or undo a commitment

_____ Helps decision makers prioritize how to allocate scare resources (time, emotional energy, and money)

_____ Uses devices to change other parties' expectations (e.g., through reality-testing questions, role reversals, metaphoric storytelling, looking at hypothetical situations, visualization, emphasizing recurrent themes)

_____ Uses constructive confrontation (e.g., helps a party to identify incongruencies between two pieces of information the party has given or between a statement and the party's behavior)

_____ Draws parties' awareness to the cost of nonagreement

_____ Uses flexibility, rigidity, tenacity, and patience for tactical purposes

_____ Secures details for implementation of decisions, as well as monitoring, evaluation, and follow-up (date, time, place, who is responsible)

Written Advocacy

_____ Writes clearly and concisely

_____ Presents arguments in logical manner

_____ Presents facts to support opinions

_____ Uses nonjudgmental language

_____ Clarifies the issues or problems

_____ States goals and objectives

_____ Appeals to concerns of the decision makers

_____ Provides balanced evaluation of various options for solution (demonstrating understanding of the positions of various parties)

_____ Suggests preferred options for solution

_____ Highlights areas of mutual interest

_____ Offers concrete plans for implementation, follow-up, and evaluation

_____ Uses creative techniques to ensure written brief captures the interest of its target audience (e.g., metaphors, vivid language, pictures, case examples)

In order to provide feedback to colleagues during role-plays, make photocopies of the inventory, and put each advocate's name at the top of the page. Use the following scale to give feedback on specific skills:

1—Demonstrated in exceptional manner

2—Demonstrated effectively

3—Demonstrated, but could use practice to be more effective

X—Not demonstrated

You may also provide descriptive comments on the reverse side of the photocopies.

ETHICAL ISSUES

Ethical issues are pervasive in advocacy (Menkel-Meadow & Wheeler, 2004). Helping professionals need to be aware of potential problems and consider the following factors: legal and professional restrictions, agency mandate, individual versus group interests, client authorization, professional values, and futile causes.

1. Legal and Professional Restrictions

Although helping professionals have an ethical obligation to advocate for clients and social causes, their advocacy role is also subject to many legal and ethical restrictions. For example, defamation laws limit what one can say about another person in a public forum. In the heat of advocacy, helping professionals might be tempted to discredit another person with verbal or written attacks. If the information is untrue and causes the person harm (including harm to personal or professional reputation), the helping professional could be sued for damages. Similarly, some jurisdictions have hate crime laws that prohibit promoting hate against a particular group. An overzealous advocate must be careful not to cross the bounds of rhetoric and incite people to commit hate crimes (e.g., an advocate who opposes same-sex marriage making statements that provoke hate crimes against gay men or lesbians).

Also, professionals have ethical responsibilities to act honestly and with integrity. This means that professionals cannot use any means necessary, regardless of how worthy the goal or cause they are advocating (Florida Bar, 2004).

2. Agency Mandate

Advocates who work in an agency context are limited by the mandate and policies of their agencies. If an agency is designated as a charitable foundation for tax purposes, that agency may be prohibited from engaging in legislative or political advocacy. Likewise, many agencies that receive government funding have restrictions on whether and how they can criticize government policies or services. Advocates who act on their own behalves may have more latitude than advocates who act on behalf of the agency. Still, it may be difficult for a helping professional to take a stand as a personal citizen when that person also works as a professional for a public agency.

Ethical dilemmas for advocates frequently arise when a conflict surfaces between the interests of the agency and the interests of the client (Dolgoff et al., 2005). Although many helping professionals would like to give precedence to the interests of their clients, this may put them at risk of dismissal or other sanctions from their agencies. By using collaborative CR approaches, advocates may be able to avoid ethical dilemmas. In other words, by focusing on the mutual interests of the client and agency, an advocate may not have to choose between them.

3. Individual versus Group Interests

Another type of dilemma arises when advocating for one client takes away resources from another person or group (Corey et al., 2007; Dolgoff et al., 2005). How should advocates prioritize? Unfortunately, codes of ethics give little guidance. If the only obligation of helping professionals is to pursue their own clients' best interests, then helping professionals may be depriving others who may be more needy or deserving. If helping professionals do not act as staunch advocates for their clients, then whom can clients look to for support? Once again, helping professionals can use CR processes to work toward win-win solutions. In some situations, consensus may be possible. If not, at least the parties can analyze the issues and develop mutual understanding of one another's positions.

Advocacy can be directed at different levels: to produce change for a specific client or to produce change for broader causes. This may present professionals with a number of difficult choices:

- Advocating for an individual client is generally faster and less expensive than trying to advocate for broader change—at least in the short run.
- However, if resources are continuously used for individual clients, then how will broader change ever occur?
- How does a helping professional determine how to advocate when an agency is mandated to act on behalf of specific clients, but the professional's code of ethics obliges the professional to advocate for broader social change?
- Does a client have a right to advocacy, even when the client's wishes contravene values or causes that the agency and helping professional represent?

4. Client Authorization

When professionals advocate on behalf of clients, they should have the clients' consent to act on their behalves. Unfortunately, many professionals advocate for clients without gaining explicit consent to do so. Although the professional may be well meaning, advocacy engenders many risks: costs in time and other resources, potential backlash, and the chance that advocacy will not bring about the expected changes. If a client is not properly informed or the professional does not have the client's consent, then the professional may be putting both the client and the professional at risk. The client could also claim breach of confidentiality. Advocates must be aware of issues related to the capacity of certain clients to consent, including young children and people with severe cognitive impairments (Corey et al., 2007). In such instances, the advocate may need to secure consent from a parent, guardian, or other representative.

Authorization for cause advocacy can be even trickier than consent for individual advocacy. Ideally, the professional seeks informed consent from all of the people in the group or community affected. If members of the community or group have disparate views on how the advocate should proceed, then the advocate may need to use mediative skills to bring the group to consensus (as per the gun control case in Chapter 4). Often, a helping professional derives authority to advocate for a certain cause from the agency or organization that pays the professional. This type of authority provides the professional with some safeguards should the professional's work be challenged.

5. Professional Values

Advocates must develop an awareness of their own values and priorities in order to ensure that they do not impose their values on clients (refer back to your values inventory from Chapter 2, Exercise 2). When the client's and advocate's values are consonant, the advocate can easily pursue the aims of the client. But what happens when their values clash? In fact, value conflicts between clients and advocates are quite common. Sometimes the conflicts relate to methods of advocacy; for instance, a client wants the advocate to fight in a manner that inflames conflict, while the advocate values the peaceful resolution of conflict. Other times, the values conflict relates to differences over the goal of advocacy: a client asks an advocate to argue in favor of capital punishment, whereas the professional values the sanctity of life. When helping professionals do not feel right about their advocacy work, they should ask themselves the following questions: (a) Why are they doing it? (b) Is their goal ethical? and (c) Are the means of attaining the goal also ethical? (See Menkel-Meadow & Wheeler, 2004.) If an advocate determines that it would be inappropriate to advocate for a particular cause or in a particular manner, the advocate may need to use conflict resolution skills with the client in order to determine whether they can continue to work together. If the values conflict persists, the advocate may need to terminate work with the client. This gives the client an opportunity to look for another advocate who feels that he or she can advocate ethically and effectively for the client. Ethical decisions should not be made in isolation. Consulting with others allows professionals to explore various alternatives and hear how others might deal with difficult decisions.

6. Futile Causes

Some helping professionals question whether they should become involved in causes that seem overwhelming or futile. Too often, this excuse is an easy way out. One person can make a difference, even when the odds seem enormous. Remember the Chinese student in 1989 who stood before a row of tanks in Tiananmen Square? The Chinese government brought in the military to quash prodemocracy demonstrations by the students. One young man, standing alone, stopped the progression of the tanks. In doing so, he captured the imagination and support of a world audience. Although the demonstrations were eventually stopped, his image lives on to inspire others.[6]

KEY POINTS

- The role of an advocate is to promote changes in favor of particular clients or causes.

- Helping clients advocate on their own behalves is generally more empowering than advocating for them.

- Advocates can influence change at three levels: individual, agency, and policy.

- Advocates who have a positive relationship with decision makers are able to use collaborative approaches to influence change; advocates with an adversarial relationship with decision makers may need to build a more constructive relationship before trying to influence decision making.

- If competitive strategies are required, advocates should use the least force necessary to achieve key objectives.

- Selection of advocacy strategies depends on the following factors: the nature of the problem, the objectives of the client, the theoretical orientation of the helping professional, available resources, and the likelihood of success among various alternatives.

- Advocates can utilize 10 sources of power in order to influence change: expertise, associations, possession of resources, control of procedures, legitimacy, sanctions, nuisance, habit, morality, and personal attributes.

- An advocate's choice of skills will vary depending on the forum for conflict resolution—for example, private negotiation, mediation, administrative hearing, debate, and public campaign.

- In order to analyze whether an advocacy intervention is ethical, advocates must consider both the means and objectives of the intervention.

DISCUSSION QUESTIONS AND EXERCISES

1. OBLIGATIONS: Refer to the code of ethics of your professional association. What does it say about your professional obligation to advocate? Identify three causes that you value as a helping professional.

2. ADVOCATES AND NEGOTIATORS: Compare and contrast the role of an advocate with the role of a negotiator.

---

[6] When I raised this example in class, one student asked, "You're telling us we have to put ourselves in front of a line of tanks?" Perhaps. Can you think of a cause that is very dear to you? What would you be willing to risk in order to defend this cause?

3. ADVOCATES AND MEDIATORS: Compare and contrast the role of an advocate with the role of a mediator (Barsky, 1993).

4. LEVELS OF ADVOCACY: You work in a family counseling agency in a remote community with a large indigenous population. About two-thirds of your clients suffer from depression. Eighty percent of your clients with depression are unemployed. What are the advantages and disadvantages of advocating for clients individually versus advocating at a policy level? What type of advocacy strategy would be most effective?

5. POWER AND PROFESSORS: Review your notes for Role-Play 3.2—"Negotiating for Grades." What are the power issues raised by this scenario? Having read this chapter, what would you do differently in the role of the student? How could you use different sources of power in an ethical and effective manner? What are the short- and long-term implications of using power-based strategies in this situation?

6. POWER ANALYSIS: Identify a client who could use assistance in advocating. Consider the sources of power identified in this chapter. What are your client's strengths as a negotiator? What are your client's limitations? As an advocate trying to help the client negotiate on the client's own behalf, what types of interventions would you suggest (Kirst-Ashman & Hull, 2005)?

7. VENUS/MARS: What are the differences, if any, between the ways that men and women tend to approach advocacy? When dealing with conflicts between women and men, what is the relevance of power, patriarchy, and privilege (Kolb & Williams, 2003)?

8. ROLE REVERSAL: A *role reversal* is a method of observing a conflict from the other person's perspective. It can be used to help you gain empathy with someone who has a different view, as well as how to advocate more effectively since you will have greater insight about what is behind the other person's thoughts, feelings, and behaviors. Select one of the following issues that raises strong feelings for you:

> Euthanasia—right to die with dignity versus sanctity of life
>
> Definition of civil marriage—inclusive of same-sex couples or only different-sex couples
>
> Mandatory prosecution of wife assault allegations
>
> Legalization of marijuana (or heroin)
>
> Sterilization of the mentally challenged
>
> Criteria justifying a declaration of war—pre-emptive strike, defense to an attack, regime change and promotion of democracy, genocide

With the help of at least one other person, identify and write down the following:

a. What is my position on this issue?
b. Why do I hold this position? What values, attitudes, or beliefs is this position based on?
c. What other points of view could one have on this issue?

Select the point of view that is furthest (most polar) from your own preferred perspective. Role-play a debate with another person in which you are defending the point of view that you have just identified as most polar to your own perspective.

Debriefing: Which types of arguments were most effective in persuading you? Which types of arguments were most effective in persuading the person taking your original position? What were the three most important things you learned from this exercise?

9. ADVOCACY RELATIONSHIPS: The Society for the Protection of Fruits and Vegetables (SPFV) is concerned about violence toward nonanimal food products. People slice, dice, chomp, boil, and otherwise mutilate fruits and vegetables without concern for their feelings. SPFV is advocating for greater respect for fruits and vegetables as living, benevolent sources of vitamins, protein, and fiber. Assume the role of an advocate for SPFV. Develop three advocacy strategies based on influencing three target groups: carnivores (who share a deep alliance with you), omnivores (who see you as a neutral), and herbivores (who view you as an adversary).

10. CULTURAL ACCOMMODATIONS: Assume you are working with a client who has been mistreated by another social agency in your city. Your client comes from an Eastern culture that values peace, harmony, and nonconflictual relationships. She does not want to confront the agency in order to assert her rights. You assess that a linear problem-solving approach to advocacy is inappropriate, because the client has more of a circular sense of time and structure. How would you adjust the intervention strategies in this chapter, if at all, in order to ensure that your approach respects the client's culture?

11. ETHICAL ISSUES: Select one of the following situations. Analyze the ethical issues and suggest how you might try to resolve them. How would your approach differ if you adopted a conflict resolution approach versus a framework for ethical decision making from the literature (e.g., Corey et al., 2007; Dolgoff et al., 2005; Menkel-Meadow & Wheeler, 2004)?

a. One of your clients self-identifies as a neo-Nazi. She wants you to help her get into a social work program at a local college. Personally, you do not believe she is an appropriate candidate. Your job, however, is to help clients apply to school programs.

b. A group of elderly clients asks you to help them advocate for a new recreation center for seniors. You do not believe that this center has much of a chance of succeeding. You would prefer to focus on more feasible advocacy projects.

c. A young man suffering from cancer has been denied social assistance because he has parents who are able to support him. The man does not have a good relationship with his parents and does not want to receive their support. There is an internal appeals procedure for social assistance; however, you would have to establish a new precedent. The stress of going through with the appeals procedures might take its toll on this client, already quite ill from cancer. He is unsure about how to proceed and seeks your advice as an advocate. You think it would make a great test case, but the likelihood of success is relatively low.

d. You work with an advocacy group that promotes the interests of women who have been abused by husbands or other intimate partners. During a public awareness campaign, one of your colleagues publishes information that grossly exaggerates the extent of abuse in the community. She also makes up fictitious stories about clients who have been abused. When you confront her, she says, "Exaggerating is necessary in order to make a point. Besides, it's for a good cause."

e. You are advocating for a community group that wants the city to build affordable housing on a publicly owned vacant lot. During negotiations with city officials, you do not believe they have been forthright with you. They have withheld information, used scare tactics, and tried to intimidate you with vague threats about withdrawing funding from the social agency that employs you. Although you cannot prove city officials have done anything illegal, you believe they have been soliciting bribes from a sleazy developer that wants to build an upscale shopping center on the lot. The community you represent asks you to respond with "whatever it takes" to persuade the city to do the right thing. As a professional advocate, do you "treat others as you would have them treat you," or can you justify "treating others as they have treated you"? As one community member put it, "If you're being attacked by sharks, it does no good to offer your hand as a gesture of peace."

12. RESEARCH AS ADVOCACY: You are working with a client who is claiming refugee status because of emotional torture he suffered in his country of origin. He claims to have post-traumatic stress disorder as a result of threats to himself and family over a 3-year period. The tribunal hearing his case is skeptical about his claims. They question whether someone can be a victim of torture if there are no signs of physical abuse. Conduct a literature review in order to gather information that may be helpful in advocating for the client (Mnookin, Susskind, & Foster, 1999). Develop an advocacy brief that could be provided to the refugee tribunal.

ROLE-PLAY 6.1: "ICE CREAM ALIENS"—ASSESSING DECISION MAKERS

This role-play allows you to practice assessing decision makers in order to determine what types of advocacy affect their decision making. The whole class takes part. Assign two people to role-play Aliens. The rest of the class will role-play Earthlings.

Chafe and Veej are from another planet, Huggendaz. Their supreme master, Benjer, has sent them down to Earth to advocate for a certain type of ice cream.

Chafe must advocate for chocolate ice cream; Veej must advocate for strawberry. These just happen to be the flavors that they actually like best. In order to prepare for this exercise, Chafe and Veej will be sent out of the room. Each of them will write down a list of reasons why they like their flavor of ice cream best. Their role is to advocate for their favorite type of ice cream, persuading as many Earthlings as possible to vote for their flavor. The ice cream with the fewer votes will be banished from Huggendaz forever. Chafe and Veej will have 13 minutes to do their advocating.

Confidential Facts for Both Chafe and Veej (not to be read by Earthlings)

In order to prepare for this case, consider various ways of influencing the Earthlings. Try to assess how each person might be persuaded: Consider which groups of Earthlings view you as an ally, a neutral, or an adversary. Ensure that your tactics are appropriate for each of these groups. How can you win over people who view you as adversaries? Consider both ethical and unethical tactics. Have fun.

Confidential Facts for Earthlings (not to be read by Aliens)

Each of you will only have certain ways of being persuaded:

- People with glasses: You are affected by emotional appeals. You view both aliens as neutrals.
- People with contact lenses: You are affected by rational appeals. You feel an alliance with Veej and adversarial relations with Chafe.
- People with neither glasses nor contact lenses: You are affected by humorous appeals. You feel an alliance with Chafe and adversarial relations with Veej.
- Females: You tend to be more persuaded by loud voices.
- Males: You tend to be more persuaded by soft voices.
- People with detached ear lobes: You are persuaded by bribes (particularly subtle ones)
- People with joined ear lobes: You are turned off by bribes.

Check off the rules that affect you and try to remember them. Do not disclose them directly to either of the Aliens. Engage in normal conversation with the aliens and cooperate with any of their questions. At the end of the exercise, role-players should vote according to the above rules.

Debriefing: The facilitator should ask each Alien the following questions: (a) Which people viewed you as allies? as neutrals? as adversaries? (b) How did you find out? (c) As an advocate, which skills or strategies worked well? (d) Which skills or strategies did not seem to work?

The facilitator should then ask each Earthling the following questions: (a) How did it feel to be a decision maker in this case? (b) Which specific skills or strategies influenced you the most?

ROLE-PLAY 6.2: "PERRY'S PAROLE"—ORAL AND WRITTEN SKILL DEVELOPMENT

This role-play involves one person playing a therapist (Therma) and three people playing members of a parole board. The purpose is to provide the therapist with an opportunity to practice advocacy skills.

Therma is a therapist on contract with the Conflictia Justice Center. She has been working with Perry, a 34-year-old man who has been convicted of sexual assault of a minor. Perry is coming up for parole. Therma has been asked to prepare a report for the parole board. Therma believes that Perry now has a very low risk for re-offending, as he has developed insights and empathy regarding the impact of sexual abuse on children. He has consented to the use of drug therapy to control his sexual drive and wants to continue in counseling.

Confidential Facts for Therma

In order to prepare for the role-play:

1. Write down a list of concerns/criteria that you believe the parole board will be considering when they read your report.
2. Draft a report advocating for Perry's parole—separate the facts from your expert opinions, address the concerns that you have identified in (1), and consider language that would be most persuasive.
3. Consider how to handle information that may go against Perry's application for parole. Do you present both sides of the issue?
4. Prepare how you will present your case as an advocate in front of the parole board.

When you role-play, you will be making submissions to the members of the parole board. One of them will facilitate the process. The board will be making a decision about whether to release Perry on parole and, if so, with what conditions.

Confidential Facts for Parole Board

Prior to the oral hearing, consider the therapist's written advocacy brief. In order to prepare for the role-play, consider the following questions:

1. What criteria will you use to make your decision about Perry's parole?
2. What information do you need to make a decision based on these criteria?
3. Where will you get this information from (aside from what you will get from the therapist)?
4. How important will the therapist's information be? Why?
5. What types of strategies could the therapist use in order to make her submission to you most persuasive?
6. What types of strategies would turn you off?
7. Review the Inventory of Advocacy Skills and Activities, so that you can give Therma feedback on her use of skills following the role-play.

During the role-play, your function will be to hear submissions. You will be in control of the process (appoint one member to be the facilitator). You will have the task of making the decisions at the end of the process: Will Perry be released on parole? If so, under what conditions?

Debriefing: What are the strengths of the written brief? What oral advocacy skills did the therapist demonstrate most effectively? What other strategies could an advocate use under similar circumstances?

ROLE-PLAY 6.3: "WORKFARE CASE"—SKILL DEVELOPMENT

The Right of Center (ROC) government of Conflictia has proposed a workfare program, in which people will be required to work in state-sponsored jobs in order to be eligible for welfare payments. The Left of Center (LOC) Party opposes this proposal. The Somewhere in the Middle (SIM) Party keeps flip-flopping on its position.

For this role-play, work in groups of three. One person will play an advocate who opposes the workfare proposal. The second person will role-play a member of one of the three parties (to be decided by your group). The third person will act as an observer, to provide feedback. During the interaction between the advocate and the party member, the advocate will try to develop a positive relationship with the party member and then try to influence the way the member votes in the upcoming vote on the workfare proposal. The advocate should identify three or four advocacy items from the Inventory of Advocacy Skills that the advocate wants to practice.

The position of LOCs who oppose workfare can be summarized as follows.

- Mothers on welfare are already working: they are raising children.
- Many others on welfare are also working outside the home. They supplement their inadequate welfare payments by working "under the table." However, they are not reporting their incomes to avoid being cut off welfare and health insurance benefits.
- It is mean to require welfare recipients to train for tedious jobs that do not offer career advancement or benefits (such as health insurance or vacations).
- These jobs pay so little that many would remain on welfare rolls even if they retained their jobs following the workfare program.
- Where good jobs are offered through workfare, employers are displacing regular salaried employees with a cheaper, "second-class" workforce.
- Previous work-training programs have not worked.
- Governmental policy makers should quit "blaming the victim." Instead, reform the inequitable education system; banish racism; pay a living wage; and provide decent housing, adequate nutrition, healthcare, and childcare.
- In terms of welfare reforms, substantially raise benefits and allow welfare mothers to choose whether they will work or not. Offer them incentives and opportunities to work (e.g., through subsidized daycare or job training for meaningful careers).

The position of ROC members who favor workfare can be summarized as follows:

- Work is inherently good. It is a core value of life in this society.
- Most parents today, even those with young children, are in the labor force.
- Welfare recipients act as a drain on the economy and are exploiting taxpayers who work.
- Getting rid of people on welfare who exploit the system will allow tax revenues to be used for other public purposes.
- Benefits for the truly needy can be increased if those on workfare enter the productive economy.
- People who work have better self-esteem and will be more likely to find productive places in the community than those who stay home collecting welfare.
- Public sector jobs could be given to those on welfare.
- If people cannot depend on welfare, they will be more likely to pull themselves up by the bootstraps.

Role-play for about 45 minutes. Break up the role-play into short segments, so you have ample opportunity to provide feedback during the role-play.

Debriefing: What were the objectives of the advocate? What skills did the advocate use to work toward these objectives? Which skills did the advocate use most effectively? Which skills does the advocate want to prioritize for future practice?

MAJOR ASSIGNMENTS

The following four role-plays are designed to be conducted in class and can be used for the purposes of writing a major assignment (see the section in Chapter 3 on Major Assignments for instructions on how to prepare the written analysis). You can use these role-plays to practice both advocacy and facilitation skills and strategies.

For each role-play, everybody in the class will be assigned one of three types of roles: an advocate, a decision maker (on a panel with other decision makers), or an observer. All parties should read the common facts for the role-play. In addition, read the confidential facts for your specifically assigned role. One person in each role-play will also be designated to play the facilitator. The facilitator will choose the type of CR process to use for the meeting (e.g., debate, dialogue, mediation, town hall meeting, court trial, administrative hearing, or other process from Chapter 5). The facilitator should let all participants know the type of CR process in advance, so that they can prepare. The facilitator can decide whether advocates should have input into the type of process or not.

Each role-play will last 45 to 70 minutes. You may also decide to have preparatory meetings outside of class time. Allow a few minutes before each role-play for setting up, as well as 20 minutes after each role-play for debriefing and filling out the feedback forms. During debriefing, the advocates will be asked to identify the key strategies they used and how effective they were. They may also explain why they did not use certain types of strategies (e.g., if their assigned role asked them to take a positional stance, then they may have chosen not to focus on interests). On agreement of the people in the role-play, you may audio- or video-record the assignment to help you with your written analysis of the role-play.

During the role-plays where you are not an advocate or a panel member, your job will be to observe the role-play and complete a feedback form for each of the people playing an advocacy role-play. Make photocopies of the Inventory of Advocacy Skills and Activities, and use these to provide detailed feedback to colleagues in your class.

ASSIGNMENT 6A: ANTIDISCRIMINATION PROTEST CASE

The Coalition Against Ethnic Profiling (CAEP) has requested permission from the municipality of Conflictia to conduct an antiracism demonstration this Saturday. The date was chosen to commemorate the 2-year anniversary of a mass suicide in a detention center by a group of Muslim inmates who were being held on charges of conspiracy to commit terrorist acts. The coalition represents people of Muslim, Pakistani, and Arab backgrounds, who believe they have been the target of governmental and police discrimination. Since the September 11, 2001, attacks on the U.S. Pentagon and World Trade Center, more than 1,200 people have been charged and held on the premise that they had ties to Al Qaeda or other terrorist organizations. The coalition believes that most of these people have been held merely because of their ethnic or religious background. They believe they have been made scapegoats for Conflictia's war on terrorism.

Many government officials do not want the proposed protest to take place. Although they recognize that peaceful protest is a right within a free and democratic society, they believe the proposed protest will become violent. In fact, it might become a magnet for hooligans or even actual terrorists. They also believe that the protestors will make the job of homeland security more difficult. If the law enforcement officials are not permitted to detain people suspected of terrorist affiliations, this will increase the chances of another terrorist strike. They are also concerned that CAEP itself has terrorist ties.

Other officials support the protest, noting that freedom of association and freedom of expression are guaranteed in the Conflictia Declaration of Rights and Freedoms. They contend that other cities have had demonstrations concerning the war on terrorism and they did not become violent. In fact, trying to stop the demonstration might actually provoke violence. They downplay some of the violence that erupted during protests in other cities, including Quebec City, Buenos Aires, Madrid, and London. They believe Conflictian citizens have been well educated in means of peaceful conflict resolution.

In an effort to involve the community in the decision-making process, the municipality has invited the following people to participate in a closed meeting.

- Collette, a representative of the CAEP, who is requesting the demonstration
- Stonewall, a store owner, on the proposed route of the demonstration
- Sgt. Pilar Polgat, a representative of the police force
- Arabella, the president of a student run Anti-Racism Group from Conflictia University
- Socrates, a social worker who works in an agency that serves immigrants and refugees from the Middle East

The panel conducting the hearing will consist of Miranda (the mayor and facilitator), Miguel, Mavis, Martin, and Maya (municipal councilors). They have decision-making authority over whether to grant a permit for a public demonstration.

This group has been brought together for a 45-minute meeting. Its task is to make recommendations to the municipality about what it should do in response to the coalition's request for a demonstration permit. No one knows for sure what consequences will result, whether or not a permit is granted.

Confidential Facts for Collette

You would like to see the demonstration go ahead, with approval of the municipality. The members of your coalition, however, may go ahead with their demonstration regardless of whether it is approved. You are CAEP's spokesperson, although you do not have a lot of influence over them. CAEP represents a variety of interests and does not agree about how best to proceed with their "antiracist" agenda. Moving the protest to a less commercial or less trafficked area is not a good solution for you. You want high visibility. Furthermore, people will only start to listen to your concerns if you cause them some discomfort. You are particularly offended by those who equate all Arabs, Muslims, or Pakistanis with terrorists. You self-identify as an American Muslim, and you know firsthand the fear that your coalition members have regarding racial profiling and police harassment.

Confidential Facts for Stonewall

You believe that having the demonstration would be a big mistake. You do not agree that racial profiling is a big issue, but you are also unsure about how people would react to your saying so. You are mostly concerned about the loss of business and the potential risk to your property if the demonstration goes ahead. Saturday is your best day for sales. A protest would keep shoppers away—particularly Connie's group from the Conflictia Seniors Center (Chapter 4), who hold their self-defense classes at your store on Saturdays. Your store sells antiques, including knives and swords that you have collected from around the world. You are very concerned that protesters might loot your store to use these as weapons. You have spoken to people in Sydney, Los Angeles, and Quebec about riots they have had. Even well-planned demonstrations can spark fires. Other businesses on the demonstration route share your concerns.

Confidential Facts for Sgt. Polgat

You have a lot of experience working with people from the Middle East and Pakistan. You can empathize with their concerns. Even though you do not like to discriminate against any group, you understand that racial profiling is a necessary tool for keeping the country safe from terrorism. You believe that CAEP has good intentions—to raise awareness of racism issues—but you do not believe the cost of policing a demonstration is justified. Demonstrations in public places can put the interests of a few above the interests of the majority. People have a right to freedom of expression, but they do not have the right to inconvenience others, particularly at the expense of taxpayers. A demonstration would require retaining extra police for a Saturday, paying overtime, and putting the riot squad on alert. If there is a riot, it is your head that is put on the line.

Confidential Facts for Arabella

You are not an Arab, Muslim, or Pakistani, so you have not directly experienced their concerns about racism and police treatment. You have been working with these groups in your antiracism work, so you are aware of many incidents where people have been thrown in jail for no cause. This issue has literally torn families apart, some of them fearing that maybe a family member does have terrorist ties. You have a large student group behind you. You have also started to prepare for the demonstration in conjunction with CAEP. You have lined up a number of celebrity speakers, including Sasha Lizte (leader of the LOCs). The local newspapers and radio stations have also received copy to promote the demonstration. If the protest is blocked, considerable time and effort will have gone for naught.

Confidential Facts for Socrates

As someone who works in an agency that serves immigrants and refugees from the Middle East, you have been helping many clients and families deal with issues related to racial profiling. Even families that have had no arrests have experienced stress and fear. Many have experienced taunts and threats from neighbors and coworkers, telling them to go home where they belong. Some of your clients have lost jobs because they were arrested on charges related to terrorism. Even when they were cleared of criminal charges, they were not rehired. You believe that the demonstration would be a great way to raise the awareness of the plight of Arabs, Muslims, and Pakistanis in Conflictia. You believe that racial profiling is discriminatory and does not make the country any safer. You feel the protest will help sway the public to put pressure on the government to use alternate strategies to fight terrorism.

Confidential Facts for Committee Members—Miranda (the mayor and facilitator), Miguel, Mavis, Martin, and Maya (municipal councilors)

Try to put yourselves into the roles of mayor and municipal councilors. Jot down some of your concerns, questions, and biases. During the role-play, try to be sensitive to the types of arguments and strategies that would persuade you. Remember, an election is coming up next year. Miranda will facilitate the meeting and can choose what type of format to use. One possibility would be to open the meeting as if it were a town hall meeting. After about 20 minutes, try switching to an interest-based mediation process.

ASSIGNMENT 6B: TO HOLD OR NOT TO HOLD

Diversity Plus operates three group homes for children with emotional disturbances. The ages of the children range from 7 to 16 years old. The Office of the Ombud in

Conflictia has recently received complaints from three children in the group homes. Each stemmed around a different incident in which group home staff used physical force to discipline children. The Office of the Ombud has initiated a conflict resolution process in which it will hear from all interested parties before rendering its recommendations. Ideally, the parties will come to a consensus on how to proceed. At present, consensus does not seem possible.

The current policy of the group homes allows staff to physically restrain children who pose a risk to themselves, others, or property. Three or four staff members hold down a child who is acting out. Both arms and legs are restrained in order to ensure that the child is safe. Agency staff say that "holdings" are a therapeutic intervention, providing the child with structure, boundaries, and a sense of being cared for (similar to a hug from a parent). Staff are not permitted to strap, hit, or otherwise discipline children with physical force.

This role-play involves five advocates:

* Chet, a child advocate who opposes the use of holdings in group homes
* Urania, a union steward who represents the group home staff
* Amelia, the administrator of the group homes
* Dr. Parker, a psychologist who is advocating for a group of parents whose children have laid complaints against the group homes
* Matilda, the distraught mother of a child who was injured by another child in the group home

The Office of the Ombud has appointed five people to hear the case: Orillia (who will facilitate the process), Ovide, Omer, Obadiah, and Oprah.

Confidential Facts for Chet

As a child advocate, you value the civil liberties of children. You believe that holdings infringe the autonomy of children. Staff can use other methods in order to ensure the safety of themselves and others. Many staff members are poorly trained, leading to frequent crises in the group home that could be avoided with more effective verbal interventions. You realize that the group homes are under-resourced and have a difficult time retaining good staff.

About 45 percent of the children in the group homes have a history of being sexually abused. Holdings are particularly scary and demeaning for this group. Consider different options that may be more empowering to the children.

Confidential Facts for Urania

You have a background in social work and organizational behavior. As a representative of the union representing childcare staff at the group homes, you are concerned about the charges that have been laid against childcare staff by various children. The group homes have used holdings for over 25 years, with no complaints until this past year. You believe that the children have raised charges against staff as a way of manipulating them. Some of the children have been violent: punching walls, throwing dishes at staff, and bullying smaller children. The staff is paid not much more than minimum wage, even though most of them have 2-year diplomas in child-care or early childhood development. The rate of turnover is high, which is not good for the union, the agency, or the children. Personally, you are unsure about the therapeutic value of holdings.

Confidential Facts for Amelia

As administrator for the group homes, you strongly believe in the use of holdings. Under certain circumstances, you also advocate for the use of reasonable physical force to discipline children. Otherwise, the children you serve will have no respect for staff and will become uncontrollable. You believe so strongly in this that you are prepared to resign if the Office of the Ombud recommends prohibition of holdings. You have worked in this field for 30 years. In that time, you have never seen a child who has been injured by a holding. On the other hand, many staff have come away from holdings with significant cuts and bruises.

You are particularly concerned about how complaints from children have been portrayed in the media. You believe that this publicity infringes on the privacy of others in the group home. Also, charitable donations to the group homes have dropped since the publicity started.

Dr. Parker conducts groups for parents, as part of his contract with your agency. You respect his professional opinion but believe that he does not have the right to advocate against the policies of Diversity Plus. You may have to terminate his contract if he continues to argue against your agency.

Confidential Facts for Dr. Parker

You are a psychologist who has worked with many of the parents now complaining about the group home. Parents are concerned about the competence of the group home staff. Some parents report that the behavior of their children has been deteriorating, not getting better. You may want to review the literature, to look at the impact of holdings or other physical discipline on children with emotional disturbances. You have a contract with Diversity Plus, so you have concerns about how your stance on this issue will affect your future relationship with the group homes. Still, your ethical code tells you to do what is right for your clients, even if it means risking your job.

Confidential Facts for Matilda

Your little angel, Angela, is a 12-year-old who was placed in the group home because of an "emotional disturbance." You believe the group home has actually made problems worse for Angela because the children are completely out of control and staff members are scared to enforce the rules. You believe Angela was hurt because staff members were slow to react to a child who struck Angela with a broomstick. If staff had initiated a holding more quickly, Angela would have been protected. During the advocacy, you are very scattered, angry, disruptive, and melodramatic. You use nuisance power to try to get others to listen to you. You actually like the staff in the home and believe that they just need policies and training to enable them to physically restrain potentially violent clients. Perhaps karate lessons would help.

Confidential Facts for the Ombuds: Orillia, Omer, Ovide, Obadiah, and Oprah

As members of the Office of the Ombuds, you would like to see the parties resolve this matter themselves. Set up a process that will allow you to gather information from the parties, share it with one another, and determine whether there is common ground. If the parties cannot reach an amicable resolution, then your mandate is to make suggestions about how the group homes should proceed. Orillia will facilitate the process and may designate others to play timekeeper, note taker, and ground rule enforcer. Orillia could set up the meeting as an administrative hearing, a dialogue, a settlement-oriented mediation, or another process from Chapter 5. Orillia should let the advocates know in advance what type of process she will use.

ASSIGNMENT 6C: HELGA'S HEART

Helga is a 15-year-old girl who was born with a moderate case of Down syndrome. She functions at the level of a 5-year-old but is generally a happy child. Helga has recently been diagnosed as suffering from a heart condition requiring a heart transplant. Her doctors believe that she cannot survive beyond the next 40 days without a transplant. Transplant surgery is expensive. However, the main concern is that hearts appropriate for this type of surgery are in short supply. Even if Helga's name is put on the top of the list, there is no guarantee that a suitable heart will be found for her in time (in fact, the chances are about 40 percent). If she is put at the middle of the list, her chances are 15 percent. If she is placed at the bottom of the list, then her chances are zero. Some of the other people already on the list include a 40-year-old single actress, a 24-year-old married mother of two (ages 2 and 4), and a 64-year-old retired army sergeant who is a heavy smoker. The hospital administration and representatives from the Department of Health need to decide how to handle Helga's situation. The have assembled a panel to hear the views of a number of interested parties. The parties that they will hear today include the following people:

- Seth, a social worker who is acting as an advocate for Helga and her family
- Rhonda, a medical researcher, specializing in heart transplant surgery. She believes that Helga is a poor candidate for this surgery.
- Praba, a psychiatric nurse who advocates for people with cognitive impairments. The group she represents believes that they should be treated with the same respect and rights as anyone else.
- Cwan, a counselor from the Department of Defense, advocating for the retired army sergeant
- Alistair, an advocate for the actress who is paying Alistair large sums of money to advance her case and help her obtain the heart she needs so desperately

The panel listening to these representations includes: Dr. Hadad (hospital administrator and designated facilitator), Drs. Dudley and Doright (two doctors), and Ms. Holloway (a representative from the Conflictia Department of Health).

Confidential Facts for Seth

You are personally unsure whether Helga is a good candidate for this surgery, given that she lacks the basic abilities to take care of herself. Even if the surgery goes well, she will always be highly dependent on others. You do share Helga's family's concern for her and will advocate for her to be given high priority for a heart transplant. You are concerned that the actress is trying to buy herself a heart, and you do not believe that this is a valid way to determine this issue. You are also concerned that the army sergeant may receive high priority because some regard the sergeant as a military hero. You may lapse into name-calling—out of anger at the insensitivity of some of the others who are advocating against Helga. Otherwise, you can use whichever strategies you believe will be most effective.

Confidential Facts for Rhonda

Your research shows that the effectiveness of heart surgery depends significantly on the postoperation cooperation of the patient. The patient must be able to follow strict instructions in terms of diet, activities, cleanliness, and rehabilitation therapy. Your information about Helga is that she has bad nutritional habits and that she is not very cooperative with being given instructions. Given the shortage of hearts, you believe that tough decisions have to be made and that the best candidates for surgery need to be the ones selected. You do not want to play God or evaluate which person is more deserving.

You expect some sort of trouble from Cwan. About a year ago, you applied for a position with the Department of Defense, and Cwan was responsible for torpedoing your chances. You think Cwan feels defensive with you because you have such strong academic credentials.

You do not know the name of the actress, but you have heard that her life is not currently in danger. She has severe damage to her heart valves, meaning that she has little energy. She is basically housebound, but she is not likely to die within the next 3 to 5 years as long as she follows proper diet and exercise plans. Your preferred style of conflict resolution is rights based, though you may also use other advocacy strategies (particularly if the facilitator or other advocates use persuasive techniques with you).

Confidential Facts for Praba

You believe that all people who need surgery should be given equal consideration. No one has the right to judge which of two or more people should live or die. If there is such a choice to be made, then your initial solution would be to use a random generating device (e.g., drawing names whenever a suitable heart became available). You are particularly incensed by people who would rate a girl with Down syndrome as a second-class citizen. You know Helga personally and believe that her life is as worthy as anyone else's on the list. You fear that the mother of two has already been given top priority and this hearing is just a way to placate the others by giving them a chance to be heard.

Confidential Facts for Cwan

You have nothing against Helga. You do not even know her. However, your role is to advocate for Amy Salk, an army sergeant who has served her country and deserves high priority on this decision. You (and Amy) fear that her age and smoking will be held against her. In fact, you have seen research that shows that people in her situation are not as good candidates as younger, nonsmoking patients. Your focus, however, is that the decision should be made on the basis of merit—or at least respect for all people. You never know which individual will actually make the best candidate. You do not have a lot of respect for Rhonda. You believe that her research methods are not very good. You also know she is angry because you did not hire her for a research position at the Department of Defense.

Confidential Facts for Alistair

The client you represent, Halle Canary, is a rich and famous actress. She has authorized you to offer the hospital a $40 million donation if her case is prioritized so that she is able to receive the next heart. The notoriety of her situation will also help the hospital garner additional donations. You know you must be careful to avoid the appearance of buying a heart. You also know that Madam Canary's situation is not the most urgent, because doctors have advised her that she can probably live for years with her heart condition. The issue for Madam Canary is quality of life: her heart condition is so severe that she can hardly walk. As long as she does not move around too much, however, she is fine.

Confidential Facts for the Hospital and Ministry of Health Panel: Dr. Hadad, Drs. Dudley and Doright, and Ms. Holloway

Try to put yourselves into the roles of the hospital and Department of Health representatives. Jot down some of your concerns, questions, and biases, based on your professional views. During the role-play, try to be sensitive to the types of arguments and strategies that would persuade you. None of you actually has decision-making authority. You will be using this consultation to develop a report to the Conflictia Council of Representatives, which will make the ultimate decisions. There is precedent for assigning priority based on who is expected to have the best quality and longevity of life, postoperation. You have already had input from other advocates who made a strong case for giving the 24-year-old mother top priority, based on these criteria. Dr. Hadad and Ms. Holloway are big fans of the actress, Halle Canary, and would like to accommodate her. Drs. Dudley and Doright believe that Madam Canary's acting abilities are irrelevant. As the facilitator, Dr. Hadad should choose one or two styles of meetings for this role-play (e.g., start as a public hearing and switch after 30 minutes to transformative mediation). Let the advocates know which style of meeting you plan to open with (do not let them know in advance that you plan to switch halfway through).

ASSIGNMENT 6D: ARCHIE'S ADOPTION

Peabody's Adoption Services (PAS) is a privately based agency acting as an intermediary to facilitate voluntary adoptions. Archie is a 38-year-old single male, who has applied to PAS to be considered as an adoptive parent. He is willing to adopt a boy or a girl. Although he would prefer to adopt an infant, Archie realizes that the waiting list for infants is long. He would be willing to adopt an older child (for which there is greater need).

Slobodan is the social worker for PAS who conducted the intake interview with Archie. During the intake interview, Archie explained that he is a gay man who is financially secure given his job as an architect for the city. Archie has always wanted to raise children, but he had decided to wait until he was in a relationship of some permanence. He believes that given his age, now would be a good time to adopt. Although he does not have a partner, he does have support from family and friends. Slobodan advised Archie that before going further in the adoption process, he would have to consult with the agency. Although Conflictia has no law against a gay, single man adopting, Slobodan was not aware of any prior situations where a gay, single man had adopted through PAS. Archie gave Slobodan permission to discuss his situation but was concerned about whether the agency would discriminate against him. Slobodan said that he did not have a problem with Archie's application. However, Slobodan did not have final say for the agency. Personally, Slobodan is not sure about the right way to deal with this situation because he feels he does not have enough knowledge about the relevant issues. He does not want to hurt Archie.

Clarice is Slobodan's clinical supervisor. She was glad that Slobodan brought this case to her attention, because it was long past due that the agency developed a policy about these issues. She believes strongly that sexual orientation should not be a factor in eligibility criteria for adoption. She also believes that the biological parent should not have any say about whether a child goes to a heterosexual or homosexual adoptive parent. She believes homophobia should not be tolerated.

Elvira is the Executive Director of PAS. Elvira believes that the agency does not have any obligation to serve gay men or women who want to adopt, because the agency is a private agency. Elvira thinks that the agency should restrict its eligibility to legally married couples. In support of this position, Elvira notes that same-sex couples are not legally sanctioned relationships in Conflictia and that many biological parents may not want their children raised by homosexual parents. Elvira fears that biological parents may not use the agency if it starts to work with gay adoptive parents. She states there is no research about whether gay men make good adoptive parents, adding that this is not being homophobic; it is just being pragmatic.

Colleen is a child psychologist who does assessments for PAS. Colleen believes that it may be advantageous for gay children to be placed with gay adoptive parents, for modeling and for support. However, most of the children that PAS deals with have not clearly developed a sexual orientation. Colleen believes that there are far more important factors than a parent's sexual orientation that would determine whether someone would make a good adoptive parent. Colleen does feel strongly that couples have more time and resources to provide for a child's needs than does a single parent. Also, older children should have some say about the sexual orientation of their adoptive parents.

Father Connell is a Catholic priest. His congregation has 3,500 members, many of whom have been big contributors to PAS. Three of his congregants sit on the Board of Directors of PAS (Betty, Bruce, and Brandy). Father Connell believes that homosexuality is immoral; accordingly, gay men should not be considered as potential adoptive parents. Even though Conflictia has no law against gay men adopting, there is a higher law—God's law. Father Connell also has research saying that children of gay men are more likely to become gay and are more likely to use drugs, commit crimes, and become atheist. Father Connell is not an employee of PAS but believes that his input is important. Clarice respects him as a spiritual leader in the community but objects to his presence in private agency meetings.

The decision about how to deal with Archie's adoption application is being referred to the agency's Board of Directors. Boris, Betty, Bruce, Brandy and Bob serve on PAS's Board. During past, informal discussions, they came to a consensus that biological parents had the right to decide whether their children are adopted by gay or straight parents. In a local survey by another agency considering this issue, less than 8 percent of biological parents would consent to having their child adopted by a gay couple. The figure would be even lower for a single gay man. Given these statistics, very few children would be placed with gay parents. They believed that it would be misleading to gay men to say they are eligible when, in fact, they would just sit on the waiting list forever.

These professionals have come together for a consultation to decide whether Archie should be considered further as a potential adoptive parent. Elvira, as Executive Director of PAS, will facilitate the process. She may start out by setting ground rules and asking everyone to agree to them.

There are no confidential facts for this case.

Hate is too great a burden to bear. It injures the
hater more than it injures the hated.

—Coretta Scott King

7 CHAPTER | Additional Third-Party Interventions

Although mediation, facilitation, and advocacy are all methods of helping people involved in conflict, they are by no means the only ways to assist. This chapter describes six additional processes in which helping professionals can serve as conflict resolution practitioners: fact finding, trust building, peacebuilding, parenting coordination, family group conferencing, and spiritual healing.[1] While the roles and goals of helping professionals in each of these methods of intervention will differ, there are overlaps in the skills, strategies, and theoretical approaches that can be used. As you work through this chapter, pay close attention to the similarities and differences between each method of conflict intervention.

FACT FINDING

Fact finding refers to using a strategic process to collect reliable information or evidence related to issues in dispute (Conflict Research Consortium, 1998). Sometimes, the parties act as fact finders for themselves, perhaps with the aid of CR practitioners. Other times, the parties agree to the help of a fact finder or have fact finders imposed on them (e.g., a jury in a court trial). Obviously, fact finding is appropriate when the nature of the dispute is a factual disagreement (Shultz, 2004). Fact finding may relate to historic facts or current ones. For instance, "Did Iraq have weapons of mass destruction?" or "Does Iraq still have weapons of mass destruction?" Fact finding may also be helpful with conflicts that are based on concerns other than facts, because determining facts may lead to resolution of issues at other levels. For instance, "What are the child's special needs?" is a factual question that assists with resolution of "What types of parenting arrangements are in the child's best interests?" Similarly,

---

[1]This chapter focuses on collaborative processes. Helping professionals can also act as decision makers (e.g., as arbitrators, enforcers, referees, or evaluators), though these processes tend to promote adversarial relations.

resolving factual questions may assist with resolving differences related to positions, values, needs, identities, and emotional concerns. Sometimes, fact finding is used early in a CR intervention. Sometimes, other concerns require intervention before the parties can move into fact finding. For instance, if anger and suspicion are running high in a divorce situation, the parents may require an intervention dealing with emotions before they can participate effectively in a fact-finding method.

Factual disputes arise when there are rumors, mistrust, lack of information, misinformation, different views on what is relevant, or different assessments concerning the importance or consequences of different information. Sometimes, people are looking at different data. Other times, they are interpreting it differently. Effective fact finding ensures the parties have access to all data. It also provides strategies to determine what data to pay attention to and how to interpret data rationally.

Different types of fact finding are required for different types of factual disputes. Accordingly, professionals must help parties assess the nature of their factual dispute before determining a strategy that effectively addresses the nature of the dispute. The following scenario demonstrates a range of fact-finding strategies:

> Pino is a pedophile who was convicted for molesting young girls. He alleges prison guards have intentionally left him alone with other inmates so they could beat him. Although the prison has a policy against this practice, the prison administrator, Dr. Addams, denies any wrongdoing. He insists that Pino is fabricating the story in order to win preferential treatment. Pino contacts Mrs. Oliver, the ombud responsible for the prison.

An *ombud* (or ombudsperson) is a specific type of CR professional who uses fact finding. Section 1 of the United States Ombudsman Association (2004) standards defines an *ombud* as "an independent, impartial public official with autonomy and responsibility to receive, investigate, or informally address complaints about government actions, and when appropriate, make findings and recommendations, and publish reports." The traditional role of an ombud is to protect members of the public against abuse, bias, unfairness, and other improper treatment by state institutions (Ombudsman Association, 2004).[2] An ombud has no authority to impose decisions on government or anyone else. He or she merely provides an independent investigation of facts. To the extent that the parties and the public view the investigation as unbiased and credible, they are likely to abide by the ombud's findings and recommendations. In Pino's case, the factual question concerns whether prison guards have deliberately subjected Pino to abuse from other prisoners. In order to promote a successful conclusion to this process, Mrs. Oliver will need to investigate what has actually happened.

An ombud or other fact finder needs to determine (a) what types of data are important to gather, (b) what processes will be used to collect data, and (c) whether to use third-party experts to gain outside opinions or break deadlocks (Moore, 1996). Typically, an ombud determines each of these issues unilaterally, though cooperation

---

[2]This website contains a detailed explanation of the role of an ombud, which includes fact finding but also roles such as confidential consulting, evaluation, reporting recommendations, and problem solving.

from the parties may be needed in order to implement the decisions on the fact-finding process. In other fact-finding approaches, the fact finder mediates with the parties to gain agreement on how to proceed with fact finding.

Mrs. Oliver determines that it is important to gather various types of information, including medical-physical records, reports from potential witnesses, and videotapes of Pino's cell. Pino expresses concern that he may be at greater risk from prison staff, who are angry at his allegations. Mrs. Oliver works with Dr. Addams to put safeguards in place, including re-assigning guards who were specifically charged with misconduct. Furthermore, because this is an ongoing investigation, prison guards know their actions may be monitored.

Some facts are relatively easy to prove, whereas others are more difficult or even impossible. Consider the mediation between sisters Suzie and Selma in Chapter 4. Selma accused Suzie of selling their parents' furniture. To resolve this dispute, the mediator could simply arrange for the two sisters to go to the parents' home to see whether the furniture is still there (perhaps with an escort to monitor their interaction). Pino's allegations may be more difficult to prove or disprove. If he had any physical injuries, these would show up on a medical examination. But how do you know what caused the injuries? Perhaps videotapes of the cell block show other prisoners beating Pino. The videos might not indicate, however, whether the prison guards intentionally left Pino to be abused. Costs of fact finding must also be taken into account. Mrs. Oliver might be able to gather better information if she conducts in-depth interviews with every prison staff member and inmate. How much would this cost, would the additional costs be worthwhile, and who will be responsible for paying these costs?

Fact finding might lead to a firm determination of facts. Often, the results of fact finding are not so certain, and decisions must be made on incomplete information (Conflict Research Consortium, 1998). Mrs. Oliver might conclude, "Pino's medical records clearly indicate he suffered from extensive bruising all over his torso, as well as a broken arm. Surveillance cameras demonstrate that he was beaten at least twice by other inmates, though Pino suggests that he was beaten on at least seven occasions. Interviews with prison staff and inmates were contradictory and inconclusive. Some witnesses expressed fear over possible repercussions if they provided information against the prison or certain staff." Although the investigation did not settle all factual issues in dispute, it might still serve to lead to a resolution, particularly concerning future conflict. Mrs. Oliver might offer recommendations, for instance, on how to ensure that Pino (and others like him) are not subjected to prisoner abuse: offering segregated areas for prisoners likely to be attacked by other prisoners; providing staff with training on how to avoid prisoner abuse; instilling a climate of respect for the basic dignity of all prisoners regardless of the nature of the crimes they committed. Dr. Addams may adopt these recommendations or work with Mrs. Oliver to make other changes that deal with these issues. For Pino, Mrs. Oliver's findings do not give him everything he wanted, but he should be relieved to know he will receive better protection going forward.

Helping professionals possess a number of attributes that fit well with the fact-finding role. First, helping professionals have specific training in assessment, interviewing, and research, all of which involve fact-finding processes. Helping professionals are also skilled in the use of critical thinking and literature reviews to gather and evaluate information. Consider a community group that is concerned about rates of teen pregnancy and is advocating for schools to promote an abstinence-only education program. If school officials are denying that teen pregnancy is a common issue, helping professionals could help community advocates construct research to document the extent of the problem. If community members and school officials disagree over the efficacy of an abstinence-only approach, helping professionals could help them organize a joint fact-finding team to look at the effectiveness of different programs around the country. The helping professional could also teach them how to evaluate the credibility of different pieces of research (e.g., taking research design, reliability, and validity of measures into account). By helping school officials and community members conduct the fact finding jointly, the results are more likely to be accepted than if either group conducted its own search for research evidence.

Second, helping professionals can play an important role in fact finding if they are seen to be independent and impartial. If a particular counselor is known to be a staunch advocate of abstinence-only sex education, then that counselor is unlikely to be accepted as a professional to assess the relative effectiveness of different types of programs. If the parties see the counselor instead as a person with an open mind, then they will be more likely to accept the person as someone who can gather and produce an unbiased set of facts. In situations where helping professionals are perceived as partisan, they might be able to construct bipartisan committees to handle fact-finding missions. Consider a dispute between Hindu and Muslim neighbors. While a Muslim community organizer or a Hindu community organizer might be viewed with skepticism by the other group, a team comprising both groups might be acceptable to everyone.

The following framework can be used by a CR professional for engaging clients in a dialogue about whether to the use of fact finding:

1. **Explain what fact finding is.** "Fact finding is a strategic method of gathering information that people can rely on for making decisions."
2. **Identify the purpose of fact finding.** "In our situation, one of the conflicts is about . . . [describe the facts in dispute]. Fact finding might be able to help us deal more effectively with the conflict by . . . ." [Explain possible advantages of fact finding, such as providing credible research evidence, identifying data that is necessary to make specific decisions, providing an objective set of facts that both parties can trust, and informing a larger conflict resolution process.]
3. **Describe various approaches to fact finding.** "Some ways to gather the information we need are . . . ." [Describe relevant approaches, such as hiring an expert, conducting a joint investigation, setting up a special commission of inquiry,[3] and referring the issue to an ombud.]
4. **Discuss the advantages, disadvantages, and costs of each approach.** Topics to consider include the perceived fairness and transparency of each fact-finding

---

[3]One way to determine contested facts is to design a "truth commission" such as those used to deal with the crimes of the apartheid era in South Africa (Schirch, 2004).

process; the perceived credibility of the outcomes; the chances both parties will accept the outcomes; the chances that the process will lead to a clear set of facts and/or interpretation of facts; the costs in time, emotional strain, and money of going through the fact-finding process; and potential ethical issues such as confidentiality, safety, and fear of retribution among potential witnesses who provide information.

5. **Obtain consensus on how to proceed.** Use mediation skills (Chapter 4) to help parties determine the best alternative. Obtain their commitment to specific guidelines governing the fact-finding process: who will be responsible for what (tasks, costs); when will each step be completed; how the results of fact finding will be reported (orally, written report, graphics, live demonstration); what the parties will do with the findings (e.g., use data or facts in the next step of the CR process, accept recommendations, treat recommendations as binding); and how the parties will treat the possibility that the report will provide uncertain or contradictory findings. A written agreement on the process can ensure the parties are clear about the fact-finding process and how they will handle the findings.

6. **Implement and monitor fact finding.** The CR professional can provide oversight to ensure that everyone is performing his or her expected roles—for instance, conducting the investigation, cooperating with the fact finders, or developing and delivering a report. The CR professional can help problem-solve any issues that arise in the process and encourage everyone to follow through. Where problems arise that imperil the credibility, transparency, or fairness of the fact-finding process, the professional may need to inform the clients and engage them in discussions about how to proceed (Conflict Research Consortium, 1998).

Fact finding may be integrated into other CR processes, but there may be advantages to separating fact finding and dealing with it as a distinct intervention. In some cases, the process of fact finding itself will be sufficient for dealing with a conflict. In other cases, the results of fact finding can be used by the parties to facilitate subsequent CR processes.

TRUST BUILDING

Just as fact finding can be used as a distinct CR method or as part of a larger CR intervention, so can trust building. *Trust building refers to strategies directed toward overcoming undue fears, suspicions, and wariness between the parties.* When parties have high levels of mistrust, they may find it difficult just to be in the same room, never mind talking civilly and rationally, or trying to address major issues. Trust is often at the core of conflict resolution. With trust, people can collaborate. Without trust, people are afraid to do so (Menkel-Meadow et al., 2005). By using trust-building measures,[4] CR professionals can prepare parties for further work together.

Although trust-building strategies can have immediate impact, trust building can also take considerable time. When a conflict has endured for years, a relatively

---

[4]Sometimes called *confidence building*.

brief intervention such as mediation—which occurs over hours, weeks, or months—cannot be expected to overcome the mistrust that has developed. Consider the following scenario:

> Recent newspaper reports concerning the death of Byron, a 12-year-old boy with cancer, have roused the long-standing conflict between mainstream healthcare professionals and naturopaths. A naturopath treated the boy with herbs and other natural substances. She advised his parents against the use of radiation or chemotherapy, so they refused to take the boy to mainstream healthcare professionals (MHPs). MHPs have responded to this story by calling naturopaths "quacks" and "reckless snake oil merchants." Naturopaths have charged MHPs with poisoning people with artificial and foreign substances, and denying the benefits of alternative medicine in order to maintain their monopoly and huge profits from the medical system. The Department of Health determines that this mudslinging feud is not in the best interests of public health. It assigns Tracy to "do something" to end the hostilities.

At this stage, bringing naturopaths and MHPs together to work through their conflict might be fruitless. Both groups are belittling one another and are likely to resist attempts at encouraging collaboration between them. Rather than inviting the groups to participate in a CR process, Tracy could invite them to try some of the following trust-building approaches (Menkel-Meadow et al., 2005).

- **Develop new avenues of communication.** Recently, the only communication between naturopaths and MHPs has been through newspapers and other media. They have not communicated directly or outside the public spotlight. Tracy could help them arrange more effective lines of communication. They might not be ready for formal, direct communications, such as mediation or a public dialogue session. Representatives from each group, however, might agree to private, unofficial meetings, perhaps at a remote location in Norway (as per the Oslo Accords between Israelis and Palestinians). Alternatively, they might engage in a scholarly discussion through articles in an academic journal on the effectiveness of various cancer treatments. Different lines of communication could be opened to serve different purposes—for instance, a town hall meeting to allow each other to express their needs, wants, and preferences, or a special task force to develop rules of engagement between the counterparts.
- **Encourage predictable behavior.** Acting in an unpredictable manner spurs mistrust.[5] If MHPs are unsure about what services naturopaths offer cancer patients, MHPs are more likely to question their credibility. For instance, do naturopaths discourage, encourage, or remain neutral about combining the use of traditional medicine with naturopathy? If MHPs knew where naturopaths stood on this issue, they would be more likely to trust naturopaths during future negotiations. Tracy could explain the importance of predictability to naturopaths, perhaps

---

[5]Consider a couple where a man has had an extramarital affair. In spite of unexplained absences, credit card charges for fancy restaurants, and nylons in the glove compartment of the car, his spouse does not see these signs or interprets them away. He has always been predictable and trustworthy, so why even entertain the thoughts of an affair? Once she breaks through the denial and accepts the affair has happened, however, she may never trust him again. He may need to demonstrate fidelity for years, and even then, mistrust may linger.

helping them develop standards of practice that naturopaths could follow. Even if naturopaths determined that they would discourage use of radiation, for instance, MHPs would know where they stood and could negotiate with them on this basis. If different naturopaths conveyed different views on this matter, MHPs would not know who to believe or who they could trust if they wanted to engage naturopaths in a collaborative CR process.

- **Facilitate mutual experiences.** Mistrust often arises and endures because the parties have little or no direct contact with each other. When they do have contact, it may revolve solely around the conflict. This dynamic creates fertile ground for hearsay, rumors, polarization, and misconceptions about each other. Tracy could facilitate trust between MHPs and naturopaths by bringing them together for events that have nothing to do with their primary conflict—for instance, inviting representatives from both groups to a weekend retreat on how to write grant proposals to fund new programs. By engaging with each other in a non-threatening environment, they will gain direct information about each other and may even learn how to work together. When you have never met someone, it is easy to rely on hearsay and demonize that person. When you spend time together, seeing (or experiencing) is believing.

- **Foster joint affiliation, goals, or values.** According to similarity-attraction theory, people are more likely to trust others who they view as similar. In the case scenario, MHPs and naturopaths view each other as if they come from different planets, with completely different goals and values. The use of the term *mainstream* for MHPs reinforces the divide, implying that naturopaths are inferior healthcare professionals. Tracy could use names that foster common identity, such as "cancer treatment providers." She could then help representatives develop and issue public statements of their shared goals and values (e.g., preservation of life, evidence-based practice, and accountability).

Stereotypes are assumptions people make concerning the characteristics of all members of a group, based on a generalized image about what people in that group are like. During conflicts, people tend to develop particularly negative stereotypes of the other side (see attribution theory in Chapter 1). Naturopaths view MHPs as greedy, self-serving, and deceitful, for example, whereas naturopaths view themselves in completely positive ways. Stereotypes by one side create defensiveness on the other side and may spur counterstereotyping. If naturopaths view MHPs as deceitful, MHPs will tend to view naturopaths as deceitful. Mutual stereotyping is exacerbated as communication is shut down and tensions rise. Overcoming stereotypes is one of the biggest challenges in trust building: How do you help people reassess their views of each other and each other's motivations (Conflict Research Consortium, 1998)?

Facilitating mutual experiences, as described here, may be helpful. Even when groups are brought together, however, stereotypes continue because people tend to look for evidence that confirms their beliefs and ignore evidence that challenges their beliefs. An MHP might meet a naturopath at the proposed retreat and develop a positive relationship with her but still say, "She was honest and professional, but she's a rare exception. Naturopaths are untrustworthy quacks."

To help people overcome negative stereotypes, a CR professional may need to help them save face as they reassess their views of the other party. Tracy could say to the MHPs, for instance:

> I realize in the past that you have expressed serious concerns about the ethics and effectiveness of naturopathy. From what I've heard, it does not sound as if you believe all naturopaths are bad or evil. In your experience, what strengths or possibilities have you heard about naturopathy? Have you heard any stories where naturopathy has been helpful?

Note how Tracy helps MHPs consider alternate stories about naturopaths (Winslade & Monk, 2000) without implying that their original views or stereotypes were wrong. Tracy even provides MHPs with language they can use to explain what may sound like backtracking on their views ("We never said all naturopathy was bad. We have some serious concerns, but we realize naturopathy has been helpful in some cases"). Once people open themselves to alternate understandings, stereotypes begin to dissipate.

Tracy could use similar strategies to help MHPs reconsider Byron's death and the meaning they attach to this event.

> When Byron died, you believed the naturopath was at fault. When you raised concerns in the media about naturopathy, your intentions were honorable. You wanted to ensure all future cancer patients received proper care. For the past few months, the mudslinging between MHPs and naturopaths has been ferocious, which makes both groups look bad to the public. Rather than condemning all naturopaths, I wonder if you've thought of finding a group of naturopaths that you might be able to trust. . . . What would it take to start trusting this group?

Here Tracy builds on the MHPs' strengths and shows them how their initial reaction to Byron's death had a positive purpose. This builds or protects their egos. Tracy then helps them consider that although the initial reaction was justified, now may be a time to change course. The key is allowing MHPs to change their views, while protecting their own self-image and how others see them (Wilmot & Hocker, 2007). MHPs can feel good about their original motivations, but also reconsider their mistrust for naturopaths and the possibility of initiating a new direction in their relationship.

Although trust is such an integral part of CR, trust building is often viewed as part of other CR approaches. When levels of mistrust are high, however, there may be benefit in offering the parties specific trust-building processes, provided by practitioners who specialize in this area.

PEACEBUILDING

Peacebuilding refers to establishing peaceful relations between people involved in a conflict. Peace goes beyond absence of war or hostility. Peace means that people are interacting in patterns marked by trust, openness, mutual caring, cooperation, and respect. Peacebuilding is not a single strategy or role. It requires a combination of efforts (including trust building), over an extended period of time (Lederach, 2005). To be effective, peacebuilders cannot simply be naïve do-gooders. They must balance their hope, enthusiasm, and idealism with knowledge, skills, and well-planned strategies (Barash & Webel, 2002). In order to gain a sense of the depth and breadth of peacebuilding strategies, consider the following situation:

> Dorota and Edyta are the 12-year-old daughters of Pavel. The girls are constantly fighting—over clothes, over chores, over friends, over who is more childish, over everything. One day, their fighting escalates, and Dorota hits Edyta with a broom. Pavel decides it is time to get help. He meets with a counselor, Cathy. He says his goal is to build peace between his daughters.

When people are involved in protracted, violent conflict, peacebuilding sometimes begins with peacekeeping, enforced prevention of further violence (Conflict Research Consortium, 1998). Peacekeepers typically act as buffers between violent parties. Cathy engages Pavel in a discussion to jointly assess what has been happening and to determine which types of peace strategies might be most useful. Cathy explains how Pavel may need to play peacekeeper in order to maintain safety, at least in the short term. Pavel describes how sometimes he tells his daughters, "Go to your rooms." This creates *physical separation* and a safe space for each. When they are arguing in the back seat of the car, he cannot enforce physical separation. Cathy describes how he can impose *social separations*—for instance, telling his daughters not to talk to one another. "For the rest of this trip, no talking between the two of you. If you have anything to say, then say it to me." Social separation can also involve breaking up their social connections—for example, having them go to separate schools, dividing which friends each can play with, or having individual father-daughter activities rather than family activities. Pavel appreciates the suggestions but wonders, "Is this really going to promote peace between Edyta and Dorota?" Separation can provide a cooling off period, which may lead to peace. Unfortunately, enduring separation may also spur mistrust, indifference, or uneasy coexistence. Pavel does not want his daughters to merely tolerate each other. He wants them to develop a loving family relationship.

Cathy explains that Pavel can also act as a peacemaker, creating a safe time and place for his daughters to meet and discuss their concerns. In this context, safety includes both physical and emotional safety. *Peacemakers help people work through specific conflicts and formulate agreements that both sides can live with.* Cathy explains the process of interest-based mediation (Chapter 4) and how Pavel can help his daughters mediate win-win solutions. Pavel asks how this would work. He gives Cathy the example of his daughters' fighting over who gets to practice playing the piano. There is only one piano, and both like to practice just after supper. The only other time to practice is after school, but both want to participate in after-school clubs and sports, rather than practice piano at home. If he just tells them when each can play piano, they are not really learning how to cooperate. Furthermore, one or both daughters may feel that his decision is unfair. Cathy demonstrates how he can help them move from fighting over positions to problem solving around interests such as fairness, quality time for practicing piano, and opportunities to hang out with other friends. Pavel also learns about brainstorming options (e.g., selling the piano and buying two cheaper keyboards, splitting who practices on which day, playing duets for practice, or finding evening clubs and activities with friends). Through peacemaking, Pavel can help them reach a mutually acceptable agreement, a peace treaty that spells out how they will get along.

Pavel knows, from world history, that peace does not necessarily follow from having peace agreements. In Rwanda, the worst violence and genocide occurred just following the 1994 announcement of a peace agreement between the Hutus and the Tutsis. In 1993, Israelis and Palestinians signed the Oslo Accords (http://www.multied.com/Israel/Documents/Oslo.html), which provided a framework for peace, yet uprisings, murder, and terrorism have continued. If Pavel wants lasting peace between his daughters, an agreement about how they will share the piano may not be enough.

Cathy concurs. Peacebuilding is not simply helping people formulate an agreement. The process of interest-based mediation may promote understanding, empowerment, and collaboration; however, it only deals with a specific conflict. There may be other conflicts, and emotional issues, left unresolved. Even if it resolves a conflict, peacemaking does not necessarily speak to the issues of how to implement and monitor the agreement. *Peacebuilding involves strengthening the physical, psychological, and social capacities of people so they can interact in a more collaborative, respectful, and equitable manner.* Cathy educates Pavel about a number of other strategies for building sustainable peace:

- **Physical capacity building**—Peace is not possible when a person's basic needs (food, water, shelter, sleep, security, physical health) are not being met (Ury, 1999). In order to promote peaceful relations, helping professionals may need to assume the role of advocate, ensuring that the parties have necessary resources. Although this may not be a primary concern in the relations between Dorota and Edyta, Pavel does note that they tend to argue most when they are hungry or overtired. It may sound simplistic, but ensuring that they get enough food and sleep may encourage more positive interactions.

- **Psychological capacity building**—In order for people to live in peace, they must have certain psychological capacities, for instance, the ability to trust, to care, to think clearly, and to be assertive. Conversely, if a person is depressed, highly anxious, or experiencing paranoid delusions, it will be difficult to participate effectively in peaceful interactions. If individuals or groups have special psychological needs, then interventions can be designed to build capacities in these areas.[6] Assume, for instance, that Dorota has low self-esteem because she has struggled through school, piano lessons, and other tasks that 12-year-old girls are expected to master. Given her low self-esteem, she responds to conflict aggressively. She fights in order to stake her claims because she fears that, otherwise, Edyta and others will take advantage of her. If Pavel, perhaps with the help of the counselor, can help Edyta build her self-esteem and learn assertiveness skills, she will be better prepared to work through conflict more constructively. Motivational enhancement is another key component of psychological capacity building. If Dorota does not see any reason to make peace with Edyta, she will not be motivated to initiate or follow through on any proposed changes. Pavel may be able to inspire Dorota to take initiative by tapping into her motivations (e.g., to have close friends) and by providing her with visions of what could be (e.g., having her sister as her closest friend) (Combs, 2004).

---

[6]When conflict leads to loss or trauma, healing processes, discussed later in this chapter, may be appropriate.

- **Social capacity building**—The manner that an individual, family, group, or community responds to conflict is strongly affected by social context (Ury, 1999). Some people have social support systems that promote peaceful relations. Others have support systems that detract. Pavel's oldest son, Stefan, takes pleasure in his sisters' rivalry. Stefan gives his sisters ideas for practical jokes and spreads rumors to stir conflict. If Pavel focuses on his daughters, without taking Stefan's impact into account, peace becomes elusive. Stefan will continue to act in ways that promote conflict. Pavel brings Stefan into the peacebuilding process, hoping to build a more constructive relationship among all family members. Dorota and Edyta discuss their hopes and expectations, helping Stefan redefine his role as older brother. Fostering constructive relationships between individuals, families, businesses, governments, religious institutions, cultural groups, and other organizations is vital to the peacebuilding process (Schirch, 2004).

- **Action evaluation**—Action evaluation plans can be used to help implement agreements, monitoring the effectiveness of the implementation and providing a mechanism for changes if problems arise: what is working, what is not working, and what do we need to try differently (Herr & Anderson, 2005; Schirch, 2004)? Whereas traditional program evaluations are held at specific times, action evaluations are ongoing. This allows everyone to respond to needs and concerns as early as possible, using the information gained from the evaluation. Consider a plan in which Edyta has priority on use of the piano on Mondays, Wednesdays, and Fridays, and Dorota has priority on use of the piano on Tuesdays, Thursdays, and Saturdays. Stefan agrees to monitor implementation and provide feedback to his sisters on an ongoing basis. Upon talking to the piano teacher, Stefan finds that his sisters are practicing less often than they used to. The teacher suggests that daily practice, even for a shorter time, is better than alternating practice. When Stefan presents this information, Dorota and Edyta agree to adjust their plan so each has daily practice time. They are not sure this will work, but Stefan will help them monitor what happens, and they can always renegotiate.

Cathy explains how some of the most intense conflicts that people experience occur within a family context. She also notes, "What people learn within a family affects how they will deal with conflict in other contexts, including school, work, and future intimate relationships." Pavel begins to see how peacebuilding within the family is a long-term process, based on passion, vision, and action. He commits to becoming a positive role model, using active listening and collaborative responses whenever he has conflicts with his children (Weinhold & Weinhold, 2000). He commits to facilitating positive opportunities for dialogue, at dinner, during family outings, and in family meetings. He also commits to encouraging his children to express themselves openly, sharing feelings and identifying their needs, but doing so in a reciprocal manner. He notes that he has tended to avoid conflict in the past, but now he will embrace it more directly (Wilmot & Hocker, 2007). Pavel asks how his daughters' school might be able to teach and reinforce the skills, values, and theory of peacebuilding. Cathy provides Pavel with information on the "Peaceable Schools

Program," which integrates peace throughout the curriculum (Crawford & Bodine, 2005). Pavel agrees to take this resource to the next parent-teacher association meeting, inviting the school to adopt this program.

In a community context, a peacebuilder may need to help groups confront stereotypes, bigotry, and systemic discrimination. If there are deep divisions between groups, then a peacebuilder needs to help them build bridges. Rather than separating people or creating buffers, peacebuilders create space and time for people to interact. Sometimes, formal structures can be used to build peace. In order to start the healing in postapartheid South Africa, for instance, the Truth and Reconciliation Commission (2003) was created. This commission provided a forum for people to bring forth information and stories about human rights abuses during the period of apartheid. Helping professionals can help other communities develop similar forums for dialogue and building peace. Helping professionals can also play a key role in helping communities develop civil society, including organizations such as clubs, schools, conflict resolution programs, service organizations, social movements, and faith-based organizations that promote peace (e.g., Women for Peace, Amnesty International, Greenpeace, Society of Friends—Quakers). Finally, helping professionals can help schools and other organizations develop peace education curricula, including content on human rights, diversity, fears, prejudices, nonviolence, and interpersonal skills (Tidwell, 2004).

Formal structures for dialogue may be useful, but informal structures often have an even greater impact. Interactions between people in their homes, around the dinner table, or at the marketplace provide people with opportunities to get to know each other, build rapport, and work together (Lederach, 2005). There are numerous examples of peacebuilding that has occurred within common environments: Palestinians and Israelis working together in a factory, African Americans and European Americans building a community park, women from rival Somali clans in Wajir creating a violence-free bazaar, and conflicting nations from around the globe putting politics aside to participate in the Olympic Games.[7] These people did not explicitly decide to "make peace." Peace happened while they were working on other things. Helping professionals, then, can promote peace by helping develop circumstances where conflicting groups can work together, walk together, eat together, socialize together, and talk together.

Absence of violence reflects negative peace. Building positive peace requires more affirmative relations. Positive peace also requires justice, or justpeace (Barash & Webel, 2002). *Justpeace* means that the rights and freedoms of all people are respected, including the rights to life, liberty, security, and basic needs (food, shelter, clothes, medical care). Justpeace means that people have equal opportunities regarding work, family, and other aspects of social life. Justpeace means that people have freedom of speech, freedom of religion, and freedom of association. Having these principles written in laws or constitutions is not sufficient. People must actually experience these rights and freedoms. In order to promote peace, helping professionals

---

[7]Although politics and controversy have infiltrated the Olympic Games, it is actually encouraging how many nations do participate in a peaceful manner, particularly given the violent histories between some of the competing peoples.

can play an important role as advocates for social justice. In other words, peace-builders do not simply work toward ending conflict; they also work to ensure so-cially just relations (Hoeffer, 2006; Schirch, 2004).[8] When conflict seems intractable, this is often because one group is being deprived basic security, recognition, and fair access to political institutions and economic participation (Conflict Research Consortium, 1998). Although some people can be wooed into peace by appealing to their moral convictions, peacebuilders may also need more strategic methods of confronting power imbalances (see Chapter 6).

Peacebuilding is not a linear process. Even when a peace process experiences great movements forward, CR professionals should plan for possible setbacks. CR professionals can learn from the relapse prevention strategies used in the field of addictions treatment. When a person with alcoholism establishes an initial period of sobriety, work does not end there. Relapse prevention strategies provide people with ways of pre-empting problems and ways of responding to them when they arise (Barsky, 2006a). When a peace treaty or mediation agreement is signed, for instance, people may feel a certain sense of jubilation and optimism. That optimism could quickly falter if one or both sides perceive the other to be breaching the agreement. Peacebuilders can inform clients that lapses are part of the peacebuilding process. It is easy to work collaboratively when conflict levels are low. When conflict escalates, that is the true test of how well the peace process is working. Peacebuilders can use a number of relapse prevention strategies to prepare people for these tests:

- Teach people conflict resolution skills, so they can resolve their own conflicts.
- Brainstorm potential conflicts that may arise and develop plans for responding to each of these contingencies.
- Help everyone balance realistic expectations, with hope and optimism about how things could be if they are able to overcome transitional challenges.
- Offer ongoing support, including a safe place to work out conflicts should they wish mediation or other help with future conflicts.
- Build a monitoring system so conflicts can be detected early and analyzed effectively, allowing everyone to determine the best way to respond to new conflicts.

In Pavel's situation, Dorota and Edyta initially respond to peacebuilding with great enthusiasm and skill. Periodically, however, they lapse into old patterns. Pavel shows them a pre-peacebuilding video of a fight they had. This video reminds them of the problems that stemmed from their old sibling rivalry. The video acts like a booster shot, inoculating them with the motivation and insight to keep new conflicts in perspective and use peaceful means to work through them.

Throughout the peacebuilding process, Cathy's role is secondary. She provides consultation to Pavel, but it is Pavel, his family, the school, and the community that put peacebuilding into effect. She provides Pavel with an array of peacebuilding

---

[8]Schirch also describes the relationship between structural violence and other forms of violence. *Structural violence* refers to inequalities, disabilities, and deaths that result when social systems, agencies, or cultures meet some people's needs, at the expense of other's needs. Structural violence may lead to various forms of secondary violence, including self-destruction (suicide, substance abuse, depression, internalized oppression), community destruction (crime, domestic abuse), and national or international destruction (war, terrorism, social upheaval).

methods and helps him select a combination of strategies that work well in concert. She continues to offer support, monitoring implementation with Pavel and assessing new peacebuilding needs as they arise.

PARENTING COORDINATION

A parenting coordinator (PC) is a professional who helps parents involved in a high-conflict separation or divorce implement a parenting plan in a manner that promotes the best interests of the children. **Parenting coordination** *may include assessment,[9] education,[10] mediation,[11] evaluation, case management,[12] arbitration, child custody consulting, coparent counseling, monitoring, and enforcement* (Baris et al., 2001; Sullivan, 2004). Although parents can agree to the services of a PC, some jurisdictions permit the court to mandate a PC to work with high-conflict parents. This authority recognizes the fact that the most important predictor of a child's post-separation adjustment is the level of conflict or hostility between parents (Boyan & Termini, 2005).

To demonstrate the role and challenges faced by a PC, consider the following scenario:

> Marya and Felix have been separated for 3 years. They have an 8-year-old daughter named Dottie who is shy, withdrawn, and emotionally immature for her age. Felix and Marya engaged in an ugly battle over custody, with Marya alleging that Felix was a neglectful and incompetent parent and Felix alleging that Marya had narcissistic personality disorder and was using Felix to try to control his life. The family court judge ordered a custody evaluation. The evaluator recommended that Dottie should live primarily with her mother and spend alternate weekends with her father. The judge granted a custody and visitation order in accordance with these recommendations and assigned a PC, Priscilla, to help Marya and Felix implement this plan over the next 2 years.

Before the ink is even dry on the court order, Marya calls Priscilla with an emergency. It is Friday afternoon, just prior to a weekend when Felix is to pick up Dottie. Marya claims Dottie is threatening to commit suicide if she has to go to her father's house. Priscilla calmly explains that she is not actually their PC until they sign the PC agreement. She says she will schedule a meeting next week. Infuriated, Marya claims Priscilla is uncaring and incompetent. Priscilla asks Marya a few questions about Dottie's suicide plans. Marya becomes defensive and is not

---

[9]Including assessment of family dynamics, parental defenses and flash points, other key players in the conflict, and the couple's metaphors (AFCC Task Force, 2003).

[10]Education may include teaching parents about child development, parallel parenting techniques to disengage, the legal system, and how to access other resources. It may also include teaching children strategies for extricating themselves from the middle of their parents' conflict (AFCC Task Force, 2003).

[11]AFCC Task Force (2005) suggests avoiding the use of the term *mediation*, in favor of "facilitation of dispute resolution," because the process is not confidential and is therefore not the same as mediation. Still, many practitioners, policies, and training materials refer to mediation as a PC's role.

[12]Case management includes interfacing with other professionals and agencies involved with the family, such as school personnel, therapists, attorneys, social services, religious entities, and extended family members (AFCC Task Force, 2003).

able to provide specifics. Priscilla asks Marya whether she has a good pediatrician for Dottie. Marya says she does. Priscilla discusses the value of taking Dottie to a professional who already knows her and whom Marya trusts. Marya agrees to take Dottie to her pediatrician, immediately, to conduct a more comprehensive suicide screening. *PCs must establish clear boundaries with clients right from the start.* Although Marya's assertions about Dottie's suicide plans must be taken seriously, Priscilla must be careful to maintain her professional roles and refer the client to other professionals when clients raise issues that go beyond their mandate. Marya was basically asking Priscilla to rule on whether Dottie had to go to her father's that weekend. If Priscilla waded into this issue, she would risk losing her neutrality, having to do a quick assessment and perhaps allowing Marya to manipulate her into siding against Felix. When Priscilla followed up, Marya said she did not have to take Dottie to the doctor because she was able to convince Dottie to go to her father's house for the weekend.

Prior to meeting with Felix and Marya, Priscilla telephones each attorney and reviews the court order that establishes her mandate. She clarifies her role and asks them whether they have any concerns they want to pass on. Felix's lawyer suggests that she review the custody evaluation. Marya's lawyer suggests that the evaluator was biased. Priscilla confirms with both lawyers that it is safe to meet with both parents together, even though there is a high level of animosity and mistrust. Both lawyers express relief that these "difficult clients" will now be calling her instead of them. After talking with the lawyers, Priscilla takes a deep breath. She senses this is not going to be an easy conflict to manage. She already begins to feel empathy for how Dottie may feel trapped in her parents' conflict.

During the first meeting with Marya and Felix, Priscilla reviews the PC agreement with them, answers their questions, and has them sign the agreement. Priscilla notes that parenting coordination is *not* a confidential process, in that she is permitted to talk to their lawyers, family members, pediatrician, teachers, and other support systems, at her discretion. She also notes that she may be asked by the court to testify or submit her records in any future family law proceedings. Priscilla puts a photo of Dottie on a table facing Felix and Marya, reminding them that Dottie must be at the forefront of all decisions. Priscilla tries to establish control over the process, giving them specific ground rules and identifying agenda items for this meeting: identifying long- and short-term goals for the PC process, and prioritizing among them. Marya expresses a litany of complaints about Felix's ability to parent, ranging from allowing Dottie to engage in risky activities to using profane language in her presence. Felix remains quiet and emotionless, perhaps trying to dissociate from what Marya is saying. Priscilla redirects the discussion back to goal setting. Marya says her goal is to ensure that Felix cannot be alone with Dottie and that any visitation must be supervised. Felix says his goal is not to be controlled by Marya. Priscilla encourages them to focus on Dottie's best interests, but this suggestion prompts mutual allegations that the other one is at fault for the ongoing conflict. Priscilla sets up individual appointments, hoping she can work with them more effectively on a one-to-one basis.

Just as the session is ending, Felix asks whether Marya can send Dottie's cello so she can practice during weekends when she is staying with him. Marya says this is not in Dottie's best interests, because the last time the cello came back, the tuning pegs were broken. As they begin to argue about what happened, Priscilla steps in and says that they do not have enough time today to resolve this issue. She says for the time being, Marya does not have to send the cello. She invites Felix to consider alternate arrangements, perhaps borrowing or renting a cello. Realizing that Felix may sense Priscilla is siding with Marya, Priscilla offers, "I understand, Felix, that you might not consider this decision fair. It is only a temporary decision until we can figure out a parenting plan that works for everyone." *Although the main task of a PC is to implement a parenting plan that the court ordered or the parties agreed to, the PC may also be given authority to arbitrate smaller issues that are not specifically resolved by the order or agreement.* Summary arbitrations (decisions without formal testimony or hearings) can help the parties move on, without having to resort to more expensive or energy-sapping processes. On the downside, one or both parties may feel that the summary arbitration process or outcome is unfair. This may be particularly risky when one client is always more unreasonable than the other and decisions keep going against the more unreasonable client.

During individual sessions, the PC assesses each parent's functioning, as well as his or her ability to communicate, problem solve, and focus on the child's best interests. Priscilla decides not to meet with Dottie, because Dottie already has a social worker who can provide Priscilla with insights from Dottie's perspective. Upon meeting with Marya, Priscilla assesses Marya as having a narcissistic personality disorder. Marya demonstrates a sense of superiority, need for admiration, and lack of empathy for Felix or Dottie. She views herself as a victim in the marital breakdown and has a distorted view of the role she plays in the conflict. Felix probably learned not to confront Marya, because any confrontation would draw verbal attacks from her. Having a fragile ego, Marya has had extreme difficulty coping with the narcissistic injury caused by her failed marriage. Given this assessment, Priscilla decides to provide Marya with positive feedback, building her ego and self-confidence, and avoiding confrontations that may come across as rejection (Eddy, 2003). Priscilla knows that she must do most of this in individual sessions or Felix will view this as siding with Marya.

In follow-up meetings with Marya, Priscilla provides Marya with information about positive parenting following separation. To pre-empt a defensive reaction, Priscilla joins with Marya's conviction that she is the better parent, "As the better parent, it is vital that you take the lead in doing what's best for Dottie. Would you like to hear some parenting suggestions that you can use to help her, regardless of how good or bad Felix acts as a parent?" Initially, Marya complains that she should not have to put up with this, and Felix should be cut off from seeing Dottie. Priscilla notes that she has no authority to order this. Furthermore, if she believes that Felix is truly neglectful or abusive, this behavior must be reported to child protective services. Marya says that child protective services refused to open cases in the past, and she trusts Priscilla more because Priscilla sees "What a good mother I am." Priscilla is able to move Marya from her original goal of "cutting off Felix's visitation" to "being the best parent she can be."

Upon meeting Felix, Priscilla determines that, on one hand, he is not the perfect parent; for instance, his discipline is sometimes too strict and not age appropriate. On the other hand, he is not the monster that Marya portrays. Priscilla offers Felix parenting skills education, suggesting this will help him avoid conflicts with Marya, which is ultimately vital for Dottie's well-being. Felix confides that no matter what he does, Marya will find ways to raise new allegations. Marya offers to be their dispute resolution system, so that any conflicts that arise can be referred to her. Felix suggests that this just provides Marya with a forum to make up new charges against him. He also fears he will have to pay for time that Marya wastes with her. Priscilla reminds Felix that each parent will pay for his or her individual sessions, which will take away any incentive for one parent to raise the other's costs. *By meeting with each parent separately, the PC can allow them to vent without triggering the other's defense mechanisms* (Boyan & Termini, 2005).

Over time, Priscilla helps her clients build a "parallel parenting system" in which each parent takes responsibility for Dottie's parenting while she is staying in his or her home. Priscilla helps them disengage from any responsibilities that require cooperation. For example, each parent buys Dottie a separate set of clothes, each parent arranges extracurricular sports and other recreation for the times Dottie is with each, each parent goes separately to parent-teacher interviews, and each parent has a separate birthday party for Dottie. While this form of parenting system may not be ideal for Dottie or her parents, it reduces the frequency and intensity of conflicts that Dottie is exposed to.

Periodically, Priscilla suggests Marya and Felix try working through a parenting issue together—for instance, how to schedule summer times with Dottie. This gives them a chance to use the conflict resolution, problem solving, communication, and coping skills Priscilla has taught them. Unfortunately, they continue to be unable to reach any agreements on their own. Priscilla ends up assuming an ongoing conflict resolution role for them.

The PC role was developed in the 1990s, and standards of practice are still evolving (Boyan & Termini, 2005). Practitioners and theorists are still debating the clinical and ethical parameters of this role. For instance, should a PC be able to mediate or arbitrate decisions, or are there inherent conflicts between the PC's role in implementing decisions and the PC's role in facilitating or determining new decisions? How can a PC help parents resolve conflicts safely and fairly when, by definition, high-conflict couples have psychosocial concerns that impede their ability to cooperate? To what extent should a PC use therapeutic techniques, such as cognitive restructuring or strategic family therapy, as opposed to referring clients to separate therapists for such interventions? Although proponents suggest PCs can reduce litigation, promote parental collaboration, and reduce a child's exposure to harmful parental conflict, is it possible that PC involvement could actually stimulate higher levels of conflict than traditional court and evaluation processes? As Felix and Marya's case suggests, when PCs are unable to help parents work together more collaboratively, PCs may need to help them manage conflict on a long-term basis—perhaps until their children reach adulthood. How, then, do you define success in situations where one or both clients seem incapable of acting rationally or moving on?

FAMILY GROUP CONFERENCING

Family group conferences (FGCs) *empower families by bringing extended family members and helping professionals together to resolve conflict that is affecting all or part of the family* (Kumari & Brooks, 2004). FGCs were originally developed by the Maori people in New Zealand to help families deal with concerns related to child abuse and neglect. In a typical FGC, helping professionals begin by determining who to invite to the conference, such as parents, children, grandparents, aunts, uncles, cousins, and fictive kin (people who are not related by blood or marriage, but who are viewed as family members). During the conference, the professionals begin by expressing their concerns—for instance, how a child's basic needs are not being met or how they have discovered signs of physical or sexual abuse. The professionals then leave the room and allow family members to work on a plan to address the concerns. If the plan is acceptable to the professionals and the child protection court, then the court and child protective agency ratify the agreement (Hudson, Morris, Maxwell, & Galaway, 1996; Kumari & Brooks, 2004). Helping professionals continue to assist the family by monitoring implementation of the plan, as well as offering services and resources (e.g., counseling, parenting education, respite care). FGCs have also been used to address problems related to criminal activity and children's misbehavior in schools (Crow, Marsh, & Holton, 2004).

The primary advantage of FGCs relates to how they empower families to take responsibility for their own issues. Rather than having professionals take over, family members assume responsibility for assessing what is going on and how to deal with it. FGCs encourage family members to commit to their agreements, because they are personally invested in the plans and the consequences of how the plans are implemented. FGCs draw upon the resources of the extended family and community. These resources may include moral and emotional support, financial support, housing, employment, mentoring, supervision, education, counseling, and spiritual guidance. FGCs have been promoted as a means of diverting cases from court, saving emotional and financial costs, while still holding individuals accountable for their actions. If the situation involves a specific victim, FGCs can be used to bring victims and offenders together. FGCs allow them to express their concerns directly to one another, possibly leading to compensation, restitution, apology, and forgiveness. FGCs work on a consensus-building model and are adaptable to the needs of different cultural groups (MacRae & Zehr, 2004).

The following example illustrates the steps of an FGC process:

> Foster is a 15-year-old youth who has been living on the streets for the past 2 months. For much of his childhood, he bounced around various foster care and group homes. Child protective services had removed him from his parents' custody because of child abuse and neglect. Foster took to the streets, feeling he was safer there than in any group home, where he was physically and emotionally abused by group home staff. Recently, he was arrested by police for stealing a car. Police turned him over to Charna, a child protection worker who suggested the use of a family group conference.

Charna knows Foster is at risk of returning to the streets, regardless of what type of housing arrangements are made for him. She believes that he is more likely to commit to a plan if he has real input into the decision-making process. The initial challenge facing Charna is the apparent lack of family members who can offer constructive support. Foster's mother and father are still addicted to alcohol, and the rest of his relatives live more than 300 miles away.

Charna explains family group conferencing to Foster. She asks him who should be invited to such a meeting. Foster insists that his parents attend. Regardless of how they treated him in the past and regardless of their current involvement with alcohol, they are still his parents. Charna agrees, validating his wishes and his love for them. She then asks who else he sees as possible support systems or even people with whom he could confide. Foster mentions a couple of friends he made on the street, Shanta and Selby. They took him under their wings, giving him a place to sleep and showing him how to survive on his the street. To Foster's surprise, Charna agrees to invite Shanta and Selby. As Foster and Charna discuss others to invite, they eventually agree to ask Mr. Colby (who owned the car that Foster stole), Mr. Perry (Foster's probation officer), and Ms. Trump (a teacher who took a sincere interest in Foster).

Charna calls everyone on the invitation list. Everyone agrees to participate, except Shelby, who could not be located. During the pre-FGC meetings, Charna discusses the FGC process, why they might be interested in attending, and what roles they would play. Charna works with each person to ensure positive participation in the FGC. When talking to Mr. Colby, for instance, Charna ensures that Mr. Colby is agreeing to participate voluntarily and that he feels safe about attending. They discuss how Mr. Colby may confront Foster about the theft but also how Mr. Colby may contribute to a solution. When Charna meets with Foster's parents, Parker and Patsy, she says they need to be sober when they come to the conference, or they will be denied entry. She invites them to consider a broad range of ways that they could provide support for him. When they ask whether it is possible for Foster to return home with them, Charna explains that any plan will require court approval, and the court will base its decision on Foster's best interests (including protection against any risk of abuse or neglect). When Charna meets Shanta, she is initially shocked at Shanta's appearance—she is covered in tattoos and body piercing and appears quite disheveled. Charna determines not to prejudge Shanta, trusting that Foster had good reason for inviting Shanta. Shanta seems interested in the FGC process but has trouble grasping how it is going to work. Charna offers to show her a video of an FGC, which Shanta finds very helpful. Constable Perry and Ms. Trump had participated in prior FGCs, so Charna does not need to explain FGCs in depth. She simply focuses them on issues particular to Foster's situation.

Charna opens the FGC by inviting everyone to introduce themselves. She then explains the process:

> We're here to discuss how to help Foster, as well as how he can help himself and perhaps even help others in this room. Each of you has played different roles in his life, and each may play similar or different roles in the future. This situation involves two types of court involvement: a criminal charge related to theft of an automobile and a child welfare proceeding, because Foster is a minor who requires a safe and supportive place to live. The purpose of a family group conference is to empower Foster and all of you to decide what should be done about these criminal charges and child protection issues. I will have Mr. Perry explain the nature of the criminal charges and how the results of this conference will affect whether Foster's case will proceed to trial. I will then describe the child welfare concerns. We hope and believe you will be able to agree to a plan that takes all of these concerns into account. Any plans that you develop must be taken back to the courts

for approval. The courts generally trust family and community members to come up with the best plan. Still, they have the authority to determine their own plans if they do not believe concerns such as public safety and Foster's welfare needs have been adequately taken into account.

After Mr. Perry and Charna explain the criminal charges and child welfare concerns, they invite questions. Everyone is silent, making it difficult for Charna to assess whether they are adequately prepared or simply too nervous to ask questions. Charna knows she has to trust the process, so she advises that she and Mr. Perry will leave the conference so the family and community members can meet in private to discuss what has happened and what to do. She invites them to call her if they have any questions about the process, but any decisions are up to them. Charna and Mr. Perry exit.

After further silence and discomfort, Mr. Colby begins to speak. He notes that he is glad to have the opportunity to meet Foster directly and let him know the anger, fear, and frustration he felt when Foster stole his car. Although the car was eventually returned, it had about $800 worth of damage, too small to make an insurance claim, but more than Mr. Colby can afford. Ms. Trump puts her hand on Foster's shoulder and asks him whether he has anything to say to Mr. Foster. Foster describes how he was just fooling around and was not thinking that borrowing a car for a while would hurt anyone. He says if it is just a matter of $800, he'll find a way to pay this back, as long as the charges get dropped.

Parker notes that the issue is bigger than $800. He expresses his concern that Foster is headed down a path of self-destruction, living on the streets and getting into all sorts of trouble. Parker admits that he is nobody to be giving a lecture, given all his problems with alcohol and the law. Still, he had better hopes for Foster. Patsy offers that perhaps Foster could come live with them. Foster, showing bravado, explains he can take care of himself just fine.

The mood in the room begins to shift when Shanta tells her story. She explains how she took to the streets after being abandoned by her family. She describes how although she has learned to survive, she wishes she had a family, even a dysfunctional one. She encourages Foster to use this conference as a way to reconnect with his family and get off the streets. Patsy and Parker confide that although they would like to give Foster a nice home with a white picket fence and a dog named Rover, they know that it is not realistic at this time. Foster becomes sullen and starts to cry, "So are those my options, street or jail?"

Patsy asks Ms. Trump whether she would be able to take Foster in. Ms. Trump notes that although she is there to offer support, it would not be appropriate for her to take Foster into her home. Ms. Trump asks Foster whether he would consider going to an alternative school that had residential facilities. Foster agrees, so long as this is just temporary. Parker and Patsy support this agreement, saying they will check themselves into an alcohol rehab program. If they are successful, they will then ask child protective services to have Foster returned to their care. They admit that overcoming their addiction is not a sure thing, but they seem sincere in their commitment.

Mr. Colby asks, "What about the criminal charges?" Shanta, who has had personal experience with court diversion programs, explains that charges can be dropped if Foster does some sort of community work or compensates Mr. Colby, and everyone agrees that this is a good way to hold Foster responsible for what he has done. Shanta says she can find some work for Foster, so he can repay Mr. Colby over the next 4 months. Foster apologizes to Mr. Colby for taking his car and asks whether this plan works for him. Mr. Colby agrees.

Everyone helps Foster write down the agreement, including the plans for where Foster will live, go to school, and work in order to be able to repay Mr. Colby. The plan also includes Patsy and Parker's commitment to go for alcohol rehab and to remain a part of Foster's life as much as possible. They invite Charna back into the room so they can present their agreement. She does a reality check with each of the participants to ensure that they are truly committed and to see whether the plans are feasible. She notes that the plans will only work if everyone follows through on their commitments, whether they are to help Foster apply to the alternative school, to connect him with a job, or to go to alcohol rehab. They work through what will happen if any problems arise in implementing the plan. Charna agrees to support the plan and to advocate for its approval in the upcoming criminal and child protection proceedings.

As the forgoing example indicates, FGCs are not just touchy-feely meetings where everyone gathers for a group hug. People are confronted and held accountable for their actions. In some instances, the consequences determined by an FGC are more severe than the consequences that would ordinarily be imposed on the accused by a criminal court. FGCs are not meant to be punitive, however. They incorporate the concept of restorative justice, where matters are put right for the victim and the community, as well as addressing underlying problems that led to the conflict (MacRae & Zehr, 2004).

SPIRITUAL HEALING

Spiritual healing refers to transcending painful feelings generated by conflict and restoring balance in one's life. Spiritual healing can occur within individuals, between individuals, between groups, or among the entire community (Fuertes, 2004). There is no right or wrong way to foster healing, though some groups (including religious ones) have specific ceremonies and traditions for healing (Moodley & West, 2005).

Some professionals shy away from spiritual healing as a specific approach to CR, thinking it is too religious, too amorphous, or beyond their professional mandates. Although spirituality may encompass religious aspects, there are many ways to foster spirituality without imposing religiosity—for instance, encouraging everyone to embrace the conflict and bringing peace, love, fulfillment, or other ideals into the dialogue and relationship. Spirituality may sound amorphous to some. In practice, however, CR professionals can foster spiritual experiences for parties through the use of specific strategies and skills. Invoking spirituality may be as simple as asking, "Why did you have this conflict? What meaning can you give to the conflict? And how can you use this conflict to make more meaningful connections with each other?" These questions give people the opportunity to look into their hearts (or perhaps their higher powers) for guidance and vision. In some circumstances, cultivating spirituality requires a more complex intervention, making use of a range of strategies over a longer period of time.

In terms of mandate, CR professionals must be aware of their roles, competencies, and limits of their roles. When people have experienced significant loss or trauma, for example, the type of healing they need may require a professional psychotherapist. A psychotherapist can help clients explore the root causes of the trauma, work through emotions and physiological effects, re-establish a sense of personal control, and work to alleviate them.[13] Often, psychotherapy incorporates a spiritual component, helping clients work through loss or trauma by finding spiritual meaning. Still, many CR approaches can incorporate trauma healing without becoming psychotherapy. In victim-offender mediation, for instance, the person who committed the crime meets with the person traumatized by the crime. By having them talk and listen to each other, they may experience a spiritual connection. The offender may not have appreciated the impact of his actions on the victim. The victim may not have understood the offender's circumstances, which may have contributed to the crime. They may move from a place of ignorance, anger, fear, or hate to a place of understanding, love, security, or caring (Schirch, 2004). All of this is spiritual, without being psychotherapy.

Some CR approaches in this book focus on problem solving or settling disputes at a surface level (e.g., power-based negotiation or rights-based advocacy). Other approaches go beyond the mundane aspects of resolving conflict and are more likely to involve spiritual healing. Transformative mediation, for instance, encourages parties to connect with each other at a deep and meaningful level through mutual empathy and recognition. Justpeace encourages parties to build relationships that are not only conflict-free but socially just. The following subsections describe additional means of spiritual healing: art, ritual and prayer, deep listening, circles, and apology and forgiveness. These means can be used separately or incorporated into other CR interventions.

To illustrate various means of facilitating spirituality, consider the following situation:

> Cali is a counselor who had been helping Deepak (82 years), a client experiencing depression. Shortly after a session with Cali, Deepak committed suicide. When Deepak's sons, Surya and Sanjiv, discovered that Cali was the last person Deepak saw, they became infuriated with Cali, blaming her for their father's death.

If Surya and Sanjiv contacted a lawyer, the lawyer might suggest suing Cali in court or initiating a professional disciplinary action for malpractice with the organization that regulates Cali's profession. Cali might feel compelled to hire her own lawyer, setting up a classic adversarial battle. If this case proceeded through court or disciplinary hearings, it would be resolved by a tribunal that would determine whether Cali was at fault. If Cali was found negligent (e.g., for not conducting a proper suicide screening or safety plan), a court might order Cali to compensate Surya and Sanjiv. A regulatory tribunal might suspend or terminate Cali's license to practice. In either process, the parties would be unlikely to experience spirituality. Although Deepak's death and the ensuing conflict might not seem like the most obvious opportunity for

---

[13]Trauma healing helps people move from victims to survivors. If healing processes are not used, people may remain depressed or may become perpetrators themselves.

spiritual transcendence, the following sections demonstrate ways in which transcendence could be fostered. For discussion purposes, assume that the parties have hired Spinoza, a CR professional who embraces spirituality in his work.

1. Art

Art refers to an expression of creativity through words, sounds, movements, color, structure, or any other medium. Even though helping professionals may not ordinarily think of art as an approach of CR, art has the potential for profound conflict transformation. Consider a song that has the power to lift spirits or a novel that invites people to reflect back on their own history and see it from a different perspective. Consider how dance, operas, musical concerts, and other types of performance art bond people through common sensory and emotional experiences. Consider a painting or statue that encapsulates the consequences of violence or inspires hope for peace. Art can be used to help people transcend mundane experiences. Art can also be used to motivate people to act. Consider Martin Luther King's "I Have a Dream" speech, which created a visionary story using poetic imagery to inspire action on issues of racism and social justice.

When artists create their masterpieces, they may or may not intend to convey social or political messages. CR professionals, however, can work with communities and artists to generate and disseminate art strategically. In regions fraught with violence, for instance, communities have developed multimedia presentations documenting the brutality and carnage. Such presentations bring the community together and raise awareness of conflicts requiring attention. A picture may be worth a thousand words. Just think of the spiritual impact of a montage of photographs, set to music, and presented to thousands of people (Lederach, 2005). Art can be displayed in museums or concert halls. Art can also be shared with much larger audiences through street productions, television, radio, magazines, websites, blogs, newspapers, and other media.

Art has an impact on its creators and audiences. For the creators, art provides a means of self-expression going beyond traditional conversation. In the case scenario, Sanjiv may not be very verbal, perhaps feeling overwhelmed by emotion or feeling self-conscious about his foreign accent. During an individual session, Spinoza invites Sanjiv to draw something reflecting his feelings toward Cali. Drawing provides Sanjiv with a natural outlet for his emotions. He does not have great artistic talent, but this is not necessary for the art to have meaning. With Spinoza's support, Sanjiv shares his drawing with Cali. As they discuss the drawing, Cali is moved to tears. She feels Sanjiv's anger but also his colossal sense of loss. They sit together quietly and calmly, joined emotionally by their experience with the drawing.

Art may be especially helpful when working with children. Young children in particular may have limited ability to express themselves through words. They may also feel anxious about public speaking. Child-friendly modes of art—puppet shows, painting, singing—can provide children with fun and nonthreatening outlets for expression. They also allow children to convey thoughts and feelings about conflict or trauma, even when they do not have the language skills to articulate them (Kajosevic, 2003).

Like any approach to CR, art is not a panacea. CR professionals must be cautious when using art. The potential for strong emotional impact may be negative as well as positive. Consider a poem, for instance, that satirizes a political debate by representing politicians as children fighting over a toy. The poet may have intended the poem to encourage politicians to reflect on their self-indulgent in-fighting, seeing how juvenile they appear. The politicians, however, might interpret the poem as a mean-spirited attack and respond aggressively.

Art also entails risks for the creator. An artist depicting trauma in a song, movie, or whatever, may re-experience the trauma. This can open old wounds or inflame current ones. Professional art therapists have training to reduce these risks, as well as skills for helping clients work through emotions raised by the art. CR professionals without such training must be careful about engaging clients in artistic endeavors. In fact, they might want to engage the services of art therapists to help with their interventions.

For examples of art as a means of promoting peace, see the National Film Board videos listed in Appendix 4. These animated shorts are set to music but have no spoken language. They allow the audience to interpret the conflict scenarios from their own cultural and cognitive frames. They demonstrate how art cuts across culture, language, literacy, and even age. The videos were developed for children up to age 12, but adults can also relate to and learn from them.

2. Ritual and Prayer

Akin to art, rituals and prayers can be used to help people feel safe, open up, and create special feelings or connections between people (i.e., a sacred space or a special bond between participants). *Rituals refer to behaviors with symbolic meanings* (Moodley & West, 2005). Often, rituals are associated with religion—for instance, candle lighting, purification baths, feasts, fasts, sacrifices, pilgrimages to a sacred place, and individual or communal prayers. Some rituals are associated with specific cultures: Native American sweat lodges, sharing circles, pow-wows, smudging, potlatches (feasts), and pipe ceremonies (Pflug, 1996). There are also many rituals that cut across religions and cultures or have no religious significance: meditation, breathing exercises, spending a moment together in silence,[14] shaking hands, hugging, giving gifts, or sharing a meal. Some rituals have been developed specifically for resolving conflict, such as signing, sealing, and delivering a contract once agreement has been reached. Within CR process, rituals can be used to establish order and signify transformations by marking beginnings, transitions, and endings (Lichtenstein, 2005). The breadth of rituals available for CR is virtually limitless, because parties may draw rituals from their religions or cultures, or create their own.

Prayer refers to communicating with one's deity, whether the person defines this as God, Allah, Nature, or another higher power. Prayers may involve reading sacred texts or asking questions. Examples of prayers relevant to CR include asking

---

[14]Silence provides people with an opportunity to collect thoughts and emotions, to feel interconnections, and to focus on the reason that the group has gathered (Lichtenstein, 2005).

for insight, strength, courage, wisdom, or patience. Cali, who happens to belong to Alcoholics Anonymous, decides to use the Serenity Prayer:

> God, grant me the serenity
> To accept the things I cannot change,
> The courage to change the things I can,
> And the wisdom to know the difference.

Prior to praying, Cali felt frustrated and angry that Sanjiv and Surya were blaming her for Deepak's death. Her prayer calls on her higher power to help her accept that she may not be able to change how Sanjiv and Surya feel, but she takes control of her own responses. She begins to feel more at peace.

Rituals and prayers can be used at various stages of a CR process, from initial preparations for a CR process through to dialogue, agreement, implementation, and follow-up. Prior to engaging with others, prayers and rituals can be used to help people center themselves, as per the Serenity Prayer example. Other centering techniques include meditation, taking a walk, and giving oneself positive self-messages. Centering helps people become clear and focused, eliminating thoughts and feelings that might impede effective participation in the CR process (Chodron, 2001). By fostering inner peace within each party, centering improves the conditions for interpersonal peace. Centering is also useful for the CR professional. Because centering is a method of raising self-awareness, it can help professionals establish appropriate mind-sets and boundaries as they prepare themselves emotionally and spiritually for work with clients. Some professionals conduct their centering in private. This ensures the parties do not feel the professional is imposing prayers or starting from a place of bias (e.g., if Spinoza were to pray, "Allow me to keep my personal feelings from interfering with my obligation to remain neutral," this statement might raise more concerns for clients hearing it).

To respect client self-determination and religious sensitivities, CR professionals can use separate meetings to discuss the possible use of rituals or prayers. This enables parties to discuss freely whether they want to use specific rituals or prayers as part of the CR process. If parties wish to use particular rituals or prayers privately, they avoid the risk of offending one another by their practices. During preparations for a joint meeting, Spinoza explores Sanjiv and Surya's spiritual background. They disclose that they are Hindu, though they practice Bhuddist forms of meditation, *shamatha-vipashyana* (tranquility-insight) and *lojong* (mind training) (Chodron, 2001). They suggest that meditation would be a good way to start the first joint meeting. Spinoza explains that Cali's consent would be required in order to bring meditation into the session. They instruct Spinoza to ask Cali for permission. Cali refuses, saying that she does not believe in meditation and feels it would bias the whole process. Spinoza shuttles back to Sanjiv and Surya, giving them the option of conducting their meditation in a separate room prior to the joint meeting.

If all parties are agreeable to including certain rituals in their joint meeting, this creates greater opportunity for bonding between the parties. With permission from Cali, Sanjiv, and Surya, an elder begins the meeting with a special invocation:

> As we come together, we are entering the eye of the spirit. We must step outside the confines of our traditional feelings and thought processes. Remember that feelings are

emotional reactions to particular moments. We are not bound to stay locked in partisan perceptions or strong feelings such as hurt and loss. The spirit allows us to reach deeper into our hearts, illuminate the darkness of uncertainty, and make our own decisions about what could be.

This invocation inspires everyone to enter a space filled with spirituality, providing them with new vantage points and openness to make wiser decisions (Fox & Gafni, 2004).

One risk of using prayers and rituals is that one party might try to use this approach as a weapon against the other. A person invoking prayer might intentionally choose language that puts other parties on the defensive, perhaps denouncing them as heathens, ingrates, or sinners ("We pray for Cali's soul, that she may be redeemed for her transgressions"). Accordingly, a CR professional should be fully apprised of what the prayers or rituals will be, prior to agreeing to their inclusion. One safeguard is to have an independent third party (e.g., a cleric or spiritual leader) lead the prayer or ritual.

During the dialogue or negotiation stage of a CR process, parties may want to bring in teachings from religious texts. Cali, for instance, introduces this quote from Matthew 18:15–18:

> If your brother sins (against you), go and tell him his fault between you and him alone. If he listens to you, you have won over your brother. If he does not listen, take one or two others along with you, so that every fact may be established on the testimony of two or three witnesses. If he refuses to listen to them, tell the church. If he refuses to listen even to the church, then treat him as you would a Gentile or a tax collector. Amen, I say to you, whatever you bind on earth shall be bound in heaven, and whatever you loose on earth shall be loosed in heaven.

Spinoza asks Cali how she interprets this passage. She says that one message to be drawn is that when conflict arises, first try to sort it out with the person privately and informally. If this does not work, then you may need to bring others from the community to help resolve the matter. Cali is Christian, and the lesson draws from her sacred text; therefore, it has a more profound effect on her than a lesson that was not tied to the Bible.

Because Surya and Sanjiv are not Christian, Spinoza asks whether this lesson resonates with them or whether they have contrasting teachings from their own spiritual texts. This question provides the clients with the freedom to comment directly on the biblical quote or speak from their own sources of spiritual thought. Often, interfaith dialogue leads people to understand that the basic teachings of different religions are very similar—for instance, the importance of sharing, doing good deeds, and being honest (Nelson, 1999). Once again, this newfound understanding provides a special bond between the parties.

One of the most common uses of ritual within a CR process is at the agreement stage. This stage marks the transition between how the parties have interacted in the past and how they hope to interact in the future (Schirch, 2004). Agreement rituals include handshakes, speeches, feasts, drinks, and celebrations. Different rituals may have different meanings. Gestures such as "burying the hatchet" (or some other symbol of the conflict) can be used to put closure on past troubles. A public handshaking[15] ceremony between leaders of two groups could be used to demonstrate to their constituencies that a period marked by violence and injustice has ended, and a new era of peace and reconciliation has begun. After Spinoza has helped his clients reach agreement, he asks them how they would like to memorialize it. Part of their agreement was to develop an online training program for helping professionals to ensure they are familiar with how to screen elderly clients for risk of suicide. Sanjiv suggests they launch the new website on what would have been Deepak's next birthday. Cali and Surya like the idea and suggest they organize a party to demonstrate the program to friends and colleagues. These rituals help Sanjiv and Surya with their grieving process, as well as helping Cali with her feelings of guilt about what more she could have done for Deepak. The online course helps them put meaning to Deepak's death, inspiring them to raise consciousness and knowledge about suicide among the elderly. The launching party commemorates not only the resolution of the conflict but also their good-faith commitment to implementing their vision.

Although a CR professional should not impose religion or spirituality on the clients, a CR professional may bring rituals or prayers into a CR process in a number of appropriate ways. First, the CR professional may ask parties about their traditional use of prayers and rituals, exploring whether they could contribute to the CR process. Second, when there is conflict between parties about the possible use of prayers and rituals, the CR professional can help them find solutions that meet everyone's needs. Third, when parties have agreed to bring rituals or prayers into the process, the CR professional can help them plan and implement their use. This may include bringing an elder or spiritual **healer** into the process. In some cases, the CR professional also has the status of spiritual leader or healer—for instance, through training, experience, and community recognition. If all parties are agreeable, the CR professional may be able to provide additional services, such as spiritual education, guidance, and facilitation of rituals and prayers. The ethical appropriateness of doing so, however, depends on how the CR professional's role is defined. If hired as a "neutral professional mediator," these additional services could put the mediator's neutrality in jeopardy. If hired as a spiritual guide who happens to have CR training, these roles would be appropriate. Perhaps the most important criterion concerning whether a CR professional can lead prayers or rituals, however, is informed consent, letting the parties decide freely and voluntarily what the CR professional's role should be.

3. Deep Listening

Deep listening[16] refers to an interviewing approach that uses questions strategically to encourage deeper levels of discussion and understanding (Kraybill, 2005a). Deep listening is similar to active listening (Chapter 2) in that both use paraphrase and reflection of feeling to let clients know the professional is listening, understanding, and

---

[15]Historically, handshaking indicated a laying down of arms, because people could not hold weapons as they were shaking hands.

[16]For related approaches, see research on appreciative inquiry or compassionate listening.

valuing what they are saying. Deep listening goes beyond active listening, however, by helping clients think deeper and differently about their situation and possibilities for the future (Schirch, 2004). Deep listening may be used as a distinct process or as part of another CR process. Nongovernmental organizations promoting civil society have used deep listening with various groups occupied by intractable conflicts, including Israelis and Palestinians, as well as Irish Catholics and Protestants. Business organizations have used deep listening as a means of transforming work environments (Appreciative Inquiry Commons, n.d.).

As with other helping processes, deep listening starts where the client is. During an individual meeting, Spinoza asks Surya, "Would you like to talk about your father?" This question not only gives Surya control over whether to talk about his father but also allows Surya to choose what he wants to say about his father. He responds, "I can't talk about my father without thinking about that horrible counselor. Why didn't she call us to say he needed help?" In order to build a positive working rapport, Spinoza reflects back Surya's anger, validating his feelings and encouraging Surya to elaborate. Surya tells the whole story of how his father had depression, but it was supposedly under control. He vents and vents about Cali's incompetence.

Although venting can be cathartic, it can also reinforce harsh feelings and negative belief systems. Deep listening questions help people look underneath their feelings and beliefs. Spinoza asks Surya, "What do you think lies underneath your feelings of anger?" Surya asks what he means, and Spinoza responds, "Help me understand why you feel so angry?" Surya needs time to think about this but eventually discloses that he's not just angry at Cali—he's angry at himself, too. As Surya goes back over his story, he adds how he referred his father to Cali and how he felt personally guilty for his father's suicide.

Another key to deep listening is to pay attention to the culturally based meanings behind the words used by clients. Even words such as *healing, trauma,* and *spirituality* have vastly different connotations in different languages and dialects (Fuertes, 2004). When Spinoza hears Surya say that he feels guilty, Spinoza understands guilt to mean personal responsibility or liability, as if Surya feels that he has committed a crime. Rather than assuming his interpretation is correct, Spinoza asks Surya, "What do you mean by 'I felt personally guilty'?" Surya explains that his grasp of English is not so good, so perhaps he is using the wrong word. Spinoza asks Surya to use Hindi if that is more comfortable for him. Surya says the Hindi word would be "*khata.*" He explains *khata* as a "failure" or "blunder." He feels deficient in the eyes of his family. Although he is explaining khata to inform Spinoza, Surya is gaining a deeper understanding of his own thoughts and feelings.

Deep listening fosters spiritual healing by putting people in touch with the deeper meaning of past experiences and visionary possibilities for the future. The following examples demonstrate questions that facilitate these insights and connections:

* Asking clients about prior positive experiences related to the topic of inquiry
* Asking what the client values about him- or herself as a member of the family, organization, or community system
* Asking the client what might help with healing and moving forward (Germany, 2004).

Building on this last example, Spinoza asks Surya, "What would it take for you to make amends for the khata?" Surya says that he needs to act in a way that would make his father and family proud. As they discuss what this means, Surya realizes that blaming or attacking Cali does nothing to achieve this greater purpose. He says that he will use his father's image as a guide for the future. Spinoza congratulates Surya for bringing spirituality into the process.

This example shows how deep listening can bring spirituality into the CR process. In order to keep the illustration brief, unfortunately, the example may sound contrived. In practice, a CR professional must use proper pacing, allowing sufficient time for venting thoughts and feelings about the past before redirecting the client to future visions. Although the focus is on listening and helping the clients achieve deeper understanding, this process can lead to restoration or renewal of relationships, and transcending the base issues that led to the conflict.

4. Circles

Circles are dialogues between members of a community who sit in a round configuration, with no beginning, no ending, and no breaks in between. This configuration reinforces the ideas that all people are equal and all people are interconnected. Traditionally used in Native American communities, circle processes promote communication, understanding, harmony, and healing (Pranis, 2005). "The peacemaking community is a container strong enough to hold: anger, frustration, joy, pain, truth, conflict, diverse world views, intense feelings, silence, paradox" (Pranis, 2005, p. 6).

Whereas mainstream CR approaches such as mediation and arbitration engage only those immediately affected by a conflict, circle processes involve a whole community. Circles operate on the premise that conflict affects not only the immediate conflictants but also extended family members, friends, neighbors, and coworkers (Bear Chief, Barsky, & Este, 2000). Because circles are based on the premise that everyone in a community is interconnected, the whole community can serve as a resource for the resolution of conflict and as a vehicle for restoring harmony.

Traditionally, circles are facilitated by community elders, though they may also be facilitated by other community leaders. The facilitator (sometimes called a "circle keeper") initiates a space that is respectful and safe. The facilitator encourages sharing, but is generally nondirective, letting the process unfold on its own (Pranis, 2005). The facilitator is not specifically a neutral, because the facilitator can share his or her own stories and lessons. In some circles, the facilitator circulates a talking piece, such as a stone, feather, or branch. Whoever holds the talking piece is permitted to speak, uninterrupted and for as long as it takes.

The primary means of communicating in a circle is storytelling. People recall experiences and relate them to each other. Participants know in advance—from prior experience in circles or from preparation by those calling the circle—that they are not there to judge, advise, or rebuke others. Each storyteller plants images or thoughts in the minds of the listeners. Storytelling helps listeners acknowledge the wisdom of others in a noncompetitive and noncoercive process (Moodley & West, 2005). Healing occurs through the sharing of experiences, helping community members reconnect and establish harmony. Although some circles involve a problem-solving component, others focus only on storytelling and healing.

In the case involving Deepak's suicide, assume that a *sadhu* (holy person) from the Hindu community convenes a circle. Sudheer (the sadhu) invites not only Surya and Sanjiv but also their extended family members and community. Sudheer invites Cali, not as a person accused of any misbehavior but rather as just another community member to participate in the healing process. Many community members have never participated in a circle before. Spinoza (who has extensive experience with circles) helps Sudheer prepare community members for the circle. Spinoza meets with each invitee separately to describe the nature of the circle and how everyone can participate. Spinoza explains to Cali:

> Circles bring communities together to help them heal from loss and conflict. Deepak's death has affected many people. In order to help everyone move on, the circle allows community members to share their stories about Deepak's life, about the way he died, or about the ways they have dealt with similar losses in their lives. Just like everyone else, you are free to speak or not speak. Your presence is what is most important.

Initially, Cali is concerned about being an outsider who may become the target of anger from Deepak's relatives. As she comes to understand the circle process, however, she believes that her participation will be good for both herself and the community.

Participants are prepared in advance, so the facilitator does not need to make an opening statement or set ground rules during the actual circle. Sudheer opens the circle with an incantation, inviting everyone to bring the values of honesty, humility, sharing, courage, empathy, trust, forgiveness, compassion, interpersonal connection, benevolence, and love into the room (Pranis, 2005). The incantation sets the tone, establishing that this is a special time and place for the community. Although Sudheer has not specifically mentioned spirituality, circle members begin to feel its positive energy permeate the room (Cloke, 2005). Sudheer passes a brass ring to an elderly woman on his right. The woman explains how Deepak was one of her longest and dearest friends. She relates stories from their childhood, conveying the playfulness and creativity that Deepak brought to everything he did in life. She concludes by describing her sense of emptiness since Deepak committed suicide. She passes the ring to Sanjiv.

Sanjiv tells the story of how he learned about his father's death. As he describes how Cali was the last person to see Deepak, Sanjiv's voice becomes louder and angrier. Nobody asks him to calm down. Everyone listens, quietly and patiently. Sanjiv goes on for almost 20 minutes, eventually completing what he had to say. He looks a bit more relaxed, but he is still flushed and breathing heavily.

As the ring makes its way around the room, various community members relate their stories about Deepak. Some tell of the loss of their own parents and how they struggled to cope. When the ring passes to Cali, she says, "Thank you," holds the ring for a few moments, and passes it to the next person. Although she says just two words, everyone hears her sadness.

Deepak's cousin, Chetan, is next to speak. Chetan recounts a conversation he had with Deepak. Deepak had been feeling depressed for some time. He said that he felt like a burden to his family and he felt bad about that. Chetan encouraged Deepak to talk to his children, knowing they would tell him he was not a burden but a source of love and sustenance. Deepak said he did not want to bring any more stress to the family, so he decided not to discuss his feelings with anyone else in the family. Deepak found talking to Cali to be helpful, because she was outside the family.

When the ring returns to Sudheer, he explains the Hindu concept of reincarnation, that the spirit of a deceased person may live again in another person or animal. Surya adds that while he does not believe in reincarnation literally, he believes that family and community members are affected by his father's spirit. He pledges that he will live by his father's spirit of integrity, compassion, and understanding. Others are moved to convey similar pledges.

Although circling processes may sound foreign to some, most cultures possess some type of circling process. It may be as simple as a family gathering around the dinner table or neighbors gathering around a campfire to talk. No single strategy turns a circle into a healing experience. Healing emerges from the process and the moment itself. The most important role of the facilitator is to create a safe place for people to share stories. Storytelling often involves one generation teaching the next, based on narratives of past experience. Storytelling engages people emotionally and spiritually, not just intellectually. Personal narratives convey insights, pain, happiness, and other feelings. As people are touched by each other's stories, they gain a sense of connectedness. The facilitator may invite participants to discuss how their behavior has affected others or what they need in order to heal (Pranis, 2005). Generally, however, the facilitator trusts the process and lets it unfold without asking participants to answer specific questions.

Helping professionals often play a limited but important role in circle processes. Although the circle keeper (facilitator) is typically an elder or community leader, a helping professional can provide a number of supportive functions, particularly in the preparation and follow-up stages:

- Help the circle keeper and community determine who to invite to the circle: who are the people affected by the conflict or loss, who are the people that may contribute in a constructive manner, and who can participate safely (e.g., if a person has an uncontrolled substance abuse problem, would it be safe and constructive for that person to participate)?
- Educate community members about the circle process and how they can participate constructively (e.g., listening quietly, conveying stories, and offering support).
- Help implement any plans made during the circle (working with individuals or small groups who made commitments, helping them plan the best way to implement agreements, and helping them monitor and evaluate implementation) (Pranis, 2005).

In some situations, circles are used in conjunction with mainstream social services, such as the criminal justice system (to determine appropriate sentencing for a crime) or child welfare system (to determine how to take care of children when concerns about child abuse or neglect have been raised). In these situations, helping professionals act as the liaison between the circle and the social service system, ensuring that decisions from one are conveyed and followed through by the other. In other situations, circles operate independently, and minimal formal follow-up is required. The healing that occurs within the circle is both the means and the end of the process (Pranis, 2005).

5. Apology and Forgiveness

Apology and forgiveness are interactive processes between people who have caused harm and people who have suffered from the harm. In order to simplify the discussion, I will use the term *transgressor* to indicate the person who has caused the harm and *victim* to indicate the person who suffered from the harm. In practice, I avoid these terms, because they connote blame and accentuate polarization of the parties. Furthermore, in many conflicts, responsibility for harm may be shared or ambiguous. These labeling problems can be avoided in practice by simply referring to clients by their names.

When people suffer harm, emotional responses such as anger, hurt, sadness, and loss may keep them stuck in the past. At the same time, transgressors may become stuck in feelings such as shame, guilt, fear, or anxiety. Apology and forgiveness help transgressors and victims move on (Cloke, 2005). Both apology and forgiveness can be experienced at different levels: change of head, change of heart, and change of hand. *Change of head* refers to a change in the way a person thinks about the harm done. *Change of heart* refers to a deeper level of change, relating to the person's underlying feelings about the harm done (Kraybill, n.d.). *Change of hand* refers to actual changes in the person's behavior, reflecting and reinforcing the changes in head and heart. Full apology or forgiveness transcends the head, heart, and hand. Partial apology or forgiveness, however, may involve just one or two of these domains.

Apologizing refers to admitting responsibility for acts or omissions that caused harm. Although merely saying "I'm sorry" may have a profound impact on everyone involved in a conflict, there is also an art and a science about how to offer apologies. Helping professionals can assist transgressors by helping them (a) see the value of apology, (b) make an informed decision about whether to apologize, and (c) learn how to make an apology as effectively as possible.

The value of an apology extends to both the victim and transgressor. For the victim, apology validates the person's experience of being harmed and demonstrates the transgressor feels remorseful for the harm done. Receiving a simple apology may help the victim's sense of worth. If the apology is conveyed in public, it may also clear the victim's name or reputation. For the transgressor, apology offers the chance to take responsibility for causing harm, perhaps freeing the transgressor from feelings of guilt or self-reproach. For both parties, apology opens up the possibilities of collaboration, reconciliation, compensation, and restitution.

Deciding whether to offer an apology can be an arduous emotional task. When a person causes harm to another, initial reactions may be to withdraw, conceal responsibility, or blame the victim. Transgressors may feel too ashamed or afraid to apologize. Helping professionals can help them work through this shame or fear. They can also help transgressors consider the pros and cons of making an apology, so they can make informed decisions. Questions to facilitate insight may include the following (Cloke, 2005):

- What roles have you played in this conflict, by either action or inaction?
- Is there anything you might like to apologize for?
- What has made it difficult for you to apologize until now?
- How might an apology affect your future relationship?

Ideally, people offering apologies should do so because they truly feel sorry. "Act without a why" (Combs, 2004, p. 201). If a transgressor offers an apology merely because she expects a positive response from the victim, the victim may feel manipulated and resentful. If the victim does not accept the apology, the transgressor may also feel resentful and angry.

There are many cultural aspects to giving and receiving apologies. Within some cultures, saying "I'm sorry" is relatively easy. In other cultures, it is much more difficult. A person with a high sense of machismo, for instance, may view apologizing as a sign of weakness or lack of masculinity. A person with a strong sense of family honor, in contrast, may be very quick to offer an apology so as not to dishonor the entire family. Women, who are generally more comfortable discussing feelings, may find it easier to offer and accept apologies than men. Religion may also offer suggestions on how to convey an apology—for instance, "extending an olive branch" or "praying for forgiveness." When helping clients determine whether to offer apologies, helping professionals need to take gender, religion, and culture into account.

Decisions to offer apologies should also take legal issues into consideration. Offering an apology may be tantamount to accepting legal responsibility for causing harm. Lawyers often advise clients not to admit liability, so that they do not prejudice any court case that may arise. In court, a victim has to prove the transgressor caused the harm; sometimes, the victim cannot do this unless the transgressor has admitted fault. The risk of not apologizing, however, is that the victim may become even angrier. Consider a situation in which a client is upset because you did not show up for one of her appointments. If you apologize, the client's frustration may subside. If you withhold an apology, the client may become more incensed and more likely to lay a complaint against you. When legal issues are at stake, clients should consider the advice from their lawyers—which may include withholding an apology until after a court case or settlement of the legal issues. Clients should also consider the positive roles that apology can play, including the possibility of a collaborative settlement (Robbennolt, 2003).[17] If the parties are involved in a confidential and privileged process, such as mediation, the transgressor may be able to offer an apology without the risk of it being used in a future court process. Sometimes, apologies are included as part of the settlement process.

Apologies may be issued in many different ways: unilaterally or mutually, individually or collectively, privately or publicly, and fully or partially. With a *unilateral apology*, one person offers an apology without preconditions. By offering an apology unilaterally, the transgressor demonstrates genuine remorse and good faith since no strings are attached to the apology. In some instances, nobody involved in a conflict wants to make the first move towards apology. This may be due to dueling egos, fear of losing face, or fear of becoming legally responsible to pay damages or serve time for committing a crime. If parties can agree to offer apologies to each other at

---

[17]Some jurisdictions have passed legislation stating that certain types of apologies cannot be used as evidence of admission of guilt. These laws acknowledge the value of apologies in encouraging settlement of disputes. Some laws pertain specifically to apologies by healthcare workers. These laws cover some types of apologies but not others. For example, expressions of sympathy may be exempted from court but not expressions admitting responsibility. You may require legal advice to help you understand what types of apologies are protected or not.

the same time, they can both save face. They may also agree that issuing apologies will not affect their legal rights or responsibilities. The downside of mutual apologies is that each side may perceive the other's apology as conditional or limited. Although each side coolly issues words of apology, they may perceive that the other's heart was not into the apology. Cool apologies are unlikely to lead to a spiritual connection or full reconciliation between the parties.

An *individual apology* refers to the issuing of an apology by a particular individual. This individual acknowledges personal responsibility. *Collective apologies* refer to the issuing an apology by a group of people. The president might say, for instance, "On behalf of the people of the United States, I offer our sincere regret and apology to the African American community and to all those who were affected by the Tuskeegee syphilis research conducted from the 1930s to 1970s." In such a statement, the president is not admitting personal responsibility. He is admitting communal responsibility. Both individual and collective apologies may be effective, depending on the circumstances. If a person was individually responsible for causing harm, for instance, it would sound disingenuous to issue a collective admission. Likewise, issuing an individual admission may not ring true if the actual responsibility for harm was collective.

Whether an apology should be issued privately or publicly also depends on the circumstances. When a conflict is truly private, and perhaps embarrassing, a private apology may be sufficient. Taking the issue public may cause unwarranted stress or shame to both the transgressor and victim. If a matter is already known to the public, a public apology may be useful in order to set the public record straight. A public apology may also clear a victim's name and social standing, if the public was blaming the victim or otherwise had a negative view of the victim. Public apologies may also demonstrate that the transgressor is truly remorseful and wants to make amends. Often a transgression is not just a private issue but a matter of public concern. Consider the spate of Catholic priests who have been charged with child molestation since the 1980s. When the Catholic Church kept matters quiet, further children were put at risk. When the issues became more open, the church, parishioners, and others could take more effective steps to ensure that children were safeguarded.

People are more likely to accept an apology if it is a full apology, rather than a partial one (Robbennolt, 2003). A *full* apology includes

- a sincere admission of behaving in a way that caused harm;
- taking responsibility for causing the harm;
- showing remorse for causing the harm;
- demonstrating empathy towards the victim; and
- changing behavior to demonstrate that the apology goes beyond words or gestures to deeds or actions (e.g., compensating the victim or taking steps to improve the relationship with the victim).

In order to demonstrate the different levels of apology, consider a situation where Ed, the executive director of a social agency, hires a man from outside the agency to be the new clinical supervisor for the program. A front-line worker, Fatima, contends that she was overlooked for this position because of sexism. Ed wants to apologize, but he is not sure how. He meets with Claire, a CR professional to help him construct an effective apology. Clair asks him to role-play what he might say to Fatima. Ed responds:

> Fatima, I'm sorry you feel angry because you think I overlooked you for the supervisor's position.

Claire asks Ed to consider how Fatima would hear this apology. She helps Ed understand that his example conveys that he feels sorry, but only for Fatima's feelings. He takes no responsibility for his actions and shows no remorse. With this feedback, Ed tries again:

> Fatima, I understand that you feel angry because I overlooked you for the supervisor's position. I want to apologize for not even interviewing you for the position. After all you've contributed to the agency, I should have at least offered you an interview. I guess I was just so busy, I wasn't thinking.

Claire congratulates Ed for showing more accurate empathy regarding Fatima's feelings. She adds that Ed takes personal responsibility for not interviewing Fatima, and his apology sounds sincere. Claire notes that saying he was too busy sounds like an excuse and may not go over well with Fatima. Ed agrees. Claire asks him what he might be able to offer Fatima in terms of a change in behavior, explaining that actions often speak louder than words. She asks whether there is some way that he can offer restitution, making right the wrong, or at least ensuring better treatment in the future. Ed provides the following example:

> I apologize for overlooking you when I hired someone from outside the agency for the clinical supervisor's position. I understand that you might take this as indicating sexism, though I assure you this was not my intent. I respect your work and feel bad that my oversight caused you such hurt. I realize my oversight in not even letting you know about the opening was insensitive. You have contributed so much to our agency and have great clinical skills. It's too late for me to interview you for this position, but I will commit to considering you for any future openings. In fact, if you'd like to participate in the up-coming training for new supervisors, you would be more than welcome to attend.

Ed critiques this apology, noting that he admits the wrong, he says he's sorry, he empathizes with her hurt, he takes responsibility, and he says he will make sure that he will not do it again. He wonders whether he needs to admit he was sexist, even if he doesn't think he was sexist. Claire notes that he needs to be honest in order to sound honest. She adds that he can demonstrate that he is not sexist by his future actions much better than he can by his words. Ed thanks Claire for helping him develop and practice making an apology. He says that it will be difficult to admit making a mistake, because he likes to convey an image of competence to his employees. Claire notes that being able to apologize for making a mistake is a sign of competence. After all, the apology may be a way to strengthen his working relationship with Fatima, a valued employee.

The last area where a CR professional can help people with apologies is timing. Problems may arise if an apology is provided too soon or too late. If a transgressor causes harm and immediately says, "I'm sorry," the advantage may be that the apology was issued before feelings of anger or hurt have a chance to fester. One risk of an immediate apology may be that the apology does not sound sincere. Have you ever had someone brush by you in a crowded store, and as she elbows you, she says, "Excuse me"? If the apology is too soon, the victim may perceive that the transgressor did not even think about the harm she caused or the impact on the victim. Furthermore, the victim may be in no shape to hear the apology. The victim may be in shock, denial, or anguish from the transgression, unable to appreciate the value of an apology. Sometimes, it is better to hold off on providing an apology or perhaps extend a second apology at a more appropriate time.

When apologies are delayed, one risk is that the conflict will become exacerbated. The victim may impute negative attributes to the transgressor—for instance, she is evil, rude, uncaring, or unfeeling. If the victim retaliates, then the transgressor may become more disinclined to offer an apology. "I was ready to apologize, but if that's the way you're going to treat me, then you deserved what you got—and worse." Once a conflict escalates, it becomes more difficult for parties to apologize. When CR professionals are working with clients, however, they can help parties understand that just because an apology is difficult does not mean that they should not apologize. In fact, an apology typically has even greater meaning if it comes during a period of escalating conflict. A well-timed apology may be just what is needed to turn the parties to a more peaceful and productive course.

When a transgressor issues an apology, the victim may be moved to offer forgiveness. Although apology and forgiveness are often linked, they can take place independently. A victim, for instance, can feel and offer forgiveness even if the transgressor has not formally apologized.

Forgiving refers to offering a sincere, personal pardon to someone who has caused harm. Forgiving involves cognitive, affective, and behavioral aspects. The victim must reflect on the harm, trying to make sense of what has happened. The victim must also work through feelings such as shock, anger, fear, vengefulness, or resentment. By offering forgiveness, the victim conveys a desire to transcend all ill feelings toward the transgressor (Wilmot & Hocker, 2007). Forgiving does not mean denying these feelings but rather freeing oneself from being controlled or overstimulated by them. In order to demonstrate forgiveness, the victim must not only offer words of forgiveness but behave in a way that reflects forgiveness. Consider the following remarks from a woman talking to a student who broke into her apartment:

> Ever since you broke into my home, I have lived in fear. I have not been able to sleep at night. I am constantly checking to see if the doors are locked. I'm constantly ridden with anxiety. I am glad, though, that I was able to meet you through this Victim-Offender Reconciliation Program. I've been able to explain all I've gone through, and I know that you have heard me. I could tell from your eyes that your apology was sincere. I accept your apology, and I hope that we can move on as neighbors rather than victim and offender. Perhaps I could help you with your studies.

Some individuals and some cultural groups view forgiveness as a sign of weakness. In Western society, for instance, women tend to be more comfortable offering forgiveness than men. CR professionals can help people understand that forgiveness does not mean condoning, giving in, or forgetting harm that has transpired. In fact, forgiveness requires incredible moral and personal strength to look deeply inside oneself, in order to determine readiness to transcend feelings of denial, embarrassment, anger, hurt, resentment, or sorrow (Wilmot & Hocker, 2007).

Forgiveness can be incredibly powerful within a CR process. Forgiveness frees people from thoughts, feelings, and behaviors that have led to destructive patterns of interaction in the past. Forgiveness allows people to put past issues in their proper place and move on. Forgiveness gives people the opportunity to renegotiate or reconcile their relationships.

In spite of the benefits of forgiveness, people often find it difficult. CR professionals can assist people in moving towards forgiveness by:

- helping the transgressor make an apology (e.g., teaching the components of a full apology, as already described);
- providing the victim with psychotherapy[18] to help work through the cognitive, emotional, and behavioral reactions to the loss or hurt (Kübler-Ross, 1997);
- helping the victim explore the personal, relational, spiritual, or economic consequences of offering forgiveness, as well as the consequences of not offering forgiveness;
- clarifying how forgiveness does not mean condoning, forgetting, or being indifferent to past transgressions;
- role-playing the skills required to offer forgiveness;
- helping the victim identify what he or she needs in order to be able to forgive (e.g., compensation, opportunity to talk to the transgressor, apology, time) and mediating with the transgressor in order to work out a solution;
- providing the transgressor and victim with time and space to interact, feel safe, and share their feelings, thoughts, and experiences.

People should not be pressured to forgive. Pressure may further victimize a person. Sometimes, pressure results in a half-hearted statement of forgiveness ("That's all right"), which does nothing to transcend the conflict. It might be better to help a person explain why they cannot offer full forgiveness rather than try to coerce one: "Thank you for your apology. I know it was difficult to give. As you can imagine, it's also difficult for me to offer forgiveness, but I'm just not ready. Still, I would like to work through some of our other concerns." Partial but genuine forgiveness is more helpful than full but artificial forgiveness (Wilmot & Hocker, 2007).

Sometimes, forgiveness is something that people feel in their heart but do not convey to the transgressor—for instance, when the transgressor has died or when the victim is ready to feel forgiveness but not ready to offer it. Although this does not allow for reconciliation of their relationship, feeling forgiveness can help the victim transcend feelings of anger, hurt, loss, and so on. In other words, forgiveness can be spiritually uplifting whether or not it is conveyed directly from the victim to the transgressor.

* * *

As this chapter demonstrates, the range of CR roles for helping professionals is broad and still growing. Given the extent of conflict within society, the availability of many approaches to conflict resolution is a good thing. Now that we have covered a broad spectrum of CR approaches, the next challenge is to determine how do we know which approaches to use, and when. This is one of the main topics of Chapter 8.

---

[18]If the practitioner has proper training in this field. If not, the practitioner can refer clients to qualified psychotherapists.

KEY POINTS

- Many CR strategies can be used as either distinct interventions or as part of a larger intervention strategy.
- Fact-finding strategies may be useful when conflict relates to rumor, misinformation, lack of information, or competing evidence.
- Trust-building strategies help each party act in a manner that is reliable, credible, open, and honest, in order to foster a more positive relationship between the parties, fostering their ability to work through conflict more effectively.
- Peacebuilding strategies go beyond stopping violence or reaching an agreement. Peacebuilding includes a combination of interventions aimed at promoting open, cooperative, caring, and respectful relationships between people.
- True peace requires justice, meaning that the rights and freedoms of all people are respected, and their physical, psychological, and social needs are being fulfilled.
- Parenting coordinators help divorcing or separating families implement a parenting plan by providing a combination of services, including assessment, education, monitoring, enforcement, and conflict resolution.
- Helping professionals may use family group conferences to bring extended family members together to work through issues such child abuse, child neglect, or criminal activity by a family member, empowering families to take responsibility and develop their own solutions.
- Although helping professionals should not impose spirituality or religion on clients, they may offer processes that allow for spiritual healing, helping clients transcend conflict and give it meaning through means such as art, ritual, prayer, deep listening, circles, apology, and forgiveness.

DISCUSSION QUESTIONS AND EXERCISES

1. UNITED WE STAND: Assume that the agency where you work is unionized, and you are a member of the collective bargaining team for the union. The main sticking point in negotiations is salary. Both sides have agreed to the principle that salaries should reflect market salaries for comparable professionals in comparable agencies. Management says that it has evidence that the average salary for your profession is $53,000 per year. The union claims that its research shows the average salary is $66,000.

   a. To help resolve the salary dispute, you suggest a joint fact-finding strategy. Explain how fact finding would work in this particular case. Also, how would you present this alternative to maximize chances that both the union and management would accept this process?

   b. Assume negotiations break down. Both sides mistrust each other. Management claims that the union is not acting in good faith, presenting false information about the agency to union members and the public. The union claims that management cannot be trusted, that it has backed down on previous offers and has been hiring replacement employees to take over the jobs of unionized employees. What type of trust-building interventions might be helpful at this stage? How could you persuade one or both sides to engage in trust building?

c. Assume that the union goes on strike. Hostilities flare during the strike, with managers accusing employees of not caring about clients and professional employees claiming that management has mishandled its budget, wasting money that could be used to pay descent salaries. Eventually, the parties settle the salary dispute. Although the strike ends, the morale among management and employees is poor. Describe how peacebuilding or spirituality strategies could be used to improve management-employee relations and morale. How would you present your suggestions so that everyone is more likely to accept them?

2. APOLOGY DILEMMA: Assume you are working with Allie, a woman in recovery from alcoholism. Allie attends AA and is using its 12-step approach to recovery. Allie tells you in confidence that she stole $20,000 from her employer, who never discovered who stole it. Allie wants to apologize and make amends, as is suggested by her 12-step program. Allie is concerned that if she admits her crime, she could be charged with theft and could also lose her job. How would you respond to Allie's request for advice on whether she should apologize? What ethical guidelines from your profession do you need to consider? Would you refer Allie for legal advice? What would you tell her about how to balance the legal issues with her need to make amends under the 12-step program? Is there a way Allie can issue an apology in a manner that improves the chances of beneficial consequences and reduce ethical, legal, and clinical risks?

3. INSPIRATION: Locate a text from a religious or spiritual group that you are affiliated with (e.g., Christian Bible, the philosophies of Confucius, Kabbalah, a classic Yoga book, or a Sufi text). Identify a passage in this text related to conflict resolution. Describe how this passage could help people deal with conflict more effectively, more ethically, or more spiritually.

4. RELIGIOUS RIFT: Assume that you are working in a halfway house where two residents, Tessa and Katie, have been embroiled in a battle ever since Tessa started calling Katie "the little whore." When you invite both of them to agree to treat one another with respect, Tessa says that Katie deserves no respect. Tessa cites her religious scriptures, which say, "Those who sell their flesh shall be treated with contempt, as they have shown contempt for their own bodies." How can you help Tessa and Katie, without imposing your religious beliefs or invalidating Tessa's?

5. MATCHING STRATEGIES: The following examples demonstrate brief exchanges between clients and CR practitioners. For each example, identify the type of strategy being used by the practitioner and also which type of CR process this strategy fits with (fact finding, trust building, peacebuilding, parenting coordination, family group conferencing, spiritual healing):

a. *Client* (in a child custody dispute): My ex-wife just went nuts when she found out that I was having an affair. There is no way she'll agree to anything when we get together."
CR practitioner: Perhaps we need to give her some time to work through her feelings. In the meantime, what do you think you could do to help her see you as a good father?

b. *Manager* (in a workplace conflict): I will not tolerate disrespect from my employees. They were incredibly rude and offensive.
   CR practitioner: I think you've made your point. You feel they treated you with disrespect. I can hear that it would not be reasonable to ask you to simply excuse their behavior, but what do you think they could do now, in order for everyone to move forward?

c. *Human rights activist* (planning a civil disobedience protest over Social Security benefit cuts proposed by government): Once again, government is taking from the poor to give to the rich. We will do whatever is necessary to stop this, even if we have to take the law into our own hands. If the police shoot at us, at least we'll have made our point.
   CR practitioner: You obviously feel very strongly about these cuts, enough to put your lives on the line. That's the ultimate commitment people can make. Excuse me if this sounds a bit morbid, but what would you want your loved ones to say at your funeral?

d. *Client* (who has been skipping school): What's the point of going to school if I'm going to fail anyhow? Let's face it—I'm stupid. Just save everybody the time and pain, and kick me out of school right now.
   CR practitioner: Perhaps we can go around the room, so each of your family members, teachers, and friends can tell us whether you're too dumb to be successful at school.

e. *Nurse* (in a conflict over discharge plans for a patient with AIDS): I don't care what the case manager says. This patient has nowhere to go and nobody to take care of him if we discharge him now.
   CR practitioner: It sounds as if people are operating on different information. Some believe the patient has a supportive place to stay, whereas others believe he doesn't. Rather than argue about this now, perhaps two of you could agree to meet with the patient and ask about family, friends, and other possible support systems for when he leaves the hospital.

f. *Senator* (after a frenzied debate between parties on whether to teach school children "intelligent design" as an alternative to the "theory of evolution"): Well, it's not as if everybody is friends, but at least the Speaker of the House put an end to all the barbs and insults.
   CR practitioner: What you're describing suggests that you've moved from a state of hot war to a state of cold war. Discussions over values and beliefs can be very divisive. I wonder whether it would be helpful at this point for both parties to work on important educational issues where there is broad agreement. Perhaps you could start with a retreat in more serene venue, away from the Capitol. You may be more productive, and it will give relations a chance to warm up.

g. *Client* (in a high-conflict divorce): Every time the children are scheduled to be with me, my ex comes up with an excuse for why they cannot come. Either the kids are sick, or they have soccer practice, or she fabricates some sort of family emergency.
   CR practitioner: You have an agreement about how time will be shared with the children. The issue seems to be how to implement and enforce it. What would you think about working with a professional whose role would be to

help both of you put the agreement into practice, making sure everyone follows through on their commitments?

h. *Client* (accused of vandalism): All I did was paint a drawing on the side of a building. They call it graffiti, but I call it art. What happened to freedom of expression?

Probation officer: You're right. What is graffiti to some is art to others. Still, you drew on public property, without permission, and now you are being held accountable. We have a restorative justice program where people can do community service to make up for the harm they have caused. Because you like to express yourself through painting, would you like to see whether any community service programs involve beautification of public places?

6. TASER TROUBLE: An ombud is investigating a case where police used a taser gun on a 15-year-old girl. Police claim they stopped the girl in relation to a robbery, but she resisted arrest, and they needed to use the taser in self-defense. The girl claims she did not hear them call her and was walking away when they shot her. She sustained a concussion when she fell. Some community members are outraged that police would fire a taser on such a young girl. Which CR intervention(s) from this chapter do you think would be most useful at this point? Why?

7. SPIRITUAL ETHICS: Although spirituality can play an important role in CR, it can also raise important ethical questions: Because many forms of spirituality are "accepted on faith," how do we know that they are effective? Is it ethical to use a spiritually based intervention (e.g., prayer) if there is no research evidence to support it? If a CR professional is not expert in the clients' religious or spiritual traditions, is the CR professional competent to help the clients plan and implement a religious or spiritual intervention? If a CR professional does not take the spiritual world of the client into account, is the professional liable for malpractice—in other words, is spirituality a required component of CR assessment and intervention?

7. GOING DEEP: Deep listening provides clients with a sense of validation. It helps them move to deeper levels of understanding and insight. But what are the risks of using deep listening with clients? Given these risks, what type of training or certification should CR professionals have before they provide this sort of service with clients? Does deep listening require a degree in psychology, family therapy, or some other mental health profession?

7. QUASI-APOLOGIES: Review the following apologies. Identify their strengths and weaknesses. Then, rewrite each apology so it reflects a full apology, as described in this chapter.

   a. *Child to teacher*: I am sorry I got you mad because I cheated on the math test.
   b. *Advocate to client*: I know you wanted me to help you file an appeal with your health insurance company. I have been working for other clients with more pressing needs, so I haven't been able to get to your case yet. I feel badly, and I will make it up to you.
   c. *Granddaughter to grandmother*: I cannot tell a lie. I was the one who broke your glasses. I was playing with them, and they fell. I feel better now that I have 'fessed up.

8. FORGIVENESS FORESTALLED: Robbie was raised in a family where whatever he did, it was never good enough. His brother Raymond was the shining star in the family. Raymond took advantage of this. He would always ask his parents for the biggest piece of pie, the newest bike, or the most powerful computer. He would get what he wanted, often at Robbie's expense. As adults, Raymond decides to make amends. He apologizes and promises to do whatever he can to compensate Robbie for all the grief he caused Robbie during their childhood. Robbie says that he cannot find it in his heart to forgive Raymond. He feels that he was unjustly treated and he keeps replaying his painful childhood memories in his mind. It burns a whole in his heart, and all he wants is revenge. If you were working with Robbie, what type of help would you offer him, and why (take your professional role and code of ethics into account)? Would you start where the client is, honoring his self-determination, and help him plan revenge?

9. ART FROM THE HEART: If you are going to ask others to create art as a means of CR, try doing it yourself first in order to gain a better sense of what you are asking and how you will ask. Try the follow exercise, which uses poetry to express thoughts, feelings, and visions about conflict (Combs, 2004):

   a. Select a time and location where you can sit and write, comfortably and without disruption.
   b. Think of a current conflict at home, at work, with friends, or in the news. Visualize the players and how they are responding to the conflict, including their thoughts, feelings, and actions.
   c. List everything that comes to mind about the conflict, including colors, emotions, people, and other images. Do not be concerned about the order, importance, normality, or strangeness about what you are writing. Just take at least 5 minutes to write a list of points.
   d. Take your list of items, mixing up the order, matching common or contrasting themes, and create a poem. The poem need not rhyme, maintain a standard rhythm, or follow any other conventions of poetry.
   e. Read your poem aloud. Ask others for feedback on how your poem resonates with them.

ROLE-PLAY 7.1: "WET FOOT, DRY FOOT"—DEEP LISTENING PRACTICE

Cammy is a community development worker responsible for a Miami neighborhood consisting primarily of Cuban and Haitian Americans. Relations between these groups have been fractious. Many Haitians have expressed resentment toward Cubans, believing that they enjoy special, undeserved status. Cubans are granted automatic legal standing when they set a foot on dry American soil. Haitians believe that Cubans receive disproportionate support to help with them settle. In contrast, Haitian asylum seekers are often put into detention or returned to Haiti, where they may be persecuted by the government. Haitians who are allowed to stay face discrimination in housing, jobs, and treatment by police. Many Cubans say that Haitians have nobody to blame but themselves. They accuse Haitians of bringing HIV, crime, poverty, poor education, and other social problem to the United States. Cammy has tried bringing the two groups together, but they refuse. She decides to use deep listening with members of each group. For this role-play, Cammy will meet with Javier, a Cuban American who resents sharing his neighborhood with Haitian immigrants and refugees. To prepare for this role-play, Cammy should review the section on deep listening. This role-play can be repeated with an interview between Cammy and a Haitian American, Hennie).

Debriefing: What questions or comments did Cammy use to promote deep listening? What changes, if any, did Javier experience in his feelings or beliefs about Haitians? Did Javier change his views on what type of relationship between Haitians and Cubans was possible? Did anything spiritual arise during this deep listening process?

ROLE-PLAY 7.2: "PEYOTE PLACE"—WHEN RITUALS CLASH

Howie manages a public housing development where there has been an ongoing feud between people of Native and non-Native backgrounds. Howie invites both groups to a community meeting so they can work through their concerns. While organizing the meeting, Earl (an elder from the Native community) asks to open the meeting with a traditional prayer to Mother Earth and a smudging ritual, involving the burning of sacred herbs. This role-play consists of a meeting between Howie and Novia, an informal leader for the non-Native community. During this role-play, Howie will present Earl's proposal for the prayer and smudging ritual. Novia will initially reject this idea, saying she should not have anyone imposing their weird prayers or practices on them. Novia will also note that Earl uses peyote for smudging, which is an illegal hallucinogen. Howie will try to persuade Novia and her backers to allow the prayer and smudging.

Debriefing: What were the main challenges Howie faced in trying to gain agreement on whether the community meeting would begin with a Native prayer and smudging ritual? Which strategies were most effective in trying to reach resolution? Would the use of prayer and ritual at this type of meeting be helpful and ethical? Why or why not? What other options could they have considered?

ROLE-PLAY 7.3: "INTERN, OUT OF TURN"— TIME TO APOLOGIZE?

Nina is a nurse intern at Conflictia Hope Hospital. During grand rounds, Dr. Cranium, chief of the cardiology department, describes a new procedure for heart surgery to a group of healthcare staff. Nina thinks he made a mistake in his description of the procedure and corrects him. Although she intended to be helpful, she comes across as condescending. Dr. Cranium, known for having a big ego, responds defensively, asking whether this young "whippersnapper" thinks she knows more than a doctor who has been practicing medicine for more than 30 years. Nina runs out of the room, crying. This role-play consists of a meeting between Nina and her supervisor, Savannah. Savannah will raise the possibility of Nina apologizing to Dr. Cranium. Savannah will cover why an apology might be helpful and assist Nina in making an informed decision about whether to apologize. Savannah may also offer to help Nina practice making an apology. Nina will initially resist the idea of apologizing, feeling it is up to Dr. Cranium to apologize to her.

Debriefing: What were the potential benefits and risks of Nina's apologizing in this situation? What did Savannah do that helped Nina make an informed decision about whether and how to apologize?

MAJOR ASSIGNMENTS

Choose one of the following two scenarios, and develop a conflict resolution plan using one of the CR approaches described in this chapter. As you develop this plan, consider the following questions:

1. According to my chosen approach, what is the underlying cause of the conflict?
2. What type of forum for interaction would be best suited for this situation and the chosen approach?
3. What strategies and skills will be necessary in order to carry out an intervention according to this approach?

Once you have designed an intervention, determine who will play which roles in order to role-play the intervention. The role-play could include as few as two role-players (one client and a CR professional) or as many as there are in the whole class (e.g., a CR professional, clients, and members of the community or extended family). The person playing the CR professional should take primary responsibility for setting up the rest of the role-play scenario (e.g., who will meet, where, when, and with what type of interaction). Use the instructions in Chapter 3 for how to prepare a written analysis of the role-play.

ASSIGNMENT 7A: HURRICANE XENA

Three weeks ago, Conflictia was hit by Hurricane Xena, a Category 5 storm that virtually wiped out a neighborhood called Trailer Park Heaven (TPH). Conflictia has been traumatized not only by this natural disaster but also by the deep societal divisions that this hurricane exposed. Emergency services were slow to respond to hurricane warnings, which some say lead to the deaths of 374 residents of TPH. While many wealthier areas of Conflictia were evacuated, most TPH residents stayed in their homes. TPH was not only an economically depressed community but also a community composed primarily of Hispanic and African residents.

Given that no mobile homes survived Xena, European and Asian community leaders suggest that TPH should be turned into a community with proper houses. TPH residents and advocates believe this is a plot to gentrify the area, basically cleansing it of Hispanics, Africans, and poor people. Most TPH residents were renting space and did not have windstorm insurance. They fear that redevelopment plans will not make room for affordable housing, including rental properties. Town leaders view redevelopment as an opportunity to build homes that are safer, particularly during heavy winds. The fact that new single-family homes could attract wealthier residents also means that redevelopment would enhance the community's tax base. When asked what will happen to former TPH residents, the mayor of Conflictia responded, "Their mobile homes were pretty dismal, so they'll actually be better off in new and better homes. They were on welfare before, and they'll be able to stay on welfare. I'm more concerned about people who have lost their jobs because of the hurricane." With all the tension and trauma between different community groups, Conflictia decides to hire a CR professional to design and implement an appropriate CR process (this process does not need to deal with all levels of the conflict or all stages of conflict resolution; just select one intervention that seems appropriate at this stage).

ASSIGNMENT 7B: MAME AND FRITZ

Mame (33) and Fritz (34) were unhappily married for 15 years. They had two children, Ikis (15) and Daphne (13). Ikis was conceived out of wedlock. Fritz and Mame both came from evangelical Christian families, so they wanted to do the "right thing" and get married before Ikis was born. Fritz moved out of the house 3 years ago, hoping to free himself from an intolerable situation. He felt Mame was controlling, emotionally abusive, and erratic. Mame was also unhappy in the marriage, wanting to have more children and yearning for a husband who would be more supportive of her wishes.

Separation has been horrible for the whole family, perhaps even worse than staying together. Fritz's parents, Gail and Gord, believe that Fritz had a duty to stay with Mame and the kids "'until death do you part." Gord and Gail have made Fritz feel very guilty about leaving them. Mame's sister Myrtle has been encouraging Mame to "make Fritz pay!" Myrtle referred Mame to a lawyer of questionable ethics who has been known to drag families through courts for years, initiating mudslinging and false claims. Mame has accused Fritz of everything from being a transsexual to having hidden millions of dollars in offshore bank accounts, with her lawyer prodding her on. Although none of Mame's accusations have proven true, Fritz and Mame have spent more than $190,000 in legal fees. Family court judges required them to try mediation on three separate occasions. During the last mediation, they finally reached an agreement about custody, visitation, and financial issues. Unfortunately, conflict has continued, with both making allegations and counterallegations. Last week, Ikis committed suicide. He left a note saying, "All I wanted was peace." Fritz blames Mame, whom he views as a narcissistic nutcase who has used the children as pawns in their separation process. Mame blames Fritz, whom she accuses of being immoral and unfit to parent, particularly because he is now living with a young bimbo named Bambi. Bambi and Mame have never met. Daphne actually likes Bambi, but Daphne has become very broody and isolated since her brother's suicide. The court has assigned Francine, a family court counselor, to help the family deal with their current issues. Francine has experience using many different types of CR interventions and is well suited to designing and implementing an appropriate intervention for this family.

Peace is not an absence of war. It is a virtue, a state of mind,
a disposition for benevolence, confidence, justice.

—Baruch Spinoza

Conclusion

The "conclusion" of a book usually tries to resolve unanswered questions and bring outstanding issues to closure. Hopefully, the readings and exercises in this text have raised many questions, and hopefully, you have begun to find answers for yourself. As when you practice CR with clients, finding answers for yourself is more empowering than having others impose their answers. Given the enormity of issues raised in this text and the fact that many have no universal truths, trying to bring closure to all issues would be infeasible. Instead, this conclusion focuses on five questions:

- Is conflict resolution a collection of strategies, techniques, and skills; a group of practice models; or a distinct profession?
- If it is a profession, what type of qualifications are required to practice as a CR professional?
- How can helping professionals develop a comprehensive CR system, rather than a loose patchwork of CR processes that may or may not address the needs of the community or organization it serves?
- How can a helping professional develop an integrated model of practice to guide his or her work?
- How can helping professionals participate in the ongoing development of the CR movement?

Although this chapter answers some questions, it is likely to raise even more. After all, learning CR is an ongoing process.

STRATEGIES, TECHNIQUES, SKILLS, MODELS, OR PROFESSION

Conflict resolution is a dynamic and growing field. Although many aspects of CR can be found in the long-standing practices of the helping professions, these were not always viewed as CR interventions. Some writers question whether CR is a collection of techniques, a group of practice models, or a distinct profession. Perhaps it is all three.

First, CR offers a range of strategies, techniques, and skills that helping professionals can use in various contexts: clinical interventions, interactions with coprofessionals, advocacy for clients, and negotiation with systems in the client's social environment (families, workplaces, schools, healthcare providers, etc.). Viewed in this way, CR allows practitioners to select various strategies, techniques, or skills based on their own methods and models of practice. Practitioners who operate in this manner would not identify themselves as mediators, arbitrators, or other types of conflict resolution practitioners but rather as psychotherapists, social workers, nurses, educators, family counselors, or whatever other professional identifications they have. In other words, conflict resolution is something that helping professionals do, but it does not govern their entire practice, and it does not define who they are.

CR could also be seen as a bundle of practice models—for example, interest-based negotiation, therapeutic mediation, identity-based facilitation, and rights-based advocacy. A practitioner jointly assesses a situation with a client (or clients), and they determine which CR model is most likely to be effective. The practitioner's choice of strategies, techniques, and skills is driven by the theoretical approach of the chosen CR model.

Finally, some helping professionals not only adopt CR models or techniques but also adopt the persona of a CR professional. This includes a distinct value system and knowledge base. From this perspective, CR pervades not only what helping professionals do but who they are (Mayer, 2004a). Helping professionals possess a variety of skills and attributes that allow them to move smoothly into CR personas, such as negotiators, mediator, group facilitators, evaluators, and advocates. As Chapter 7 illustrates, new roles such as parenting coordinators are emerging, and traditional roles such as spiritual healers continue to evolve, providing new ways for helping professionals to incorporate CR into how they practice and how they self-identify.

In spite of optimistic trends in CR, this field still faces a number of serious challenges. Although the evolving nature of CR is dynamic and exciting, CR does need to define itself more clearly. What does it stand for, what does it mean in practice, and is it truly distinct from other approaches to practice among helping professionals? Among CR methods, mediation and negotiation possess the most advanced levels of theoretical development, ethical codification, standards for accreditation, and empirical research (English & Neilson, 2004; Menkel-Meadow & Wheeler, 2004). Practitioners, ethicists, and scholars need to continue to work together to refine various methods of CR, ensuring they are value driven, theoretically sound, and clinically effective. Do not be surprised if some methods and models of CR that are in vogue today fall into disrepute as we gain more experience and research knowledge.

The following section looks at the qualifications required to claim status as a CR professional (as opposed to "just anyone" who uses a smattering of conflict resolution techniques, strategies, skills, or models of practice).

QUALIFICATIONS

The interdisciplinary nature of CR encourages helping professionals to work together and learn from one another. However, CR professionals are not immune to turf wars as various groups lay claim to different areas of practice. To deal with such problems, CR professionals need to use CR skills not only with clients but among themselves.

One of the key issues is the question of what standards, if any, should be required for a practitioner to qualify as a specific type of CR professional. Family mediators and attorneys are two examples of CR professionals with specific systems for accreditation and licensing. Although some people view mandatory regulation as a way of ensuring competent, responsible CR practice, in some areas of CR, restricting practice to "qualified professionals" may not be appropriate. These include peer mediation in schools, informal or emergent CR roles assumed by helping professionals as part of their ordinary practice, and lay advocacy to promote health, justice, and other social causes.

When determining what types of qualifications, if any, are needed to practice CR, the following guidelines should be considered:

- In order to provide broad access to CR services, restricting CR practice to certain groups should be avoided unless the risks of unregulated practice are too high (where there are severe legal issues or safety concerns, where CR users are particularly vulnerable because of mental capacity, etc.).
- Any requirements for qualification should be based on what a practitioner needs in order to practice in a competent manner—that is, what values, skills, and knowledge a practitioner must possess in order to provide effective CR services.[1]
- Different qualifications are required for different CR processes and different contexts of practice. A victim-offender mediator, for example, needs to know about the effects of victimization, whereas a patient advocate needs to know about hospital procedures.
- If practice in certain areas of CR is restricted to "qualified" professionals, ensure that the qualifications do not have any systemic biases against particular cultural groups.[2]
- Any association that establishes standards for CR should have broad-based representation to ensure that it does not become self-serving or biased. Include consumers of the CR services, if possible.
- Any association that regulates CR professionals should adopt CR processes that are consistent with CR values and knowledge—for example, using mediation to try to resolve client concerns before moving toward more adversarial processes, such as disciplinary hearings (Feld & Simm, 1998).

---

[1]Historically, some CR licensing and accreditation requirements have required degrees in law or mental health, or "any master's-level" professional education. Such standards, though easy to apply, do not necessarily relate to the actual values, skills, and knowledge required to practice CR. They may be impeding competent people from practicing, simply because they do not have the right degrees, and allowing others to practice even if they do not have the requisite skills, values, and knowledge base (e.g., some people with law degrees have no specific training in negotiation, mediation, or other collaborative approaches to CR; they are only trained in the adversarial model).

[2]For instance, people from some cultural groups have stigmas about mental health and may be less likely to pursue a degree in psychology or another mental health profession. If CR accreditation is limited to mental health professionals, this cultural group will be underrepresented, even if there are many people from the group capable of serving in a competent manner. High costs for training may also be a barrier for cultural groups with high rates of low income.

Recent trends suggest, on one hand, greater movement toward professionalization and accreditation of CR practitioners (see Appendix 4 for a list of professional associations). On the other hand, grassroots organizations such as neighborhood justice centers continue to use lay community members to provide mediation and other CR services. When considering whether to regulate CR, heed concerns about who regulation benefits and how.

Now that we have explored different systems for regulating CR professionals, we turn next to developing systems that can help organizations deal with conflict more effectively.

DESIGNING CONFLICT RESOLUTION SYSTEMS

Throughout much of this text, we have explored how to intervene once specific conflicts have arisen. Although helping people work through conflicts on a case-by-case basis is useful, we can often achieve broader, more effective, and more efficient results by establishing a CR system that helps people handle conflict as it arises and on an ongoing basis. Having a comprehensive CR system ensures that CR processes are appropriately matched to the needs of the people it serves. It also ensures smooth links and transitions between various stages of the CR process (Mayer, 2000). The purpose of a CR system is not to prevent or stop conflict altogether but rather to help people deal with conflict in a positive manner. As noted throughout this book, different professionals and different clients will have different ideas about what is a positive way of handling conflict. Accordingly, when helping a particular group develop a CR system, you will need to help the group articulate its core goals and values—for instance, peace, harmonious relations, social justice, mental health, democracy, economic efficiency, respect, high morale, spiritual growth, fairness, freedom from reprisal, or mutual understanding. Rather than imposing a "one-size-fits-all" CR system, you will then tailor the system to meet the goals and values of the group. The following guidelines provide a framework for developing a CR system.

1. *Building a culture of CR*—Whether you are working with a family, business organization, community, or other social system, each unit develops its own norms, values, and preferred methods for dealing with conflict. Rather than imposing a completely foreign conflict resolution system, assess the current CR culture. For instance, do people tend to avoid conflict or embrace it? Who traditionally plays which CR roles within the system? What are people's attitudes toward authority, status, and saving face? When do people from the system seek outside CR help? What types of CR are viewed positively and negatively? Once you have an understanding of the current culture, you can help the system build on its strengths in a manner that respects existing culture but also encourages it to evolve in a positive manner (Lederach, 2005). If a social agency values "working as a team," for instance, various employees may interpret this as everyone must think alike and agree with everyone else. In working with this agency, you could validate its value for the team concept but help build a culture where expressing differences in a respectful manner is an integral part of being a team. By working with the unit to enhance its CR system in an incremental

manner, you can ensure broad-based buy-in. People must have confidence in the system or they will resist using it (Brahm & Ouellet, 2003).

2. *Self-determination*—Promote CR alternatives where people make decisions themselves. Choices within the CR system should be should be transparent, accessible, easy to understand, and easy to use (Mayer, 2000). Providing people with choice helps them feel more empowered and trusts them to identify the processes which best meet their needs. A CR system may include incentives to try certain types of CR that promote overall organizational interests or public policy. If the system requires people to use certain types of CR processes, the justification for doing so should be clearly articulated. When concerns about patient abuse arise, for instance, a healthcare system may be required to appoint an advocate to assist the patient. A CR system might involve CR consultants whom individuals can consult on a confidential basis for help determining the best approach to handling a conflict. Sexual harassment officers, for example, often play this type of role. Victims of harassment may not know what alternatives are available, or they may have concerns about retribution. By talking to a CR consultant or harassment officer, they can make informed decisions about the best way to proceed.

3. *Loop-backs*—The system should allow for loop-backs, meaning that if a conflict progresses to more formal and adversarial stages, mechanisms should allow the parties to circle back to less formal or less adversarial stages (Ury, Brett, & Goldberg, 1988). Unfortunately, once people enter a formal CR process, they tend to be swept along, without having an opportunity to turn back. A CR system could include cooling-off periods or structured time-outs, to help people consider whether they want to revert back to a more informal or more collaborative process. When people initiate a proceeding in court or arbitration, for instance, they do not necessarily have to continue the process through to fruition. Often, the parties realize which direction a case is headed, and they decide to settle before a final determination is made, potentially helping them save costs, save face, and come up with a more creative solution than adjudication might offer (Brahm & Ouellet, 2003).

4. *Proactive CR*—As you are developing a system, consider potential conflict situations and employ processes that can address them before they arise: (a) scheduling periodic planning meetings; (b) providing clients with clear policies, indicating the expectations, services, and limitations of the agency; and (c) providing CR training so that people know how to manage conflict in constructive manners, before critical problems arise. Remember, the purpose is not to quash all conflicts but to provide mechanisms for handling them more effectively.

5. *Informal CR*—When conflict arises, encourage parties to deal with it informally, on a face-to-face basis. Third-party interveners may be unnecessary, costly, and disempowering. When people resort to formal means too quickly, they may also become more adversarial (Ury et al., 1988). Although informal CR suggests the parties involved in the conflict must take primary responsibility for resolving it, the CR system can provide them with various forms of support, for instance, teaching them communication skills and problem-solving frameworks. Leaders within the family, community, or organization can also offer support by modeling

constructive CR skills and approaches (e.g., using active listening skills and being open to receiving criticism). The informal level of the CR system should be easy to access and unfettered by bureaucracy. If two neighbors are having an argument, for instance, the local community center could provide them with a free meeting room, without requiring them to hire a mediator or other CR professional. Unless there are significant power imbalances or safety issues, encourage people to first try to negotiate on a one-to-one basis, without the use of advocates.

6. *Formal collaborative CR*—If informal CR is ineffective or inappropriate, a more formal process may be necessary. This does not mean, however, that the process has to be adversarial. Interest-based negotiation, transformative mediation, and structured dialogues are examples of collaborative processes to consider. These approaches help people resolve conflict on the basis of needs, interests, mutual understanding, and empowerment, rather than by rights or power. They also help parties improve relationships and communication, as well as simply resolving the immediate conflict (Mayer, 2004a). Helping professionals may assume roles as mediators, advocates, or facilitators. Decision-making power rests with the parties. Still, helping professionals may assume power-balancing roles, to ensure the process is fair.

7. *Formal adjudicative processes*—This stage removes decision-making power from the parties and gives it to an impartial third party who uses a rights-based approach to determining conflicts. Judges, arbitrators, assessors, and investigators are examples of adjudicators. Helping professionals can assume the roles of arbitrators, assessors, investigators, witnesses, and advocates in such processes. Because most helping professionals value client self-determination, they may be reluctant to assume a role where they make decisions for clients. Such a role may be justified if other processes have failed.

8. *Separate power-based action*—More forceful interventions may be necessary in order to secure mental health, social justice, or other client needs (Germain & Gitterman, 1996). Using the least force necessary to achieve such results minimizes costs and risks of retaliation. Even if one must resort to competitive strategies, consider the possibility of healing relationships in the future (Pruitt & Carnevale, 1993).

9. *Peacebuilding*—CR systems should include components for building peace in the broadest sense. Rather than merely focusing on ending conflicts, a peacebuilding approach promotes respect, reconciliation, openness, mutual caring, and collaboration (see Chapter 7 for details on how to build physical, psychological, social, and spiritual capacities for peace). Whereas people involved in disputes may often settle for absence of violence or overt conflict, families, communities, and organizations can promote more positive forms of peace, which benefits both the individuals and the social unit as a whole.

10. *Ethical issues*—The system should provide clear policies on how it will manage ethical concerns such as informed consent, confidentiality, power imbalances, conflict of interest, and safety issues (British Columbia Ministry of the Attorney General, 2003). For instance, how will the system ensure that people are properly informed about their choices and feel free to decide whether to participate in a particular CR process, without fear of coercion or retribution? To what

extent will information shared by specific individuals be kept confidential, and when (if ever) will information be shared with others? What types of safety concerns are likely to arise, and how can these be managed?

11. *Feedback*—CR systems should include mechanisms for monitoring and evaluating CR processes. This will allow the system to determine how well it is working, as well as how it might be improved (Grinnell & Unrau, 2005). Some systems, for example, look great in theory but have problems in implementation: too few resources, insufficient training for CR staff, lack of coordination between different parts of the CR system, poor communication concerning the availability of different types of support for CR, or hidden disincentives from using CR processes. Program evaluations typically provide feedback for CR professionals, but evaluators may also provide feedback to the parties about their CR efforts and how they could improve on them when future conflicts arise. Although it may be expedient to have CR professionals gather data on their work, it may be helpful to have independent evaluators gather information from people using the CR system. By having external evaluators, people can provide feedback on a confidential basis, without fear of repercussions should their feedback be negative.

No CR system is perfect, so there is always room for improvement. Helping a family, organization, or community improve its CR system may take time, so CR professionals must look at developing CR systems as a longer-term venture. Some initiatives may be implemented relatively quickly. Others may take longer, in order to garner support, ensure that there are proper resources, and ensure that implementation has a high chance of success (British Columbia Ministry of the Attorney General, 2003).

AN INTEGRATIVE MODEL OF PRACTICE

The previous section explored how to develop a comprehensive CR system for an organization, community, or other social unit. This section describes how individual CR practitioners can develop their own models of practice, whether or not they are working within a comprehensive CR system. CR training materials often prescribe what to do and how to do it. For instance, if you take a course on interest-based mediation, all you will learn is interest-based mediation, and you may be left with the impression that this is the only valid approach to mediation. Throughout this text, I have tried to present a range of approaches to CR, so that you can select the most appropriate ones for you and the clients or people you will be serving. Some practitioners say they are *eclectic,* meaning that they pick and choose CR skills, strategies, and approaches as they see fit. The problem with an eclectic approach is that it is not guided by a specific set of values and theories. Rather than adopting an eclectic approach, I suggest developing an integrative model of practice. An integrative model draws from different approaches, but it clearly articulates the values, theories, and research that guide the practitioner's choice of what to use and when (Corey & Corey, 2006).

In terms of values, you will need to consider your own values, as well as the values of your agency and clients. Refer back to the personal values about CR that you identified for yourself in Chapter 2, Exercise 2. Consider whether these have changed given your readings and experiences throughout this course. Consider also your professional values as expressed in your profession's code of ethics. For instance, nurses value caring, social workers value social justice, and psychologists value mental health. Your model of CR practice should be consonant with your value system. A teacher who values knowledge, for example, may choose to focus on methods of CR that educate students—that is, providing them with the knowledge they need to practice CR on their own rather than acting as a mediator, judge, or other third-party conflict resolver for the students. In contrast, a lawyer who values civil rights may focus her model of practice on rights-based advocacy.

Although professionals' own values affect their choice of how to practice, professionals must also consider the values of the agency and clients they serve. Agency values are typically reflected in its mission statement, goals, and policies. A shelter serving survivors of intimate partner abuse, for instance, will place high value on the safety of its clients. Given this value, it would not be appropriate for shelter staff to use methods of CR that put their clients at risk of being further abused (e.g., reconciliation counseling).

In terms of client values, professionals should consider the general value systems of the client groups they typically serve, as well as the specific values of the actual clients they are serving. When I began working with the Ismaili community, for instance, I needed to learn more about the values of this community (e.g., care, compassion, and community). I also needed to consider within-group differences, not assuming that all Ismailis shared exactly the same values. The Ismaili community has a worldwide structure of conciliation and arbitration boards (Keshavjee & Whatling, 2005). Whereas many Ismailis prefer to use these services because they reflect community values, some prefer to use services that are not Ismaili-specific, because, for instance, they want to keep their issues private from their close-knit community.

As noted in Chapter 1, many theories can be used to help make sense of why conflict arises and how practitioners can intervene to help people deal with conflict more effectively. If you believe that conflict primarily arises because of problems in communication, your model of practice may incorporate specific skills, strategies, and approaches that reflect communication theory. If you believe that some conflicts become intractable because the parties have fixed views of themselves as victims and of the others as evil doers, then you may adopt identity-based approaches in your model of practice.

Most practitioners will not limit themselves to one theory to guide their practice, recognizing that no single theory can explain all conflict situations. However, saying that you accept and use all theories is equally problematic. First, some theories may not be valid. Second, some theories conflict with each other, meaning that you cannot apply both equally. Bush and Folger (2005), for instance, argue that interest-based mediation is incompatible with transformative mediation, and they should not be mixed. Third, in order to be able to apply theory to practice in a rational manner, a model of practice must indicate the relationships between theories and how they apply in different situations. When I mediate with separating couples, for instance, I make use of family systems theory, recognizing that I can use this theory to help couples negotiate new roles, rules, and boundaries (Irving & Benjamin, 2002). When I mediate with community organizations, however, family systems theory is not relevant. Instead, I incorporate organizational theories, such as management styles theory, to guide my CR processes (Kirst-Ashman & Hull, 2005).

Research should also inform your CR practice. Helping professionals have an ethical duty to provide services that are based on the current state of knowledge in the field. A CR professional who uses a particular intervention that is known to be ineffective may be liable for malpractice. Because many CR approaches are new or still evolving, there may be limited research on their effectiveness. If you decide to be a parenting coordinator, for instance, you will need to pay particular attention to emerging research: Under what situations, if any, is it helpful? What are the risks of parenting coordination? How can parenting coordinators practice in a manner that maximizes the benefits and minimizes the risks?

Your model of CR practice is likely to grow as you develop as a professional. As a novice, you may decide to focus on one particular approach, learning how to apply its strategies, techniques, and skills. Initially, you may limit your practice to cases that fit with this model and your current level of competence. As you develop professionally, you may add other theories, methods, and approaches to your repertoire, and you may be able to serve a broader range of clients. You will also learn how to respond to particular conflict situations more fluidly and more artistically, being acutely conscious of what is going on and making deliberate decisions about how to proceed.

SUPPORTING DEVELOPMENT OF CONFLICT RESOLUTION

For many helping professionals, CR is not just a set of skills, theories, interventions, or models of practice but rather a passion or a way of life. If you feel the passion of CR and want to become more connected with the CR movement, you can participate in its development in several ways:

- Training CR practitioners
- Providing public education and CR promotion
- Planning and developing community-based CR programs
- Working with CR associations
- Advocating for public policies that foster the CR movement

The following sections discuss each of these roles.

1. Training CR Practitioners

People who learn CR often become so enamored with it that they want to share it with others. Teaching others CR strategies, techniques, and skills helps spread their use and empowers people to resolve conflicts on their own. Because CR is a practice-based profession, prospective trainers must ensure that they are not only competent at practicing CR but also competent at teaching it (Honeyman, Hughes, & Schneider, 2003; Wheeler, 2006).

The role of a trainer is similar to that of a coach: to provide knowledge, strategies, constructive feedback, and motivational support. Trainers must be able to model effective CR, because people learn by seeing as well as by hearing about, discussing, and doing CR themselves.

Some branches of CR have specific requirements for training. Family mediation courses are typically 40 to 60 hours long. Their content may be determined by specific bodies that accredit mediators. Some jurisdictions have laws mandating certain types of training and accreditation standards. In other jurisdictions, independent associations have their voluntary standards (see Appendix 4 for a list of CR associations). Some courses provide certificates for completion of the course, without any testing to ensure that students have actually learned what they were supposed to learn. Other courses use written tests, live role-plays, or videotaped role-plays to test student knowledge and skill (English & Neilson, 2004).

Ideally, training is individualized to meet the needs of the particular trainees: (a) the trainer identifies the core competencies required for practice, (b) the trainer assesses which competencies each participant possesses and which each needs to work on, (c) the course is tailored to provide knowledge and experience where needed, and (d) the participants are tested at the end of the training to determine whether they have reached required levels of competence. For example, helping professionals may enter CR training with excellent facilitation skills. If they do not know the legal issues relevant to their proposed area of CR practice (e.g., child welfare), the course should focus on filling this need. Interdisciplinary classes are useful, so that people from different professional backgrounds can learn from one another (Severson, 1998). In contrast to the ideal, most existing courses have fixed content and do not allow for individualized learning based on the specific needs and interests of the trainees.

Written materials for training programs generally focus on one approach to CR practice (Folger & Bush, 2001). Hopefully, this model has a theoretical basis and empirical research support, though trainees should not assume this is always true. Trainers use case examples and illustrations to demonstrate how the model is put into practice (Kestner & Ray, 2002). Supplementary readings can be used to broaden the scope of the training.

One of the most important parts of training is a CR internship or practicum (Birkhoff & Warfield, 1997). Lectures, readings, discussions, and role-plays provide trainees with CR basics. An internship ensures that trainees are ready to practice on their own. Ideally, an internship offers trainees the opportunity to observe an experienced CR practitioner, as well as the opportunity to cofacilitate with the experienced practitioner. During the first two or three sessions, the experienced practitioner takes most of the responsibility for facilitating the process. Gradually, the trainee assumes more and more responsibility. The experienced practitioner provides feedback and support and is able to intervene to assist the trainee where necessary. This type of cofacilitation ensures that clients receive competent CR services, even when one of the practitioners is inexperienced. Eventually, the experienced practitioner determines that the trainee is ready to handle cases without a cofacilitator.

Unfortunately, many training programs do not offer internships. Internships can be time-consuming and costly. In addition, trainers with private CR practices are often reluctant to expose their clients to inexperienced trainees. An alternative to internships is for the newly trained practitioners to hire experienced CR practitioners to act as consultants during their first few cases. New CR practitioners can also volunteer at community CR centers in order to gain experience.

In addition to training people to be formal CR professionals, some trainers teach people conflict resolution skills that they can use as emergent CR practitioners. Some CR courses are designed specifically for groups such as students, business managers, clergy, politicians, or community leaders from different cultural groups.

In order to develop as a professional trainer, consider taking courses in teaching and learning, as well as reading adult education literature (Knowles, 2005; Schwarz, Davidson, Carlson, & McKinney, 2005; Severson, 1998). Obtain feedback from trainees and cotrainers. If resources permit, conduct follow-up research so that you can receive more structured feedback.

2. Public Education and Promotion

Unless specific CR methods have already been entrenched in your community and culture, public education and promotion are crucial to the development of such services. Consider a proposal to use family group conferences (FGCs) in a particular community. Public education informs people about the FGC process, its uses, its advantages, and its disadvantages. Rather than describing FGCs as a panacea, presenting a balanced view of FGCs offers greater credibility. Public education can take many forms: articles in newspapers or local newsletters, speaking engagements with community groups, or workshops for potential referral sources, such as lawyers and helping professionals. Two of the best ways for the public to learn about mediation are to see it in action and to participate in role-plays. Radio, television, the World Wide Web, and other media can be used to reach mass audiences. Court-TV broadcasts trials 24 hours a day. Why not at least one weekly spot on mediation, FGCs, or healing circles?

Promotion can be aimed at the general public or specific referral sources (e.g., teachers, physicians, counselors, community leaders, lawyers, clergy). Business cards, brochures, posters, telephone book advertisements, and other promotional materials should be customized for each intended audience: language should be clear, claims about the particular method of CR should have empirical support, and the format should project professionalism.

Promotional materials generally include a description of the specific CR process, the CR practitioner's credentials, the types of cases that are appropriate, and how to contact the practitioner for further information or referral. Some practitioners offer a free information session for each party. Referral sources and prospective clients often find it useful to have the practitioner's curriculum vitae in order to determine the practitioner's level of training and experience. Reputation and word of mouth tend to be the most powerful forms of promotion.

Some CR associations produce listings of CR practitioners and promotional materials for their members. Public education and promotion are time-consuming and expensive. In order to share the burden, some private mediators work in partnership to promote their practices or CR in general.

3. Planning and Developing CR Programs[3]

Conflict resolution has a certain allure that gets people excited about creating new programs. After all, various CR programs promote peace, collaboration, and self-determination. Who can argue with goals like these? Successful implementation of a CR program, however, requires more than just a good idea and well-intentioned enthusiasm. Many programs have failed because of a lack of planning and follow-through.

When planning a CR program, developers should consider the following issues: program goals and objectives, target population, appropriate issues, alternative CR approaches, qualifications of practitioners, program policies, and research. To illustrate, consider a mediation pilot project designed for students at Conflictia Elementary School. The guidance counselor, Ms. Gandy, establishes a committee of teachers and students to help her develop the program.

Goals are the broad aims of the program. In this case, the committee decides that the primary goal of the program is to promote peaceful resolution of conflicts among students. *Objectives are desired, measurable outcomes that are based on the program goals* (Grinnell & Unrau, 2005). Objectives for the school program include the following: students will resolve their own conflicts; they will learn conflict CR skills; they will deal with anger and other emotions constructively; they will communicate feelings about violence; and they will think creatively about alternative solutions (Morse & Andrea, 1994).

Target population refers to the individuals or groups that the program hopes to attract to its services. The target population for the school program includes all students who are involved in conflict at Conflictia Elementary. Some school-based mediation programs include teacher-student conflict, but this does not fit with the program's initial goal and objectives. This is a peer mediation program, because both the mediators and the parties are students. The program is intended to be a voluntary program. Although teachers and fellow students may refer the parties to mediation, the parties are free to reject mediation without fear of negative consequences for refusing to mediate. In practice, students may feel pressured to participate, because teachers maintain authority over them, including the power to discipline them for inappropriate behavior during school hours. Initially, the program will be offered to Grade 4 and 5 students, with plans to expand the program to the whole school within two years.

Appropriate issues are the types of conflicts that the CR program is designed to help parties resolve. The planning committee provides broad latitude for appropriate (or mediatable) issues: cross-cultural conflicts, gang-related issues, disputes in the classroom or on the sports fields, and bullying complaints between students. Intake staff for the mediation program will screen out any cases involving immediate risks

---

[3]Whereas the earlier section on "Designing Conflict Resolution Systems" dealt with how to create a comprehensive system for dealing with conflicts, this section focuses on creating a specific program (e.g., a parenting coordination program, as opposed to a system that included mediation, family group conferences, circling, and other court diversion programs).

to either student's safety. The program will not mediate cases involving drugs and weapons, because school policy says such cases need to be handled by teachers or school administration.

The CR approaches chosen should reflect the goals of the program and the needs of the target population. The committee reviews the literature on mediation in schools (Association for Conflict Resolution, n.d.; Hessler, Hollis, & Crowe, 1998; Kaplan, 1997). Because the primary goal of the program is "peaceful resolution," the committee selects an interest-based approach. In this case, the mediators will be Grade 4 and Grade 5 students. The approach will be simplified in order to tailor it to their cognitive abilities and levels of social skills. At a very basic level, mediation can be reduced to three questions:

- What happened?
- What did you hear ___ say?
- How can we work out this problem so that both of you are happy and friendly to each other?[4]

The first question facilitates storytelling. The second question helps the parties develop mutual understandings. The last question focuses the students on collaborative problem solving. For some settings, having a choice of CR approaches is desirable. Different approaches can be used for different circumstances. Given the age of the mediators in the school program, the committee decides to keep it simple and focus on one model.

Practitioner qualifications include knowledge, skills, and values. Some school programs select peer mediators according to who already possesses the best conflict resolution skills. These tend to be the "keenest," the "brightest," and the "most well-behaved" students. Other schools select "bullies" and "troublemakers" to be their mediators. First, these are students who have the greatest need to learn constructive CR skills. Second, if the school can enlist their help, then other students with similar backgrounds will be more likely to use the services. Ms. Gandy's committee decides to empower students by allowing them to determine who the mediators will be. Each class will elect six peer mediators. The mediators will participate in a training program conducted by experts from the school board. Role-plays will be used to evaluate each mediator's level of competence. If a mediator falls below the desired level, further training and coaching will be offered.

Policy issues include terms of confidentiality, impartiality, payment, and participation of people who are not directly involved in the conflict. Because this program is offered within the context of a school system, blanket confidentiality cannot be assured. Teachers will not participate directly in the mediation sessions; however, the mediators will report to the two teachers responsible for the program for supervision and consultation. Issues pertaining to drugs and safety must be reported. Information from mediation will not be shared with other students, unless the parties agree.

---

[4]For other examples of teaching children constructive conflict resolution skills, see Association for Conflict Resolution (n.d.).

Because this is a peer mediation program, mediators will know the parties and may even be friends with one or both. If the parties do not believe that a certain mediator can be impartial, then they can request another mediator. Students will not be permitted to bring a lawyer to the mediation session (yes, some have asked to do so). The mediation services will be provided by the student volunteers, who will not receive any payments for their services. The mediators will use an oral Agreement to Mediate, in order to keep the process informal. Any agreements reached in mediation will not be legally binding agreements, also to keep the process informal. Students will not be required to pay for using the mediation services, particularly given that they are minors and may not have the means to pay. Students who participate in mediation may be invited to volunteer for mediation training and to act as peer mediators in the future.

Evaluative research explores the extent to which the program is meeting its objectives (Grinnell & Unrau, 2005). In this case, the school enlists the help of a graduate student at the local university to design and conduct the research component. The researcher establishes measures and questionnaires for each of the objectives identified. The researcher also conducts interviews with mediators and parties in order to obtain qualitative feedback. This information will be used for further program development. The principal and the school board will not allocate staff time and other resources to the program unless it can demonstrate its effectiveness.

Program start-up requires a lot of time and energy: to get stakeholders on side, to secure funding, to set up a location, to select and train CR practitioners, and to publicize for cases. Once a program is in place, continuity requires that practitioners and staff have sufficient resources and support. Because conflict tends to be emotional, CR can be very taxing. In order to reduce the risk of stress and burnout, practitioners should have opportunities for debriefing in supervision or peer consultation. They should also receive training in self-care and how to prevent vicarious trauma[5] (Trippany, White Kress, & Wilcoxon, 2004).

4. CR Associations

CR associations support the field of CR in a number of ways: providing conferences, trainings, and other educational support for practitioners; acting as regulatory bodies that license or accredit CR professionals; providing malpractice insurance and other professional benefits for practitioner-members; lobbying government to support various CR endeavors; and offering information about CR to the public and potential clients. Different associations offer different combinations of these services. The Association for Conflict Resolution is one of the largest CR associations. It comprises many fields of practice, including family mediation, spirituality, workplace dispute resolution, education, criminal justice, healthcare, and international CR (for contact information for this and other CR associations, see Appendix 4). Many national associations also have state, provincial, or regional chapters.

---

[5]Harmful reactions experienced by a helping professional who hears or is otherwise exposed to client trauma.

Because professions are regulated on a state or provincial basis, you will need to check with your own state or province to see whether it has mandated regulatory bodies. Some jurisdictions require licensing or accreditation in order to practice in a certain area (e.g., family mediation, labor arbitration, or parenting coordination). In other jurisdictions, membership in professional associations is purely voluntary. Regulation of CR practitioners is intended to ensure competence and accountability: by establishing standards for education and supervised internships, by establishing a binding code of ethical conduct, and by establishing grievance procedures for clients who have complaints.

Helping professionals have a number of incentives to join a relevant CR association, even where licensure is not required: to show support for the professionalization of the field, to show potential clients they have met certain standards and are willing to be held accountable for their practice, and to have a say in the further development of the profession.

Grievance procedures and accountability vary across CR associations. Some have no grievance procedures against their members. These associations do not warrant that their members abide by any specific standards of practice or competency. Members are simply people who have paid membership dues. Other associations require members (or certain categories of practicing members) to have certain types of training, experience, and competence. These associations require some type of mechanism to hold members accountable to their standards. Some associations offer collaborative methods, such as mediation, to help professionals and clients resolve disputes (Feld & Simm, 1998). Others hold formal disciplinary hearings, paradoxically similar to those in the court system.

Some proponents of mediation oppose the development of professional CR associations. They believe that professionalizing mediation depreciates the value of traditional mediators. As noted earlier, educational standards set by associations limit access to the profession to those who can afford the requisite courses. Professionalization also encourages conformity to certain models of practice. In the absence of research to show which models are superior, society may be better off with CR practitioners offering a broad range of models. Still, concerns about competent, ethical, and accountable practice seem to dictate the ongoing professionalization of mediation, at least in certain areas of practice.

5. Public Policy Development

Individual mediators and mediation associations have advanced the causes of CR with varying degrees of success in different jurisdictions and areas of practice. Various methods of CR have been sold to public policymakers as money-saving ventures, as ways to resolve labor disputes without strikes or work stoppages, as means of diverting cases away from court, as ways to stop violence in schools, and as ways to transform how people interact when faced with conflict. To some extent, research backs up these claims (Beck, Sales, & Emery, 2004; Bush & Folger, 2004; Crow, Marsh, & Holton, 2004; Oetzel & Ting-Toomey, 2006). Further research is obviously needed for most fields of CR (Deutch & Coleman, 2000; Druckman, 2005).

Ongoing public policy issues include

- whether licensing should be required in order for CR professionals to practice in certain fields;
- whether people should be required to try mediation, family group conferences, or other collaborative CR alternatives before they have access to adversarial processes such as court, arbitration, labor strikes, or grievance hearings; and
- whether to subsidize the cost of specific types of CR with public funding.

The answers to these matters will certainly vary depending on the method of CR, as well as the context in which it is being considered—family law, mental health, labor, community, and so on. Various CR practitioners, researchers, theorists, and program administrators have different views on these issues. Interestingly, conflict resolution within the conflict resolution community can be a greater challenge than gaining political support from government officials. When the CR community speaks with the voice of consensus, public policy makers are more likely to listen.

PARTING THOUGHTS

Whether we are talking about families, communities, social agencies, healthcare institutions, workplaces, or nations, conflict is inevitable in any social relationship. The challenge is to turn what could be demoralizing, frustrating, stressful, and damaging into something that is energizing, healing, visionary, and constructive . . . for ourselves and the people we serve.

KEY POINTS

- Helping professionals can use conflict resolution in a variety of ways: as a collection of strategies, techniques, and skills that they can incorporate into their traditional methods of practice; as a group of theory-based practice models that they can use to help people deal with conflict; or as professional personas that guide not only what they do and how they do it, but also their values, knowledge, and professional identities.

- Professional accreditation or licensing requirements can be used to raise standards of competency and provide clients with recourse for grievances, but such requirements may also unduly limit who can provide certain types of CR services.

- Developing a comprehensive CR system can help an organization or community deal with conflict more effectively and efficiently by providing members with an array of CR choices and incentives to resolve conflicts proactively, informally, and collaboratively, rather than reactively, formally, and adversarially.

- Helping professionals can develop their own integrative model of CR practice by articulating the values and theories that guide their practice and by selecting methods and approaches to practice that fit with these values and theories. An integrative model of practice must also take agency context, research evidence, and client needs and values into account.

- Helping professionals can support the ongoing development of the CR movement by becoming involved as CR trainers, educators, program planners, members of CR associations, and advocates for public policies that foster or sustain constructive methods of conflict resolution.

DISCUSSION QUESTIONS AND EXERCISES

1. ONGOING PROFESSIONAL DEVELOPMENT: Review your written exercises from throughout the course. Summarize the changes that have occurred in terms of your values and attitudes toward conflict. Identify your strengths in the field of CR. Describe the skills and models of intervention that you want to improve on. Identify readings, training programs, conferences, or practical experiences that you could use for next steps in professional development (note the professional resources listed in Appendix 4).

2. LICENSING: What are the advantages of requiring licensing for a specific type of CR professional (e.g., family mediators, workplace grievance arbitrators, parenting coordinators, governmental ombudspersons)? What are the disadvantages? How is licensing different from certifying or accrediting CR professionals?

3. CR SYSTEM: Identify an agency that you believe could use a CR element in its programming. Describe the existing concerns and a rationale for developing a CR service. Construct a CR system that addresses the agency's needs. Identify how to evaluate success of the proposed system.

4. INTEGRATIVE MODELS: For each of the following scenarios, develop and describe a CR model or approach to practice that fits with the values, theories, and contextual concerns expressed in the scenario:
   a. Ibrahim is an imam (spiritual leader in the Islamic faith) who wants to help members of his community reconcile their relationships. He is particularly concerned about families that have had long-standing feuds. Ibrahim values forgiveness and believes that existential theory could be used to inform his work.
   b. Pacita is a public health nurse. She works with people who have tested HIV-positive. She is interested in developing a CR model to help her assist clients who are reluctant to tell intimate partners that they may have been exposed to HIV. She believes that conflict styles theory may be helpful in developing the model. Pacita values honesty and creativity. Most of her clients value privacy.
   c. Delta is the Dean of the College of Community Services at Conflictia U. She is concerned about animosity between professors, some complaining that others are "dead wood" (not contributing to the teaching and scholarship of the college) and some complaining that others are self-centered, immature prima donnas. Delta values hard work and collaboration. Most faculty members value academic freedom and independence. Delta thinks that social identity theory may help her develop a CR model to guide her role as dean.

5. PROGRAM PLANNING: Diversity Plus has decided to establish a mediation program for conflicts between children who have run away from home and their

parents. The director has asked you to develop a plan for this program. Identify the goals of the program, which model(s) of mediation will be used, how mediators will be selected, and key issues for implementation of the program (as an alternative to a mediation program, you could plan a family group conferencing program or a healing circle program).

6. PROGRAM CRITIQUE: Identify an agency that has a CR component in its programs or services. Meet with a practitioner from the agency who incorporates CR into practice. Develop a critical analysis of the CR component, including strengths and recommendations for improvements. Describe the extent to which the agency and practitioner base their practice on CR theory, research, and values. If you were a consultant for this agency, how would you give feedback in a manner that encouraged change and avoided defensive responses?

7. PROGRAM EVALUATION: Identify an agency that has a CR program. Develop a proposal for evaluating the effectiveness of the CR program. Your proposal should include

   a.   a description of the program, its goals, and objectives;
   b.   a literature review examining the theoretical bases of the program and evaluative research results for similar programs;
   c.   an explanation and justification of the research design;
   d.   a description of sample;
   e.   a discussion of the methods and instruments for collecting data;
   f.   how data will be analyzed; and
   g.   how ethical issues such as confidentiality and informed consent will be handled.

   Ideally, the agency will want to implement your proposal. Maintain a journal to log any conflicts that arise between you and the agency, as well as how you and agency staff handled these conflicts. How well were you able to implement what you have learned about CR?

8. PROMOTION: Identify a segment of your community that you want to educate about a particular type of CR (e.g., educating teachers about peer mediation, making politicians aware of circle processes, informing the elderly about advocacy resources, teaching listening skills to children, or demonstrating peacebuilding techniques to a community experiencing intractable conflict). Develop a 15-minute educational video that you could show to this audience. As you prepare the video, consider what your audience already knows about the CR process (if anything), what messages you want to convey, and how to convey these messages in suitable language and format. Consider using humor, roleplays, special effects, or other devices to make the video interesting and persuasive. If you are technically inclined, your presentation could include multimedia (e.g., digital video, interactive website, and brochures).

9. PROFESSIONAL ASSOCIATIONS: Identify a field of CR that you are considering for your professional practice, such as family mediation, labor relations arbitration, community peacebuilding, spiritual healing for survivors of domestic violence, or ombudsperson for malpractice grievances. In order to practice in this field, is licensing or accreditation required? If so, what are the requirements

for licensing or accreditation? If licensing or accreditation is not required, what voluntary associations could you consider joining? What services do these associations offer to practitioner-members and the public?

10. MANDATORY MEDIATION: What are the advantages and disadvantages of "mandatory mediation"? Consider values issues and research comparing the effectiveness of mandatory versus voluntary mediation. Does it depend on the context of mediation (e.g., parent-youth mediation, adult guardianship mediation, victim-offender mediation, or labor mediation)?

11. PUBLICATION: Review your writings and assignments from this term. Select a paper that could be publishable in an edited form. Generally, to be publishable, an article must be original and must add to the knowledge base that is already available in scholarly literature. Select a journal that fits with your paper. Revise your paper to ensure that it meets the terms of reference (guidelines) set out in the journal. Appendix 4 includes a list of journals that publish CR articles, though you may also consider publishing in a non-CR journal in order to spread the word and the fervor to other disciplines.

1 APPENDIX | Decision Trees

As Chapter 1 noted, most disciplines use some type of structured problem-solving process. A generic problem-solving model includes the following steps:

1. Identify problem(s).
2. Canvass a broad array of alternative courses of action.
3. Identify objectives and values to be taken into account.
4. Gather information relevant to the choices to be made.
5. Evaluate the alternatives.
6. Select the best alternative given the identified objectives and values.
7. Implement the decision.
8. Evaluate its execution to identify any further problems (Kirst-Ashman & Hull, 2005).

Decision Tree Analysis is basically an extension of this type of problem-solving process. Decision trees offer a specific structure for exploring alternative courses of action to resolve a conflict (Elangovan, 1995; Menkel-Meadow et al., 2005). Decision trees fit with a cognitive theory of CR: by helping people think through problems on a rational basis, you can help them overcome cognitive distortions, such as those described in Chapter 1 (e.g., overconfidence about being right or overlooking a counterpart's perspective). Decision trees are commonly used in business and law to evaluate various courses of action. For example, is it better to go to court or negotiate a settlement privately? Should the company invest in research and development or use its funds for marketing and promotion? Generally, these types of decisions are based on monetary factors. However, nonmonetary factors such as emotions, values, communication, and relationships can also be factored into Decision Tree Analysis (Weitzman & Weitzman, 2000). For helping professionals, these "soft factors" are often more important than monetary ones.

Decision Tree Analysis follows six basic steps:

1. Depict the decisions to be made and possible outcomes for each decision.
2. Assign probabilities to each of the uncertain events.
3. Assign values to each of the possible outcomes.
4. Calculate the Expected Values for each possible alternative.
5. Identify soft factors that are relevant to the decisions to be made.
6. Decide on the best alternative, taking financial costs, benefits, and soft factors into account.

In order to demonstrate these steps, consider a situation in which you are trying to decide whether to confront a client, Clifford, about paying his bill for your services. To simplify for the purposes of demonstration, consider two courses of action: ignoring the late payment or confronting Clifford the next time you see him for a counseling session.

*In Step 1, depict the decision to be made and possible outcomes for each decision. To depict a decision, draw a small square with lines (or branches) extending to the right for each possible alternative. Label each alternative on this **Decision Fork** as follows:*

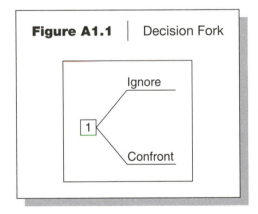

Figure A1.1 | Decision Fork

Ignore

1

Confront

Each decision choice or "alternative" is a potential course of action. The decision maker has control over these. In this case, you can decide whether to confront your client or ignore the issue of late payment. When you select an alternative, you do not know the specific outcome or solution. Possible outcomes or "options" for solution are dependent on the other person's response to your decision.[1] If you confront Clifford, he will either pay his bill or refuse to pay. *To depict each possible outcome,*

---

[1]To remember the difference between an alternative and an option, remember that *alternative* and *action* both begin with the letter *a. Option* and *outcome* both begin with the letter *o.*

draw a small circle at the end of Decision Fork 1, and draw one branch for each possible outcome. Label each outcome as follows:

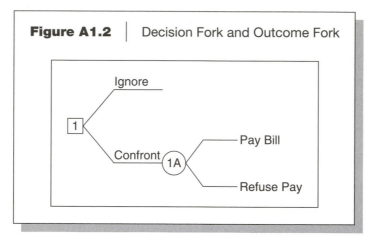

Figure A1.2 | Decision Fork and Outcome Fork

For Step 2, assign probabilities for each uncertain event. Probabilities for outcomes are often best estimates, rather than precise percentages. If you believe that there is a high likelihood of a particular outcome, then the percentage will be in the range of 70 percent to 100 percent. If you believe there is a moderate likelihood, then the percentage will be in the range of 40 percent to 70 percent. If you believe there is a low likelihood, then the percentage is in the range of 0 percent to 40 percent. You could also identify conservative and optimistic estimates in order to perform the calculations. To keep the illustration relatively simple, I will use just one set of reasonable estimates. Assuming you believe there is a 70 percent likelihood that Clifford will pay and a 30 percent chance that he will not pay, the decision tree looks as follows:

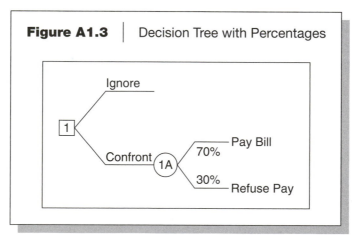

Figure A1.3 | Decision Tree with Percentages

Note that the percentages for each Outcome Fork add up to 100 percent, indicating that all possible outcomes have been identified.

*For Step 3, insert Endpoint Values for each possible outcome. The **Endpoint Value** is the difference between the benefit and cost of each outcome (i.e., the net* *benefit)*. Assuming Clifford owes $500, then his paying is worth $500, and his refusing to pay is worth $0. If you incurred any costs in order to collect these amounts, then the costs would be subtracted. If the costs exceed the benefits, then the Endpoint Value will be negative.

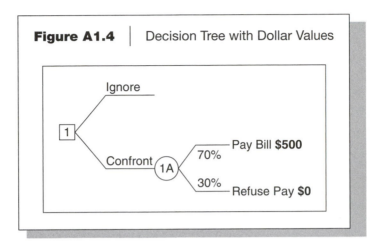

Figure A1.4 | Decision Tree with Dollar Values

In Step 4, *calculate the* **Expected Value** *for each Outcome Fork. The Expected Value is the weighted average of the End Values for each Outcome Fork.* To calculate the Expected Value, multiply each probability with the End Value, and add the results together. In the sample case, the Expected Value of Decision 1A (EV_{1A}) is

$$EV_{1A} = (70\% \times \$500) + (30\% \times \$0) = \$350.$$

To complete the decision tree, insert the Outcome Fork, End Values, and Expected Values for the second decision alternative, ignoring the issue of late payments. Assume that there is only a 20 percent chance that Clifford will pay what he owes if you do not confront him. The decision tree looks as follows:

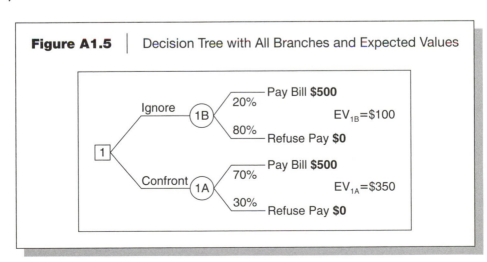

Figure A1.5 | Decision Tree with All Branches and Expected Values

At Step 5, identify soft factors, such as emotional concerns and relationship issues, that have not been factored into your economic analysis (e.g., factors that do not translate easily into dollar figures). For instance, you might find it difficult to confront a client about money. Alternatively, you might believe that confronting Clifford at this time is inappropriate because he is dealing with a crisis situation. If you are averse to taking risks, you might be particularly concerned about whether confronting Clifford about the money will put him over the edge. Once you label these concerns, the decision tree looks as follows:

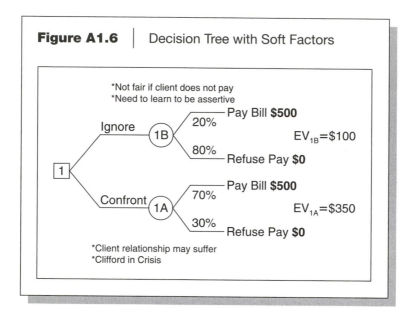

Figure A1.6 | Decision Tree with Soft Factors

I describe other soft factors, including moral sentiments about justice, in greater depth later.

Step 6 concludes the analysis by determining which course of action is preferable, given the monetary and nonmonetary concerns identified. When evaluating each decision alternative, the branch with the largest Expected Value represents the choice with the greatest economic benefit. Based on monetary concerns, confronting Clifford is preferable because the Expected Value for confronting ($350) is higher than the Expected Value for ignoring ($100). However, you also identified that Clifford is in a crisis. If you determine that helping Clifford through the crisis is more important than collecting fees that he owes, then you will choose to ignore the late payments (at least for now).

This example begins to show how Decision Tree Analysis can help you make reasoned decisions about how to proceed in conflict situations. Many other alternatives could also be considered: write Clifford a letter, confront Clifford at a later date, refuse to provide services for Clifford, or help Clifford apply for financial support to pay for counseling.

You can also analyze a sequence of alternatives and possible outcomes. For instance, if you confront Clifford and he does not pay his bill, you need to decide what to do next: write a letter, confront him again, ignore the problem, or take some other action. For each successive Decision Fork, the tree will expand to the right with further Outcome Forks.

Figure A1.6 | Decision Tree with Second Series of Decisions

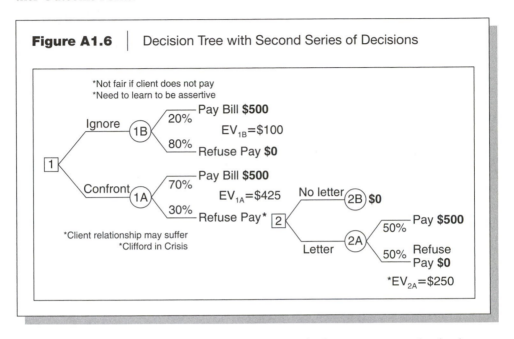

When calculating Expected Values, begin with the Outcome Forks furthest to the right and work back toward the left ("folding back the tree"). In this example, the highest Expected Value for Decision 2 is $EV_{2A} = \$250$. This suggests you should write Clifford a letter if he does not respond to your initial request for payment. The Expected Value for Decision 1A now becomes

$$EV_{1A} = (70\% \times \$500) + (30\% \times \$250) = \$425.$$

This amount is higher than in the first example, indicating that the best course of action, financially, is first to confront Clifford in person. If he does not pay his arrears, then follow up with a letter. You have increased your chances of collecting your fees by using a staged approach. Once again, soft factors need to be considered.

Some helping professionals are repulsed by the use of mathematical equations to determine how they will intervene with living, breathing human beings. Keep an open mind when you are working through the exercises in this book, because monetary factors are important for many types of decisions. For other kinds of conflict situations, the numbers and calculations are not essential. Even without the numbers, Decision Trees are useful because they can

- clarify the decisions to be made;
- help to brainstorm alternatives in a structured manner;
- indicate the possible outcomes of alternate courses of action;

- identify factors that are critical to decision making;
- encourage the decision maker to consider rational factors as well as emotions, traditions, and moral sentiments;
- provide visual representations to guide the decision-making process, enabling one to see both the broad picture and the finer points;
- help one strategize and prepare for how to deal with a conflict; and
- help two or more parties work through a conflict jointly.

The example with Clifford demonstrates how you can use decision trees to make your own decisions about how to respond to conflict. You can also use decision trees to help clients decide how to respond to their own conflict situations (Aaron, 2005). For instance, in working with a battered woman, you can use a decision tree to help her explore her alternatives. Often, such clients are so used to a particular pattern of interaction that they do not see other available choices. The client may see her choices as leaving her spouse and home versus staying in an abusive relationship. If she leaves, then she gives up the security of her home and familiar surroundings. She may believe she has no place to go except for the streets or a hostel for battered women. If she stays, she continues to be abused. By helping her look at other alternatives, she broadens her choice set and becomes more empowered to make self-determined decisions (Dan-Cohen, 1992). She may not have considered alternatives such as going to court for a restraining order and staying at home, or asking for help from a relative who may be able to offer her safe, comfortable shelter.

For an example of using decision trees for joint decision making, consider a multidisciplinary committee meeting where the participants are deciding how to regulate their professions. Ordinarily, each professional might submit a separate plan. This sets them up to have to decide whose plan is best. In a joint problem-solving exercise, the participants develop a decision tree together. Various alternatives are canvassed and evaluated without any individual owning a particular idea. The tree belongs to the whole group, and the group comes up with a mutually acceptable course of action.

When analyzing a decision tree, one of the key questions is "What do the decision makers want?" A common theme in conflict situations is that parties want "justice." Each party feels wronged by the other and wants a solution that is just. Definitions of justice vary from person to person and culture to culture. Some want retribution or punishment. Others want restitution, compensation, deterrence, healing, or protection (Umbreit et al., 2005).

Retributive justice demands that people receive appropriate punishment for their misdeeds. Criminal courts focus on retributive justice. If someone commits murder, then the punishment (typically incarceration) must be commensurate with the crime. The biblical adage "an eye for an eye, a tooth for a tooth" also suggests that punishment must be equivalent to the harm done. If, for example, Ingrid causes Dilbert to become blind, then does justice require that we make Ingrid blind? You hurt me, so I need to hurt you back. The archetypal blood feud between the Hatfields and McCoys seems irrational, until you factor in each side's desire for revenge (Frank, 1992). After three decades of fighting, it hardly mattered what originally caused the feud. Each side was bent on retribution. After a series of atrocities are committed against one another, however, can there ever be justice?

Compensation and restitution are related concepts of restorative justice. Under the notion of compensation, when one person incurs a loss caused by another, the person who caused the loss is expected to make up for the loss. Compensation could be a monetary payment or replacement of the loss "in kind." Restitution refers to putting the situation back to how it was prior to the loss. Exact restitution may not be possible, so a next best replacement may be necessary.

Ho'opono pono ("making right the wrong") is a traditional conflict resolution method among Hawaiians that is partially based on the concept of restitution (Wall & Callister, 1995). It is also based on the notion of healing. Healing is an emotional or spiritual process that enables the people to move on with their lives and relationships in a more positive fashion.

Whereas retribution, restitution, and compensation focus on making up for past wrongs, deterrence and protection focus on the future. Under these latter notions of justice, people are concerned about preventing harm from recurring.

Consider Clifford's case again. If he is late on paying his bill, what do you really want—retribution? Compensation? Restitution? Deterrence? Rehabilitation? Your decision about how to deal with this conflict depends on the type of justice you are seeking. The type of justice you choose depends, in turn, on your values and moral sentiments. There is no universally correct formula for justice.

When selecting among various models of conflict resolution, different models are better suited to definitions of justice. Mediation, for instance, is future focused, making it well suited for rehabilitation of relationships. The public court system is better suited to assigning blame, imposing punishment for past misdeeds, and setting precedents for future cases.

Certainly, Decision Tree Analysis does have its drawbacks and limitations (Zey, 1992). First, decision trees and calculations become cumbersome in complex situations. On one hand, if many choices and possible outcomes are possible, you may need to simplify the facts in order to make the analysis manageable. This may not reflect the full reality of the situation. On the other hand, decision trees help decision makers cut through complex details and focus upon the most important issues. Computer software designed to illustrate decision trees and calculate Expected Values makes it easier to depict and synthesize complex situations (Walls & Fullmer, 1995).

The second criticism is that Decision Tree Analysis (and all reasoned choice models) assume that the decision makers have perfect information (Goldstein & Hogarth, 1997). In most social conflict situations, the decision makers do not know all of the possible alternatives or all of the possible options for solution. Probabilities of various outcomes are particularly difficult to predict.[2] Decision trees help decision makers identify gaps in information. To the extent that they can fill in gaps, the quality of the choices improves. Still, decision makers must acknowledge lack of perfect

---

[2]Sometimes, all you are doing is applying your best "guestimate" of the chances. For example, if you think the chances of winning a lawsuit are vary high, you might use 90 percent; if you think the chances of winning are moderate, you might put 65 percent; and if you think the chances of winning are low, then you might put 20 percent. Even if these figures are not exact, they may provide better information than assuming your chances of winning are 100 percent. If nothing else, this type of exercise helps people strategically re-assess their confidence levels.

information, limitations of subjective factors, and possibilities of error. Conflict resolution and decision making are not exact sciences.

The third criticism is that Decision Tree Analysis suggests that rational choices are preferable to ones based on emotional, moral, or other criteria. The terminology implies that someone who is not rational is "irrational" or "crazy." To avoid this connotation, the converse of rational could be termed "nonrational." Nonrational choices can be perfectly valid choices. Whether Decision Tree Analysis actually has a bias toward rational choices depends on how one employs it. The examples provided earlier demonstrate how soft factors can be considered in making decisions. Decisions need not be based solely on monetary factors or economic efficiency. The focus of Decision Tree Analysis is "informed choice" rather than "rational choice." In order to respect a client's right to self-determination, a practitioner must respect the client's ultimate decision—even if it goes against what the practitioner believes is a rational choice. However, the practitioner does have a role in helping the client explore a range of alternatives and options so the client can make a more informed choice. As with any model of practice, helping professionals must be careful not to impose personal values on clients.

The fourth criticism is that there is no formula for how to take soft factors into account. Soft factors could be quantified. For example, how much is revenge worth to you? Would you be willing to engage in a fight, knowing it would cost you $10,000, as long as it satisfied your yen for vengeance? Quantification of soft factors is not easy or required. Even if there is a subjective element to considering soft factors, it is better to identify them rather than leave them out of the analysis altogether. Once monetary and soft factors are identified, decision makers are in a better position to make informed decisions about their priorities (Menkel-Meadow et al., 2005).

In spite of their limitations, decision trees can assist with various types of CR. Trees are tools that can be used in combination with other tools and strategies. No one tool is perfect for all types of situations or as an exclusive strategy for CR.

DISCUSSION QUESTIONS AND EXERCISES

1. LACK OF INFORMATION: Assume you are working with Molly and her 13-year-old son, Spencer. Molly wants Spencer to continue to go to private school so he will have a better chance of getting into a good college and getting a good job. Spencer wants to switch to public school so he can be with his friends. He believes that he can get into just as good a college if he goes to a public school. Draw a decision tree to help Molly and Spencer with this conflict. What types of information are missing? How can a decision tree be useful if it is missing such important facts?

2. DECISION TREE EXERCISES: The following exercises are designed to offer you practice in developing decision trees. Add additional information, as needed, in order to come up with a thorough analysis. Do not question the facts given. They have been simplified for the purposes of these exercises and are not necessarily intended to reflect "real-life" costs and risks involved. Also, remember that the other person's information may be different from yours. If you decide to use decision trees for exercises in other chapters, you will have to identify the various alternatives, costs, benefits, and chances of different

outcomes. The case facts will only give you partial information, and you will have to build the rest of the information. Just like real life. You will have lots of opportunities for creativity!

a. "Playing the Lottery"

You are trying to make a decision about whether to play the lottery. You have a one in a million chance of winning the grand prize of $2 million if you buy a ticket for $10. Assume there are no other prizes. Draw a decision tree to reflect your choices. Calculate the Expected Value for each choice. Would a rational person play the lottery? Would you? What soft factors might explain why people play the lottery?

b. "Asking for a Raise"

You have been working for Diversity Plus for the past 5 years and currently earn $60,000 per year. One year has passed since your last pay raise, so you are considering what your choices are. Being a very rational person, you would like to follow a rational process to base your decision about what course of action to take. In order to carry out this process, you have gathered the following facts.

Initially, you seem to have four choices: ask your boss for a raise; go directly to the owner for a raise; look for another job; accept the status quo (do nothing). If you ask your boss for a raise, you believe that there is a 20 percent chance you will get a raise of $5,000, a 30 percent chance of getting a raise of $3,000, a 40 percent chance of getting no raise, and a 10 percent chance of getting fired. If you go directly to the owner for a raise, then there is a 50 percent chance that he will offer a $3,000 raise but a 50 percent chance that he will refer you back to your boss. If the boss hears that you went to the owner, there will be a 10 percent chance you will get a raise of $8,000 (to avoid your going to the owner again), a 20 percent chance of getting a raise of $3,000 (to be fair), a 50 percent chance of getting no raise (because that is what the owner really wants), and a 20 percent chance of getting fired (because of anger that you went above the boss's head). If you get fired, you believe that you can get unemployment insurance benefits or part-time work, but it will cost you $7,500 in the next year before you can get another job at a comparable salary. You feel that the prospects of getting another job in less than 1 year at a comparable salary (given your specific job skills and the recession in the job market) are worse than your chances of winning the lottery. Also, if you start to look for a job and the boss finds out, the boss may make life miserable for you (without actually firing or disciplining you).

If you get fired, you also have a number of alternatives. You could go to a lawyer and sue for wrongful dismissal. The lawyer's fees would be $5,000 if you negotiate a settlement or $10,000 if the case goes to trial. If you settle, then there is a 50 percent chance of getting $15,000, a 40 percent chance of getting $10,000, and a 10 percent chance of getting $20,000. If you go to trial, there is a 60 percent chance of getting $20,000 and a 40 percent chance of getting nothing.

Create a decision tree to help you analyze this information and decide which alternatives to take. Be sure to consider soft factors such as emotional energy, pride, risk aversion, and justice.

c. "Spousal Support"

   Wanda and Harold have recently separated, following a 10-year marriage. Neither one has children. The main issue is spousal support (alimony).
Harold currently earns $30,000 per year and believes that Wanda earns
$80,000 per year. Wanda has been paying Harold $600 per month, but there
is no formal separation agreement or court order. Harold has thought about
going back to school to earn a professional degree in order to become financially independent from Wanda after he completes the degree (in about 3 years).
If he goes back to school, he believes he would need $4,000 per month to
maintain his standard of living and to pay the costs of school. If he does not
go back to school, he will need $2,500 per month support in addition to his
regular income. He feels that he "deserves" more than this because Wanda's
income is likely to rise significantly over the next few years.

   If Harold wants to go back to school, he has the following choices:

- Talk it out privately: no legal fees; 30 percent chance Wanda will agree
  to $3,000 per month; 30 percent chance of agreement at $2,000/month;
  and 40 percent chance at $1,500/month.
- Go to a lawyer: legal fees of $5,000 if they negotiate, mediate, or arbitrate
  a settlement; $10,000 if they go to court for a full trial. If Harold's lawyer
  negotiates a settlement or if they go to mediation, then they will have a
  50 percent chance of getting $3,000 per month and a 50 percent chance of
  getting $3,500 per month. A mediator would cost $500 but may help
  Wanda and Harold treat each other with more respect in the future. If they
  go to mediation, then Harold will have a 50 percent chance of getting
  $3,500 per month and a 50 percent chance of getting $4,000 per month.

   If Harold decides that it is not worth going back to school, he will have
the following choices:

- Talk it out privately: no legal fees; 30 percent chance Wanda will agree to
  $1,500 per month; 30 percent chance of agreeing to $1,000; and 40 percent chance of agreeing to $500.
- Go to a lawyer: legal fees of $5,000 if they negotiate, mediate, or arbi-
  trate a settlement; $10,000 if they go to court for a full trial. If Harold's
  lawyer negotiates a settlement or if they go to mediation, then Harold
  will have a 40 percent chance of getting $1,000 per month and a 60 per-
  cent chance of getting $1,500 per month. A mediator would cost $500
  but may help Wanda and Harold to treat each other with more respect
  in the future. If they go to court, then Harold will have a 20 percent
  chance of getting $1,600 per month and an 80 percent chance of getting
  $1,400 per month.

   Harold may also want to consider other possibilities (e.g., getting
remarried, having children; moving to a less expensive city) and how
these might affect his current decisions. Assume that Harold is your
client. Develop a decision tree that can be used to help him analyze this
information and decide which alternatives to pursue. After you have
dealt with the monetary factors, remember to consider soft factors such

as emotional energy, pride, justice, and propensity to take risks. If one decision tree becomes too complicated, you could draw separate trees for separate decisions.

d. "Olympics Community"

Conflictia has just been awarded the right to hold the Olympic Games 5 years from now. The mayor, the applicants, and local business leaders are thrilled. Advocates for homeless and poverty-stricken groups living in the proposed Olympic site (including Victorious Park) are concerned. What will the impact of the Olympics be for them? A group of advocates gets together to consider their alternatives:

- The first alternative is to do nothing. Let the planning go ahead and put their faith in the Olympic Planning Committee (OPC) to come up with a plan that will look after their rights. The best scenario that could expected under this plan would for the OPC to demolish low-cost housing in Victorious Park but use profits from the Olympics to subsidize cooperatives and public housing in other parts of the city. At worst, residents would be forced out of Victorious Park with no compensation and no support to find alternative housing. If the advocates do nothing now, they could still consider a public demonstrations or a court injunction at a later time.
- The second alternative is to advocate with the World Olympic Committee to revoke Conflictia's right to hold the Games. There is only minimal chance that this would happen, but think of the repercussions for the advocates and for the people of Victorious Park. The most likely consequence is that the World Olympic Committee will ignore the advocates, saying it is a done deal. The World Olympic Committee might put pressure on the OPC to provide support for residents who will be pushed out of Victorious Park, but the results are uncertain. Should the advocates take this route out of principle, even though "successful advocacy" is unlikely?
- The third alternative is to try to collaborate with OPC—offer expertise and support; suggest that OPC offer local residents the first right to certain types of jobs at the Olympics; provide plans for "transitional improvements" to Victorious Park, rather than leveling the community in one broad sweep. Identify one or two additional strategies that the advocates can try to raise their clout with the OPC and influence their decisions in a favorable way.

Develop a decision tree to depict the various alternatives and outcomes. What are the best courses of action for the advocates? What criteria are you using in order to determine which alternatives are best?

ROLE-PLAY A1.1: "JOINT DECISION TREE—CASEY'S CASE"

This role-play is designed to provide you with experience facilitating a joint problem-solving process using a decision tree. Three role-players are needed: Edwina (an education counselor), Parker, and Pamela (parents of a 5-year-old named Casey). Pamela and Parker are meeting with Edwina to discuss Casey's education. Casey has a mild cognitive impairment. Parker wants Casey to be enrolled in the special education program at Conflictia Elementary School. Pamela wants Casey to be placed in the mainstream program at Conflictia Elementary.

Parker believes that the teachers are better in the special education program. He does not want to see Casey fall behind. He believes that good education during a child's formative years is particularly important. Parker is also concerned that Casey will be teased by other students in the mainstream program. Casey is somewhat shy and withdrawn, so he might benefit from smaller classes in the special education stream.

Pamela is concerned that Casey's future will be limited from the outset if he is put in a special program. She fears that Casey will not have the same career opportunities and will not learn how to socialize with "normal" people. She is also concerned that some children in the special education program have behavioral problems and more severe challenges than Casey.

Edwina does not have a strong opinion about whether Casey should be placed in one program or the other. She sees her role as getting the parents to agree to one plan, and support Casey, regardless of the decision. During the role-play, Edwina will try to engage Pamela and Parker in a joint decision-making process and move them away from a debate against one another. In order to facilitate this process, consider the following steps:

1. Engage the parents in the discussion.
2. Have them briefly identify their concerns.
3. Obtain their agreement about the importance of a joint decision.
4. Explain how they can use a decision tree to help them explore alternatives.
5. Lead them through the stages of building a decision tree, identifying choices and potential outcomes, and evaluating which choices meet both of their concerns.
6. Encourage them to think of a broad range of alternatives, and to look at decisions at various points in time (e.g., now, next year, 5 years from now).

This role-play will take 20 to 30 minutes.

Debriefing: What strategies did Edwina use that helped Pamela and Parker move toward joint decision making? If it was difficult for Pamela and Parker to work together, what factors contributed to these difficulties? What, if anything, did Pamela and Parker learn from building the decision tree? How did the decision tree help (or hinder) the decision-making process? How should Edwina decide whether to bring Casey into the decision-making process? If she does bring Casey in, how should this be done?

ROLE-PLAY A1.2: "PENELOPE'S AIDS DECISIONS"

This role-play has two roles, Penelope (a person with AIDS) and Ahmad (an AIDS counselor). Assign one role to each person. Read the "Common Facts" plus the "Confidential Facts" for your own role. Not knowing the other person's Confidential Facts will help simulate real-life situations, where the counselor and client enter a situation with different information and perspectives. The role-play will take 50 to 70 minutes, with breaks in the middle for feedback and debriefing.

Common Facts

Penelope is a 35-year-old woman who has recently been diagnosed with AIDS. She did not believe she was in a high-risk group for contracting HIV but was tested after coming down with a type of pneumonia associated with AIDS. At first, she thought her test results must wrong. On a second test by another clinic, the first results were confirmed. Penelope became depressed and started to isolate herself from friends, work, and family. A clinic at Conflictia Hope for People with AIDS (PWAs) made a number of attempts at outreach with Penelope. Eventually, one of the counselors (Ahmad) connected with Penelope and began to see her on a weekly basis. Initially, Penelope and Ahmad just talked about how Penelope was coping emotionally. Ahmad's role was to listen, to demonstrate empathic understanding, develop trust, and screen for suicidal or homicidal ideation (thoughts).

Penelope has begun to come out of her depression and is starting to make plans for the future. In the session to be role-played, Penelope and Ahmad will discuss whether she will tell her boss that she has AIDS. She is a waiter in a posh restaurant. Her boss, Benita, only knows that Penelope has been taking sick leave. Benita does not know the nature of her illness. Penelope is very embarrassed about having AIDS. She sees it as an illness that only gays and drug addicts get. She is worried that if she tells anyone at work, she will lose her job. If she does not tell and Benita finds out, she may also lose her job. Penelope is also concerned that co-workers will stigmatize her at work, even if she does not lose her job.

Penelope's Confidential Facts

In order to prepare for this role-play, imagine Penelope's situation and what her fears might be: You see your boss as an adversary who will probably fire you if she finds out you have AIDS. You tend to avoid conflict situations and confrontations. You would rather not say anything to Benita, but fear what will happen if Benita finds out on her own (if you get sick again and Benita checks your medical records). You may have to hire a lawyer. Wouldn't it be easier to stay home and get family benefits (welfare) for medical reasons? What if someone at the restaurant gets HIV and it is your fault? What about finding another type of work? Once in the role-play, be co-operative with Ahmad and allow him to lead the process. The content, however, will come from your own heart.

Ahmad's Confidential Facts

To prepare for this role-play, review your notes on this chapter. Draw a decision tree to help you identify possible alternatives for Penelope. In this role-play, you view yourself as a conflict consultant to Penelope. You can either present her with suggestions or ask questions to facilitate insights about how to handle her interaction with Benita. Write down 3 or 4 strategies you hope to use in the role-play.

Debriefing: What concepts from decision-making theory did Ahmad try to employ? Which of these efforts were successful? What other concepts might have been useful?

2 APPENDIX | **Sample Assignment and Process Recording**

The Major Assignments in this book are designed to help you integrate conflict resolution theory, values, skills, self-awareness, and practice. Because these assignments may be quite different from those you are used to from other courses, I have provided the following abbreviated sample to illustrate a format you can use for completing these assignments. This format may also be useful for processing actual interventions and discussing them with your supervisor or professional colleagues (Barsky, 2006b).[1] See the guidelines for Major Assignments in Chapter 3 for further explanations of how to analyze your role-plays.

1. Heading

Assignment 4.5: Mediating with Cats and Dogs
A Bird's-Eye View

Submitted by Robin Hatch

CR101: Conflict Resolution for the Helping Professions
Conflictia University, College of Conflict
Professor Pascal Salem

March 13, 2009

---

[1]To protect the privacy of clients, change identifying information, or include a covering statement to indicate that the process recording is confidential.

2. Introduction

In my previous work placements, I have had difficulty dealing with strong emotions and clients who are not acting rationally. I have chosen this role-play to work on my affect management skills using the Dilbert and Sullivan (2006) model of "evacuative mediation." In addition, I plan to use the analysis to reflect on my affective and behavioral responses to repetitive victimization of one party . . . [1 paragraph. The *ellipsis* or three periods are included to show where I have abbreviated certain sections of this assignment. Your analysis will be complete, so you will not need to use ellipses.]

3. Preparation

For this role-play exercise, I play a budgie named Tweety B. I perform community mediation services for an agency called Diversity Plus. In recent months, Conflictia has witnessed a marked increase in gang violence among its pet population. I have been assigned to mediate between two gangs: the Felines and the Canines. Each gang has more than 30 members, so I decided to begin the process by meeting with representatives of the two groups: Tiger and Felicia who are top cats of the Felines, and Buddy and Spike who are top dogs of the Canines. Although meeting with delegates for two groups can simplify the process, I knew I would need to attend to the interests and feelings of all gang members (Snowball, 2005).

Prior to the first joint meeting, I met separately with the dogs and cats to screen for risks of scratching, clawing, and biting. See the appendix at the end of this paper to see how I completed the Feline-Canine Risk Assessment Scale . . .

The four representatives each come from a different ethnic constituency: Siamese, Calico, Labrador, and Irish Setter. I have reviewed literature describing some of the cultural preferences of these groups in relation to conflict resolution (Sylvester, 2002; Tom, 1998). I know that I could get eaten up by this group if I am not adequately prepared, so I set an agenda (Dino, 2007) and arranged the meeting room with a pentagonal table, separate drinking bowls filled with warm cream, and soft blue lights (Fido, 2005). The stated purposes for this meeting are: (1) to identify areas of individual concern and (2) to identify areas of common concern . . . [1 to 3 pages]

4. Overview of the Intervention

As noted, I had planned to use Dilbert and Sullivan's (2006) model of evacuative mediation to help the clients identify their concerns and resolve them peacefully. As this model suggests, I began with a question inviting everyone to voice their concerns. This opened the floodgates, particularly with sniping back and forth between Felicia and Spike. As their voices grew louder and louder, I didn't know what else to do, so, in panic, I began to whistle loudly. Everyone stopped arguing.

Now that I had the floor, I decided to tell Felicia and Spike what I thought of their immature behavior. Although this went against Snowball's (2005) suggestion that mediators should not impose their biases, I felt that there was no other way to help them. At this point, Buddy and Spike stood up and started to leave the room. Obviously, I offended them, as they barked on about how rude and insensitive I was. I decided it was time to be more humble, so I apologized for my outburst, as Dino (2007) suggests.

The apology had no impact and everyone continued to argue. I lost control for about 10 minutes. At this point, Tiger stepped in and settled everyone down. Tiger told a sad, personal story about losing two kittens in a recent gang fight. This was a turning point, as we talked about the need to work together. Spike acknowledged that turf wars and other negative reactions to overcrowding in the neighborhood were not just feline phenomena. Buddy and Spike noted that there is a lot of dogchismo (pride) in the canine community, making it difficult to admit problems to outsiders. We decided that we needed to develop some type of forum to discuss the needs of the community. We divided up tasks. Buddy said he would do some research into methods of conducting "town hall meetings" (Beast, 2002). I agreed to bring information about the use of surveys for a needs assessment (Snoop, 1998). Tiger said she would contact associates in Bassetville to obtain information about their "Pets Against Violence" campaign. Felicia and Spike agreed to bring refreshments . . .

[skipping to the end of the role-play]

We had been mediating for 70 minutes. Everyone looked tired. I congratulated them for working so hard and gaining agreement on four of the seven issues. In the five remaining minutes, we booked a follow-up appointment. I then asked them whether there were any additional types of homework to complete prior to the next meeting. Felicia and Tiger agreed to go back to their gang to ask for suggestions on how to resolve the outstanding issues. Spike and Buddy thought this was a good idea and agreed to do the same. I concluded the meeting by handing everyone a treat as a means of reinforcing their positive behaviors (Tom, 1998). [2 to 3 pages]

5. Process Recording

The role-play began with my shaking paws with each client in the waiting room. This allowed me to make a direct connection with each client and ensure that none of them had sharp claws (Fido, 2005). The following transcription begins with formal introductions, after I had invited everyone into the mediation room.

Narrative (*Verbatim*)	Observations of Clients and Possible Interpretations	Reflections (Thoughts and Feelings of the Professional(s))	Skills, Theory, and Alternatives
Me (Tweety): Chirp. I'd like to thank you for your time and commitment in coming to this very important meeting. Perhaps we can begin by introducing ourselves, and stating our reasons for being here. Spike, would you care to start . . .	Everyone arrived promptly and is sitting attentively around the table. Spike is tapping his left front paw. I interpret this to mean he is anxious.	Since I think Spike looks anxious, maybe I should start with him. I think I forgot to use mouthwash this morning. I'm so embarrassed. Maybe I better not sit too close to anyone today.	We are a task group (Heidi, 1999) and at the forming stage (Alvin, 2007). I need to use listening skills and gain their trust if I want to be an effective chair. I expressed my gratitude for everyone coming, hoping to reinforce their commitment Alternative: I could have explained the mediation process right away (Alvin, 2007).

Narrative (*Verbatim*)	Observations of Clients and Possible Interpretations	Reflections (Thoughts and Feelings of the Professional(s))	Skills, Theory, and Alternatives
Spike: I'm Spike and I'm tired of all these nasty fat cats who provoke us all the time and then complain that they're innocent victims.	Spike hasn't touched his warm cream.	Perhaps I wasn't culturally sensitive to his dietary needs. I feel sorry. Underlying value: respect for diversity.	I don't know what theory or skill I can use to deal with someone who is so belligerent and bigoted toward felines. I decided to just ignore the insults.
Me: What are you hoping that we can accomplish here today?	The others have moved onto the edge of their seats. Felicia's tail is straight up—a sign of anger?	I have to control my anger towards Spike—he's been hard to deal with, but he represents a large segment of the community.	Setters and Calicos have had a long history of conflict (Muttley, 2002). Skill: Open-ended question; nonjudgmental and concrete. Alternative: Using a narrative approach, I could have said, "Let's begin by sharing our stories of what happened, leading up to the conflict."
Felicia: Spike just wants to lock us up in a cage and throw away the key. Why did you invite him anyway?	Felicia's tone of voice is high and quivering. She sounds bitter, but she's likely nervous underneath.	Now I'm being attacked. I just wanted to help out.	I think we've gone into the "storming stage" too quickly. Haven't these folks read the book (Sparky, 2006)?
[Etc.]	[5 to 8 pages]		

6. Critique

On reflection, I can see both strengths and limitations in my performance as a mediator. In terms of strengths, I was able to implement the first three steps of Dilbert and Sullivan's evacuative approach quite effectively. In particular, I was able to help the clients reframe their individual concerns into community-based concerns. The fourth step proved difficult because the parties were reluctant to share affective information. Perhaps I need to find a different way to introduce this step. . .

One of my original learning objectives was to improve my affect management skills. During the opening stages of the role-play, when everyone started arguing, I lost control of my emotions and started lecturing the clients. This indicates I still need to find more deliberate ways to respond to my emotional responses, particularly when clients express anger and frustration . . .

While I had prepared to use Sylvester's (2002) cultural affect theory, it did not fit with the present situation. This theory seems to work well with cats, but it does not address many of the emotional responses that are more characteristic of dogs because . . . [3 to 6 pages]

7. Conclusion

At one point, I was hanging on by a wing and a prayer, but my prayers must have been answered. I'm not sure if I had any positive influence—Tiger did most of the work. My biggest fear is that what happened at the beginning of the meeting today is only a small sample of what will happen when we get the whole community together. In order to prepare for our follow-up meeting, I had better read Cardinal's (2006) *A Bird's-Eye View to Community Development Work with Dogs and Cats* . . .

Perhaps the most important insight I gained from this conflict was the power of storytelling (Muttley, 2002). As mentioned earlier, Tiger's narrative about friends who died in prior fights completely changed the tone of the discourse. When clients start blaming each other or arguing about who is right, storytelling can be used to help them take a step back and listen to each other's experiences . . . [1 to 3 paragraphs]

References

Cardinal, S. L. (2006). *A bird's-eye view to community development work with dogs and cats.* Leashville, KY: Collar Publishing. [5 to 10 scholarly references]

Metaphoric Storytelling

Metaphoric storytelling refers to sharing narratives, anecdotes, or analogies with people involved in a conflict. During communication, people often speak in metaphors without specifically intending to do so ("We need to play as a team," or "They're turning up the heat on us"). Advocates, mediators, and other third parties intentionally use metaphors to help people change their perceptions or move them toward agreement. Conflicting parties can also use them to gain insight into their own conflict situation (Smith, 2005). Sometimes, conflicting parties use metaphors in a manner that distorts reality or hinders their progress toward conflict resolution ("In these negotiations, I feel like I'm walking a tightrope. One false move and I'm history"); in these cases, CR professionals can help them by checking the validity of the metaphor or by suggesting alternate metaphors (e.g., "How can we restructure our discussions so you feel that you have a safety net?"). In other situations, CR professionals can reinforce or build on metaphors used by the parties ("Earlier you spoke of playing on the same team. How would team members prepare for a critical match, perhaps the most important game of their careers?").

The following three examples illustrate specific stories that can be used to promote new insights. When creating your own anecdotes for CR, use humor, creativity, and common wisdom.

"SEEKING CREATIVE SOLUTIONS"

A man died, leaving 17 camels to his three sons. The first son was to receive one-half, the second son was to receive one-third, and the third son was to receive one-ninth of their father's camels. They were unable to figure out how to divide the camels fairly. After arguing among themselves, they consulted a wise woman for a solution to this difficult problem. She offered to lend them her one camel. Of the 18 camels, the first son took 9, the second took 6, and the third took 2. One camel was left over, so the sons gave it back to the woman.[1]

"STRENGTH FROM WEAKNESS"

The director of an agency announced that she was going to retire. The obvious choices to replace her were the three senior supervisors: Jodie, Frank, and Beatrice. Everyone assumed that Jodie would be chosen, because she had the greatest experience and was a strong administrator. Frank seemed to be the second favorite, given his capacity to raise funds and develop new programs for the agency. Beatrice did not think she had a chance against the others, so she just went about her job as usual.

Frank really wanted the director's position, so he decided to do whatever Jodie did but better: he stayed late, worked harder, and tried to do everything faster. Jodie quickly saw what Frank was trying to do, and she responded in kind. Everything she did had to be perfect, and she would always go the extra step to ensure that her performance would exceed Frank's. Frank and Jodie were so anxious to impress, they even asked Beatrice whether they could do her work for her. Reluctantly, Beatrice offered each of them some of her most tedious responsibilities.

Decision time came, and Beatrice was selected for director. She demonstrated that she could delegate work and collaborate with her colleagues.[2]

"HOW FEAR SOUNDS LIKE ANGER"

I was driving to work one morning, when I saw the driver of a van cut in front of a car. The car driver had to slam the brakes in order to prevent a collision. The car driver honked, and the van driver honked back, but even louder. This seemed to enrage the car driver, as the car sped ahead and passed the van. The van then raced up and passed the car as if to play a game of chicken. By this point, both were going so fast that I lost sight and never did find out who won.

As I pondered what happened, I tried to figure out how these folks could get so angry at each other. Then I wondered whether it really was anger. When the car first honked, perhaps the driver was saying, "Hey, we almost crashed. That really scared me." The van driver must have interpreted the honk as "You idiot. You almost killed me!" The van driver honked back meaning to say, "I didn't mean it. It was an accident." Now the car driver probably heard this honking differently: "What are you

---

[1]From a Middle Eastern parable, cited in Rothman (1997, p. 53).

[2]This story is drawn loosely from game theory.

honking at me for, jerk!" And on they went. I wonder whether we need to develop a new car horn that communicates different sounds for "I'm angry" and "I'm scared." I wonder whether people could benefit from the same sort of thing.

CREATING YOUR OWN METAPHORS

People involved in conflict can create their own metaphors. Creating metaphors not only provides parties with an opportunity to view conflict from different perspectives but also externalizes problems, making it easier to think about different possibilities for solutions. The following steps can be used to facilitate creation of metaphors:

1. Provide a definition of metaphors and why they may be useful: "Metaphors are imaginative ways of describing conflict as a different process, object, or type of relationship. Sometimes metaphors help us gain insight into conflict, and how we can look at deal with it differently."
2. Provide examples of metaphors: "There are different ways to view conflict. Some people see conflict as a garden that needs to be cultivated, a quilt with pieces that must be carefully stitched together, or dance requiring people to move in synch with the same music."
3. Invite everyone to create their own metaphors: "How do you see the conflict we're trying to resolve? What metaphor or image would you use to describe it? Please take your time to think of a metaphor, and write it down."
4. Invite each person to share the metaphors: "Let's hear everyone's metaphor. I'll jot down your metaphors on this flipchart."

Ask everyone to explain the metaphors, including the messages or lessons that can be learned from them: "Great examples of metaphors. Tell us more specifically what your metaphor means to you. What can we learn from it? What does it say about what needs to be done in order to resolve this conflict?" (Wilmot & Hocker, 2007).

Sometimes, metaphors lead to specific solutions. Other times, they provide new insights and mutual understanding, which can be valuable even if they do not lead to specific solutions.

4 APPENDIX | **Additional Resources**

This appendix lists additional resources for professional development, accreditation, and training. These resources are broken down into the following topics: CR journals, research institutes and databases, professional associations, videos, codes of ethics, and practice opportunities.

JOURNALS

- *Conflict Resolution Quarterly*
- *Family Courts Review*
- *Negotiation Journal*
- *Journal of Dispute Resolution*
- *Argumentation and Advocacy Journal*
- *Peace, Environment, and Education*

RESEARCH INSTITUTES AND DATABASES

- ADR Mediation Resources: http://www.adrr.com
- Beyond Intractability: http://www.beyondintractability.org
- The Centre for Conflict Education and Research (CCER), Ottawa, Canada: http://www.carleton.ca/law/conflict/ccer.htm
- CDR Associates, Boulder, CO: http://www.mediate.org
- Conflict Resolution Information (CRInfo), Boulder, CO: http://v4.crinfo.org and http://conflict.colorado.edu (Conflict Research Consortium)

- CPR International Institute for Conflict Prevention and Resolution, New York: http://www.cpradr.org
- George Mason University, Institute for Conflict Analysis and Resolution, Fairfax, VA: http://www.gmu.edu/departments/ICAR
- Israel Center for Negotiation and Mediation, Haifa, Israel: http://www.icn.org.il
- Mediation UK, Bristol, England: http://www.mediationuk.org.uk
- National Association for Community Mediation, Washington, DC: http://www.nafcm.org
- National Multicultural Institute, Washington, DC: http://www.nmci.org
- Nova Southeastern University, Department of Conflict Analysis and Resolution, Davie, FL: http://www.nova.edu/shss/DCAR
- Program on Negotiation, Cambridge, MA: http://www.pon.org

PROFESSIONAL ASSOCIATIONS

- American Bar Association Section of Dispute Resolution, Chicago: http://www.abanet.org/dispute
- Association of Family and Conciliation Courts, Madison, WI: http://www.afccnet.org
- Association for Conflict Resolution, Washington, DC: http://www.acrnet.org (includes sections for conflict in a range of contexts, including family, workplace, education, and spirituality)
- Conflict Resolution Network, Chatswood, Australia: http://www.crnhq.org
- Family Mediation Canada, Kitchener: http://www.fmc.ca
- Conflict Resolution Network Canada, Waterloo: http://www.crnetwork.ca
- International Ombudsman Association, Hillsborough, NJ: http://www.ombudsassociation.org
- International Organization of Facilitators, St. Paul, MN: http://www.iaf-world.org
- The British and Irish Ombudsman Association, Twickenham: http://www.bioa.org.uk
- Sulha Peace Project, Jerusalem: http://www.sulha.com
- Victim-Offender Mediation Association, St Paul, MN: http://www.voma.org
- Victim-Offender Reconciliation Program (VORP), Asheville, NC: http://www.vorp.com
- United Kingdom College of Family Mediators, Bristol: http://www.ukcfm.co.uk

VIDEOS

The following animated films (from the MakePeace Series; see http://www.nfb.ca) are useful educational tools for children aged 5 to 12. Creative and humorous, these videotapes help children explore conflict resolution and learn how to deal with anger and conflict more effectively. Adults will also find the presentations entertaining and insightful.

- National Film Board of Canada. (1997a). *Dinner for two* [Videotape]. Toronto: Author.
- National Film Board of Canada. (1997b). *When the dust settles* [Videotape]. Toronto: Author.
- National Film Board of Canada. (2000). *Bully dance* [Videotape]. Toronto: Author.
- National Film Board of Canada. (2002). *Elbow room* [Videotape]. Toronto: Author.

The following video includes a series of four films designed to educate 15- to 18-year-olds about peace and conflict resolution:

- National Film Board of Canada. (2002). *Cultivating peace in the 21st Century* [Videotape]. Toronto: Author.

For videos on peer mediation for students in Grades 6 to 12, consider the following:

- Hawaii Research Center for Future Studies. (1991). *Cultural approaches to conflict resolution* [Videotape]. Honolulu: Author.
- Schrumpf, F., & Crawford, D. K. (1994). *The peer mediation video: Conflict resolution in schools*. Waterloo, ON. Research Press. (*1996 Program Guide* and *Student Manual* come separately; [800] 265-3375.)

The following video provides a good introduction to interest-based mediation, in the context of a dispute between developers and environmentalists:

- Gibson, M. (Ed.). *Mediation: An introduction* [Videotape]. Toronto: MGI Film & Television, Mackenzie Group International.

The following video demonstrates an interest-based model in a business context:

- Friedman, G. J., Himmelstein, J., & Mnookin, R. H. (2001). *Saving the last dance: Mediation through understanding* [Videotape]. Cambridge, MA: Program on Negotiation & Center for Mediation in Law (http://www.pon.org).

For an introduction to adult guardianship mediation, consider:

- Center for Gerontology. (1999). *Adult guardianship mediation: An introduction* [Videotape]. Ann Arbor, MI: Author. (Order form available at http://www.tcsg.org)

For a video on transformative mediation, see:

- Bush, R. A. B., & Folger, J. P. (2004). *The "purple" house conversations* [DVD]. Grand Forks, ND: Institute for Study of Conflict Transformation (http://www.transformativemediation.org).

CODES OF ETHICS

You can find codes of ethics and standards of practice for various CR roles at the following websites:

Advocacy

- Advocacy Network—Leeds
  http://www.advocacy-network-leeds.org.uk/standard/gpgwelc1.html

Arbitration

- American Arbitration Association
  http://www.adr.org/CodeOfEthics

Child Custody Evaluation

- Association of Family and Conciliation Courts
  http://www.afccnet.org/pdfs/CCEStandardDraft0805.pdf

Facilitation

- International Organization of Facilitators
  http://www.iaf-world.org/i4a/pages/index.cfm?pageid=3346

Mediation

- Association for Conflict Resolution
  http://www.mediate.com/articles/modelSTDSd.cfm
- Association of Family and Conciliation Courts
  http://www.afccnet.org/resources/standards_practice.asp
- Family Mediation Canada
  http://www.fmc.ca/?p=Professionals
- Uniform Mediation Act
  http://www.mediate.com/articles/umafinalstyled.cfm

Ombuds

- The Ombudsman Association
  http://web.mit.edu/negotiation/toa/TOAsop.html

Parenting Coordination

- Association of Family and Conciliation Courts
  http://www.afccnet.org/pdfs/AFCCGuidelinesforParentingcoordinationnew.pdf

CONFLICT RESOLUTION PRACTICE OPPORTUNITIES

One of the primary concerns of newly educated CR professionals is where to gain practice experience. If practice opportunities are not readily available, you may need to be creative. Consider the following possibilities:

- Practicum—some training programs and professional degree programs offer supervised internships as part of the program.

- Mediation volunteer—contact neighborhood community dispute resolution services, victim services (possibly located in the criminal court), or volunteer service listings.
- Peace volunteer—volunteer with the Peace Corps (http://www.peacecorps.gov), Red Cross (http://www.redcross.org), Amnesty International (http://www.amnesty.org), Doctors Without Borders (http://www.doctorswithoutborders.org), or another agency that does work in the fields of peace, social justice, and humanitarian work.
- Guardian ad litem—become a trained volunteer who is appointed by the court to advocate for the best interests of an abused or neglected child (there may be different names and role descriptions depending on your jurisdiction).
- Comediation, cofacilitation, or copractice—work together with a more experienced CR professional; some CR professionals charge trainees who want to copractice with them.
- Private supervision—obtain your own cases and hire an experienced CR professional to provide feedback, suggestions, and support (if you are planning to apply for licensure or accreditation, ensure that your supervisor meets the appropriate qualifications).
- Peer consultation—meet periodically with other CR professionals to discuss cases and offer one another support (be careful to protect client confidentiality).
- Career development—practice CR skills in your traditional practice on an emergent basis or work with others in your agency to develop CR programming.

Glossary

accommodative a style of conflict resolution where a party tries to satisfy the other person's interests, without trying to satisfy his or her own; relationship oriented.

adjudication a method of CR in which the parties present evidence and arguments to a neutral third party who has power to decide how the conflict will be resolved. Adjudicators are generally required to base their decisions on objective standards, laws, or precedent cases. Arbitration and litigation are forms of adjudication (cf. *judicial process*).

administrator a professional who assists with implementation of the resolution of a conflict.

adversarial a style of CR in which the party sees him- or herself in competition; a process in which there is a winner and a loser.

advocacy the act of providing CR support to a particular party or cause.

alternative dispute resolution (ADR) various methods of handling disputes; often used to refer specifically to CR methods used as alternatives to litigation.

anecdotal storytelling using narratives to demonstrate a point; using analogies or metaphors to help parties gain insight into their own conflict situation.

approaches to practice a general framework for engaging people in practice, guided by a particular theoretical perspective, such as interest-based negotiation or identity-based mediation (cf. *models of practice, theories of practice,* and *methods of practice*).

arbitration a CR method in which the parties select and agree on a neutral third person to resolve their dispute through an adjudicative process. Arbitrators receive oral and/or written evidence and arguments from the parties and issue a decision. The arbitrator's decision could be binding or nonbinding, depending on prior agreement of the parties. The parties may also have input into the rules of the arbitration process. Most arbitration processes are closed to the public.

avoidant a conflict style in which a party denies the existence of the conflict or backs away from conflict; not wanting to confront conflict directly.

balance of power the relative capacity of two or more individuals or groups to influence one another.

bargaining communication between two or more conflicting parties who are trying to work toward an agreement; sometimes used to describe a positional approach to negotiation.

bias favoritism, perceived or objective; siding with one party or cause in a conflict.

bicultural having sufficient experience in two cultures, so that one is able to understand and interpret both effectively.

brainstorming generating ideas on a topic by asking participants to list as many options as they can imagine, regardless of whether they are realistic or reasonable.

buffer an individual or agency that separates conflicting parties during an intense, destructive phase of conflict.

case advocacy supporting a particular client or client system in a CR process.

cause advocacy supporting a particular set of values or goals in a CR process.

collaborative a conflict style in which the person works together to satisfy both party's interests; a joint problem-solving style.

competitive a conflict style in which the person is focused on self-interest or individual success.

compromising a conflict style in which the person makes concessions in hopes of resolving conflict; compromisers reduce goals or demands in return for the other party also reducing its demands; a form of positional bargaining.

conciliation a problem-solving method similar to mediation, but focused on settling the presenting issues rather than dealing with underlying concerns, relational, or process issues (cf. *reconciliation*).

conflict see *social conflict*.

conflict resolution any means used by people to deal with conflict situations; for example, negotiation, mediation, fighting, and debating (sometimes referred to as *conflict management*).

conflict style an individual's preferred way of dealing with conflict (accommodating, avoiding, compromising, competing, collaborating).

consensus building any CR process that works toward agreement among all of the parties directly involved in the conflict. Consensus building includes negotiation, mediation, community development, and therapeutic processes that give the parties the power to make decisions for themselves. General consensus may not require that all parties agree; the group can agree to a certain level of consensus required to take an action.

contract an exchange of promises between conflicting parties. A contract can be binding (enforceable in court) or nonbinding (an informal commitment that the parties intend to follow, although it is not enforceable in court).

contractual conflict resolution a formal CR process in which the parties agree to a specific process, as established by contract (cf. *emergent conflict resolution*).

cultural relativism valuing all cultures, without making assumptions about one culture being better than another.

culture a system of values, language, customs, and beliefs among a group that shares a common nationality, ethnic origin, gender, sexual orientation, disability, or other background.

debate a form of discourse in which participants take a stance and argue for their preferred outcomes (cf. *dialogue*).

Decision Fork used in Decision Tree Analysis to denote the alternative courses of action that a decision maker can choose between (e.g., go to court, negotiate, initiate war); marked by a small square with one line extending from the square for each alternative.

dialogue a constructive form of discourse in which participants listen to one another and try to gain a higher level of mutual understanding.

directive an interventionist approach to CR, particularly mediation; in contrast to a facilitative approach in which the intermediary encourages the parties to communicate but avoids guiding them toward specific solutions.

emergent conflict resolution an informal CR process that emerges from a situation without an explicit contract; the person who facilitates the process is not necessarily recognized as a CR professional (cf. *contractual conflict resolution*).

empower facilitate self-determination, choice, and autonomy (Bush & Folger, 2005).

Endpoint Value used in Decision Tree Analysis to denote the value of a particular chance outcome. For example, if you negotiate and two possible outcomes are settling for $100 compensation and settling for $2,000, then the Endpoint Values are $100 and $2,000.

equilibrium according to systems theory, a balanced state between individuals in a family or other social system, in which each person in the system has a complementary role; according to game theory, a situation in which two or more parties have a singular best strategy, regardless of how the other party behaves.

ethics principles that tell individuals, groups, or organizations what is right and what is wrong; a system of studying the morality of behavior (cf. *values*).

evaluation a method of CR in which the professional conducts a structured assessment and provides the factual findings, opinions, and recommendations to the clients; the evaluator's recommendations may be binding or nonbinding, as agreed by the parties in the retainer contract with the evaluator.

Expected Value the weighted average of a series of chance events; used in Decision Tree Analysis to decide which decisions are most likely to bring about the best result. For example, if you negotiate and there is a 20 percent chance of settling for $100 compensation and an 80 percent chance of settling for $1,000, then the Expected Value is

$$(20\% \times \$100) + (80\% \times \$1,000) = \$820.$$

expert/consultant a professional who provides information, expertise, or advice to one or both interested parties to help them resolve a conflict.

face giving helping a person save face, or look credible, honest, or otherwise good to the other parties, in spite of a situation that may make the person look bad

facilitate to help parties communicate with one another (e.g., through mediation, family counseling, supervision, or group therapy).

fact finding using a strategic process to collect reliable information or evidence related to issues in dispute.

fields of practice contexts in which CR professionals practice (e.g., child welfare, criminal justice, education, mental health, public health)(cf. *methods of practice*).

healer a person who helps parties work through the underlying causes of a conflict (e.g., a psychotherapist who helps people heal emotional injuries or a clergy who helps people heal spiritual wounds).

homeostasis see *equilibrium*.

hybrid a combination of different methods of CR, such as mediation-arbitration or mediative-evaluation

identity-based CR a CR approach in which the professional helps parties explore who they are and how they see themselves, providing them with experiences that help them reconsider and redefine their identities and relationships.

impartial free from bias or favoritism, as perceived by the parties or objectively true (cf. *neutral*).

impasse a deadlock in negotiations; a point in the CR process when it looks as if there is no negotiable solution or room for agreement.

independent legal advice the right of each party involved in a conflict to advice from a separate lawyer before entering into an agreement.

interests concerns, needs, hopes, or underlying motivations; the reasons that a certain position matters to a party involved in a conflict.

interest-based negotiation an alternative to positional negotiation where parties are encouraged to look at their underlying interests (concerns) and work toward solutions that satisfy all parties' interests.

interpreter a person who helps parties understand one another, particularly if they speak different languages or have different cultural interpretations of the language being used; an interpreter conveys the meaning of language, rather than simply translate word for word.

interventionist see *directive*.

investigator a professional who gathers information in order to determine what has happened or what should happen in order to resolve a conflict.

judicial process a CR approach in which an independent third party decides how to resolve a conflict for the parties (cf. *adjudication*).

jurisdiction a municipal, state, provincial, or national government that has the power to make laws. In Canada and the United States, provinces and states generally have the legislative authority to regulate helping professions, including CR.

lateral thinking using cognitive processes in a creative manner; viewing a problem from various angles in order to consider innovative options for solution; an alternative to linear thinking.

learning style preferred way of learning; the predominant manner in which individuals acquire knowledge, skills, and understanding.

litigation a trial, where conflicting parties bring their dispute to court to be decided by a neutral judge or panel of judges; the parties have the right to present evidence and arguments, but the judge's decision is binding on the parties. Most trials are open to the public.

mediation assisted negotiation:

closed (or confidential) mediation mediation in which the parties agree that the process is completely confidential and privileged; information shared in the process cannot be disclosed by the mediator in a court hearing or any other CR process.

comprehensive mediation in divorce or separation mediation, used to describe mediation of both financial concerns (alimony, child support, possession of family home, and division of property) and parenting concerns (how major decisions such as healthcare and education will be made, where the children will live, and how they will share time with each parent).

open (or nonconfidential) mediation mediation in which the parties agree to limited confidentiality; the mediator cannot disclose information from mediation to the general public, but either party may ask the mediator to disclose information to a court or other tribunal, particularly if the conflicts are not resolved in mediation.

therapeutic mediation mediation designed not only to resolve the overt conflicts but to heal relationships, deal with underlying problems, and enhance the abilities of the parties to deal with future conflicts.

mediation-arbitration (med-arb) a hybrid model of CR, where the practitioner first attempts to mediate a resolution; if the parties are unable to reach their own agreement, the mediator becomes an arbitrator and imposes a decision.

mediative a process that has some of the qualities of mediation but does not fit the strict definition of mediation.

metaphoric storytelling a parable that provides an analogy or lesson, used in CR to help one or both parties gain insight into their conflict (cf. *anecdotal storytelling*).

methods of practice styles of conflict resolution (e.g., negotiation, mediation, advocacy) that are not tied to specific theories but could be used with a range of theories (cf. *approaches to practice*, *fields of practice*, and *models of practice*).

models of practice an approach to CR practice that has a well-defined theoretical base as well as specific guidance on what strategies, techniques, and skills to use in various practice situations (cf. *approaches to practice*, *methods of practice*, and *theories of practice*).

mutual for the benefit of all parties; for joint or shared interests.

narrative a story told from the speaker's perspective, useful in allowing parties to vent, to empathize with one another, or to construct new stories that permit them to move forward in a more positive fashion.

negotiation communication between two or more parties involved in a conflict; could include joint or independent action.

neutral unbiased; fair; disinterested; having no stake in final outcome (cf. *impartial*).

ombud or **ombudsperson** an official designated by government or another institution to investigate complaints about the institution, particularly those concerning discriminatory practices or unfair treatment. The ombud may try to mediate a solution or offer suggestions; however, he or she has no power to impose a solution. Sometimes, the recommendations will be made public, putting pressure on the parties to follow the recommendations.

Outcome Fork used in Decision Tree Analysis to denote the possible outcomes from various courses of action (e.g., a negotiation process might result in a favorable settlement, an unfavorable settlement, or no settlement); marked by a small circle with one line extending from the circle for each possible outcome.

parenting coordination a hybrid method of CR in which a professional assists parents involved in a high-conflict separation or divorce by providing a combination of services that may include monitoring, assessing, educating, counseling, enforcement, and nonconfidential conflict resolution to help them implement a court order or agreement regarding parenting issues.

participants individuals or groups who are involved in a CR process; the parties are always included as participants; however, other participants might include advocates, support persons, people required to help implement decisions, and experts.

parties individuals or groups who are involved in a conflict. *Interested parties* are directly involved in the conflict and have a stake in its outcome; *third parties* are not directly involved in the conflict and typically have no stake in a particular outcome; however, they can be brought in to facilitate resolution of the conflict.

peacebuilding fostering open, fair, respectful, and cooperative relations between conflicting parties (e.g., through mediative processes or advocating for social justice).

peacekeeping refereeing; maintaining peace by buffering the parties or by enforcing ground rules to avoid violence.

peer mediation assisted negotiation in which the mediator comes from a similar background as the conflicting parties (e.g., a student who mediates disputes between other students in their school).

penalizer an individual or agency with the power to impose sanctions on parties for misconduct.

position the preferred outcome or solution stated by a party involved in a conflict (cf. *interests*).

positional negotiation bargaining by trying to advance one's own preferred solution.

power the relative capacity of individuals or groups to influence one another.

power balancing redistributing power between the parties; helping a disadvantaged party participate fairly in a CR process (cf. *empowerment*).

power bases sources of power; ways of garnering greater capacity to have influence over others (e.g., resources, physical strength, morality, connections with others, legal authority).

power-based CR competitive CR approaches in which each party tries to influence the other through force, persuasion, or use of other power bases.

pre-empt to use a strategic intervention to avoid a problem; to identify potential barriers to CR and design interventions to prevent the problem from occurring.

professional a reflective practitioner who uses a specific set of knowledge, skills, and values to guide practice (e.g., professional teachers, social workers, nurses, psychologists, counselors, human service workers, clergy).

radical perspectives that challenge the status quo in society, including power structures, patriarchy, and various forms of systemic discrimination.

recognition understanding and demonstrating empathy to another party's situation (see *transformative mediation*).

reconciliation process of returning a relationship to its prior state; repairing or healing a relationship.

resolution dealing effectively with the underlying issues in a conflict situation; reaching an agreement that truly satisfies the parties (cf. *settlement*).

restitution returning a situation to its prior state (e.g., repairing damaged property).

restorative justice CR perspective based on compensation or restitution; encourages parties to restore losses and repair relationships.

retributive justice CR perspective based on punishment for wrongdoing; holds people accountable for their actions and deters future wrongdoing.

rights-based CR CR approaches in which parties assert competing rights, freedoms, entitlements, or privileges prescribed by the laws or policies that govern them (e.g., a court trial or a debate on civil liberties).

settlement an agreement that deals with the surface issues but does not necessarily resolve the parties' emotional or underlying issues (e.g., an agreement allowing the parties to avert a trial, fight, or strike but not fully resolving the parties' underlying concerns; cf. *resolution*).

shuttle mediation assisted negotiation in which the third party meets with each party in a different place, moving back and forth between them.

social conflict an expressed difference in values, beliefs, or interests between two or more parties (as opposed to *intrapsychic conflict*, which occurs when an individual has conflicting values, drives, beliefs, or behaviors).

stake a personal or monetary interest in the resolution of a conflict.

structural see *radical*.

system a group of interrelated parties.

theories of practice conceptualizations that provide the rationale or schematic explanations for specific models or approaches to practicing CR (e.g., cognitive theory, loss theory, attribution theory). Theories have hypotheses or propositions that can be tested through empirical research (cf. *approaches to practice*, *methods of practice*, and *models of practice*).

transformative mediation assisted negotiation in which the third party facilitates empowerment and recognition between the parties; bringing the parties to a settlement of their conflict is not a primary goal.

trust building strategies to overcome fear or lack of confidence, designed to prepare individuals or groups for collaborative conflict resolution

values deeply held preferences or priorities; principles that individuals or groups believe are good or worthy of aspiration (cf. *ethics*).

References

Aaron, M. C. (2005). Finding settlement with numbers, maps, and trees. In M. L. Moffitt & R. C. Bordone (Eds.), *The handbook of dispute resolution* (pp. 202–218). San Francisco: Jossey-Bass.

Adler, R. S., Rosen, B., & Silverstein, E. M. (1998). Emotions in negotiation. How to manage fear and anger. *Negotiation Journal, 14,* 161–179.

Alberta Agriculture, Food and Rural Development. (1997). *Finding common ground: Negotiating agreements.* Edmonton: Author.

Alinsky, S. (1971). *Rules for radicals.* New York: Vintage Press.

American Arbitration Association. (n.d.). *Welcome to the AAA.* Retrieved May 15, 2006, from http://www.adr.org

American Psychological Association (2001). *Publication manual of the American Psychological Association* (5th ed.). Washington, DC: Author.

Anderson, J., & Carter, R. W. (Eds.). (2003). *Diversity perspectives for social work practice.* Boston: Allyn & Bacon.

Aponte, H. J. (1991). Structural family therapy. In A. S. Gurtman & D. P. Kniskern (Eds.), *Handbook of family therapy* (pp. 310–358). New York: Brunner/Mazel.

Appreciative Inquiry Commons. (n.d.). *Intro to AI.* Retrieved May 24, 2006, from http://appreciativeinquiry.cwru.edu

Association for Conflict Resolution, Education Section. (n.d.). *Conflict resolution education school resources.* Retrieved May 15, 2006, from http://www.mediate.com/acreducation/pg3.cfm

Association of Family and Conciliation Courts. (2000). *Model standards of practice for family and divorce mediation.* Retrieved May 15, 2006, from http://www.afccnet.org/resources/resources_model_mediation.asp

Auerbach, J. S. (1984). *Justice without law?* New York: Oxford University Press.

Augoustinos, M., & Reynolds, K. J. (2002). *Understanding prejudice, racism, and social conflict.* Thousand Oaks, CA: Sage.

Aureli, F., & deWaal, F. B. M. (2000). *Natural conflict resolution.* Berkeley: University of California Press.

Back, A. L., & Arnold, R. M. (2005). Dealing with conflict in caring for the seriously ill: "It was just out of the question." *Journal of the American Medical Association, 293,* 1374–1381.

Balachandra, L., Bordone, R. C., Menkel-Meadow, C., Ringstrom, P., & Sarath, E. (2005). Improvisation and negotiation: Expecting and unexpected. *Negotiation Journal, 21,* 415–423.

Bandler, R., & Grinder, J. (1982). *Reframing: Neuro-linguistic programming and the transformation of meaning*. Moab, UT: Real People.

Barash, D. P., & Webel, C. P. (2002). *Peace and conflict studies*. Thousand Oaks, CA: Sage.

Bargal, D., & Bar, H. (1992). A Lewinian approach to intergroup workshops for Palestinean-Arab and Jewish Youth. *Journal of Social Issues, 48*(2), 139–154.

Bargal, D., & Bar, H. (1997). *Living with conflict: Encounters between Jewish and Palestinian youth*. Jerusalem: Jerusalem Institute for the Study of Israel.

Baris, M. A., Coates, C. A., Duvall, B. B., Garrity, C. B., Johnson, E. T., LaCross, E. R. (2001). *Working with high-conflict families of divorce: A guide for professionals*. York, PA: Aronson.

Barsky, A. E. (1993). When advocates and mediators negotiate. *Negotiation Journal, 9*, 115–122, 273–274.

Barsky, A. E. (1996). Mediation and empowerment in child protection cases. *Mediation Quarterly, 14*(2), 111–134.

Barsky, A. E. (1997a). Child protection mediation. In E. Kruk (Ed.), *Mediation and conflict resolution in social work and the human services* (pp. 117–139). Chicago: Nelson-Hall.

Barsky, A. E. (1997b). Mental illness, mental capacity, and negotiation competence. *Conflict Resolution Notes, 14*(3), 23–24.

Barsky, A. E. (2004). Mediating separation of same-sex couples. In J. Folberg, A. Milne, & P. Salem (Eds.), *Divorce and family mediation: Models, techniques, and applications* (pp. 351–377). New York: Guilford.

Barsky, A. E. (2006a). *Alcohol, other drugs, and addictions: A professional development manual for social work and the human services*. Belmont, CA: Brooks/Cole-Wadsworth.

Barsky, A. E. (2006b). *Successful social work education: A student's guide*. Belmont, CA: Brooks/Cole.

Barsky, A. E. (in press-a). Social work approaches to conflict analysis and Resolution: Causes, conditions, and conflict handling interventions. In S. Byrne, D. Sandole, J. Senehi, & I. Staroste-Sandole (Eds.), *Conflict analysis and resolution as multidiscipline: Integration and synergy across disciplines*. New York: Routledge.

Barsky, A. E. (in press-b). Social work research and the law: How LGBT research can be structured and used to affect judicial decisions. In W. Meezan & J. I. Martin (Eds.), *Research methods with gay, lesbian, bisexual, and transgender populations*. Boston: Haworth Press.

Barsky, A. E., Este, D., & Collins, D. (1996). Cultural competence in family mediation. *Mediation Quarterly, 13,* 167–178.

Barsky, A. E., & Gould, J. (2002). *Clinicians in court: A guide to subpoenas, depositions, testifying, and everything else you need to know*. New York: Guilford.

Barsky, A. E., & Wood, L. (2005). Conflict avoidance in a university context. *Higher Education Research & Development, 24,* 249–264.

Bazemore, S. G., & Umbreit, M. (2001). *A comparison of four restorative conferencing models*. Washington, DC: U.S. Department of Justice, Office of Justice Programs, Office of Juvenile Justice and Delinquency Prevention. Retrieved May 18, 2006, from http://purl.access.gpo.gov/GPO/LPS10955

Bazerman, M. H., & Shonk, K. (2005). The decision perspective to negotiation. In M. L. Moffitt & R. C. Bordone (Eds.), *The handbook of dispute resolution* (pp. 52–65). San Francisco: Jossey-Bass.

Bear Chief, R., Barsky, A. E., & Este, D. (2000). Theft by a Cree woman: Victim-offender mediation versus healing circle. In E. Geva, A. E. Barsky, & F. Westernoff (Eds.), *Interprofessional practice with diverse populations: Cases in point* (pp. 127–146). Westport, CT: Greenwood.

Beck, C. J. A., Sales, B. D., & Emery, R. E. (2004). Research on the impact of family mediation. In J. Folberg, A. Milne, & P. Salem (Eds.), *Divorce and family mediation: Models, techniques, and applications* (pp. 447–482). New York: Guilford.

Bens, I. (2005). *Facilitating with ease! Core skills for facilitators, team leaders and members, managers, consultants, and trainers*. San Francisco: Jossey-Bass.

Birkhoff, J. E., & Warfield, W. (1997). The development of pedagogy and practicum. *Mediation Quarterly, 14,* 93–110.

Bossy, J. (Ed.). (2003). *Disputes and settlements: Law and human relations in the West*. Cambridge: Cambridge University Press.

Bowling, D., & Hoffman, D. (2003). *Bringing peace into the room: How the personal qualities of the mediator impact the process of conflict resolution*. San Francisco: Jossey-Bass

Boyan, S. M., & Termini, A. M. (2005). *The psychotherapist as parent coordinator in high-conflict divorce: Strategies and techniques*. Boston: Haworth.

Brahm, E., & Ouellet, J. (2003). *Designing new dispute resolution systems*. Retrieved May 23, 2006, from http://www.beyondintractability.org/m/designing_dispute_systems.jsp?nid=1398

Bratton, L. B. (1997). Themes of conflict theory: An integrative model for practitioners. *Journal of Teaching in Social Work, 15*(1/2), 131–146.

Brett, J. M., Adair, W., Lempereux, A., Okumura, T., Shikhirev, P., Tinsley, C., & Lytle, A. (1998). Culture and joint gains in negotiation. *Negotiation Journal, 14,* 61–84.

Brinkman, R., & Kirchner, R. (1994). *Dealing with people you can't stand: How to bring out the best of people at their worst.* Toronto: Ryerson-McGraw-Hill.

British Columbia Ministry of the Attorney General. (2003). *Reaching resolution: A guide to public sector dispute resolution systems.* Victoria: Author. Retrieved May 18, 2006, from http://www.ag. gov.bc.ca/dro/publications/guides/design.pdf

Broome, B. J. (1993). Managing differences in conflict resolution: The role of relational empathy. In D. J. D. Sandole & H. van der Merwe (Eds.), *Conflict resolution theory and practice: Integration and application* (pp. 97–111). Manchester, UK: Manchester University Press.

Bush, G. (2005). *Integrated decision management handbook.* Gainesville, FL: Probabilistic Publishing.

Bush, R. A. B., & Folger, J. P. (2005). *The promise of mediation: The transformative approach to conflict* (2nd ed.). San Francisco: Jossey-Bass.

Bush, R. A. B., & Pope, S. G. (2004). Transformative mediation: Changing the quality of family conflict interaction. In J. Folberg, A. Milne, & P. Salem (Eds.), *Divorce and family mediation: Models, techniques, and applications* (pp. 53–71). New York: Guilford.

Cappelletti, M. (1979). *Access to justice* (Vol. III). Milan: Sijthoff & Noordhoff- Alphenaandenrijn.

Cardozo, B. N. (1924). *The growth of law.* New Haven, CT: Yale University Press.

Carniol, B. (2005). *Case critical: Social services and social justice in Canada* (5th ed.). Toronto: Between the Lines.

Carpenter, S., & Kennedy, W. J. D. (2001). *Managing public disputes: A practical guide for professionals in government, business, and citizens' groups.* San Francisco: Jossey-Bass.

Center for Social Gerontology. (1997). *Adult guardianship mediation manual.* Ann Arbor, MI: Author.

Charbonneau, P. (Ed.). (1994). *Report from the Toronto Forum on Woman Abuse and Mediation.* Guelph, ON: Network Interaction for Conflict Resolution.

Chasin, R., Herzig, M., Roth, S., Chasin, L., Becker, C., & Stains, R. R. (1996). From diatribe to dialogue on divisive public issues: Approaches drawn from family therapy. *Mediation Quarterly, 13,* 323–344.

Chetkow-Yanoov, B. (1997). *Social work approaches to conflict resolution: Making fighting obsolete.* Binghamton, NY: Haworth.

Chia, H., Lee-Partridge, J. E., & Chong, C. (2004). Traditional mediation practices: Are we throwing the baby out with the bath water? *Conflict Resolution Quarterly, 21,* 451–462.

Chodron, P. (2001). *Start where you are: A guide to compassionate living.* Boston: Shambhala Classics.

Christie, D. J., Wagner, R. V., & Winter, D. D. (2001). *Peace, conflict, and violence: Peace psychology for the 21st Century.* Upper Saddle River, NJ: Prentice Hall.

Cloke, K. (2001). *Mediating dangerously: The frontiers of conflict resolution.* San Francisco: Jossey-Bass.

Cloke, K. (2005, Fall). Why every conflict breaks your heart: Conflict as a spiritual crisis. *ACResolution,* 16–21.

Cohen, J. (2003). Adversaries? Partners? How about counterparts? *Conflict Resolution Quarterly, 20,* 433–440.

Cohen, M. H. (2004). Negotiating integrative medicine: Framework for provider-patient conversations. *Negotiation Journal, 20,* 409–433.

Combs, D. (2004). *The way of conflict: Elements of wisdom for resolving disputes and transcending differences.* Novato, CA: New World Library.

Conflict Research Consortium. (1998). International online training program on intractable conflict, University of Colorado. Retrieved May 18, 2006, from http://www.colorado.edu/conflict/peace/ !treating_core.htm

Conley, J. M., & O'Barr, W. M. (1990). *Rules versus relationships: The ethnography of legal discourse.* Chicago: University of Chicago Press.

Coogler, O. J. (1978). *Structured mediation in divorce settlement.* Lexington, MA: Lexington.

Corey, G., Corey, M. S., & Callanan, P. (2003). *Issues and ethics in the helping professions* (7th ed.). Belmont, CA: Brooks/Cole.

Corey, M. S., & Corey, G. (2006). *Groups: Process and practice.* Belmont, CA: Brooks/Cole.

Craig, Y. J. (Ed.). (1998). *Advocacy, counseling, and mediation in casework.* London: Kingsley.

Crawford, D. K., & Bodine, R. J. (2005). Youths, education, and dispute resolution. In M. L. Moffitt & R. C. Bordone (Eds.), *The handbook of dispute resolution* (pp. 471–486). San Francisco: Jossey-Bass.

Crow, G., Marsh, P., & Holton, E. (2004). *Supporting pupils, schools and families: An evaluation of the Hampshire Family Group Conferences in Education Project, Family and Welfare Findings Series, 7.* Retrieved May 23, 2006, from http://www.shef.ac.uk/%7efwpg/documents/Supporting_ Pupils_000.doc

Culler, J. (1982). *On deconstruction: Theory and criticism after structuralism.* Ithaca, NY: Cornell University Press.

Cummings, E. M., & Davies, P. (1994). *Children and marital conflict. The impact of family dispute and resolution.* New York: Guilford.

Dana, D. (1996). *Managing differences: How to build better relationships at work and home.* Overland Park, KS: MTI.

Dan-Cohen, M. (1992). Conceptions of choice and conceptions of autonomy. *Ethics, 102,* 221–243.

Denzin, N. K., & Lincoln, Y. S. (2005). *The Sage handbook of qualitative research* (3rd ed.). Thousand Oaks, CA: Sage.

Desivilya, H. S. (2004). Promoting coexistence by means of conflict education: The MACBE model. *Journal of Social Issues, 60,* 339–356.

Deutsch, M. (1973). *The resolution of conflict.* New Haven, CT: Yale University Press.

Dingwall, R., & Miller, G. (2002). Lessons from brief therapy? Some interactional suggestions for family mediators. *Conflict Resolution Quarterly, 19,* 269–287.

Dodd, S., & Jansson, B. (2004). Expanding the boundaries of ethics education: Preparing social workers for ethical advocacy in an organizational setting. *Journal of Social Work Education, 40,* 455–465.

Dolgoff, R., Loewenberg, F. M., & Harrington, D. (2005). *Ethical decisions for social work practice* (7th ed.). Belmont, CA: Brooks/Cole.

Douglas, A. (1962). *Industrial peacemaking.* New York: Columbia University Press.

Druckman, D. (1993). An analytical research agenda for conflict and conflict resolution. In D. J. D. Sandole & H. van der Merwe (Eds.), *Conflict resolution theory and practice: Integration and application.* Manchester, UK: Manchester University Press.

Druckman, D. (2005). *Doing research: Methods of inquiry for conflict analysis.* Thousand Oaks, CA: Sage.

Dubinskas, F. A. (1992). Culture and conflict. In D. M. Kolb & J. M. Bartunek (Eds.), *Hidden conflict in organizations* (pp. 187–208). London: Sage.

Dubler, N. N., & Liebman, C. B. (2004). *Bioethics mediation: A guide to shaping shared solutions.* New York: United Hospital Fund.

Dugan, M. (2003). Understanding power. Retrieved on May 18, 2006, from http://www.beyondintractability. org/m/culture_conflict.jsp

Dworkin, R. M. (1977). *Taking rights seriously.* Cambridge, MA: Harvard University Press.

Edelman, J., & Crain, M. B. (1993). *The Tao of negotiation.* New York: Harper.

Elangovan, A. R. (1995). Managerial third-party dispute intervention: A prescriptive model of strategy selection. *Academy of Management Review, 20,* 800–830.

Eller, J. (2004). *Effective group facilitation in education: How to energize meetings and manage difficult groups.* Thousand Oaks, CA: Sage.

Ellis, D., & Stuckless, N. (1996). *Mediating and negotiating marital conflicts.* Thousand Oaks, CA: Sage.

Ellis, D., & Wight, L. (1998). Theorizing power in divorce negotiations: Implications for practice. *Mediation Quarterly, 15,* 227–244.

Emery, R. E. (1994). *Renegotiating family relationships: Divorce, child custody, and mediation.* New York: Guilford.

English, P., & Neilson, L. C. (2004). Certifying mediators. *Divorce and family mediation: Models, techniques, and applications* (pp. 483–515). New York: Guilford.

Erikson, E. H. (1950). Eight stages of man. In *Childhood and society* (pp. 219–234). New York: Norton.

Ertel, D. (1991). Conflict resolution/negotiation styles. In *Negotiation course materials.* Toronto: University of Toronto Faculty of Law.

Evans, A. F., & Evans, R. A. (2001). *Peace skills: Leaders' guide.* San Francisco: Jossey-Bass.

Evans, D., Hearn, M., Uhlemann, M., & Ivey, A. (2004). *Essential interviewing: A programmed approach to effective communication* (6th ed.). Belmont, CA: Brooks/Cole.

Ezell, M. (2000). *Advocacy in the human services.* Belmont, CA: Wadsworth.

Family Mediation Canada. (n.d.). *Code of Professional Conduct.* Retrieved May 18, 2006, from http://www.fmc.ca/?p=Families

Favaloro, G. J. (1998). Mediation: A family therapy technique? *Mediation Quarterly, 16,* 33–36.

Feld, L., & Simm, P. A. (1998). *Mediating professional conduct complaints.* Waterloo, ON: Network for Conflict Resolution Canada.

Fisher, R., & Brown, S. (1988). *Getting together: Building relationships as we negotiate.* New York: Penguin.

Fisher, R., & Shapiro, D. (2005). *Beyond reason: Using emotions as you negotiate.* New York: Viking.

Fisher, R., & Urtel, D. (1995). *Getting ready to negotiate.* New York: Penguin.

Fisher, R., Ury, W., & Patton, B. (1997). *Getting to yes: Negotiating agreement without giving in* (3rd ed.). New York: Penguin.

Fisher, R. J. (1997). *Interactive conflict resolution.* Syracuse, NY: Syracuse University Press.

Fisher, T., Alol, M., & Wingate, R. (2005). *Mindfulness for mediators: Theory and practice.* Paper presented at the Association for Conflict Resolution, Fifth Annual Conference, Workshop Proceedings, Minneapolis, MN.

Florida Bar, Family Law Section. (2004). *Bounds of advocacy: Goals for family lawyers*. Tallahassee: Author.

Flynn, D. (2005). The social worker as family mediator: Balancing power in cases involving family violence. *Australian Social Work, 58,* 407–418.

Folberg, J., Milne, A., & Salem, P. (Eds.). (2004). *Divorce and family mediation: Models, techniques, and applications*. New York: Guilford.

Folger, J. P., & Bush, R. A. B. (2001). *Designing mediation: Approaches to training and practice within a transformative framework*. New York: Institute for the Study of Conflict Transformation.

Fong, L. (2005). Milan mediation model. In *Conference proceedings of the Association for Conflict Resolution Annual Conference* (pp. 59–64). Washington, DC: Association for Conflict Resolution.

Fowler, M. D. M. (1989). Social advocacy. *Heart & Lung, 18*(1), 97–99.

Fox, E. A., & Gafni, M. (2004, Spring). Negotiating wisely: The third eye of decision making. *Dispute Resolution Magazine,* 18–21.

Frank, R. H. (1992). A theory of moral sentiments. In M. Zey (Ed.), *Decision making: Alternatives to rational choice models* (pp. 158–184). Newbury Park, CA: Sage.

Freire, P. (1994). *Pedagogy of hope: Reliving pedagogy of the oppressed*. New York: Continuum.

Freshman, C. (1997). Privatizing same-sex "marriage" through alternative dispute resolution: Community enhancing versus community-enabling mediation. *University of California Los Angeles Law Review, 44,* 1687–1771.

Freshman, C. (2005). Identify, beliefs, emotion, and negotiation success. In M. L. Moffitt & R. C. Bordone (Eds.), *The handbook of dispute resolution* (pp. 99–117). San Francisco: Jossey-Bass.

Freud, S. (1963). *The complete works of Sigmund Freud*. London: Hogarth.

Friedman, M. (2004, Summer). The so-called high-conflict couple. *Family Mediation News, Association for Conflict Resolution, 1,* 5–6.

Fuertes, A. B (2004). In their own words: Contextualizing the discourse of (war) trauma and healing. *Conflict Resolution Quarterly, 21,* 491–501.

Fulghum, R. (2003). *All I really need to know I learned in kindergarten* (15th Anniversary Edition). New York: Bantam.

Furlong, G. T. (2005). *The conflict resolution toolbox: Models and maps for analyzing, diagnosing, and resolving conflict*. San Francisco: Jossey-Bass.

Gadlin, H. (2005). Bargaining in the shadow of management. In M. L. Moffitt & R. C. Bordone (Eds.), *The handbook of dispute resolution* (pp. 371–385). San Francisco: Jossey-Bass.

Gaynier, L. (2005). Transformative mediation: In search of a theory of practice. *Conflict Resolution Quarterly, 22,* 397–408.

Gelfand, M. J., & Brett, J. M. (2004). *The handbook of negotiation and culture* [Electronic resource]. Stanford, CA: Stanford Business Books. Retrieved May 18, 2006, from http://www.netLibrary.com/urlapi.asp?action=summary&v=1&bookid=125436

Germain, C. B., & Gitterman, A. (1996). *The life model of social work practice: Advances in practice and theory*. New York: Columbia University Press.

Germany, T. (2004). *Appreciative inquiry—Something out of the ordinary*. Retrieved May 18, 2006, from http://admin.fmcs.gov/assets/files/Articles/AppreciativeInquirytgermany.doc

Girdner, L. K. (Ed.). (1990). Mediation and spouse abuse [Special issue]. *Mediation Quarterly, 7*(4).

Goldberg-Wood, G., & Middleman, R. (1991). Advocacy and social action: Key elements in the structural approach to direct practice in social work. *Social Work with Groups, 14*(3/4), 53–63.

Goldstein, W. M., & Hogarth, R. M. (1997). *Research on judgment and decision making: Currents, connections, and controversies*. Cambridge: Cambridge University Press.

Gould, J. W. (2004). Evaluating the probative value of child custody evaluations: A guide for forensic mental health professionals. *Journal of Child Custody, 1*(1), 77–96.

Gould, K. H. (1987). Life Model versus Conflict Model: A feminist perspective. *Social Work, July–August,* 346–351.

Gould, P., & Gould, G. (1988). *From no to yes: The route to constructive agreement* [Videotape]. Toronto: International Telefilm (with John Cleese).

Green, R. G. (1998). *Justice in aboriginal communities: Sentencing alternatives*. Saskatoon, SK: Purich.

Grellert, E. A. (1991). The self of the therapist: Attending to countertransference. *Treating Abuse Today, 1*(4), 22–25.

Grinnell, R. M, & Unrau, Y. A. (2005). *Social work research and evaluation: Quantitative and qualitative approaches* (7th ed.). New York: Oxford University Press.

Hackley, S., Bazerman, M., Ross, L., & Shapiro, D. L. (2005). Psychological dimensions of the Israeli settlements issue: Historic opportunities and challenges. *Negotiation Journal, 21,* 209–219.

Haggis, P. (Director). (2005). *Crash* [DVD]. Los Angeles: Lions Gate Entertainment.

Halabi, R. (1998). *Working with conflict groups: The educational approach of The School for Peace*. Unpublished manuscript, Neveh Shalom—Wahat Al-salam, Nahshon, Israel.

Hammer, M. R. (2003). *Intercultural conflict styles inventory: Interpretive guide and instructor's manual.* North Potomac, MD: Hammer Consulting Group.

Hermann, M. S., Hollett, N. L., Eaker, D. G., & Gale, J. (2003). Mediator reflections on practice: Connecting select demographics and preferred orientations. *Conflict Resolution Quarterly, 20,* 403–427.

Herr, K., & Anderson, G. L. (2005). *The action research dissertation: A guide for students and faculty.* Thousand Oaks, CA: Sage.

Hessler, R. M., Hollis, S., & Crowe, C. (1998). Peer mediation: A qualitative study of youthful frames of power and influence. *Mediation Quarterly, 15,* 187–198.

Hoeffer, R. (2006). *Advocacy practice for social justice.* Chicago: Lyceum.

Honeyman, C., Hughes, S. H., & Schneider, A. K. (2003). How can we teach so it takes? *Conflict Resolution Quarterly, 20,* 429–432.

Hopkins, B. R. (1994). *Charity, advocacy, and the law.* New York: Wiley.

Howick, D., Daily, S., & Sprik, A. (2002). *The new compleat facilitator: A handbook for facilitators.* Madison, WI: Howick.

Hudson, J., Morris, A., Maxwell, G., & Galaway, B. (1996). *Family group conferences: Perspectives on policy and practice.* Monsey, NY: Willow Tree.

Hunt, D. E. (1987). *Beginning with ourselves: In practice, theory, and human affairs.* Cambridge, MA: Brookline Books.

Institute for the Study of Conflict Transformation. (n.d.). *The transformative framework.* Retrieved May 18, 2006 from http://transformativemediation.org/transformative.htm

International Association of Facilitators. (2004). *IAF code of ethics.* Retrieved May 18, 2006, from http://www.iaf-world.org/i4a/pages/index.cfm?pageid=3346

International Debate Education Association. (n.d.). Teaching debate: Debate format. Retrieved May 18, 2006, from http://www.idebate.org/resources/debate_formats.php

Irving, H. H., & Benjamin, M. (1995). *Family mediation: Contemporary issues.* Thousand Oaks, CA: Sage.

Irving, H. H., & Benjamin, M. (2002). *Therapeutic family mediation: Helping families resolve conflict.* Thousand Oaks, CA: Sage.

Isenhart, M. W., & Spangle, M. (2000). *Collaborative approaches to resolving conflict.* Thousand Oaks, CA: Sage.

Ivey, A. E., & Ivey, M. B. (2007). *Intentional interviewing and counseling: Facilitating client development in a multicultural society* (6th ed.). Belmont, CA: Brooks/Cole.

Jabbour, E. J. (1996). *Sulha: Palestinian traditional peacemaking process.* House of Hope. Bethlehem: Wi'am Palestinian Conflict Resolution Center.

Jameson, J. K., Bodtker, A. M., & Jones, T. S. (2006). Like talking to a brick wall: Implications of emotion metaphors for mediation practice. *Negotiation Journal, 22,* 199–207.

Johnson, D. W. (2000). *Reaching out: Interpersonal effectiveness and self-actualization.* Boston: Allyn & Bacon.

Kadushin, A. (2002). *Supervision in social work* (4th ed.). New York: Columbia University Press.

Kajosevic, I. (2003). *Arts in conflict resolution.* Retrieved December 15, 2005, from http://www.beyondintractability.org/10614.audio

Kaminski, L., & Walmsley, C. (1995). The advocacy brief: A guide for social workers. *The Social Worker, 63*(2), 53–58.

Kaner, S. (1996). *Facilitator's guide to participatory decision-making.* Philadelphia: New Society.

Kaplan, N. M. (1997). Mediation in the school system: Facilitating the development of peer mediation programs. In E. Kruk (Ed.), *Mediation and conflict resolution in social work and the human services* (pp. 247–262). Chicago: Nelson-Hall.

Katsh, M. E., & Rifkin, J. (2001). *Online dispute resolution: Resolving conflicts in cyberspace.* San Francisco: Jossey-Bass.

Kauffman, N. (1991). The idea of expedited arbitration two decades later. *Arbitration Journal, 46*(3), 34–38.

Kavanaugh, K. H., & Kennedy, P. H. (1992). *Promoting cultural diversity.* Newbury Park, CA: Sage.

Keshavjee, M., & Whatling, T. (2005). *Reflective learnings from the training programmes of the Ismaili Muslim Conciliation and Arbitration Boards, globally.* The Institute of Ismaili Studies. Retrieved December 28, 2005, from http://www.iis.ac.uk/learning/life_long_learning/reflective_learnings/reflective_learnings.htm

Kestner, P. B. (2005). *The mediator and the mediative mind.* Paper presented at the Association for Conflict Resolution, Fifth Annual Conference, Workshop Proceedings, Minneapolis, MN.

Kestner, P. B., & Ray, L. (2002). *The conflict resolution training program: Participant's workbook* [and Leader's Mannual]. San Francisco: Jossey-Bass.

Kirst-Ashman, K., & Hull, G. (2005). *Generalist practice with organizations and communities* (3rd ed.). Belmont, CA: Brooks/Cole.

Knowles, M. S., Holton, E. F., & Swanson, R. A. (2005). *The adult learner: The definitive classic on adult education and training* (6th ed.). Houston, TX: Gulf.

Kolb, D. A. (1974). Management and learning processes. In D. A. Kolb, I. M. Rubin, & J. McIntyre (Eds.), *Organizational psychology: A book of readings* (pp. 27–42). Upper Saddle City, NJ: Prentice Hall.

Kolb, D. M., & Williams, J. (2003). *Everyday negotiation. Navigating the hidden agendas in bargaining.* San Francisco: Jossey-Bass.

Kosmoski, G. J., & Pollack, D. R. (2000). *Managing difficult, frustrating, and hostile conversations: Strategies for savvy [school] administrators.* Thousand Oaks, CA: Sage.

Kraybill, R. S. (n.d.). *From head to heart: When reconciliation is your goal.* Retrieved May 18, 2006, from http://journeytowardforgiveness.com/mapping/article2.asp

Kraybill, R. (1985). Teaching children how to fight. *MCS Conciliation Quarterly, 4*(1), 8–9.

Kraybill, R. S. (2005a). *Group facilitation: Skills to facilitate meetings and training exercises to learn them.* Harrisonburg, VA; Riverhouse ePress.

Kraybill, R. S. (2005b). *Structured dialogue: Cool tools for hot topics.* Harrisonburg, VA: Riverhouse ePress.

Kraybill, R. S. (2005c). *Style matters: The Kraybill Conflict Response Inventory.* Harrisonburg, VA: Riverhouse ePress.

Kruk, E. (Ed.). (1997). *Mediation and conflict resolution in social work and the human services.* Chicago: Nelson-Hall.

Kübler-Ross, E. (1997). *On death and dying.* New York: Macmillan.

Kumari, V., & Brooks, S. L. (2004). *Creative child advocacy: Global perspectives.* Thousand Oaks, CA: Sage.

Lang, M. (2004). Understanding and responding to power in mediation. In *Divorce and family mediation: Models, techniques, and applications* (pp. 209–224). New York: Guilford.

LeBaron, M. (n.d.). *Culture and conflict.* Retrieved May 18, 2006, from http://www.beyondintractability.org/m/culture_conflict.jsp

LeBaron, M. (1997). Mediation, conflict resolution and multicultural reality: Culturally competent practice. In E. Kruk (Ed.), *Mediation and conflict resolution in social work and the human services* (pp. 315–335). Chicago: Nelson-Hall.

LeBaron, M. (2003). *Bridging cultural conflicts: A new approach to a changing world.* San Francisco: Jossey-Bass.

LeBaron Duryea, M., & Grundison, J. B. (1992). *Conflict and culture: A literature review and bibliography.* Victoria, BC: UVic Institute for Dispute Resolution.

Lederach, J. P. (1986). *Mediation in North America: An examination of the profession's cultural premises.* Unpublished manuscript, University of Colorado, Denver.

Lederach, J. P. (1995). *Preparing for peace: Conflict transformation across cultures.* Syracuse, NY: Syracuse University Press.

Lederach, J. P. (2005). *The moral imagination.* New York: Oxford University Press.

Lens, V. (2005). Advocacy and argumentation in the public arena: A guide for social workers. *Social Work, 50*(3), 231–238.

Leviton, S. C., & Greenstone, J. L. (1997). *Elements of mediation.* Belmont, CA: Brooks/Cole.

Lewicki, R. J. (1997). Teaching negotiation and dispute resolution in colleges of business: The state of the practice. *Negotiation Journal, 13,* 253–269.

Lewicki, R. J., Litterer, J., Minton, J., & Saunders, D. (1998). *Negotiation* (3rd ed.). Burr Ridge, IL: Irwin.

Lewin, K. (1948). Action research and minority problems. In G. W. Lewin (Ed.), *Resolving social conflicts* (pp. 56–70). New York: Harper & Row.

Lichtenstein, M. (2005). Creating awareness of the spiritual dimensions of conflict: Resolution by contemplating organizational culture. *Negotiation Journal, 23,* 225–236.

Love, L. P. (1997). The top ten reasons why mediators should not evaluate. *Florida State Law Review, 24,* 937–939.

Lowry, L. R. (2004). Evaluative mediation. In J. Folberg, A. Milne, & P. Salem (Eds.), *Divorce and family mediation: Models, techniques, and applications* (pp. 72–91). New York: Guilford.

Lundy, C. (2004). *Social work and social justice: A structural approach to practice.* Peterborough, Canada: Broadview Press.

Macduff, I. (2006). Your pace or mine? Culture, time, and negotiation. *Negotiation Journal, 22,* 31–45.

MacFarlane, J. (1999). *Dispute resolution: Readings and cases.* Toronto: Emond Montgomery.

MacKearcher, D. (1997). *Making sense of adult learning.* Toronto: Culture Concepts.

MacRae, A., & Zehr, H. (2004). *The little book of family group conferences.* Intercourse, PA: Good Books.

Marlow, L. (1987). Styles of conducting mediation. *Mediation Quarterly, 18,* 85–90.

Marlow, L. (1997). *Divorce mediation: A practice in search of a theory.* Syracuse, NY: Syracuse University Press.

Marx, K. (1964). *Selected writings in sociology and social psychology.* T. B. Biltmore (Trans.). New York: McGraw-Hill.

Maryama, G. (1992). Lewin's impact on education: Instilling cooperation and conflict management skills in school children. *Journal of Social Issues, 48*(2), 155–166.

Maslow, A. H. (1987). *Motivation and personality* (3rd ed.). New York: Harper & Row.

Mayer, B. (1987). The dynamics of power in mediation and negotiation. *Mediation Quarterly, 16*, 57–86.

Mayer, B. (1997). Mediation and dispute resolution in the field of social policy. In E. Kruk (Ed.), *Mediation and conflict resolution in social work and the human services* (pp. 297-314). Chicago: Nelson-Hall.

Mayer, B. (2000). *The dynamics of conflict resolution: A practitioner's guide.* San Francisco: Jossey-Bass.

Mayer, B. (2004a). *Beyond neutrality: Confronting the crisis in conflict resolution.* San Francisco: Jossey-Bass.

Mayer, B. (2004b). Facilitative mediation. In J. Folberg, A. Milne, & P. Salem (Eds.), *Divorce and family mediation: Models, techniques, and applications* (pp. 29–52). New York: Guilford.

McCormick, M. A. (1997). Confronting social injustice as a mediator. *Mediation Quarterly, 14*, 293–307.

McGuire, A. P., & Inlow, L. (2005). Interactive reflection as a creative teaching strategy. *Conflict Resolution Quarterly, 22*, 365–379.

McMurtry, L., & Ossana, D. (Writers). (2005). *Brokeback Mountain* [DVD]. Los Angeles: River Road Entertainment.

Menkel-Meadow, C., & Wheeler, M. (2004). *What's fair: Ethics for negotiators.* San Francisco: Jossey-Bass.

Menkel-Meadow, C., Love, L. P., Schneider, A. K., & Sternlight, J. R. (2005). *Dispute resolution: Beyond the adversarial model.* New York: Aspen.

Miller, B. (1997). Great powers and regional peacemaking: Patterns in the Middle East and Beyond. *Journal of Strategic Studies, 30*(1), 103–172.

Miller, E. (2001). Gender, power, and politics. In I. Skjelsboek & D. Smith (Eds.), *Gender, peace, and conflict.* Thousand Oaks, CA: Sage.

Milne, A. (2004). Mediation and domestic abuse. In *Divorce and family mediation: Models, techniques, and applications* (pp. 304–335). New York: Guilford.

Milne, A. L., Folberg, J., & Salem, P. (2004). The evolution of divorce and family mediation: An overview. In J. Folberg, A. Milne, & P. Salem (Eds.), *Divorce and family mediation: Models, techniques, and applications* (pp. 3–28). New York: Guilford.

Mnookin, R. H., & Kornhauser, L. (1979). Bargaining in the shadow of the law: The case of divorce. *Yale Law Journal, 88*, 960–997.

Mnookin, R. H., Susskind, L. E., & Foster, P. C. (1999). *Negotiating on behalf of others: Advice to lawyers, business executives, diplomats, politicians, and everyone else.* Thousand Oaks, CA: Sage.

Montville, J. V. (1993). The healing function in political conflict resolution: In D. J. D. Sandole & H. van der Merwe (Eds.), *Conflict management* (pp. 112-128). Manchester, UK: Manchester University Press.

Moodley, R., & West, W. (2005). *Integrating healing practices into counseling and psychotherapy.* Thousand Oaks, CA: Sage.

Moore, C. (1996). *The mediation process: Practical strategies for resolving conflict.* San Francisco: Jossey-Bass.

Morse, P. S., & Andrea, R. (1994). Peer mediation in the schools: Teaching conflict resolution techniques to students. *NAASP Bulletin, 78*(560), 75–82.

Murdach, A. D. (1980, November). Bargaining and persuasion with non-voluntary clients. *Social Work,* 458–461.

Murray, H., Gillese, E., Lennon, M., Mercer, P., & Robinson, M. (1996). *Ethical principles in university teaching.* Toronto: Society for Teaching and Learning in Higher Education, University of Toronto, OISE.

Myers, I. M. (1987). *Introduction to type in organizations.* Palo Alto, CA: Consulting Psychologists Press (Instruments may be ordered from http://www.myersbriggs.org.)

Nader, L. (1992, Winter). Trading justice for harmony. *Forum,* 12–14.

National Association of Social Workers. (1999). *Code of ethics.* Retrieved May 18, 2006, from http://www.socialworkers.org/pubs/code/code.asp

National Institute for Dispute Resolution. (1987). Dispute resolution and higher education: A brief introduction. *MCS Conciliation Quarterly, Spring Issue,* 2.

Nelson, C. (1999). Common ground between Islam and Christianity. *Fountain: A Magazine of Critical, Scientific, and Spiritual Thought, 27,* 18–20.

Nelson, H. W., Netting, F. E., Huber, R., Borders, K. (2001). The social worker-ombudsman partnership: Using a resident-centered model of situational conflict tactics. *Journal of Gerontological Social Work, 35*(3), 65–82.

Newhill, C. E. (2003). *Client violence in social work practice: Prevention, intervention, and research.* New York: Guilford Press.

Nicol, A. (1997). *Advocacy.* Unpublished manuscript, Alberta Child Advocates, Edmonton.

Nicoterra, A. M. (1995). *Conflict and organizations: Communicative processes.* Albany: State University of New York Press.

Noble, C., Dizgun, L. L., & Emond, D. P. (1998). *Mediation advocacy: Effective client presentation in mediation proceedings.* Toronto: Emond Montgomery.

Noonan, M. (1998). Understanding the "difficult" patient from a dual person perspective. *Clinical Social Work Journal, 26,* 129–140.

Noone, M. (1996). *Mediation.* Essential Legal Skills series. London: Cavendish.

Oetzel, J. G., & Ting-Toomey, S. (2006). *The SAGE handbook of conflict communication: Integrating theory, research, and practice.* Thousand Oaks, CA: Sage.

Ombudsman Association. (2004). *Generic organizational ombudsperson job description.* Retrieved August 9, 2005, from http://www.ombuds-toa.org/downloads/genorgombpd.doc

Pearson, J. (1997). Mediating when domestic violence is a factor: Policies and practices in court-based divorce mediation programs. *Mediation Quarterly, 14,* 319–335.

Pennell, J., & Ristock, J. R. (1997). Feminist links, post-modern interruptions toward a critical social work education. *Social work discussion papers: Trends in social work education.* St. John's, NF: Memorial University.

Pflug, M. A. (1996). "Pimadaziwin": Contemporary rituals in Odawa community. *The American Indian Quarterly, 20,* 489–514. (Special issue: To Hear the Eagles Cry: Contemporary Themes in Native American spirituality.)

Phelan, A., Barlow, C., Myrick, F., Rogers, G., & Sawa, R. (2003). Discourses of conflict: A multidisciplinary study of professional education. *Alberta Journal of Educational Research, 59*(2), 201–203.

Picard, C. A. (2002). *Mediating interpersonal and small group conflict.* Ottawa: Golden Dog Press.

Picard, C., Bishop, P., Ramkay, R., & Sargent, N. (2004). *The art and science of mediation.* Toronto: Emond Montgomery.

Picard, C. A., & Melchin, K. R. (1988). *Conflict management in a church context.* Ottawa: Picard and Associates.

Pinderhughes, E. (1989). *Understanding race, ethnicity, and power: The key to efficacy in clinical practice.* New York: Free Press.

Platow, M. J., & Hunter, J. A. (2001). Realistic intergroup conflict: Prejudice, power, and protest. In M. Augoustinos & K. J. Reynolds (Eds.), *Understanding prejudice, racism, and social conflict* (pp. 195–212). Thousand Oaks, CA: Sage.

Pranis, K. (2005). *The little book of circle processes.* Intercourse, PA: Good Books.

Pruitt, D. G., & Carnevale, P. C. (1993). *Negotiation in social conflict.* Pacific Grove, CA: Brooks/Cole.

Pruitt, M. K., & Johnston, J. (2004). Therapeutic mediation with high conflict parents: Models and strategies. In J. Folberg, A. Milne, & P. Salem (Eds.), *Divorce and family mediation: Models, techniques, and applications* (pp. 92–111). New York: Guilford.

Rabie, M. (1994). *Conflict resolution and ethnicity.* Westport, CT: Praeger.

Rahim, M. A., & Blum, A. A. (1994). *Global perspectives on organizational conflict.* Westport, CT: Praeger.

Raiffa, H., Richardson, J., & Metcalfe, D. (2002). *Negotiation analysis: The science and art of collaborative decision-making.* Cambridge, MA: Harvard University Press.

Raines, S. S. (2005). Can online mediation be transformative: Tales from the front. *Conflict Resolution Quarterly, 4,* 437–451.

Rapoport, A. (1974). *Fights, games and debates.* Ann Arbor: University of Michigan Press.

Rave, E., & Larson, C. (1995). *Ethical decision making in therapy: Feminist perspectives.* New York: Guilford.

Rawls, J. A. (1971). *Theory of justice.* Cambridge, MA: Harvard University Press.

Reisch, M. (1990, January). Organizational structure and client advocacy: Lessons from the 1980s. *Social Work,* 73–74.

Ricci, I. (2004). Court-based mandatory mediation: Special considerations. In J. Folberg, A. Milne, & P. Salem (Eds.), *Divorce and family mediation: Models, techniques, and applications* (pp. 397–419). New York: Guilford.

Rifkin, J., Millen, J., & Cobb, S. (1991). Toward a new discourse for mediation: A critique of neutrality. *Mediation Quarterly, 9,* 151–164.

Robbennolt, J. K. (2003). Apologies and legal settlement: An empirical examination. *Michigan Law Review, 102,* 460–517.

Robbins, S. P. (1998). *Organizational behavior: Concepts, controversies, applications* (8th ed.). Upper Saddle City, NJ: Prentice Hall.

Robin, A. L. (2003). *Negotiating parent-adolescent conflict: A behavioral-family systems approach.* New York: Guilford.

Rogers, C. (1957). The necessary and sufficient conditions of therapeutic personality change. *Journal of Counseling Psychology, 21,* 95–103.

Rossides, D. W. (1998). *Professions and disciplines: Functional and conflict perspectives.* Upper Saddle City, NJ: Prentice Hall.

Roth, B. J., Wulff, R. W., & Cooper, C. A. (1993). *The alternative dispute resolution practice guide.* Rochester, NY: Lawyers Cooperative Publishing.

Rothman, J. (1997). *Resolving identity-based conflict—In nations, organizations and communities.* San Francisco: Jossey-Bass.

Rothman, J. C. (1998). *Contracting in clinical social work.* Chicago: Nelson-Hall.

Ryan, E. (2006). Building the emotionally learned negotiator. *Negotiation Journal, 22,* 209–225.

Sandole, D. J. D., & van der Merwe, H. (1993). *Conflict resolution theory and practice: Integration and application.* Manchester, UK: Manchester University Press.

Schirch, L. (2004). *The little book of strategic peacebuilding.* Intercourse, PA: Good Books.

Schittekatte, M. (1996). Facilitating information exchange in small decision-making groups. *European Journal of Psychology, 26,* 537–556.

Schneider, R. L., & Lester, L. (2001). *Advocacy in social work: A new framework in action.* Belmont, CA: Wadsworth.

Schwarz, R., Davidson, A., Carlson, P., & McKinney, S. (2005). *The skilled facilitator: A comprehensive resource for consultants, facilitators, managers, trainers, and coaches.* San Francisco: Jossey-Bass.

Severson, M. (1998). Teaching mediation theory and skills in an interdisciplinary classroom. *Journal of Social Work Education, 34,* 185–194.

Shienvold, A. (2004). Hybrid processes. In J. Folberg, A. Milne, & P. Salem (Eds.), *Divorce and family mediation: Models, techniques, and applications* (pp. 112–128). New York: Guilford.

Shulman, L. (2006). *The skills of helping individuals, families, groups, and communities* (5th ed.). Belmont, CA: Brooks/Cole.

Shultz, N. (2004). *Fact-finding.* Retrieved May 24, 2006, from http://www.beyondintractability.org/m/fact-finding.jsp

Simons, H. W. (2001). *Persuasion in society.* Thousand Oaks, CA: Sage.

Skinner, D. C. (2003). *Introduction to decision analysis: A practitioner's guide to improving decision quality* (2nd ed.). Gainesville, FL: Probabilistic Publishing.

Skjelsbaek, I., & Smith, D. (Eds.). (2001). *Gender, peace, & conflict.* Thousand Oaks, CA: Sage.

Smith, T. H. (2005). Metaphors for navigating negotiations. *Negotiation Journal, 21,* 343–364.

Sosin, M., & Caulum, S. (1983). Advocacy: A conceptualization for social work practice. *Social Work, 28*(1), 12–17.

Southwest Educational Development Laboratory. (n.d.). Normative-re-educative/cultural/fix the school. In *Facilitative leadership: The imperative for change.* Retrieved May 18, 2006, from http://www.sedl.org/change/facilitate/approaches.html

State Justice Institute. (1998). *An interim report of the mediator skills project: Assessing and supporting effective mediation.* Atlanta: Author.

Stewart, D. D., & Stasser, G. (1998). The sampling of critical unshared information in decision-making groups: The role of an uninformed minority. *European Journal of Social Psychology, 28,* 95–113.

Stone, D., Patton, B., & Heen, S. (2000). *Difficult conversations: How to discuss what matters most.* New York: Penguin.

Strunk, W., & White, E. B. (2000). *The elements of style* (4th ed.). Boston: Allyn & Bacon.

Stuart, B. (1997). *Building community justice partnerships: Community peacemaking circles.* Ottawa: Aboriginal Justice Section, Canadian Department of Justice.

Stulberg, J. B., & Keating, J. M. (1983). *An introduction to mediation: A manual for beginning mediators.* New York: Conflict Management Resources.

Sue, D. W. (2006). *Multicultural social work practice.* Hoboken, NJ: Wiley.

Sullivan, M. J. (2004). Ethical, legal, and professional practice issues involved in acting as a psychologist parenting coordinator in child custody cases. *Family Court Review, 42,* 576–582.

Susskind, L. E. (2005). Consensus building and ADR: Why they are not the same thing. In M. L. Moffitt & R. C. Bordone (Eds.), *The handbook of dispute resolution* (pp. 358–370). San Francisco: Jossey-Bass.

Tannen, D. (1998). *The argument culture: Moving from debate to dialogue.* New York: Random House.

Taylor, A. (1997). Concepts of neutrality in family mediation: Contexts, ethics, influence and transformative process. *Mediation Quarterly, 14,* 215–236.

Taylor, A. (2002). The handbook of family dispute resolution: Mediation theory and practice. San Francisco: Jossey-Bass.

Thoennes, N. (1991). Mediation and the dependency court: The controversy and three courts' experiences. *Family and Conciliation Courts Review, 29,* 246–258.

Thomas, K. W., & Kilmann, R. H. (1974). *Thomas-Kilmann Conflict Mode Instrument.* Tuxedo, NY: Xiacom. (Instruments may be ordered from http://www.cpp.com.)

Tidwell, A. (2004). Conflict, peace, and education: A tangled web. *Conflict Resolution Quarterly, 21,* 462–470.

Ting-Toomey, S., & Oetzel, J. G. (2001). *Managing intercultural conflict effectively.* Thousand Oaks, CA: Sage.

Tjaden, P. G. (1994). Dispute resolution in child protection cases. *Negotiation Journal, 10,* 373–390.

Torré, D. A. (1986). *Empowerment: Structural conceptualization and instrument development.* Unpublished doctoral dissertation, Cornell University, Itasca, NY.

Trippany, R. L., White Kress, V. E., & Wilcoxon, S. A. (2004). Preventing vicarious trauma: what counselors should know when working with trauma survivors (Practice & Theory). *Journal of Counseling and Development, 82*(1), 31–38.

Truth and Reconciliation Commission. (2003). *Truth: The road to reconciliation.* Retrieved May 18, 2006, from http://www.doj.gov.za/trc/index.html

Turner, D., Hibbs, T., Lopez, E., & Sparks-Ngenge, C. (2001, June). *Critical perspectives on conflict resolution theory and process: Through the eye of the beholder – Confronting some key myths.* Paper presented at the Research and Higher Education Symposium, National Conference on Peacemaking and Conflict Resolution, Fairfax, VA. (Available from the University of Victoria Institute for Dispute Resolution.)

Umbreit, M. S. (2001). *The handbook of victim offender mediation: An essential guide to practice and research.* San Francisco: Jossey-Bass.

Umbreit, M. S., Coates, R. B., & Voss, B. (2005). Victim offender mediation: Evidence-based practice over three decades. In M. L. Moffitt & R. C. Bordone (Eds.), *The handbook of dispute resolution* (pp. 455–470). San Francisco: Jossey-Bass.

Uniform Mediation Act. (2003). *National Conference on Commissioners on Uniform State Laws.* Retrieved on May 18, 2006, from http://www.law.upenn.edu/bll/ulc/mediat/2003finaldraft.htm

United States Ombudsman Association. (2003). *Governmental ombudsman standards.* Retrieved May 18, 2006, from http://www.usombudsman.org/en/references/standards.cfm

Ury, W. (1999). *Getting to peace: Transforming conflict at home, at work, and in the world.* New York: Penguin.

Ury, W. L., Brett, J. M., & Goldberg, S. B. (1988). *Getting disputes resolved: Designing systems to cut the costs of conflict.* San Francisco: Jossey-Bass.

Van Es, R. (1996). *Negotiating ethics: On ethics in negotiation and negotiating ethics.* Delft, The Netherlands: Eburon.

van Ginkel, E. (2004). The mediator as face-giver. *Negotiation Journal, 20,* 475–487.

Wall, J. A., & Callister, R. R. (1995). Ho'opononopono: Some lessons from Hawaiian mediation. *Negotiation Journal, 11,* 45–54.

Walls, R. T., & Fullmer, S. L. (1995). Decision support services: Determining eligibility for human services. *Rehabilitation Counseling Bulletin, 38*(3), 248–261.

Wanis-St. John, A. (2005). *Cultural pathways in negotiation and conflict management.* In M. L. Moffitt & R. C. Bordone (Eds.), *The handbook of dispute resolution* (pp. 118–134). San Francisco: Jossey-Bass.

Warfield, W. (1993). Public policy conflict resolution: The nexus between culture and process. In D. J. D. Sandole & H. van der Merwe (Eds.), *Conflict management.* Manchester, UK: Manchester University Press.

Weinhold, B. K., & Weinhold, J. B. (2000). *Conflict resolution: The partnership way.* Denver: Love.

Weitzman, E. A., & Weitzman, P. F. (2000). Problem solving and decision-making in conflict resolution. In M. Deutsch & P. T. Coleman (Eds.), *Handbook of conflict resolution* (pp. 185–209). San Francisco: Jossey-Bass.

Werner, D., Thuman, C., & Maxwell, J. (2003). *Where there is no doctor: A village health care handbook.* Berkeley, CA: Hesperian.

Wheeler, M. (2006). Is teaching negotiation too easy, too hard, or both? *Negotiation Journal, 22,* 187–197.

Wilhelmus, M. (1998). Mediation in kinship care: Another step in the provision of culturally relevant child welfare services. *Social Work, 43*(2), 117–126.

Williams, J. M. (2005). *Styles: Ten lessons in clarity and grace* (8th ed.). Boston: Longman.

Wilmot, W. W., & Hocker, J. L. (2007). *Interpersonal conflict* (7th ed.). Boston: McGraw-Hill.

Winslade, J., & Monk, G. (2000). *Narrative mediation: A new approach to dispute resolution.* San Francisco: Jossey-Bass. (Summarized online at http://v3.crinfo.org/narrative_mediation.)

Yilmaz, M. R. (1997). In defense of a constructive, information-based approach to decision theory. *Theory and Decision, 43,* 21–44.

Young, P. T. (1961). *Motivation and emotion: A survey of the determinants of human and animal activity.* New York: Wiley.

Zastrow, C. (2003). *The practice of social work* (7th ed.). Belmont, CA: Wadsworth.

Zey, M. (Ed.). (1992). *Decision making: Alternatives to rational choice models.* Newbury Park, CA: Sage.

Index

TO THE OWNER OF THIS BOOK:

I hope that you have found *Conflict Resolution for the Helping Professions,* Second Edition, useful. So that this book can be improved in a future edition, would you take the time to complete this sheet and return it? Thank you.

School and address: _____

_____

Department: _____

Instructor's name: _____

1. What I like most about this book is: _____

_____

_____

2. What I like least about this book is: _____

_____

_____

3. My general reaction to this book is: _____

_____

_____

4. The name of the course in which I used this book is: _____

_____

5. Were all of the chapters of the book assigned for you to read? _____

   If not, which ones weren't? _____

6. In the space below, or on a separate sheet of paper, please write specific suggestions for improving this book and anything else you'd care to share about your experience in using this book.

_____

_____

DO NOT STAPLE. PLEASE SEAL WITH TAPE.

FOLD HERE

 BROOKS/COLE
CENGAGE Learning

NO POSTAGE
NECESSARY
IF MAILED
IN THE
UNITED STATES

BUSINESS REPLY MAIL
FIRST-CLASS MAIL   PERMIT NO. 34   BELMONT CA

POSTAGE WILL BE PAID BY ADDRESSEE

Attn: Social Work Editor

Brooks/Cole
20 Davis Drive
Belmont, CA 94002-9801

Il.l..I..lll..ll....l.lll.l..l.l.ll.....lll..ll

FOLD HERE

OPTIONAL:

Your name: _____   Date: _____

May we quote you, either in promotion for *Conflict Resolution for the Helping Professions,* Second Edition, or in future publishing ventures?

Yes: _____   No: _____

Sincerely yours,

Allan Edward Barsky